ART IN PARIS
1845-1862

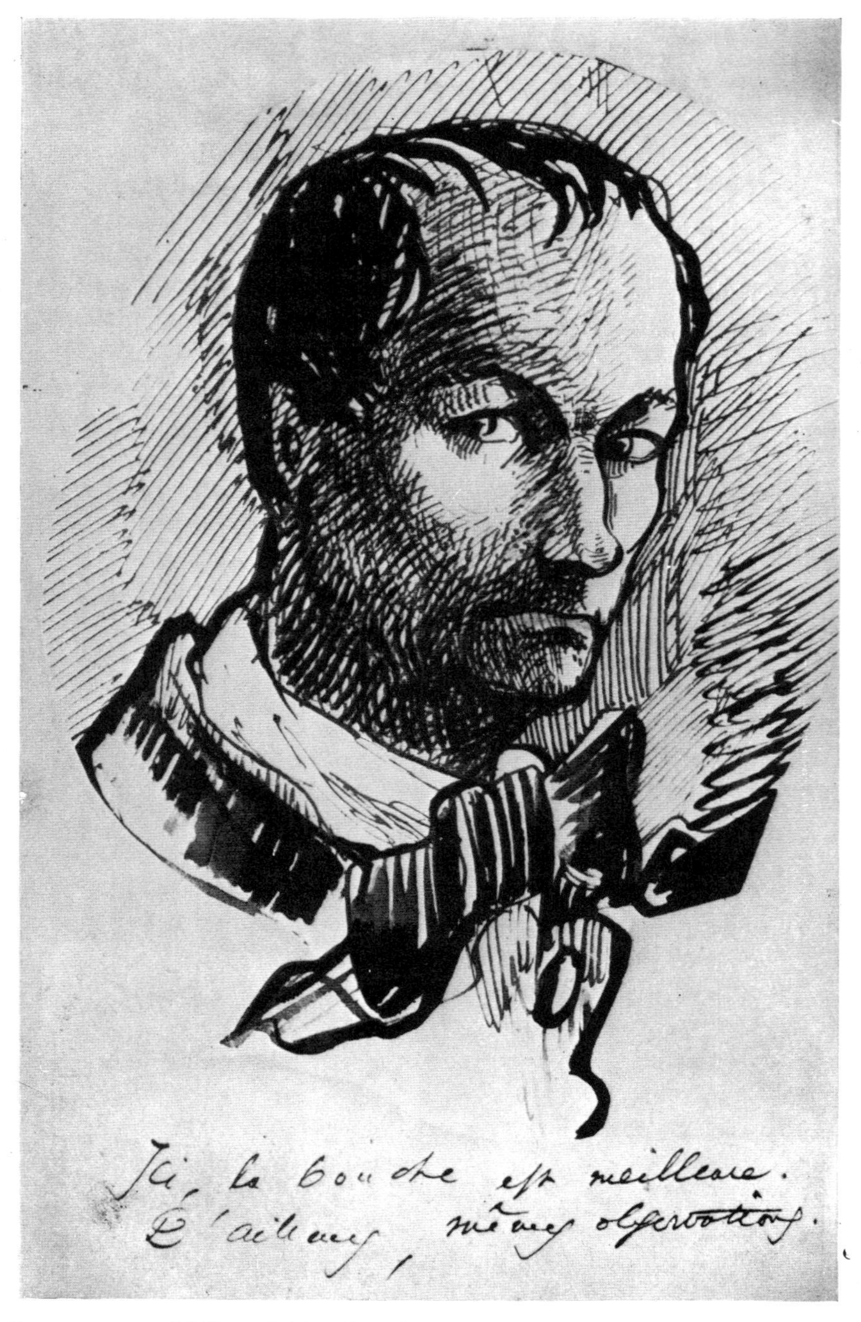

I. BAUDELAIRE: *Self-Portrait*. Drawing, about 1860. Chantilly, Spoelberch de Lovenjoul.

ART IN PARIS 1845-1862

SALONS AND OTHER EXHIBITIONS

REVIEWED BY
CHARLES BAUDELAIRE

TRANSLATED AND EDITED
BY JONATHAN MAYNE

PHAIDON · OXFORD

PHAIDON PRESS LIMITED, LITTLEGATE HOUSE,
ST EBBE'S STREET, OXFORD OX1 1 SQ

FIRST PUBLISHED 1965
SECOND EDITION (PHOTOGRAPHICALLY REPRINTED) 1981

British Library Cataloguing in Publication Data

Baudelaire, Charles
Art in Paris, 1845–1862.—(Landmarks in art history)
1. Painting, French
2. Painting, Modern—19th century—France
I. Title II. Mayne, Jonathan III. Series
759.4 ND547

ISBN 0-7148-2138-1

PRINTED AND BOUND IN U.S.A. BY VAIL-BALLOU PRESS, INC., BINGHAMTON, N.Y.

CONTENTS

PUBLISHER'S NOTE

This volume has been photographically reprinted from the first edition, published by Phaidon Press in 1965.

The companion-volume referred to in the Editor's Note (p. vii) and Editor's Introduction (p. ix)—*The Painter of Modern Life and Other Essays* by Charles Baudelaire (Phaidon Press, 1964)—has not been reissued in the Landmarks in Art History series.

EDITOR'S NOTE AND ACKNOWLEDGEMENTS

As in the companion-volume, The Painter of Modern Life, *the present translation has been made from the Conard editions of* Curiosités esthétiques *(1923) and* L'Art Romantique *(1925), both edited by the late Jacques Crépet. Reference has also been made to the Pléiade edition of the* Oeuvres complètes, *edited by Y. G. le Dantec, and revised by Claude Pichois (1961), and to the late André Ferran's fully-annotated edition of the* Salon de 1845 *(Toulouse 1933). To these editions I am indebted for much of the material contained in those footnotes which are preceded by a numerical reference. All footnotes, or parts of footnotes, included between an asterisk and the initials 'C.B.' are Baudelaire's own. To some of these I have added a further note after the initials.*

The main principles governing my attempts at the identification of works mentioned and discussed by Baudelaire, and my indication of existing reproductions elsewhere when they are not included among the plates, remain the same as in The Painter of Modern Life. *It should perhaps be pointed out that, where reproductions in* L'Illustration *are noted, these will merely be small wood-engravings, giving little more than the general design of a picture or a sculpture.*

My greatest personal debts are owed to the late Margaret Gilman; to Mr. Felix Leakey, of Glasgow University, who has been most helpful and patient; and to M. Claude Pichois, who now has the position in Baudelaire studies formerly occupied by Jacques Crépet. Among those others who have assisted me in a variety of ways, and whom I should like to take this opportunity of thanking once again, are: M. Jean Adhémar, of the Bibliothéque Nationale; Mr. John Beckwith, of the Victoria and Albert Museum; M. Raoul de Broglie, of the Musée Condé, Chantilly; Mr. Gordon Crocker; Miss Bernice Davidson; Mr. Wolf Drost; Miss Helen Darbishire; Mr. Maurice Harris; Mrs. Marie-Louise Hemphill; Dr. Robert von Hirsch; Dr. Arthur Kauffmann; Mrs. Dora Lykiardopulo; Mrs. F. J. Mather, Jr.; Mr. Peter Mayne; Mr. O'Hana; Mr. Peter Quennell; Mr. Graham Reynolds; and Mr. Denys Sutton. My thanks are also due to the authorities of the following Museums and Galleries who have kindly granted permission for works of art in their care to be reproduced here: the British Museum, the National Gallery, the Victoria and Albert Museum and the Wallace Collection, London; the Bibliothèque Nationale and the Musée du Louvre, Paris; the Musées Royaux, Brussels; the Fodor Museum, Amsterdam; the Frick Collection, New York; the Smithsonian Institution, Washington; the Museum of Fine Arts, Boston, Massachusetts, and the Museums at Autun, Bordeaux, Bourg-en-Bresse, Chantilly, Lille, Lyon, Metz, Montauban, Montpellier, Nantes, Nîmes, Rouen, Saint-Lô, Toulouse and Versailles.

J.M.

EDITOR'S INTRODUCTION

In a companion-volume, *The Painter of Modern Life*, I have traced the main lines of Baudelaire's critical thought and method, and their development through his working life. In the present Introduction I want rather to show how some of these ideas originated for him, and to indicate something of the breadth of influence and interest that helped to form his critical mind. Inevitably there will be some overlapping and repetition; but the emphasis will be somewhat shifted.

In making his début in 1845 with a Salon-review, Baudelaire was following a literary tradition that was within two years of being a century old. The first critical account of a Salon, entitled *Réflexions sur quelques causes de l'état présent de la peinture en France*, by La Font de Saint-Yenne, had appeared in 1747. The real father of the genre, however, was Diderot, whose first Salon appeared in 1759—exactly a hundred years before Baudelaire's last. Appropriately enough it is Diderot's influence that has been most often remarked in Baudelaire's earlier art-criticism. After his death in 1784, Diderot's reputation suffered a partial eclipse, but by the time that Baudelaire came to write, a number of his *Salons* had been reprinted, the short *Salon de 1759* having reappeared as recently as March 1844 in the magazine, *l'Artiste*. It is a fair assumption that Baudelaire had read this, and its easy, conversational tone is sharply reflected by him in his own first *Salon*. This was already noticed by contemporary critics. Champfleury, reviewing Baudelaire's *Salon de 1845*, observed: 'M. Baudelaire-Dufaÿs (the name under which his earlier writings were published) est hardi comme Diderot, moins le paradoxe.' And he went on to note certain resemblances with Stendhal also—another important early influence, whom we shall shortly discuss. Diderot, described by Sainte-Beuve as 'le créateur de la critique émue, empressée et éloquente', is certainly one of the great-grandfathers of that criticism which Baudelaire, in his *Salon de 1846*, applauded as 'partiale, passionnée, politique'. His manner, particularly in dismissing pictures which he did not like, is strikingly adopted by Baudelaire. Where Diderot writes: 'Si vous êtes curieux de visages de plâtre, vous verrez . . . les portraits de Drouais', we find Baudelaire parallelling him with: 'Les têtes de M. Pérignon sont dures et lisses comme des objets inanimés. Un vrai musée de Curtius.' And the mocking conclusion to Baudelaire's 1845 and Diderot's 1759 *Salons* are remarkably close to one another. According to his early biographer and friend, Charles Asselineau, Baudelaire was constantly saying 'Pas de grande peinture sans de grandes pensées.' Can this essentially eighteenth-century notion have been derived from Diderot's remark in his *Salon de 1759*: 'Ces gens-ci croient qu'il n'y a qu'à arranger des figures; ils ne savent pas que le premier point, le point important, c'est de trouver une grande idée . . .'?

Although the influence of Stendhal could already be detected in the *Salon de 1845*, as Champfleury had observed, it was not until the *Salon de 1846* that it became really noticeable. The 1845 *Salon* was concerned more with facts than general ideas: one of the most important of the ideas, however—the call for a painter to interpret the epic quality of modern life, which was only to reach its complete statement years later in the essay on Guys, *Le Peintre de la Vie Moderne*—certainly derives from hints dropped by Stendhal in his *Histoire de la peinture en Italie*. The *Salon de 1846* is constructed very differently from its predecessor. It is a combination, in roughly equal proportions, of facts and philosophy. The exhibition itself seems somehow to have been used as an excuse for a series of self-consistent observations on modern art. It is significant to note that the cover of the *Salon de 1845* had already announced as 'sous-presse' a work entitled 'De la peinture moderne'. This never appeared, and it is reasonable to suppose, as has been suggested before, that large portions of it were incorporated in the *Salon de 1846*. These were clearly the philosophical chapters and it is here that the ideas—and sometimes even the very words—of Stendhal are to be recognized. As Miss Gilman has pointed out, it is often difficult to disentangle the influences of Delacroix from those of Stendhal in this *Salon*. The insistence on originality was common to them both, but Baudelaire's idiosyncratic use of the word 'naïveté' he probably took over, and developed, from Delacroix. The key-word of the *Salon* however is 'idéal', and this is certainly of Stendhalian inspiration. It is not only general ideas, however, but direct, unacknowledged verbal quotation that finally proves the point. Miss Gilman, whose brilliant *Baudelaire the Critic* has suggested many of these observations, as it has those of most of the English writers who have concerned themselves with this subject, has made this devastatingly clear. In the chapter 'De l'idéal et du modèle', which ends with an admitted quotation from Stendhal, there are whole paragraphs which reproduce, idea for idea, what Stendhal had written. And when we come to the sentence: 'Toute la différence, c'est qu'en faisant tout d'une venue les bras et les jambes de leurs figures, ce n'étaient pas eux qui fuyaient les détails, mais les détails qui les fuyaient; car, pour choisir il faut posséder', it is no longer idea for idea, but word for word.

The third, and most lasting, influence on Baudelaire's critical mind was of course that of Delacroix. Each one of the *Salons*, and the review of the Exposition Universelle, contained extended appreciations of the painter who was the

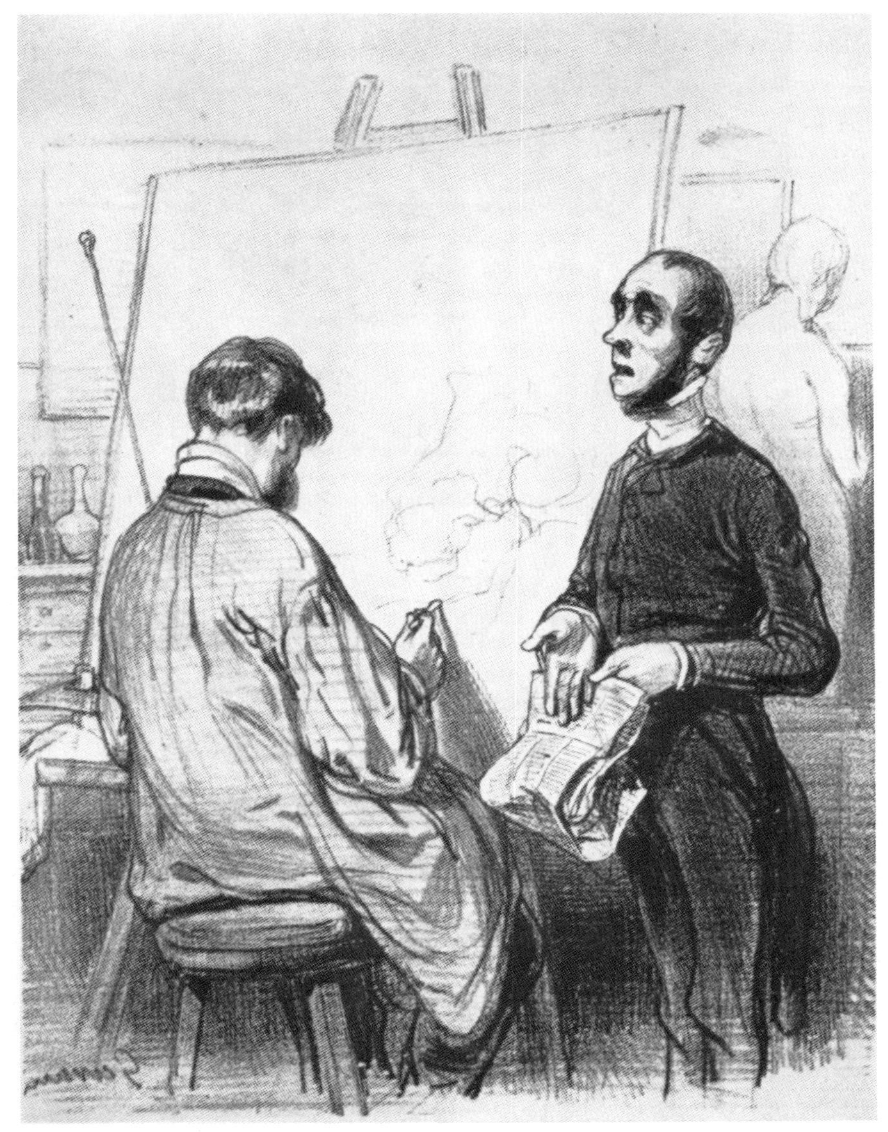

II. Gavarni: *The Artist and his Critic*. Lithograph. London, Victoria and Albert Museum.

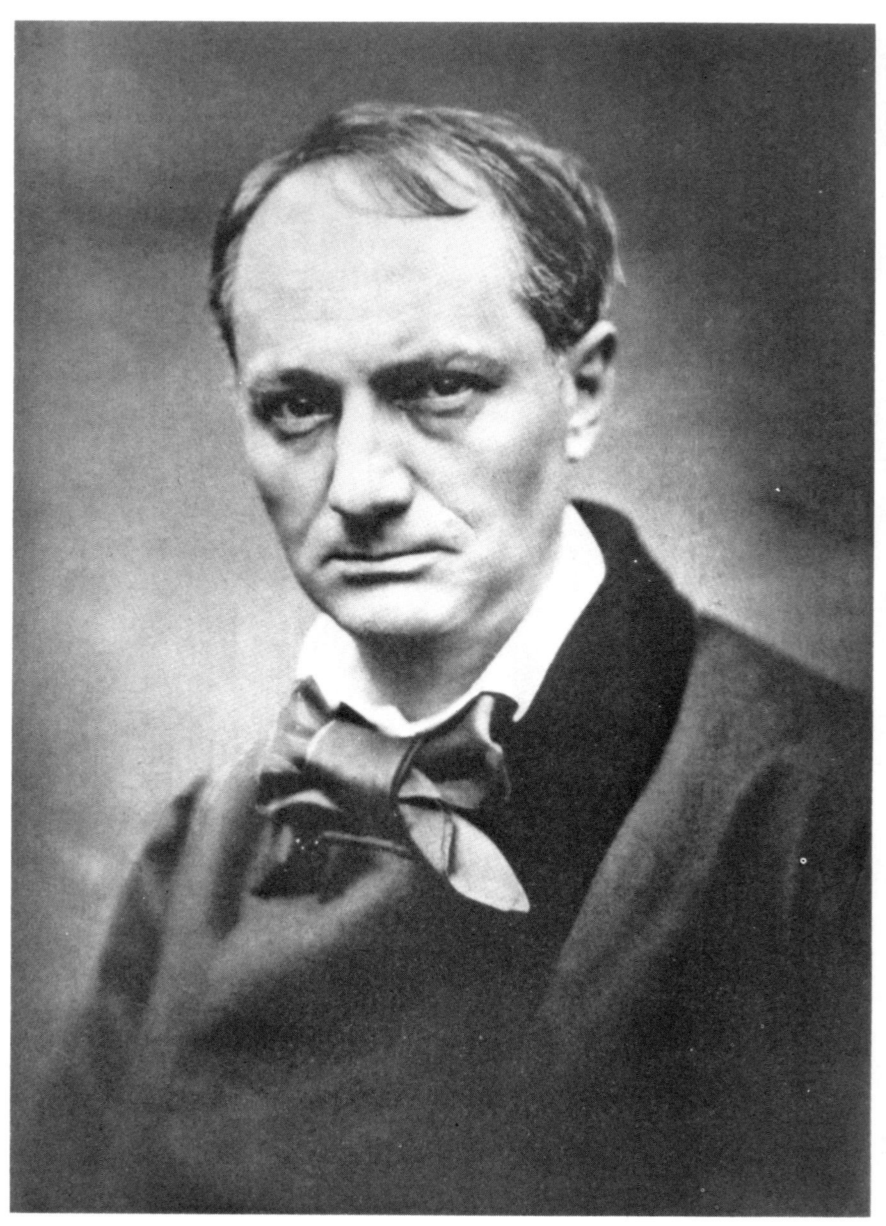

III. CARJAT: *Photograph of Baudelaire*. About 1861–2.

major hero of Baudelaire's life: and one of Baudelaire's last published prose works was the long obituary article in which he summed up all his ideas on Delacroix, and of which a translation appears in *The Painter of Modern Life*. It seems that Baudelaire first met Delacroix about 1845, and from the casual way in which he refers to him and quotes from his conversation one would suppose that the two men were on intimate terms. The evidence of Delacroix's Journal, however, as far as it goes, tends to contradict this assumption. 'Tends' only, because Delacroix kept no journal during the first three years of their acquaintance, so for this possibly crucial period there is no record on Delacroix's side. The very few references to Baudelaire, in the later Journals, however, suggest no kind of intimacy, or even friendship, and Delacroix is reported to have said of Baudelaire, 'il m'ennuie à la fin'. This is perfectly credible, particularly as Baudelaire's interpretations of Delacroix's paintings were highly subjective and idiosyncratic. Nevertheless many of the ideas touched on, or elaborated, in the Journal (which Baudelaire of course cannot have known) run parallel to Baudelaire's own, which may well have derived partly from conversations.

The famous notion, 'la nature n'est qu'un dictionnaire', first stated by Baudelaire in the *Salon of 1859* (p. 139), and repeated in the obituary article, though not exactly parallelled in any of Delacroix's published writings or journals, seems to originate from the painter's statement 'les formes du modèle . . . ne sont que le dictionnaire où l'artiste va retremper ses impressions fugitives . . .', and the insistence on the essential importance of the memory, which, like many of Baudelaire's aesthetic ideas, was to reach its full elaboration in the essay on Guys, can also be traced back to Delacroix's artistic theorizing. Baudelaire's ideas on execution, as expressed for example in the *Salon of 1859* (p. 160), are suggestively close to those of Delacroix, as revealed in various passages of the Journals, and almost certainly originate therefrom. Again, his observations concerning the interrelations of line and colour have their counterparts in Delacroix's known views.

Many other writers could be, and often have been, cited as sources of Baudelaire's ideas: the eighteenth-century philosopher, Joseph de Maistre, for example, Heine, Poe (and through him, Coleridge), Hoffmann. Why then do we bother to read him, if he was no more than such a rag-bag of other, detectable, influences? The first answer to this question is developed in Baudelaire's early—and unique—work of fiction, *La Fanfarlo*, in which the recognizably autobiographical hero, Samuel Cramer, is presented as 'comédien par tempérament': 'he was at one and the same time all the artists he had ever studied, and all the books he had ever read, and yet, despite this gift for mimicry, he remained profoundly original.' It is this that helps to explain the Baudelairean Delacroix whom we find so often evoked in the following pages, and the Baudelairean Wagner who is to be encountered in the companion-volume (portrayed of course by a Wagnerian Baudelaire); it is precisely this *faculté comédienne* that enabled Baudelaire to recognize Poe, when he first discovered him, as a spiritual and artistic brother—for he was in fact recognizing something of himself.

This is the first answer, and it is also the last. We read Baudelaire because we read him. Delacroix said of Raphael: 'Son originalité ne paraît jamais plus vive que dans les idées qu'il emprunte. Tout ce qu'il trouve, il le relève et le fait vivre d'une vie nouvelle.' It is once more this extraordinary gift, far exceeding Samuel Cramer's gift for mimicry, that confers such a remarkable immediacy on almost every word that Baudelaire wrote about the fine arts, whether visual, literary or musical. It may have been himself that he was all the time writing about—and we know from his volume of autobiographical exclamations, *Mon coeur mis à nu* (it is significant that the very title, so apparently Baudelairean, was literally lifted from Poe's *Marginalia*), that one of his earliest ambitions was to be an actor—but there was an originality, a *naïveté*, about him that added to every word and idea a specially acute novelty that enhanced and transformed its source. He may have been a literary and social monster, as probably he was: but borrower, pilferer, even plagiarist (by demonstration), he paradoxically remains one of the great originals of the nineteenth century.

JONATHAN MAYNE

BIBLIOGRAPHICAL NOTE

THE SALON OF 1845

The exhibition opened on 15 March at the Musée Royal (Louvre). Baudelaire's review appeared in the form of a booklet. Although it was officially recorded as published on 24 May, Baudelaire himself wrote to his mother that it was appearing on his birthday, 9 April. The present translation of this *Salon* is somewhat abridged. Omissions are indicated where they occur.

THE MUSEUM OF CLASSICS

This article first appeared in the *Corsaire Satan*, 21 January 1846, signed Baudelaire-Dufays (as were the poet's first two *Salons*, 'Dufays' being part of his mother's maiden name). The name *Bazar Bonne-Nouvelle* was given to the extensive arcades on the Boulevard Bonne-Nouvelle, near the Porte Saint-Denis, where there were shops of all kinds, as well as the largest café in Paris. In 1846 the management had the idea of opening a gallery and holding there a retrospective exhibition of eighteenth- and early nineteenth-century French painting; the exhibition opened on the 11 January. The title 'Musée classique' which he gave to this review seems to have been Baudelaire's own invention.

THE SALON OF 1846

The exhibition opened on 16 March at the Musée Royal. Baudelaire's review appeared as a booklet on 13 May.

THE EXPOSITION UNIVERSELLE 1855

The *Exposition Universelle* opened at the Palais des Beaux-Arts (the new *Palais de l'Industrie*), Avenue Montaigne, on 15 May 1855. Baudelaire had been commissioned to write a series of articles on the subject for *Le Pays*, but only the first and third of the articles here printed were published in that paper (26 May and 3 June); the second article was published later in *Le Portefeuille* (12 August). It seems that Baudelaire's approach to his task was not acceptable to his employers, and from the 6 July a journalist called Louis Enault took over the succession.

To judge by its opening paragraph, and the fact that it appeared in *Le Pays* a week after the introductory article, the article on Delacroix seems clearly to have been intended as the second, and not the third, of the series. We are, however, retaining the order in which the three articles were first printed together in *Curiosités esthétiques*.

THE SALON OF 1859

This article was published in four instalments, between 10 June and 20 July 1859. The name of the editor of the *Revue Française*, to whom the article was addressed in the form of letters, was Jean Morel. The Salon opened on 15 April at the Palais des Champs-Elysées. In a letter to Nadar of 14 May, Baudelaire claimed that he was writing this *Salon* without having seen it; a few days later he admitted (also to Nadar) that he had been once.

PAINTERS AND ETCHERS

This article derives from a shorter piece entitled 'L'Eau-forte est à la mode' which appeared, unsigned, in the *Revue Anecdotique*, 2 April 1862; the developed version, here translated, appeared as 'Peintres et Aqua-fortistes' in *le Boulevard*, 14 September 1862. The earlier version is printed by Crépet among his notes (*L'Art Romantique*, pp. 466–7).

Margaret Gilman's *Baudelaire the Critic* (New York 1943) contains a list of works on Baudelaire's criticism. Martin Turnell's *Baudelaire* (London 1953) contains a good general bibliography. For a detailed examination of the art-criticism of the period 1848–70, see Joseph C. Sloane's *French Painting between the Past and the Present* (Princeton 1951). The most convenient source of information concerning the Salon-exhibits of nineteenth-century French artists is Bellier de la Chavignerie's *Dictionnaire général des artistes de l'école française* (2 vols., Paris 1882–5).

ABBREVIATIONS USED IN THE FOOTNOTES

Escholier	Raymond Escholier. *Delacroix*. 3 volumes. Paris, 1926–9
Gilman	Margaret Gilman. *Baudelaire the Critic*. New York, 1943
Illustr.	*L'Illustration. Journal universel*
Journal	*The Journal of Eugène Delacroix*. London (Phaidon Press), 1951
Painter of Modern Life	Baudelaire. *The Painter of Modern Life and other Essays*. London (Phaidon Press), 1964
Robaut	Alfred Robaut. *L'Oeuvre complet d'Eugène Delacroix*. Paris, 1885
Wildenstein	Georges Wildenstein. *The Paintings of J.A.D. Ingres*. London (Phaidon Press), 1956

ART IN PARIS
1845—1862

THE SALON OF 1845

I. A FEW WORDS OF INTRODUCTION

WE CAN claim with at least as much accuracy as a well-known writer claims of his little books, that no newspaper would dare print what we have to say. Are we going to be very cruel and abusive, then? By no means; on the contrary, we are going to be impartial. We have no friends—that is a great thing—and no enemies. Ever since the days of M. Gustave Planche,[1] an honest fellow whose learned and commanding eloquence is now silent to the great regret of all right-thinking minds, the lies and the shameless favouritism of newspaper criticism, which is sometimes silly, sometimes violent, but never independent, have inspired the bourgeois with a disgust for those useful handbooks which go by the name of Salon-reviews.*

And at the very outset, with reference to that impertinent designation, 'the bourgeois', we beg to state that we in no way share the prejudices of our great confrères in the world of art, who for some years now have been striving their utmost to cast anathema upon that inoffensive being whom nothing would please better than to love good painting, if only those gentlemen knew how to make it understandable to him, and if the artists themselves showed it him more often.

That word, which smells of studio-cant from a mile off, should be expunged from the dictionary of criticism.

The 'bourgeois' ceased to exist the moment he himself adopted the word as a term of abuse—which only goes to prove his sincere desire to become artistic, in relation to the art-critics.

In the second place, the bourgeois—since he does, in fact, exist—is a very respectable personage; for one must please those at whose expense one means to live.

[1] Gustave Planche (1808–57), who had written regularly for the *Revue des Deux-Mondes*, had been absent in Italy for the last few years.

* Let us record a fine and honourable exception in M. Delécluze, whose opinions we do not always share, but who has always managed to preserve his integrity, and, without roaring or ranting, has often been responsible for bringing new and unknown talents to light. (C.B.)

And finally, the ranks of the artists themselves contain so many bourgeois that it is better, on the whole, to suppress a word which does not define any particular vice of caste, seeing that it is equally applicable to those who ask no more than that they should cease to incur it, as to those who have never suspected that they deserved it.

It is with the same contempt for all systematic nagging and opposition—opposition and nagging which have become banal and commonplace;* it is with the same orderliness, the same love of good sense, that we are banishing far from this little booklet all discussion both of juries[1] in general and of the paintings-jury in particular; of the reform of the jury, which we are told has become necessary, and of the manner and frequency of exhibitions, etc. . . . First of all, a jury is necessary—so much is clear; and as for the annual recurrence of the exhibition,[2] which we owe to the enlightened and liberally paternal mind of a king to whom both public and artists owe also the enjoyment of six museums,** a fair-minded man will always see that the great artist cannot fail to gain by it, considering his natural productiveness, and that the mediocre artist will only find his deserved punishment therein.

We shall speak about everything that attracts the eye of the crowd and of the artists; our professional conscience obliges us to do so. Everything that pleases has a reason for pleasing, and to scorn the throngs of those that have gone astray is no way to bring them back to where they ought to be.

Our method of address will consist simply in dividing our work into categories—History-paintings and Portraits—Genre-paintings and Landscape—Sculpture—Engravings and Drawings; and in arranging the artists in accordance with the rank and order which the estimation of the public has assigned to them.

8th May 1845

* The complaints are perhaps justified, but they count as nagging, because they have become systematic. (C.B.)

[1] I.e. selection-committees, about which there was much current dissatisfaction. Under the Empire and the Restoration, the works of new exhibitors only were subject to the jury; in 1831 new rules were formed according to which all were so subject.

[2] It was not until 1833 that the Salon became an annual event. In recent years there had never been less than two years between each, and often more.

** The *Galerie des Dessins*, the extension to the *Galerie Française*, the *Musée Espagnol*, the *Musée Standish*, the *Musée de Versailles*, and the *Musée de Marine* (C.B.). The first two and the last two of these exist today. The *Musée Espagnol* comprised Spanish pictures belonging to the Orléans family. The *Musée Standish* consisted of works bequeathed by Lord Standish to King Louis-Philippe. A list of the Spanish paintings in the Musée Standish and the Musée Espagnol is given in G. Guillaume-Reicher's *Théophile Gautier et l'Espagne* (1936), pp. 495–502.

II. HISTORY PAINTINGS

DELACROIX.—M. Delacroix is decidedly the most original painter of ancient or of modern times. That is how things are, and what is the good of protesting? But none of M. Delacroix's friends, not even the most enthusiastic of them, has dared to state this simply, bluntly and impudently, as we do. Thanks to the tardy justice of the years, which blunt the edge of spite and shock and ill-will, and slowly sweep away each obstacle to the grave, we are no longer living at a time when the name of Delacroix was a signal for the reactionaries to cross themselves, and a rallying-symbol for every kind of opposition, whether intelligent or not. Those fair days are past. M. Delacroix will always remain a somewhat disputed figure—just enough to add a little lustre to his glory. And a very good thing too! He has a right to eternal youth, for he has not betrayed us, he has not lied to us like certain thankless idols whom we have borne into our pantheons. M. Delacroix is not yet a member of the Academy, but morally he belongs to it.[1] A long time ago he said everything that was required to make him the first among us—that is agreed. Nothing remains for him but to advance along the right road—a road that he has always trodden. Such is the tremendous feat of strength demanded of a genius who is ceaselessly in search of the new.

This year M. Delacroix has sent four pictures[2]:

1. *La Madeleine dans le désert.*[3] A head of a woman, upturned, in a very narrow frame. High up to the right, a little scrap of sky or rock—a touch of blue. The Magdalen's eyes are closed, her mouth soft and languid, her hair dishevelled. Short of seeing it, no one could imagine the amount of intimate, mysterious and romantic poetry that the artist has put into this simple head. It is painted almost entirely in visible brush-strokes, like many of M. Delacroix's pictures. Far from being dazzling or intense, it is very gentle and restrained in tone; its general effect is almost grey, but of a perfect harmony. This picture demonstrates a truth which we have long suspected, and which is made clearer still in another work of which we shall shortly speak; it is that M. Delacroix is stronger than ever, and on a

[1] In fact Delacroix had already sought election to the Institut in 1837, but he was not finally elected until 1857.

[2] A fifth, his *Education de la Vierge*, was rejected by the jury.

[3] Robaut 921: on the art-market in 1958; repro. *Burlington Magazine*, June 1958.

path of progress which ceaselessly renews itself—that is to say that he is more than ever of a harmonist.

2. *Dernières paroles de Marc-Aurèle.*[1] Marcus Aurelius commits his son to the Stoics. A half-draped figure, on his death-bed, he is presenting the young Commodus—a young, pink, soft voluptuary, seemingly a little bored—to his austere friends, grouped around him in attitudes of dejection.

A splendid, magnificent, sublime and misunderstood picture. A well-known critic has sung the painter's praises for having placed Commodus—that is to say, the future—in the light; and the Stoics—that is to say, the past—in the shade. What a brilliant thought! But in fact, except for two figures in the half-shadow, all the characters have their share of illumination. This reminds us of the admiration of a republican man of letters who could seriously congratulate the great Rubens for having painted Henri IV with a slovenly boot and hose, in one of his official pictures in the Médicis gallery.[2] To him it was a stroke of independent satire, a liberal thrust at the royal excesses. Rubens the revolutionary! Oh criticism! Oh you critics! . . .

With this picture we are in mid-Delacroix—that is to say, we have before us one of the most perfect specimens of what genius can achieve in painting.

Its colour is incomparably scientific; it does not contain a single fault. And yet what is it but a series of triumphs of skill—triumphs which are invisible to the inattentive eye, for the harmony is muffled and deep? And far from losing its cruel originality in this new and completer science, the colour remains sanguinary and terrible. This equilibrium of green and red delights our heart. M. Delacroix has even introduced into this picture some tones which he had not habitually employed before—at least, so it seems to us. They set one another off to great advantage. The background is as serious as such a subject requires.

Finally—let us say it, since no one else does—this picture is faultless both in draughtsmanship and in modelling. Has the public any idea of how difficult it is to model in colour? It is a double difficulty. In modelling with a single tone—that is with a stump—the difficulty is simple; modelling with colour, however, means first discovering a logic of light

[1] Now in the Lyons Museum; see pl. 35.

[2] The paintings executed by Rubens for the Palais du Luxembourg are now in the Louvre.

and shade, and then truth and harmony of tone, all in one sudden, spontaneous and complex working. Put in another way, if the light is red and the shadow green, it means discovering at the first attempt a harmony of red and green, one luminous, the other dark, which together produce the effect of a monochrome object in relief.

'This picture is faultless in drawing.' With reference to this vast paradox, this impudent piece of blasphemy, must I repeat, must I re-explain what M. Gautier gave himself the trouble of explaining in one of his articles[1] last year, on the subject of M. Couture—for when a work is well suited to his literary temperament and education, M. Gautier expounds well what he feels finely? I mean, that there are two kinds of draughtsmanship—the draughtsmanship of the colourists, and that of the draughtsmen. Their procedures are contrary; but it is perfectly possible to draw with untrammelled colour, just as it is possible for an artist to achieve harmonious colour-masses while remaining an exclusive draughtsman.

Therefore when we say that this picture is well drawn, we do not wish it to be understood that it is drawn like a Raphael. We mean that it is drawn in an extempore and *graphic* manner; we mean that this kind of drawing, which has something analogous to that of all the great colourists, Rubens, for example, perfectly renders the movement, the physiognomy, the hardly perceptible tremblings of nature, which Raphael's drawing never captures. We only know of two men in Paris who draw as well as M. Delacroix—one in an analogous and the other in a contrary manner. The first is M. Daumier, the caricaturist; the second M. Ingres, the great painter, the artful adorer of Raphael. This is certainly something calculated to astound both friends and enemies, both partisans and antagonists of each one of them; but anyone who examines the matter slowly and carefully will see that these three kinds of drawing have this in common, that they perfectly and completely render the aspect of nature that they mean to render, and that they say just what they mean to say. Daumier draws better, perhaps, than Delacroix, if you would prefer healthy, robust qualities to the weird and amazing powers of a great genius sick with genius; M. Ingres, who is so much in love with detail, draws better, perhaps, than either of them, if you prefer laborious niceties to a total harmony, and the nature of the fragment to the nature of the composition, but . . . let us love them all three.

[1] In *La Presse*, 28 March 1844.

3. *Une Sibylle qui montre le rameau d'or.* Once more the colour is fine and original. The head reminds one a little of the charming hesitancy of the Hamlet designs. As a piece of modelling and texture it is incomparable: the bare shoulder is as good as a Correggio.

4. *Le Sultan de Maroc entouré de sa garde et de ses officiers.*[1] This is the picture to which we were referring a moment ago when we declared that M. Delacroix had advanced in the science of harmony. In fact, has anyone ever shown a greater musical seductiveness, at any time? Was ever Veronese more enchanting? Were melodies more fanciful ever set to sing upon a canvas? or a concord more wondrous of new, unknown, delicate and charming tones? We appeal to the honesty of anyone who knows his Louvre to mention a picture by a great colourist in which the colour is as *suggestive* as in M. Delacroix's picture. We know that we shall only be understood by a small number, but that is enough. In spite of the splendour of its hues, this picture is so harmonious that it is grey—as grey as nature, as grey as the summer atmosphere when the sun spreads over each object a sort of twilight film of trembling dust. Therefore you do not notice it at first; its neighbours kill it. The composition is excellent; it has an element of the unexpected, because it is true and natural. . . .

P.S. It is said that praises can be compromising, and that it is better a wise enemy, etc. . . . We, however, do not believe that it is possible to compromise genius by explaining it.

HORACE VERNET. This African painting[2] is colder than a fine winter's day. Everything in it is of heart-breaking whiteness and brightness. Unity, none; rather, a crowd of interesting little anecdotes—a vast tavern mural. These kinds of decoration are generally divided up as though into compartments or acts, by a tree, a great mountain, a cavern, etc. M. Horace Vernet has followed the same method—that of a serialist—thanks to which the spectator's memory duly finds its landmarks; namely a huge camel, some deer, a tent, etc. . . . It is truly painful to see an intelligent man floundering about in such a mess of horror. Good Heavens, has M. Horace Vernet never seen the works of Rubens, Veronese, Tintoretto, Jouvenet?

[1] Now in the Toulouse Museum; see pl. 38.

[2] The *Prise de la Smalah d'Abd-el-Kader*, now in the Versailles Museum. The colossal size of this painting (over ninety feet long) ensured it overwhelming critical and popular attention. The military operation which it illustrated took place in 1843. See pl. 5.

William Haussoullier. M. Haussoullier must not be surprised, first of all, at the violence of the praises which we are about to heap upon his picture, for we have decided to do so only after having conscientiously and minutely analysed it; nor, in the second place, at the brutal and unmannerly reception which a French public is according it—at the passing bursts of laughter which it occasions. We have seen more than one important newspaper critic tossing it his little meed of mockery, over his shoulder. Let the artist take no notice. It is a fine thing to have a success like *St. Symphorian.*[1]

There are two ways of becoming famous—by the accumulation of annual successes, or by a bolt from the blue. The second way is certainly the more original. Let M. Haussoullier remember the outcries which greeted *Dante and Virgil,*[2] and then persevere along his own path. A lot of miserable catcalls are yet in store for this work, but it will abide in the memory of anyone with eyes and feelings. May its success continue ever widening—for success it ought to have.

After M. Delacroix's wonderful pictures, this is truly the capital work of the exhibition. Let us rather say, it is, in a certain sense at least, the unique picture of this year's Salon. For M. Delacroix has for long been an illustrious genius, a granted and accepted glory; and this year he has given us four pictures. Whereas M. William Haussoullier was unknown yesterday; and he has only sent one.

To begin with, we cannot deny ourselves the pleasure of describing it—such a joyful and delicious task does it seem. The subject is the Fountain of Youth.[3] In the foreground are three groups. At the left a young, or rather a rejuvenated couple, gazing into one another's eyes and talking close together—they appear to be practising Platonic love. In the middle, a half-nude woman, with skin white as snow, and brown crimped hair—she too is smiling and chatting with her partner; there is a greater air of sensuality about her, and she still holds a mirror in which

[1] Ingres's *Martyre de saint Symphorien*, painted for the Cathedral of Autun and exhibited at the 1834 Salon, was the centre of violent controversy.

[2] By Delacroix; exhibited at the 1822 Salon.

[3] This painting, long believed lost, was acquired in London shortly before the war by Mr. Graham Reynolds; see pl. 2. A preliminary drawing for it was published by J. Crépet in the *Figaro*, 15 November 1924. The painting itself had been exhibited at the Royal Academy in London a year before being shown in Paris. As well as Baudelaire, Théodore de Banville was much struck by it and described it in a poem of the same title (dated May 1844), which was later published in *Les Stalactites* (1846).

she has just been looking at herself. Finally, in the right-hand corner, a robust elegant man—a ravishing head, this, with forehead a trifle low and lips a shade forceful; he smiles as he puts down his glass on the turf, while his companion is pouring some wondrous elixir into the glass of a long, thin young man standing in front of her.

Behind them, on the second plane, is another group, lying at full length on the greensward, in one another's arms. In the middle stands a nude woman; she is wringing from her hair the last drops of the health-giving and fertilizing stream. A second woman, also nude, and half recumbent, seems like a chrysalis still clothed in the last shift of its metamorphosis. Delicate of form, these two women are vaporously, outrageously white; they are just beginning to re-emerge, so to speak, into life. The standing figure is in the strong position of dividing the picture symmetrically in two. This almost-living statue is admirably effective, and, by contrasting with them, stresses the violent hues of the foreground which thereby acquire an added vigour. The fountain itself, which will doubtless strike some critics as a little too 'Séraphin'[1] in style—this fairy-tale fountain is much to our liking; it divides into two sheets of water, and is tapered, or cleft, into wavering fringes, thin as air. Along a winding pathway, which leads the eye right into the background of the picture, come happy sixty-year olds, bent and bearded. The background to the right consists of a grove in which a kind of joyful ballet is taking place.

The sentiment of this picture is exquisite; it shows us people making love and drinking—a sight that thrills the senses—but they are drinking and making love in a deeply serious, almost a melancholy manner. Far from the storms and ferments of youth, this is a second youth which knows the value of life and can enjoy it in tranquillity.

In our opinion this picture has one very important quality, especially in a Museum—it is very showy. There is no chance of not seeing it. Its colour is of a terrible, an unrelenting rawness, which might even be accounted rash, if the artist were a weaker man; but . . . it is *distinguished*—a merit so sought after by the gentlemen of the school of Ingres. Moreover it contains some happy tonal combinations; it is possible that the artist will one day become a genuine colourist. This painting possesses another prodigious quality, and one which makes men—true men; it has faith—faith in its own beauty; this is absolute, self-convinced painting,

[1] The 'Théâtre du sieur Séraphin', a marionette-theatre for children, was well known for its sensational production-effects.

which cries aloud 'I will, I will be beautiful, and beautiful according to my own lights; and I know that I shall not lack an audience to please!'

The drawing, too, suggests great determination and finesse; the facial expressions are pretty. All the attitudes are felicitous. Elegance and *distinction* are the particular mark of this picture throughout.

Will it have a swift success? We cannot tell. It is true that every public possesses a conscience and a fund of good will which urge it towards the true; but a public has to be put on a slope and given a push, and our pen is even more unknown than M. Haussoullier's talent.

If it were possible to re-exhibit the same work at different times, and on different occasions, we could guarantee the justice of the public towards this artist.

Nevertheless his painting is quite bold enough to support attack, and it suggests a man who can assume responsibility for his works; so he has only to go off and paint a new picture.

Now that we have so openly displayed our sympathies, dare we . . . ?—but our wretched duty compels us to think of everything!—dare we, I say, admit that after our happy study of this work the names of Giovanni Bellini and of one or two other early Venetian painters crossed our mind? Is M. Haussoullier perhaps one of those who know a little too much about their art? That is a truly dangerous scourge, and one that represses the spontaneity of many an excellent impulse. Let him beware of his erudition, let him beware even of his taste—but that is a glorious failing—and this picture still contains enough originality to promise a happy future.

DECAMPS. Let us hurry on quickly—for Decamps kindles the curiosity in advance—you can always promise yourself a surprise—you count on something new. This year M. Decamps has contrived for use a surprise which surpasses all those on which he worked for so long and with so much love in the past—I mean the *Crochets* and the *Cimbres*.[1] This year M. Decamps has given us a bit of Raphael and Poussin. Yes, by Heaven, he has!

Let us hasten to correct any exaggeration in that sentence by saying that never was imitation better concealed, nor more skilful; it is perfectly permissible, it is praiseworthy, even, to imitate thus.

[1] The *Supplice des crochets* (Wallace Collection) was exhibited in 1839, and the *Défaite des Cimbres* (Louvre) in 1834.

But frankly—in spite of all the pleasure it gives us to peruse an artist's works for the various transformations of his art and the successive preoccupations of his mind—frankly, we miss the old Decamps a little.

With the sense of choice which particularly distinguishes him, he has hit upon that one among all biblical subjects which best suits with the nature of his talent; it is the strange, the epic, fantastic, baroque, mythological story of Samson, the man of impossible labours, who could overturn houses with a push of his shoulder—Samson, that antique cousin of Hercules and the Baron von Münchausen.

The first of these designs[1]—the sudden appearance of the angel in the midst of a wide landscape—makes the mistake of recalling things that we know too well; that raw sky, those rocky boulders, those horizons of granite have for long been familiar to the whole of the younger school, and although it is true to say that it was M. Decamps who first taught them, nevertheless it pains us to be reminded of M. Guignet when we are in front of a Decamps.

Several of these drawings have, as we have already said, a very Italian cast to them; and this mingling of the spirit of the great masters with that of M. Decamps himself—a very Flemish intelligence, in certain respects—has produced a most curious result. For example, you will find figures comporting themselves happily enough in the grand manner, side by side with an effect of an open window and the sun streaming through it to light up the floor, such as would rejoice the heart of the most industrious Fleming. In the drawing, however, which represents the overturning of the temple—a drawing composed like a great and magnificent picture, with gestures and attitudes of historical grandeur—you will find the purest essence of this artist's genius in a flying silhouette of a figure who is taking several steps in his stride and remains eternally suspended in mid-air. How many others would have dreamt of this detail? or if they had, would not have realized it in a different way? But M. Decamps loves to capture nature in the very act, in her simultaneous

[1] Decamps's *Histoire de Samson* in nine drawings was unanimously praised by the critics. The drawings were dispersed at the Delessert sale in May 1911, but a set of lithographic reproductions by Eugène le Roux exists. Decamps himself made a set of reduced replicas, of which one is now in the Lyons Museum. Pierre du Colombier (*Decamps*, 1928) reproduces three of the set, including that which shows Samson at the mill; the same three are reproduced in the Delessert sale catalogue. The statement in Bénézit's dictionary that such a set is in the Musée des Arts Décoratifs, Paris, is incorrect.

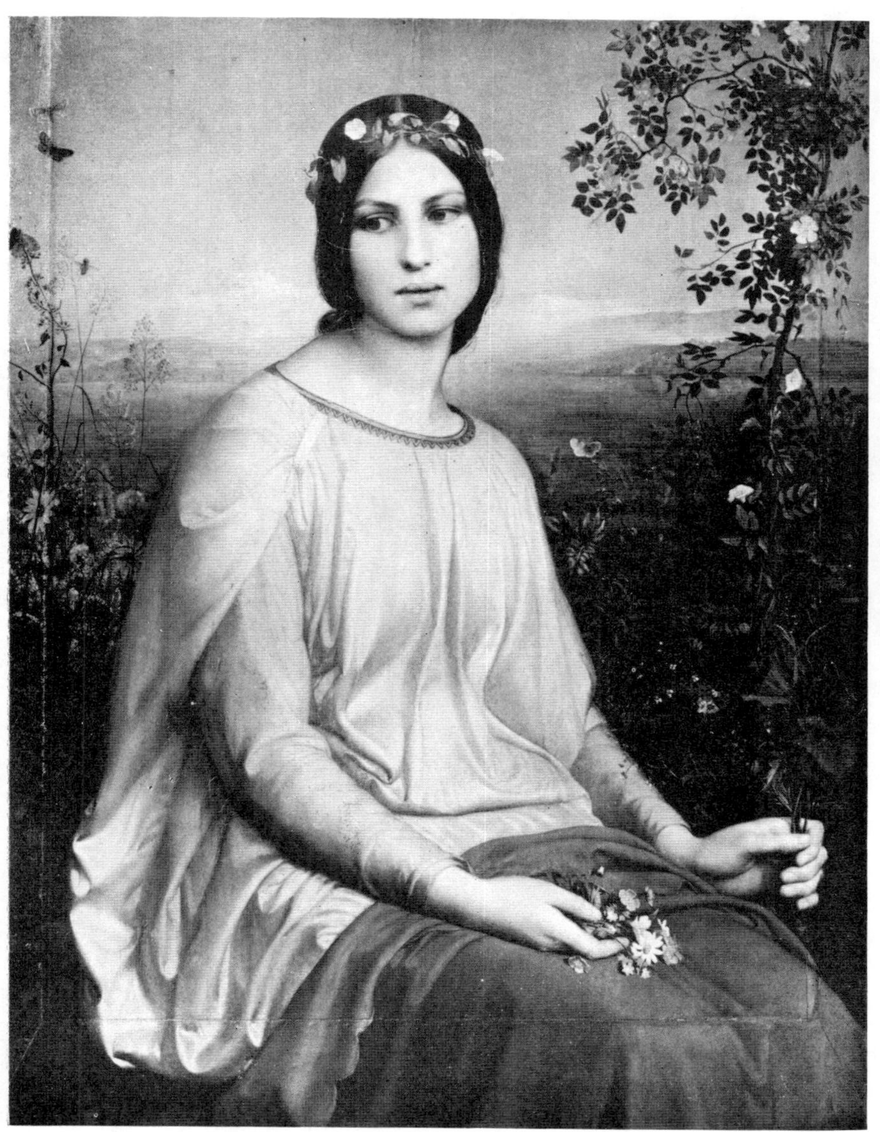

1. JANMOT: *Flowers of the Field*. Salon of 1845. Lyon, Musée des Beaux-Arts.

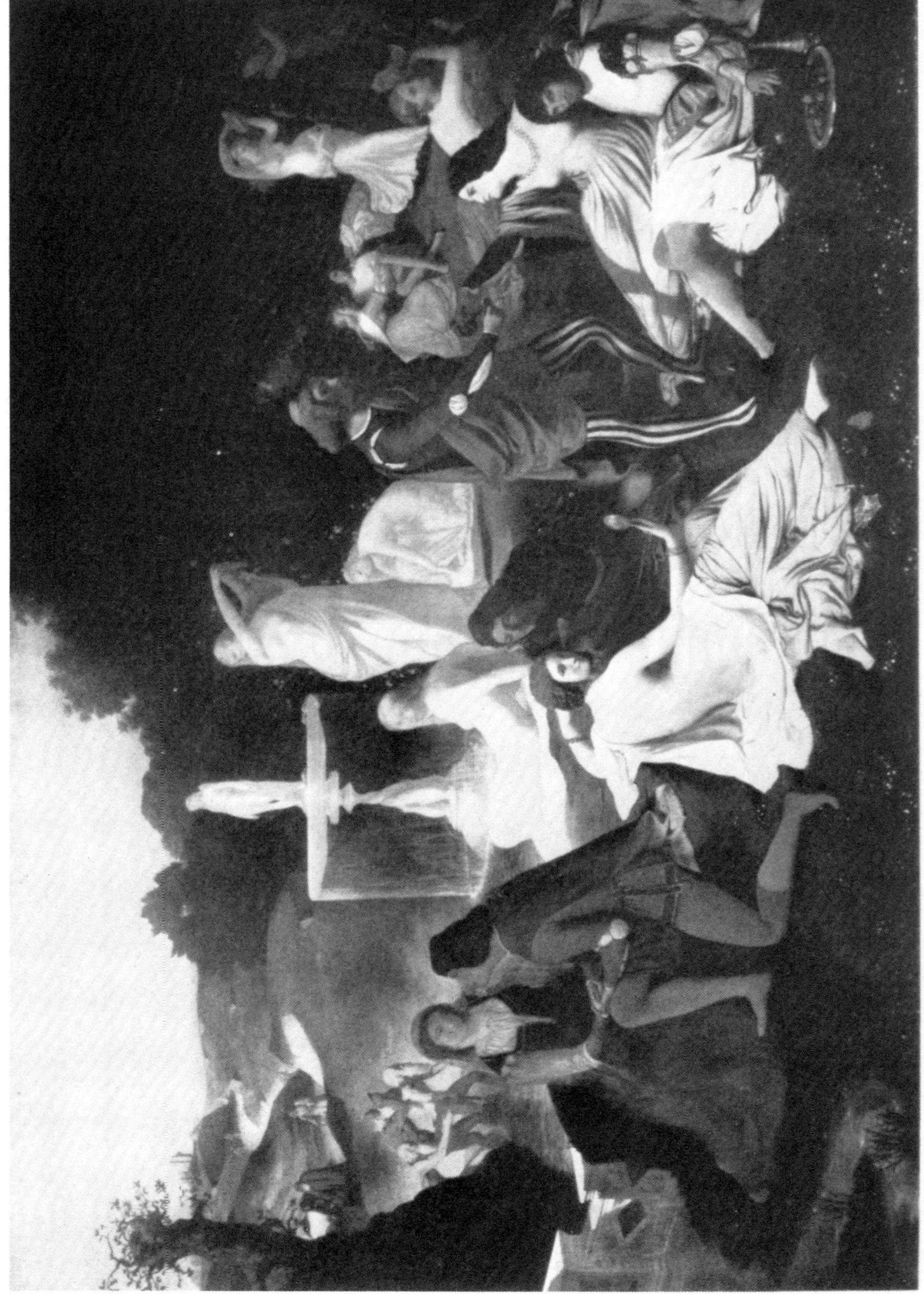

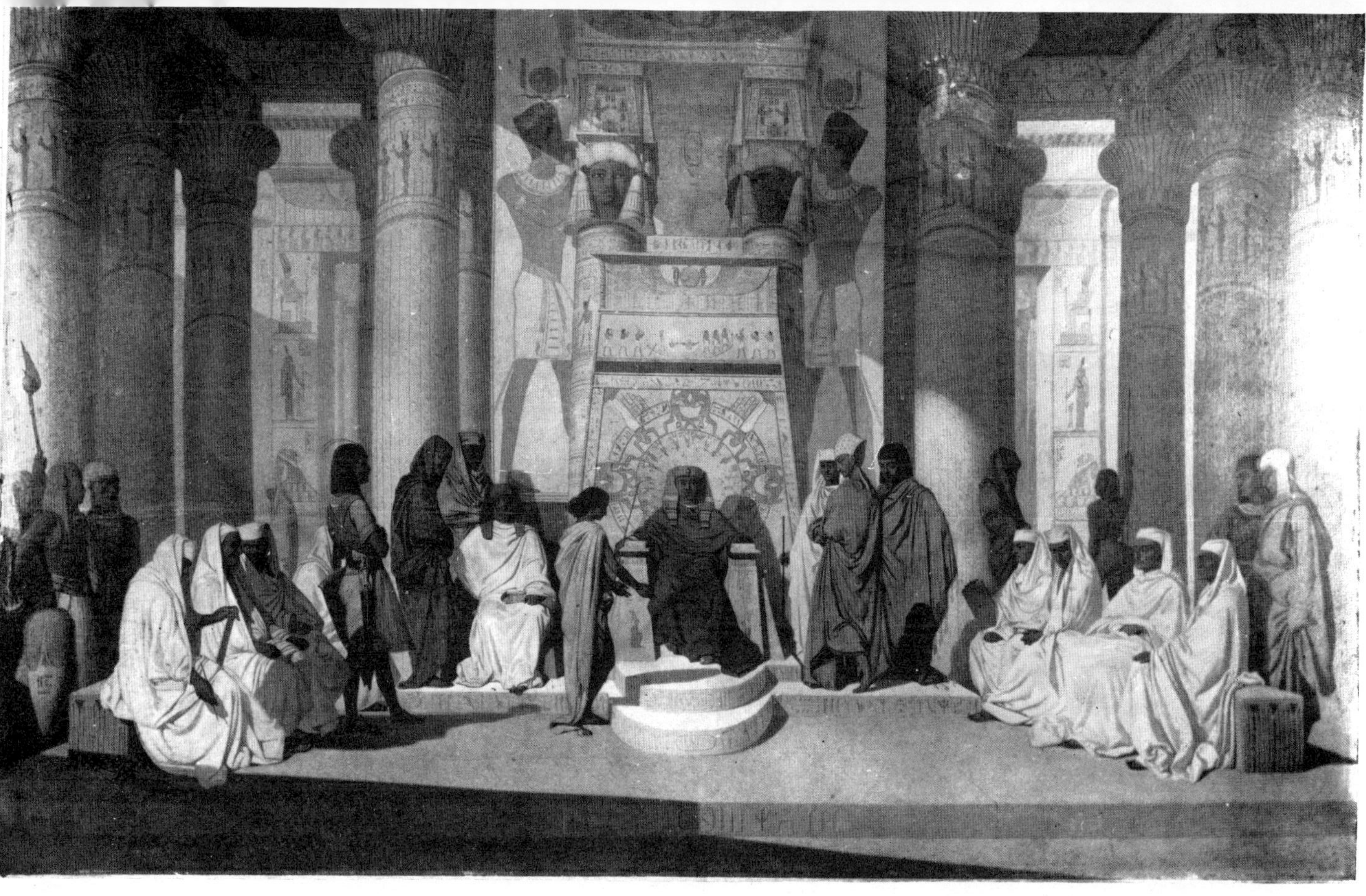

3. GUIGNET: *Joseph interpreting the Dreams of Pharaoh*. Salon of 1845. Rouen, Musée des Beaux-Arts.

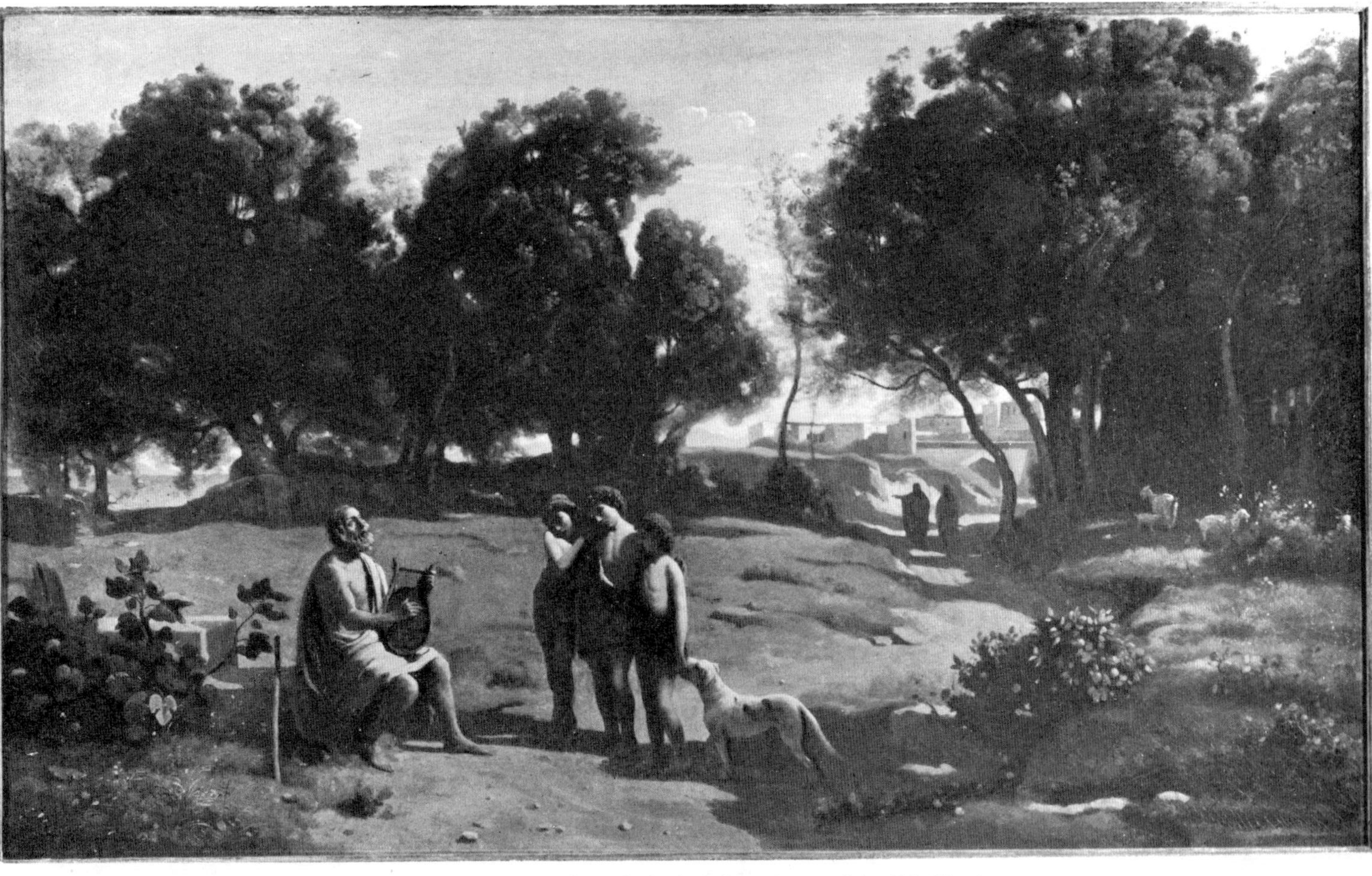

4. COROT: *Homer and the Shepherds*. Salon of 1845. Saint-Lô, Musée.

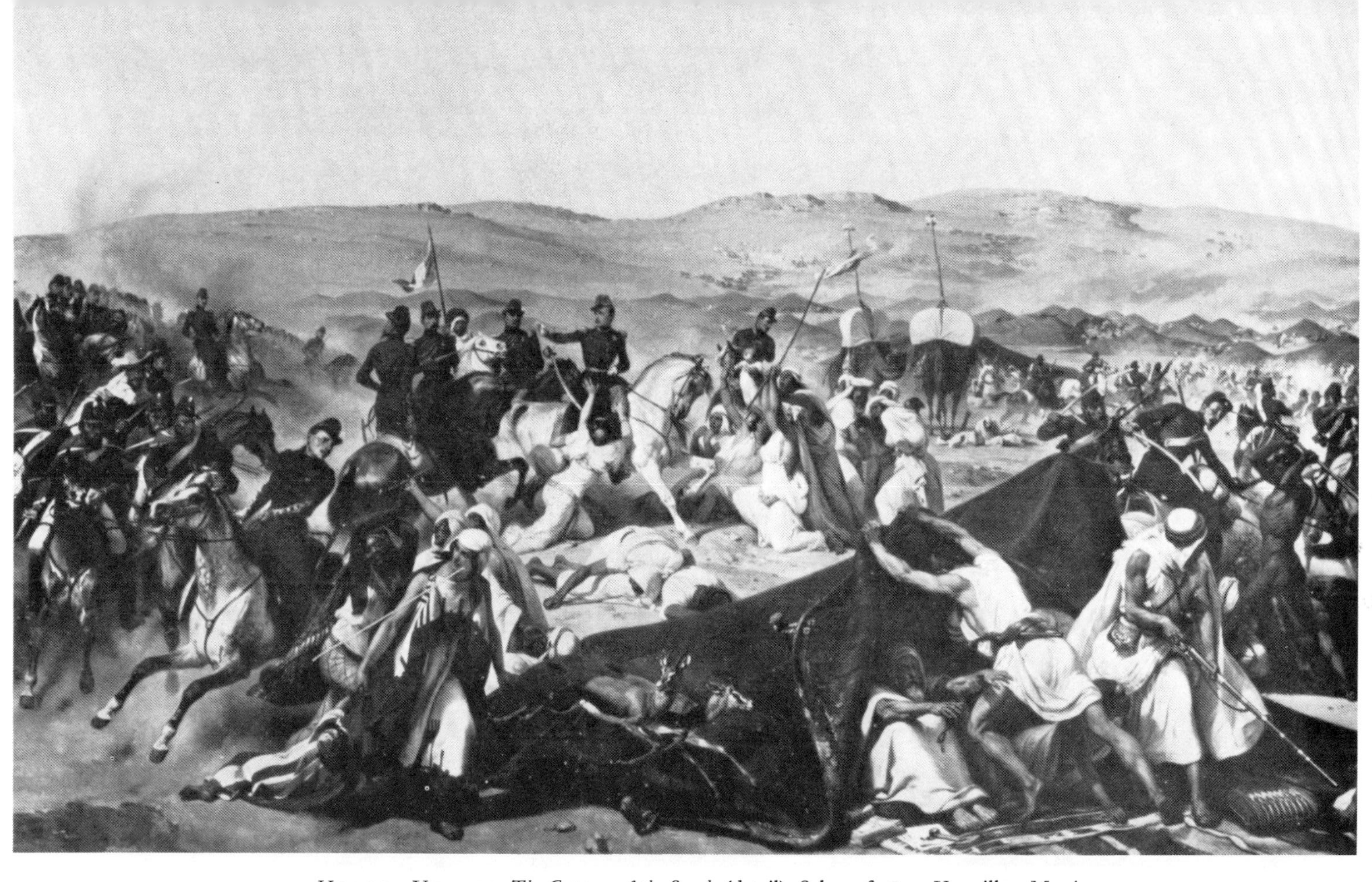

5. Horace Vernet: *The Capture of the Smala* (detail). Salon of 1845. Versailles, Musée.

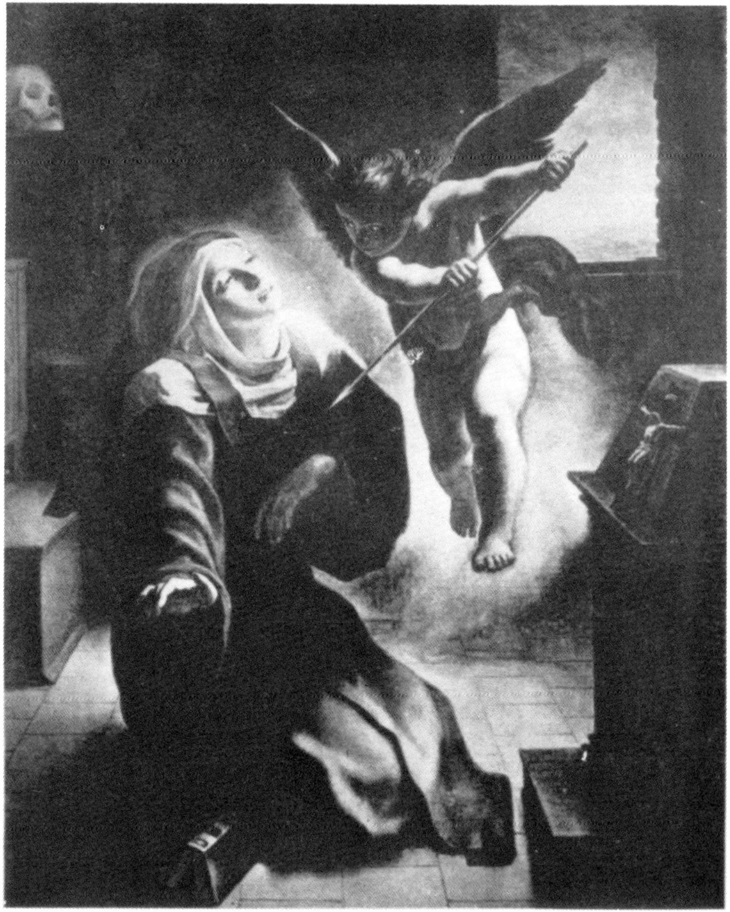

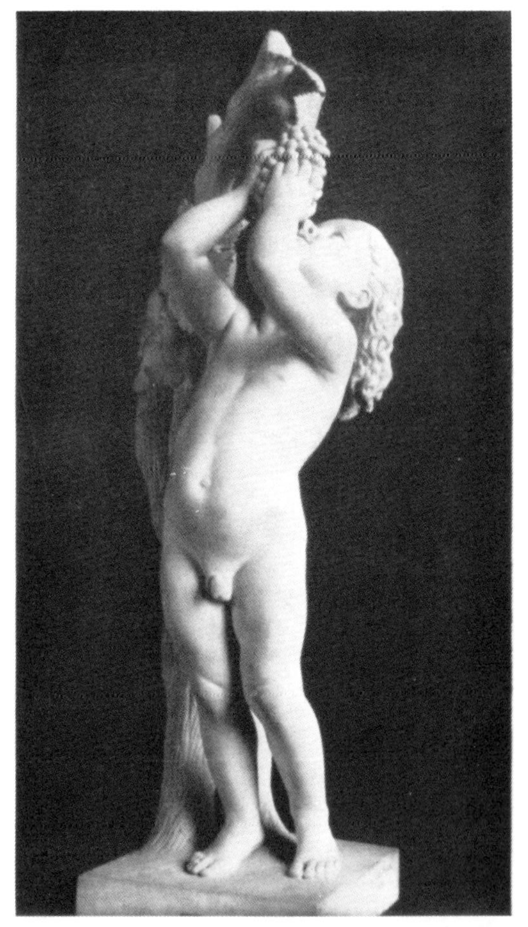

6. PLANET: *The Vision of St. Teresa.* Salon of 1845.

7. DAVID D'ANGERS: *Child with a Bunch of Grapes.*

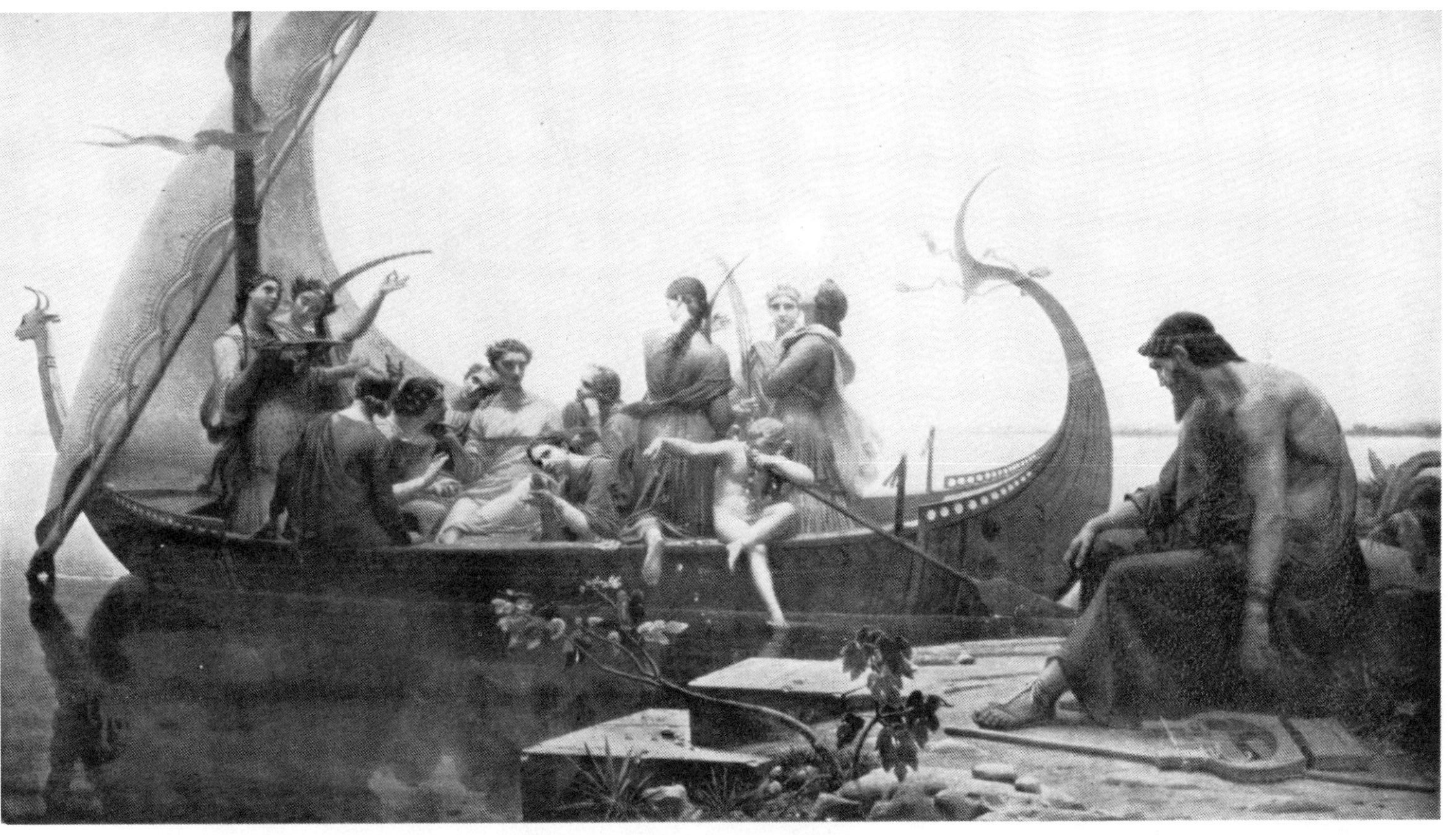

8. GLEYRE: *Evening*. Salon of 1843. Paris, Musée du Louvre.

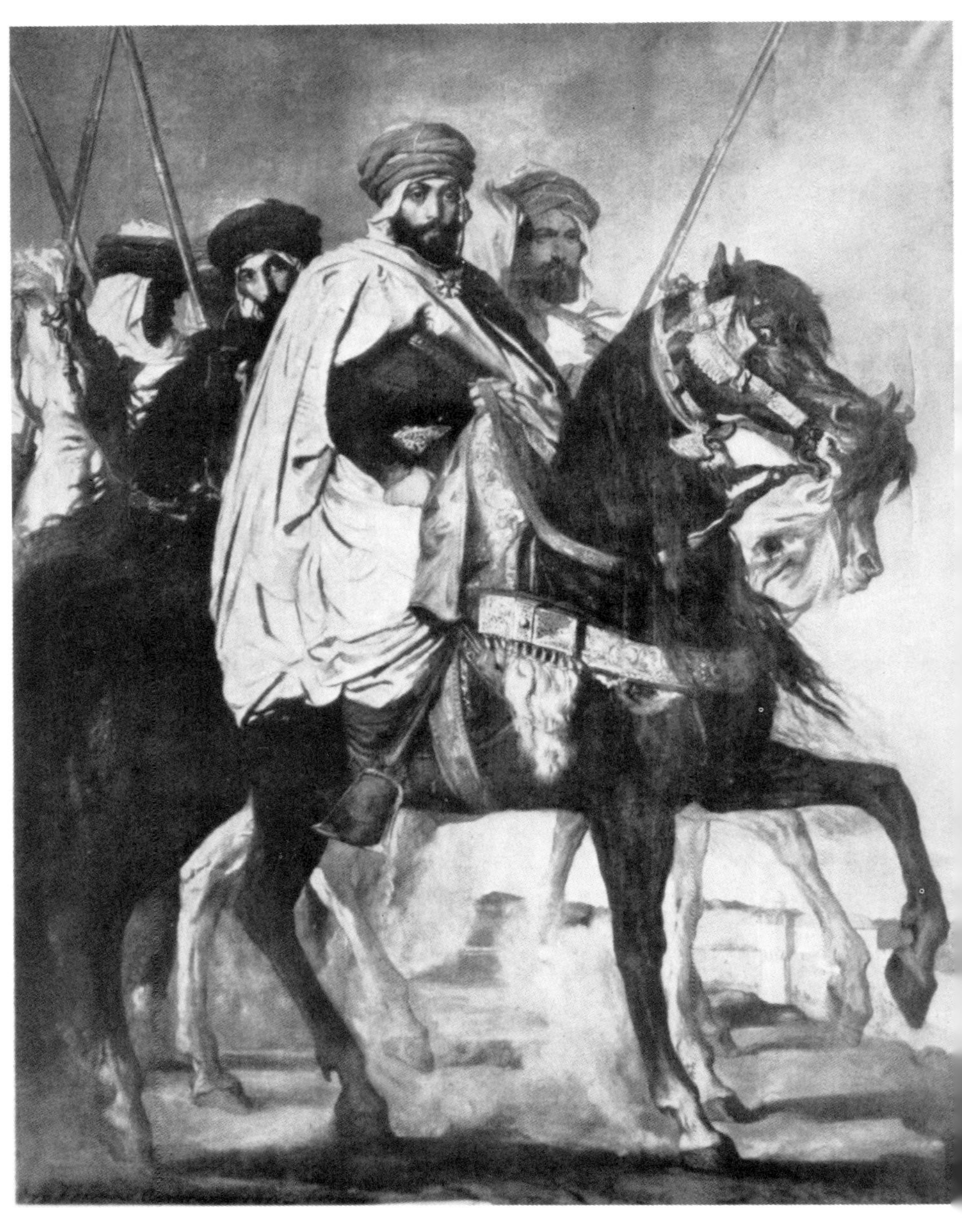

9. CHASSÉRIAU: *The Caliph of Constantine with his Bodyguard*. Salon of 1845. Versailles, Musée

moments of fantasy and reality—in her most sudden and most unexpected aspects.

The finest of all is undeniably the last, in which the broad-shouldered and invincible Samson is condemned to turn a millstone—his head of hair, or rather his mane, is no more—his eyes are blinded—the hero is bending to his toil like a draft-animal—trickery and treachery have mastered that terrible strength which was capable of overturning the very laws of nature. Here, then, at last is a true bit of Decamps, and of the best vintage; here at last we find that sense of irony, of fantasy, I was just about to say that sense of the comic, which we missed so much in the earlier drawings. Samson is turning the wheel like a draft-horse; he walks ponderously, stooping with a rude naivety—the naivety of a dispossessed lion, the resigned sadness, the almost brute abasement of the king of the forests made to drag a cartload of manure or of offal for cats.

In the shadowed foreground an overseer—a jailor, no doubt—is silhouetted against the wall, in an attentive attitude, and is watching him work. What could be more *complete* than these two figures and the millstone? And what more interesting? There was no need even to introduce those inquisitive onlookers behind a grill in the wall—the thing was already fine, and fine enough.

And so we may say that M. Decamps has produced a magnificent illustration, a set of heroic vignettes, to the strange and poetic story of Samson. And although one might perhaps find fault with the over-literal treatment of a wall here and an object there, or with the meticulous and artful mixture of painting and pencil, nevertheless, just because of the new aims which it reveals, this series of designs constitutes one of the finest surprises which this prodigious artist has yet produced. But no doubt he is already getting some new ones ready for us.[1]

ACHILLE DEVÉRIA. And now for a fair name; now for a true and noble artist, to our way of thinking.

The word has gone round among critics and journalists to start intoning a charitable *De Profundis* over the defunct talent of his brother, M. Eugène Devéria;[2] and each time the fancy takes that glorious old veteran

[1] *Paragraphs on* Robert-Fleury *and* Granet *are omitted here.*

[2] This probably refers to the article by Gautier in *La Presse* (28 March 1844), in which Eugène Devéria's *Naissance de Henri IV* (1827; now in the Louvre) was praised at the expense of his most recent work.

of romanticism to show his face, they devoutly enshroud him in the *Birth of Henri IV*, and burn a few candles in honour of his ruined genius. So far so good; it proves that those gentlemen have a conscientious love of beauty, and it does honour to their feelings. But how comes it that no one thinks of tossing a few sincere blossoms, of plaiting a few loyal tributes to the name of M. Achille Devéria? For long years, and all for our pleasure, this artist poured forth from the inexhaustible well of his invention a stream of ravishing vignettes, of charming little interior-pieces, of graceful scenes of fashionable life, such as no Keepsake—in spite of the pretensions of the new names—has since published. He was skilled at colouring the lithographic stone; all his drawings were distinguished, full of feminine charms, and distilled a strangely pleasing kind of reverie. All those fascinating and sweetly sensual women of his were idealizations of women that one had seen and desired in the evening at the *café-concerts*, at the Bouffes, at the Opéra, or in the great Salons. Those lithographs, which the dealers buy for three sous and sell for a franc, are the faithful representatives of that elegant, perfumed society of the Restoration, over which there hovers, like a guardian angel, the blond, romantic ghost of the duchesse de Berry.[1]

But what ingratitude! People speak of them no longer, and today all our routine-minded and anti-poetic asses have turned their loving eyes towards the virtuous asininities and ineptitudes of M. Jules David,[2] or the pedantic paradoxes of M. Vidal.[3]

We are not going to say that M. Achille Devéria has painted an *excellent* picture in his *Sainte Anne instruisant la Vierge* but he has painted a picture whose great value consists in qualities of elegance and clever composition. It is more a patchwork of colour than a painting, it is true, and in these days of *pictorial criticism* of *Catholic art* and of *bold handling*, a work like this must of necessity seem somewhat naive and out of its element. But if the works of a famous man who was once your joy seem today to be naive and out of their element, then at least you might bury him to the accompaniment of a chord or two on the orchestra, you mob of egotists!

[1] The duchesse de Berry (1798-1870), daughter-in-law of Charles X, and mother of the comte de Chambord.

[2] In 1837 Jules David had published a set of moralistic lithographs entitled *Vice et Vertu*. He exhibited three water-colours at the 1845 Salon.

[3] See pp. 28–29.

BOULANGER'S *Sainte famille*[1] is detestable.

His *Bergers de Virgile*—mediocre.

His *Baigneuses*—a little better than Duval Lecamuses or Maurins;[2] but his *Portrait d'homme* is a good piece of painting.

Here we have the last ruins of the old romanticism—this is what it means to come at a time when it is the accepted belief that inspiration is enough and takes the place of everything else; this is the abyss to which the unbridled course of Mazeppa has led.[3] It is M. Victor Hugo that has destroyed M. Boulanger—after having destroyed so many others; it is the poet that has tumbled the painter into the ditch. And yet M. Boulanger can paint decently enough—look at his portraits. But where on earth did he win his diploma as history-painter and inspired artist? Can it have been in the prefaces and odes of his illustrious friend?

BOISSARD. It is to be regretted that M. Boissard,[4] who possesses the qualities of a good painter, has not been able to show us this year an allegorical picture of his representing Music, Painting and Poetry. The jury, who doubtless found its irksome task too fatiguing that day, did not deem it proper to admit it. M. Boissard has always contrived to keep his head above the troubled waters of that bad period of which M. Boulanger prompted us to speak, and thanks to the serious and what one might call the *naïve* qualities of his painting, he has preserved himself from danger. His *Christ en croix* is solidly painted and its colour is good.

SCHNETZ. Alas! what is to be done with these vast Italian pictures? We are in 1845—but we are very afraid that Schnetz will still be giving us the same kind of thing ten years from now.

CHASSÉRIAU. *Le Kalife de Constantine suivi de son escorte.*[5] The immediate attraction of this picture lies in its composition. This procession of horses and noble riders has something that suggests the spontaneous boldness

[1] Now in the church of Saint-Médard, Paris.

[2] The Duval-Lecamuses (father and son) were pupils of David and Delaroche respectively; Antoine Maurin was a pupil of Ary Scheffer.

[3] Boulanger achieved his first great success in 1827 with *Le Supplice de Mazeppa* (Rouen Museum).

[4] Boissard de Boisdenier, painter, musician, writer and dandy, was a friend of Baudelaire's in the days of the Club des Haschischins.

[5] Now in the Versailles Museum; see pl. 9.

of the great masters. But to anyone who has carefully followed M. Chassériau's studies, it must be obvious that many a revolution is still going on in this youthful mind, and that the struggle is not yet over.

The position which he wants to create for himself between Ingres, whose pupil he is, and Delacroix, whom he is seeking to plunder, has an element of ambiguity for everybody—and of embarrassment for himself. That M. Chassériau should find his quarry in Delacroix is simple enough; but that, in spite of all his talent and of all the precocious experience that he has acquired, he should make the fact so obvious—that is where the evil lies. And so this picture contains contradictions. Here and there it already achieves *colour*; elsewhere it is still only a patchwork of *colouring*. Nevertheless its general effect is pleasing, and its composition, we are glad to repeat, is excellent.

As early as the Othello illustrations[1] everyone had noticed how concerned he was with imitating Delacroix. But given tastes as distinguished and a mind as active as those of M. Chassériau, there is every ground for hoping that he will one day become a painter, and an eminent one.[2]

VICTOR ROBERT. Here is a picture which has been very unlucky. We think however, that it has been quite sufficiently *roasted* by the pundits of the press, and that the time has now come to right its wrongs. And yet what a curious idea it was to show these gentlemen *Europe being enlightened by Religion, Philosophy, the Sciences and the Arts*,[3] and to represent each European people by a figure occupying its geographical position in the picture! How could one hope to make something bold acceptable to those scribblers, or to make them understand that allegory is one of the noblest branches of art?

The colour of this enormous composition is good—in bits, at least; it even reveals a search after fresh tones. The attitudes of some of the beautiful women who symbolize the various nations are elegant and original.

It is unfortunate that the eccentric idea of assigning its geographical position to each people should have damaged the ensemble of the composition and the charm of the groups, and that the figures should thus have

[1] A series of fifteen etchings which appeared in 1844.

[2] *A paragraph on* Debon *is omitted here.*

[3] The catalogue contained a lengthy explanation of this picture. Gautier described it as 'cet immense tableau humanitaire et palingénésique'.

been spilt all over the canvas, as in a picture by Claude, whose little manikins are allowed to tumble about as they like.

Is M. Victor Robert a consummate artist, or a crack-brained genius? There are things to be said for either view—expert intentions side by side with the blunders of youth. But on the whole this is one of the most interesting pictures in the Salon, and one of the most worthy of attention.[1]

PLANET is one of those rare pupils of Delacroix who brilliantly reflect certain of their master's qualities.[2]

There is no joy so sweet, in the miserable business of writing a Salon-review, than to come upon a genuinely good and original picture whose name has already been made—by hoots and catcalls.

And in fact this picture really *has* been jeered at. We can perfectly well understand the hatred of architects, masons, sculptors and modellers towards anything that looks like painting; but how comes it that artists can be blind to such things in this picture as its originality of composition, and even its simplicity of colour?

We were charmed at the very start by some hint which it contains of an almost Spanish voluptuousness. M. Planet has done what all first-rate colourists do—that is, he has achieved colour with a small quantity of tones—with red, white, and brown; and the result is delicate and caressing to the eye. St. Teresa,[3] as the painter has represented her here—St. Teresa, sinking, falling, thrilling at the point of the dart with which Divine Love is about to pierce her, is among the happiest inventions in modern painting. The hands are charming. The attitude, for all its naturalness, is as poetic as could be. This picture distills an atmosphere of extreme sensuous rapture and marks its author as a man who is capable of thoroughly understanding a subject—for we are told that St. Teresa was 'afire with so great a love of God that its violence caused her to cry out aloud. . . . And her pain was not bodily but spiritual, although her body had its share in it, even a large one.'[4]

[1] *Paragraphs on* Brune, Glaize, Lépaulle, Mouchy, Appert *and* Bigand *are omitted here.*

[2] Planet's *Souvenirs* (published long after his death, in 1929) contain much useful information concerning Delacroix's methods, as well as information about the present picture.

[3] *La Vision de sainte Thérèse*, now in a private collection, is reproduced on pl. 6.

[4] Quoted, in the catalogue, from St. Teresa's *Life* (chap. XXIX, § 17).

Are we going to speak about the mystical little cupid, hanging in mid-air and about to transfix her with his javelin? No. What is the point? M. Planet is obviously talented enough to paint a *complete* picture another time.[1]

GLEYRE. He it was that captured the heart of the sentimental public with his picture, *Le Soir*.[2] And that was all very well, so long as it was only a question of painting women warbling romantic ballads in a boat—in the same way as a poor opera can triumph over its music with the delightful aid of undraped bosoms—or rather *behinds*. But this year M. Gleyre has taken it into his head to paint apostles[3]—*apostles*, M. Gleyre!—and alas! he has not proved capable of triumphing over his own painting.[4]

JOSEPH FAY. M. Joseph Fay has sent only drawings, like M. Decamps—which is our reason for including him among the history-painters. We are not concerned here with the *technique*, but with the *manner* in which an artist works.

M. Joseph Fay[5] has sent six drawings representing the life of the ancient Germans—they are the cartoons for a frieze executed in fresco in the town hall at Elberfeld in Prussia.

And as a matter of fact these things did strike us as more than a little *Germanic*, and while we were scrutinizing them with the pleasure that any honest work will always afford, we found ourselves thinking of all those modern celebrities from the other side of the Rhine, who are published by the dealers on the Boulevard des Italiens.

These drawings, of which some represent the great struggle between Arminius and the invading Romans, and others the serious and ever-martial games of Peace, bear a noble family likeness to the excellent compositions of Peter Cornelius. Their draughtsmanship is adroit and skilful, and tends towards the neo-Michelangelesque. Every movement is happily conceived and denotes a mind which sincerely loves form, if it be not actually in love with it. We were attracted to these drawings because of

[1] *A paragraph on* Dugasseau *is omitted here.*

[2] Now in the Louvre; otherwise known as *Les Illusions perdues*. See pl. 8.

[3] This painting is now in the church at Montargis; it is reproduced, after an engraving, in Clément, *Gleyre*, 1878, pl. IV.

[4] *Paragraphs on* Pilliard *and* Auguste Hesse *are omitted here.*

[5] A German artist, Joseph Fay was in Paris in 1845–6. He studied for a time with Delaroche.

their beauty; and it is for that that we like them. But on the whole, despite the beauty of this array of intellectual power, we still yearn and cry aloud for *originality*: we should like to see this same talent arrayed in support of ideas more modern—or rather, in support of a new way of seeing and of understanding the arts. By this we do not mean to refer to choice of subject—for in that respect artists are not always free—but rather to the manner in which subjects are comprehended and depicted.

In a word, what is the point of all this erudition when a man has talent?[1]

JANMOT. We were only able to find a single figure-subject by M. Janmot—it is of a woman, seated, with flowers on her knee.[2] This simple figure, which is both serious and melancholy, and whose fine draughtsmanship and slightly raw colour reminds one of the old German masters—this graceful *Dürer* made us excessively curious to find the others; but we were not successful. Here, however, we certainly have a fine painting; and quite apart from the fact that the model is very beautiful, well chosen and well attired, there is in the colour itself, and in this slightly distressing combination of green, pink and red tones, a certain mystical quality which is in keeping with the rest; there is a natural harmony here between colour and drawing.

To complete the idea that one should form of M. Janmot's talent, it will be enough to read the subject of another of his pictures in the catalogue: '*The Assumption of the Virgin*; in the upper part, the Blessed Virgin surrounded by angels, of which the two chief ones represent Chastity and Harmony; in the lower part, *The Rehabilitation of Woman*—an angel breaking her chains.'

ETEX. Oh sculptor! you who have been known to give us good statues—are you unaware, then, that there is a great difference between designing upon a canvas and modelling with clay, and that colour is a melodious science whose secrets are not revealed by merely knowing how to cope with marble? It would be possible to understand a *musician* wanting to ape Delacroix—but a *sculptor*, never! Oh great hewer of stone, why do you want to play the fiddle?[3]

[1] *Paragraphs on* Jollivet, Laviron *and* Matout *are omitted here.*
[2] Janmot's *Fleurs des champs* is now in the Lyons Museum; see pl. 1. Besides his *Assumption* (mentioned below), he also exhibited two portraits.
[3] Etex's painting is now in the Lyons Museum. See also p. 31 below.

III. PORTRAITS

LEON COGNIET has a very fine portrait of a woman, in the *Salon carré*.

This artist occupies a very high position in the middle reaches of taste and invention. If he does not aspire to the level of genius, his is one of those talents which defy criticism by their very completeness within their own moderation. M. Cogniet is as unacquainted with the reckless flights of fantasy as with the rigid systems of the absolutists. To fuse, to mix and to combine while exercising choice, have always been his role and his aim, and he has perfectly fulfilled them. Everything in this excellent portrait—the flesh-tones, the millinery, the background—is handled with an equal felicity.

DUBUFE. For several years now M. Dubufe has been the victim of every art-journalist. If it is a far cry from M. Dubufe to Sir Thomas Lawrence, at any rate it is not without a certain justice that he has inherited some of that artist's urbane popularity. In our opinion the *bourgeois* is quite right to idolize the man who provides him with such pretty women—and almost always such elegantly attired ones.

M. Dubufe has a son who has declined to walk in the steps of his father and has blundered into serious painting.

MLLE EUGÉNIE GAUTIER. Fine colour—firm and elegant drawing. This woman knows her old masters—there is a touch of Van Dyck about her—she paints like a man. Every connoisseur of painting will remember the modelling of two bare arms in a portrait which she showed at the last Salon. Mlle Eugénie Gautier's painting has nothing to do with *woman's painting* which usually makes us think of the domestic precepts of the excellent Chrysale.[1]

BELLOC. M. Belloc has sent several portraits. That of M. Michelet struck us with the excellence of its colour. M. Belloc, who is not well enough known, is among the most skilful of present-day artists. He has turned out some remarkable pupils—Mlle Eugénie Gautier is one of them, we believe. Last year at the Bonne-Nouvelle galleries we saw a child's head of his which reminded us of the very best of Lawrence.[2]

[1] The protesting husband, and father, of Molière's *Femmes Savantes*.

[2] *Paragraphs on* Tissier, Riesener *and* Dupont *are omitted here.*

HAFFNER. Another new name, for us at least. Very badly hung in the little gallery, he has a strikingly effective portrait of a woman. It is difficult to find, which is a real pity. This portrait betokens a colourist of the first order. There is nothing dazzling, sumptuous or vulgar about its colour; it is excessively distinguished and remarkably harmonious. The whole thing is carried out within a very grey tonal scale. Its effect is very skilfully contrived, so that it is at once both soft and striking. The head, which is romantically conceived and of a delicate pallor, stands out against a grey background, which is paler still at this stage, and which, by growing darker towards the edges, gives the impression of forming a halo around it. As well as this, M. Haffner has painted a landscape which is very daring in colour—it shows a waggon with a man and some horses, almost silhouetted against the uncertain brilliance of a twilight sky. Another conscientious seeker . . . how rare they are!

PÉRIGNON[1] has nine sent portraits, of which six are of women. M. Pérignon's heads are as hard and polished as inanimate objects. A real waxwork show.

HORACE VERNET. M. Horace Vernet, the portrait-painter, is inferior to M. Horace Vernet, the heroic painter. His colour surpasses that of M. Court in rawness.

HIPPOLYTE FLANDRIN. Did not M. Flandrin once give us a graceful portrait of a woman leaning against the front of a theatre box, with a bunch of violets at her bosom?[2] But alas! he has come to grief in his portrait of M. Chaix-d'Est-Ange.[3] This is but the semblance of serious painting; he has quite failed to catch the well-known expression of that fine-drawn sardonic and ironical face. It is heavy and dull.

Nevertheless it has just given us the keenest pleasure to find a female portrait by M. Flandrin—a simple head—which reminded us once more of his best works. Its general effect may be a little too gentle, and perhaps it makes the mistake of not rivetting the eye, like M. Lehmann's portrait

[1] According to the critic of *l'Illustration*, Pérignon was 'le portraitiste à la mode'.

[2] Presumably the portrait of Mme Oudiné, exhibited at the 1840 Salon; reproduced facing p. 166 in Louis Flandrin's *Hippolyte Flandrin, Sa Vie et son Oeuvre* (Paris, 1902).

[3] Jurist, statesman and barrister (1800–76): his son defended Baudelaire in the lawsuit over *Les Fleurs du Mal* (August 1857).

of the Princess Belgiojoso.[1] Nevertheless, as this picture is a small one, M. Flandrin has been able to carry it through to perfection. The modelling is beautiful, and the whole thing has the merit, which is rare among these gentlemen, of seeming to have been done all in one breath and at the first attempt.[2]

HENRI SCHEFFER. To give this artist his proper due, we dare not suppose that this portrait of His Majesty was done from the life. There are but few faces in contemporary history which are so strongly marked as that of Louis-Philippe. Toil and fatigue have printed some goodly wrinkles upon it—but of these the artist shows no knowledge. It pains us that France should not possess a single real portrait of her king. One man alone is worthy of that task—it is M. Ingres.

All of M. Henri Scheffer's portraits are painted with the same blind and meticulous honesty, the same monotonous and patient conscientiousness.[3]

DIAZ. M. Diaz usually paints little pictures whose magical colour surpasses even the fantastic visions of the kaleidoscope. This year he has sent some small full-length portraits. But it is not only colour, but lines and modelling, that go to make a portrait. No doubt our genre-painter will get his own back for this year's aberration.

IV. GENRE-PAINTINGS

BARON has taken his *Oies du père Philippe*[4] from one of La Fontaine's tales. He has made it an excuse for introducing pretty women, shady trees, and variegated colours, for all that.

Its general effect is most engaging, but it must be accounted the *rococo* of Romanticism. It contains elements of Couture, a little of Célestin Nanteuil's technique, and a lot of tints borrowed from Roqueplan and Clément Boulanger. Stand in front of this picture and reflect how cold an excessively expert and brilliantly-coloured painting can still remain when it lacks an individual temperament.

[1] Henri Lehmann's portrait of the Princess Belgiojoso was one of the great successes of the 1844 Salon. Reproduced in R. Barbiera's *La Principessa Belgioioso* (edition of 1914), as the property of the Marchese Franco Dal Pozzo.

[2] *Paragraphs on* Richardot *and* Verdier *are omitted here.*

[3] *A paragraph on* Leiendecker *is omitted here.*

[4] Reproduced *Moniteur des Arts* (I, 96).

ISABEY. *Un Intérieur d'alchimiste.*[1] These scenes always contain crocodiles, stuffed birds, vast morocco-bound tomes, fiery braziers, and an old man in a dressing-gown—that is to say, a great diversity of tints. This explains the partiality of certain colourists for so commonplace a subject.

M. Isabey is a true colourist—always brilliant, frequently subtle. He has been one of the most justly fortunate of the men of the new movement.

LECURIEUX. *Salomon de Caus, à Bicêtre.*[2] We are in a popular playhouse that has gone in for real literature for a change. The curtain has just risen, and all the actors are facing the public.

A great lord, with Marion Delorme leaning sinuously upon his arm, is turning a deaf ear to the complaints of Salomon, who is gesticulating like a maniac in the background.

The production is well-staged; all the lunatics are charming, picturesque, and know their parts perfectly. Indeed, we cannot understand Marion Delorme's dismay at the sight of such charming madmen.

The uniform effect created by this picture is one of *café au lait*. It is as russet in colour as a wretched, dust-ridden day.

The drawing—that of a vignette, an illustration. What is the point of attempting what is called serious painting when one is neither a colourist nor a draughtsman?[3]

TASSAERT. A little devotional picture, done almost like a love-scene. The Virgin is suckling the infant Jesus, beneath a coronet of flowers and little cupids. We had already taken note of M. Tassaert last year. He combines good, moderately bright colour with a great deal of taste.[4]

GUILLEMIN. Though his execution certainly has merit, M. Guillemin wastes too much talent supporting a bad cause—the cause of *wit in painting*. By this I mean providing the catalogue-printer with captions aimed at the Sunday public.

[1] Reproduced *Illustr.* vol. v (1845) p. 57.

[2] Reproduced *Illustr.* vol. v (1845) p. 41. Salomon de Caus was an engineer who in his writings foreshadowed the theory of steam-power. The story of his confinement in the asylum at Bicêtre is related in a letter from Marion Delorme, the famous seventeenth-century courtesan, which is quoted in the catalogue.

[3] *A paragraph on* Mme Céleste Pensotti *is omitted here.*

[4] *Paragraphs on* Leleux frères *and* Lepoitevin *are omitted here.*

MULLER. Can it be the *Saturday* public, on the other hand, that M. Muller thinks to please when he chooses his subjects from Shakespeare and Victor Hugo?[1] Enormous 'Empire' cupids in the guise of sylphs. So it is not enough to be a colourist in order to have taste. His *Fanny*, however, is better.[2]

GIGOUX. M. Gigoux has given us the pleasant task of re-reading the account of the death of Manon Lescaut[3] in the catalogue. But his picture is bad; it has no style, and its composition and colour are bad. It lacks all character, it lacks all feeling for its subject. Whatever is this Desgrieux? I would not recognize him.

No more can I recognize M. Gigoux himself in this picture—the M. Gigoux who several years ago was acclaimed by the public as the equal of the most serious innovators in art. . . . Can it be that he is embarrassed today by his reputation as a painter?

RUDOLPHE LEHMANN.[4] His Italian women this year make us regret those of last year.[5]

PAPETY showed great promise, they say. On his return from Italy (which was heralded by some injudicious applause), he exhibited an enormous canvas[6] in which, although the recent usages of the Academy of Painting were too clearly discernible, he had nevertheless hit upon some felicitous poses and several compositional *motifs*; and in spite of its fan-like colour, there was every ground for predicting the artist a serious future. Since then he has remained in the secondary class of the men who paint well and have portfolios full of scraps of ideas all ready to be used. His two pictures this year (*Memphis* and *Un Assaut*)[7] are commonplace in colour.

[1] Muller's *Sylphe endormi* was supported by a quotation from Victor Hugo, and his *Lutin Puck* by one by Shakespeare.

[2] *Paragraphs on* Duval Lecamus (père) *and* Duval Lecamus (Jules) *are omitted here.*

[3] Reproduced *l'Artiste*, 4th series, vol. IV, and Ferran's edition of the *Salon de 1845*, facing p. 178.

[4] Rudolphe Lehmann is not to be confused with his brother Henri Lehmann, to whose portrait of the Princess Belgiojoso there is reference above. Of the former's paintings of Italian peasant women, one is reproduced *Illustr.* vol. v (1845) p. 137, and another *Moniteur des Arts* (II, p. 41).[5]

[5] *Paragraphs on* De la Foulhouze, Pérèse, De Dreux *and* Mme Calamatta *are omitted here.*

[6] Presumably his *Rêve de bonheur*, exhibited in 1843.

[7] *Memphis*, reproduced *Illustr.* vol. v (1845), p. 137. *Un Assaut* (correct title, *Guillaume de Clermont défendant Ptolémais*) is in the Versailles Museum.

Nevertheless their general appearance differs considerably, which leads us to imagine that M. Papety has not yet discovered his manner.

ADRIEN GUIGNET. There is no doubt that M. Adrien Guignet has talent; he knows how to compose and arrange. But why, then, this perpetual *doubt*? One moment it is Decamps, and the next, Salvator. This year you would think that he had taken some motives from Egyptian sculpture or antique mosaics, and then had coloured them, on papyrus (*Les Pharaons*).[1] And yet if Salvator or Decamps were painting Psammenit or Pharaoh, even so they would do them in the manner of Salvator or Decamps. Why then does M. Guignet. . .?

MEISSONIER. Three pictures: *Soldats jouant aux dés—Jeune homme feuilletant un carton*[2]*—Deux buveurs jouant aux cartes.*

Times change—and with them, manners; fashions change—and with them, schools. In spite of ourselves, M. Meissonier makes us think of M. Martin Drolling. All reputations, even the most deserved ones, contain a mass of little secrets. Thus, when the celebrated Monsieur X. was asked what he had seen at the Salon, he replied that the only thing he had seen was a Meissonier—in order to avoid speaking about the equally famous Monsieur Y., who, for his part, said exactly the same thing! See what a good thing it is to act as a club for two rivals to beat one another with!

On the whole M. Meissonier executes his little figures admirably. He is a Fleming, minus the fantasy, the charm, the colour, the naïveté—and the pipe![3]

HORNUNG. '*Le plus têtu des trois n'est pas celui qu'on pense*'.[4]

BARD. See above.

GEFFROY. See above.

[1] *Joseph expliquant les songes du Pharaon* is now in the Rouen Museum. See pl. 3.
[2] Reproduced (*Jeune homme regardant des dessins*), *Illustr.* vol. v (1845), p. 184.
[3] *Paragraphs on* Jacquand, Roehn, Rémond *and* Henri Scheffer *are omitted here.*
[4] 'The most stubborn of the three is not the one you think', was the title of Hornung's painting; it showed a boy and a girl sitting on a donkey, and served Baudelaire with a convenient riddle with which to dismiss his last three genre-painters. See La Fontaine, *Le Meunier, son fils, et l'âne*, line 37.

V. LANDSCAPES

COROT. At the head of the modern school of landscape stands M. Corot. If M. Théodore Rousseau[1] were to exhibit, his supremacy would be in some doubt, for to a *naïveté*, an originality which are at least equal, M. Rousseau adds a greater charm and a greater sureness of execution. It is *naïveté* and originality, in fact, which constitute M. Corot's worth. Obviously this artist loves nature sincerely, and knows how to look at her with as much knowledge as love. The qualities by which he excels are so strong—because they are qualities of heart and soul—that M. Corot's influence is visible today in almost all the works of the young landscape-painters—in those, above all, who already had the good sense to imitate him and to profit by his manner before he was famous and at a time when his reputation still did not extend beyond the world of the studios. From the depths of his modesty, M. Corot has acted upon a whole host of artists. Some have devoted themselves to combing nature for the themes, the views and the colours for which he has a fondness—to fostering the same subjects; others have even tried to paraphrase his awkwardness. Now, on the subject of this pretended *awkwardness* of M. Corot's, it seems to us that there is a slight misconception to clear up. After having conscientiously admired and faithfully praised a picture by Corot, our fledgling connoisseurs always end by declaring that it comes to grief in its execution; they agree in this, that decidely M. Corot does not know how to paint. Splendid fellows! who first of all are unaware that a work of genius (or if you prefer, a work of the soul), in which every element is well seen, well observed, well understood and well imagined, will always be very well executed when it is *sufficiently* so. Next, that there is a great difference between a work that is *complete* and a work that is *finished*; that in general what is *complete* is not *finished*, and that a thing that is highly *finished* need not be *complete* at all; and that the value of a telling, expressive and well-placed touch is enormous, etc.—from all of which it follows that M. Corot paints like the great masters. We need look no further for an example than to his picture of last year,[2] which was

[1] See note, p. 109.

[2] Exhibited in 1844 as *Paysage avec figures*, this picture was extensively repainted by the artist and exhibited again thirteen years later; it is now in the Chantilly Museum (*Le Concert*).

imbued with an even greater tenderness and melancholy than usual. That verdant landscape, in which a woman was sitting playing the violin—that pool of sunlight in the middle distance, which lit up and coloured the grass in a different manner from the foreground, was certainly a most successful stroke of aesthetic daring. M. Corot is quite as strong this year as in the past—but the eye of the public has become so accustomed to neat, glistening and industriously polished morsels that the same criticism is always levelled at him.

Another proof of M. Corot's powers, be it only in the sphere of technique, is that he knows how to be a colourist within a scarcely varied tonal range—and that he is always a harmonist even when he uses fairly raw and vivid colours. His composition is always impeccable. Thus in his *Homère et les bergers*[1] there is nothing unnecessary, nothing to be pruned—not even the two little figures walking away in conversation down the path. The three little shepherds with their dog are enchanting, like those excellent little scraps of bas-relief which are sometimes to be found on the pedestals of antique statues. But is not Homer himself a little too much like Belisarius, perhaps?

Daphnis et Chloe[2] is another picture full of charms; its composition, like all good compositions—as we have often observed—has the merit of the unexpected.

FRANÇAIS is another landscape-painter of the highest merit—a merit somewhat like that of Corot, and one that we should be inclined to characterize as 'love of nature'; but it is already less naïve, more artful—it smacks much more of its painter—and it is also easier to understand. His painting, *Le Soir*,[3] is beautiful in colour.

PAUL HUET. *Un vieux château des rochers*. Can it be that M. Paul Huet is seeking to modify his manner?

But it was already excellent as it was.

HAFFNER. Prodigious originality—above all in colour. This is the first time that we have seen works by M. Haffner, so we do not know if he is by rights a landscape-painter or a portrait painter—all the more so because he excels in both genres.

[1] Now in the Saint-Lô Museum; see pl. 4.
[2] Reproduced *Moniteur des Arts* (I, 152).
[3] Reproduced *Moniteur des Arts* (I, 64).

TROYON always paints beautiful, luxuriant landscapes, and he paints them in the role of colourist and even that of *observer*—but he always wearies the eye by the unshakeable self-confidence of his manner and the restless flicker of his brush-strokes. It is not pleasant to see a man so sure of himself.

CURZON has painted a highly original view called *Les Houblons*. It is quite simply a horizon, framed in the leaves and branches of the foreground. As well as this, M. Curzon has produced a very fine drawing of which we shall shortly have occasion to speak.[1]

CALAME AND DIDAY.[2] For a long time people were under the impression that this was one and the same artist, suffering from a *chronic dualism*; but later it was observed that he had a preference for the name Calame on the days when he was painting well.[3]

BORGET. Eternal views of India and China.[4] Doubtless it is all very well done, but they are too much like travel-essays or accounts of manners and customs. There are people, however, who sigh for what they have never seen—such as the boulevard du Temple, or the galeries de Bois![5] M. Borget's pictures make us sigh for that China where the very breeze, according to M. Heine,[6] takes on a comical sound as it slips past the little hanging bells, and where nature and man cannot look at one another without laughing.

PAUL FLANDRIN. It is understandable that a man should damp down the reflected lights on a head in order to make the modelling more visible —and above all so when his name is Ingres. But who on earth was the weird eccentric who first took it into his head to 'ingrize' the countryside?[7]

[1] *Paragraphs on* Flers *and* Wickemberg *are omitted here.*
[2] Calame was the pupil of Diday. This year Calame exhibited *Un Orage* and Diday *La Suite d'un orage dans les Alpes.*
[3] *Paragraphs on* Dauzats, Frère, Chacaton, Loubon, Garnerey *and* Joyant *are omitted here.*
[4] His *Pont Chinois* was reproduced *Illustr.* vol. v (1845), p. 136. He had been exhibiting Chinese and Indian views since 1836.
[5] A favourite rendezvous in the Palais-Royal: it had already been demolished when Baudelaire wrote, and the site is now occupied by the Galerie d'Orléans.
[6] The allusion is to a passage in Heine's *Die romantische Schule* (Bk. III, chap. 1, § 1).
[7] *Paragraphs on* Blanchard, Lapierre *and* Lavieille *are omitted here.*

BRASCASSAT. Without doubt too much fuss is being made of M. Brascassat, who, man of sense and talent as he is, must really know that the Flemish gallery contains a lot of pictures of the same kind as his[1]—quite as fully realized, more broadly painted—and of a better colour.—Similarly, too much fuss is made of

SAINT-JEAN, who is of the school of Lyons, the penitentiary of painting, the corner of the known world in which the infinitely minute is wrought the best. We prefer the flowers and fruits of Rubens; they seem to us more natural. Moreover the general effect of M. Saint-Jean's picture[2] is most wretched—it is monotonously yellow. On the whole, however well executed they may be, M. Saint-Jean's pictures are dining-room pictures—not cabinet or gallery-pictures, but real *dining-room* pictures.[3]

ARONDEL.[4] A great heap of game of every kind. This ill-composed picture—more a hotch-potch than a composition, as though it was aiming above all at *quantity*—has nevertheless what is a very rare quality these days; it is painted with a great *naïveté*, without any dogmatism of school or pedantry of studio. And from this it follows that parts of it are really well painted. Unhappily some others are of a muddy brown colour, which gives the picture a certain effect of dinginess—but all the clear or rich tones are thoroughly effective. What therefore struck us in this picture, was its mixture of clumsiness and skill—blunders suggesting a man who had not painted for years, and assurance suggesting a man who had painted a great deal.

CHAZAL has painted the *Yucca gloriosa* which flowered last year in the park at Neuilly. It would be a good thing if all those people who cling so desperately to microscopic truth, and believe themselves to be painters, could see this little picture; and if the following little observations could be pumped into their ears through an ear-trumpet: 'This picture is a success not because everything is there and you can count each leaf, but

[1] Of five landscapes exhibited, one, *Vache attaquée par des loups*, was reproduced *Illustr.* vol. v (1845), p. 39, and another, *Paysage*, reproduced *Moniteur des Arts* (I, 112).

[2] *Fruits et Fleurs*, a copy of which is now in the Dijon Museum.

[3] *Paragraphs on* Kiörboe, Philippe Rousseau *and* Béranger *are omitted here.*

[4] This obscure artist was twice mentioned by Baudelaire in his salon-reviews (see p. 110 below). He is generally identified with the dealer Arondel who sold Baudelaire false Bassanos and in whose debt Baudelaire long remained. His address is given in the catalogue as the Hôtel Pimodan, quai d'Anjou, where Baudelaire also had lived.

because at the same time it captures the general character of nature; because it conveys well the raw greenness of a park beside the Seine and the effect of our cold sun; in short, because it is done with a profound *naïveté*, whereas all of you spend far too much of your time being. . . *artists*!'

VI. DRAWINGS—ENGRAVINGS

BRILLOUIN has sent five pencil-drawings which are a little like those of M. de Lemud; these, however, have more firmness and perhaps more character. Their composition on the whole is good. 'Tintoretto giving a drawing-lesson to his daughter' is certainly an excellent thing. What chiefly distinguishes these drawings is their nobility of structure, their seriousness and the characterization of the heads.

CURZON. *Une sérénade dans un bateau* is one of the most distinguished things in the Salon. The arrangement of all those figures is most happy, and the old man lying amid his garlands at the end of the boat is a most delightful idea. There is some affinity between M. Curzon's composition and those of M. Brillouin; they have this above all in common—they are well drawn, and drawn with a vivid touch.[1]

MARÉCHAL. Without doubt *La Grappe*[2] is a fine pastel, and good in colour. But we must criticize all those gentlemen of the school of Metz[3] for only as a rule achieving a *conventional* seriousness, an *imitation* of real mastery. We would say this without wishing in the very least to detract from the honour of their efforts. . . .[4]

VIDAL.[5] It was last year, to the best of our belief, that the parrot-cry

[1] *A paragraph on* De Rudder *is omitted here.* [2] Reproduced *Illustr.* vol. V (1845), p. 185.

[3] The *Société des Amis des Arts* at Metz was founded in 1834, and it was from this that the *Ecole de Metz* sprang. Maréchal was one of its leaders. See Ferran's edition of the *Salon de 1845* (pp. 272–3) for further details. See also p. 86 below.

[4] *Paragraphs on* Tourneux, Pollet, Chabal, Alphonse Masson *and* Antonin Moine *are omitted here.*

[5] Baudelaire seems to be confusing two artists of this name. *Victor* Vidal, who exhibited five drawings this year (one of them, *L'Amour de soi-même*, reproduced *Illustr.* vol. v (1845), p. 152), had not exhibited since 1841, whereas *Vincent* Vidal, who showed nothing in 1845, had exhibited five pastels in the previous year. It seems, therefore that the 'préjugé Vidal', to which Baudelaire again referred in 1846 (see pp. 87–88 below), originated with Vincent, and not Victor, Vidal.

about Vidal's drawings began to be raised. It would be a good thing to be finished with it once and for all. Every effort is now being made to present M. Vidal to us as a serious draughtsman. His are *very finished* drawings—but they are *incomplete*; nevertheless it must be admitted that they have more elegance than those of Maurin and Jules David. We beg forgiveness for insisting so strongly on this point—but we know a critic who took it into his head to speak about Watteau in connection with M. Vidal.[1]

JACQUE. Here we have a new name which will continue, let us hope, to grow greater. M. Jacque's[2] etching is very bold and he has grasped his subject admirably. There is a directness and a freedom about everything that M. Jacque does upon his copper which reminds one of the old masters. He is known, besides, to have executed some remarkable reproductions of Rembrandt's etchings.

VII. SCULPTURES

BARTOLINI.[3] We in Paris have a right to be suspicious of foreign reputations. Our neighbours have so often beguiled our credulous admiration with masterpieces which they never showed—or which, if at last they consented to reveal them, were an object of embarrassment for them, as for us—that we always remain on our guard against new traps. Thus it was only with an excessive feeling of suspicion that we approached the *Nymphe au scorpion*. But this time we have found it quite impossible to withhold our admiration from a foreign artist. Certainly our sculptors have more skill—an excessive preoccupation with technique engrosses them just as it does our painters; but it is precisely because of the qualities which our artists have to some extent forgotten—namely taste, nobility, grace—that we regard M. Bartolini's exhibit as the capital work of the Salon of sculpture. We know that more than one of the *sculpturizers* of whom we are about to speak are very well fitted to pick out the several faults of execution which this statue contains—a little too much softness

[1] Gautier had invoked the name of Watteau (and of Chardin) in *La Presse*, 16 April; and Thoré added Boucher and Fragonard. *Paragraphs on* Mme de Mirbel *and* Henriquel-Dupont *are omitted here.*

[2] This was Jacque's first Salon.

[3] Lorenzo Bartolini (1777–1850) was one of the most admired Italian sculptors of his day. His portrait had been painted by Ingres in 1806, and again in 1820.

here, a lack of firmness there; in short, certain flabby passages, and a touch of meagreness about the arms—but not one of them has managed to hit upon such a pretty *motif*; not one of them has this fine taste, this purity of aim, this chastity of line which by no means excludes originality. The legs are charming, the head graceful and coquettish; it is probable that it is quite simply a well-chosen model.* The less a workman obtrudes himself in his work and the purer and clearer its aims, the more charmed we are.

DAVID. This is far from the case with M. David, for example, whose works always make us think of Ribera. And yet our comparison is not entirely just, for Ribera is only a man of technique *into the bargain*, so to speak—in addition to that, he is full of fire, originality, rage and irony.

Certainly it would be difficult to model or to trace a contour better than M. David. His child hanging on to a bunch of grapes,[1] which was already familiar to us from a few charming lines by Sainte-Beuve, is an intriguing thing; admittedly it is real flesh and blood, but it is as *senseless* as nature—and surely it is an uncontested truth that it is no part of the aim of sculpture to go into rivalry with plaster-casts. Having made this point, let us stand back and admire the beauty of its workmanship.[2]

PRADIER. You would think that M. Pradier had wanted to get away from himself and to ascend, in one leap, towards the supernal regions. We do not know how to praise his statue;[3] it is incomparably skilful; it is pretty from every angle, though doubtless one could trace some of its detail to the Museum of antique sculpture, for it is a prodigious mixture of hidden borrowings. Beneath this new skin the old Pradier still lives, to give an exquisite charm to this figure. Certainly it is a noble *tour de force*; but M. Bartolini's Nymph, with all its imperfections, seems to us to be more original.

FEUCHÈRE. More cleverness—but Good Heavens! shall we never get any further?

* What makes us only the prouder of our opinion is that we know it to be shared by one of the greatest painters of the modern school. (C.B.)

[1] *L'Enfant à la grappe*, now in the Louvre. Sainte-Beuve's poem, 'Sur une statue d'enfant, à David, statuaire', is included in his *Pensées d'Août*. See pl. 7.

[2] *A paragraph on* Bosio *is omitted here.*

[3] *Phryné*, reproduced *Illustr.* vol. v (1845), p. 173.

This young artist has already had his good years at the Salon; his statue is evidently destined for a success. Quite apart from the fact that its subject is a happy one (for virgin purity can generally count on a public, like everything that touches the popular affections), this Joan of Arc, which we had already seen in plaster,[1] gains much by being enlarged. The fall of the drapery is good—not at all like that of the generality of sculptors; the arms and the feet are very finely wrought; the head is perhaps a little commonplace.[2]

ETEX. M. Etex has never been able to produce anything complete. His conceptions are often happy—he possesses a certain pregnancy of thought which reveals itself quickly enough and which we find pleasing; but his work is always spoiled by quite considerable passages. Thus, when seen from behind, his group 'Hero and Leander' seems heavy, and the lines do not unfold harmoniously. Hero's shoulders and back are unworthy of her hips and legs.[3]

DANTAN has done several good busts[4]—noble, and obviously lifelike—as has

CLÉSINGER, who has put a great deal of distinction and elegance into his portraits of the duc de Nemours and Mme Marie de M. . . .

CAMAGNI has done a romantic bust of Cordelia, original enough in type to be a portrait. . . .

We do not think that we have been guilty of any serious omissions. This Salon, on the whole, is like all previous Salons, except for the sudden, unexpected and dazzling appearance of M. William Haussoullier, and several very fine things, by Delacroix and Decamps. For the rest, let us record that everyone is painting better and better—which seems to us a lamentable thing; but of invention, ideas or temperament there is no more than before. No one is cocking his ear to tomorrow's wind; and

[1] At the 1835 Salon.

[2] *A paragraph on* Daumas *is omitted here.*

[3] *Paragraphs on* Garraud, Debay, Cumberworth, Simart, Forceville-Duvette *and* Millet *are omitted here.*

[4] One of them, of Soufflot, is at Versailles. The reference is to Dantan the younger; Dantan *aîné* did not exhibit this year.

yet the heroism of *modern life* surrounds and presses upon us. We are quite sufficiently choked by our true feelings for us to be able to recognize them. There is no lack of subjects, nor of colours, to make epics. The painter, the true painter for whom we are looking, will be he who can snatch its epic quality from the life of today and can make us see and understand, with brush or with pencil, how great and poetic we are in our cravats and our patent-leather boots. Next year let us hope that the true seekers may grant us the extraordinary delight of celebrating the advent of the *new*![1]

[1] This conclusion is taken up and developed in the closing section of the *Salon of 1846*.

THE MUSEUM OF CLASSICS AT THE *BAZAR BONNE-NOUVELLE*

Every thousand years or so a brilliant idea arises. Let us count ourselves fortunate therefore to have numbered the year 1846 in the tale of our existence, for this year has enabled all sincere enthusiasts of the fine arts to feast their eyes on ten pictures by David and eleven by Ingres. Our annual exhibitions, those turbulent, noisy, riotous bedlams, can give no idea of this one, which is as calm, gentle and serious as a scholar's study. Without counting the two eminent artists whom we have just named, you will be able once more to enjoy noble works by Guérin and Girodet, those remote and delicate masters, those proud continuers of David, himself the proud Cimabue of the genre called Classical; and ravishing pieces by Prud'hon, that brother in Romanticism to André Chénier.

But before giving our readers an account and an appraisal of the most important of these works, let us record a somewhat curious fact which will no doubt provide them with food for some melancholy reflections. This exhibition was organized in aid of the Benevolent Fund of the Society of Artists[1]—in other words, in aid of a certain class of the poor, themselves the noblest and the most deserving, since they minister to society's noblest pleasure. The poor—the others, that is—immediately rushed forward to levy their rights. In vain were they offered an advance settlement; our crafty weaklings, acting like experienced businessmen, and scenting an excellent piece of business in this, held out for proportional rights. Is it not time to be a little on our guard against this clumsy humanitarian frenzy, which day after day makes us, poor as we are too, the victims of the poor? Charity is doubtless a beautiful thing: but could it not enact its benefits without sanctioning these deadly *razzias* on the purse of the workers?

One day a musician dying of hunger organized a modest concert; the poor descended upon it; the outcome being dubious, they accepted an advance settlement, two hundred francs; the poor flew off, their wings

[1] According to the printed catalogue, 'au profit de la caisse de secours et pensions de la Société des Artistes'.

loaded with booty; the concert made fifty francs, and the starving violinist was reduced to imploring a position as supernumerary *cranke* in Beggars' Town[1]!—We are simply reporting facts; the conclusions, dear reader, are up to you.

The classical exhibition achieved at first no more than a loud guffaw from our young artists. The majority of these presumptuous gentlemen—we would prefer not to name them—who in art correspond well enough to the adepts of the false Romantic school in poetry—whom we would prefer not to name either—can learn nothing from these austere lessons of Revolutionary painting, that painting which voluntarily denies itself all unhealthy sugar and spice, and whose life is primarily one of thought and soul—as bitter and despotic as the Revolution from which it sprang. But our young daubers are far too clever and know much too much about painting to rise to these heights. Colour has blinded them; and they can no longer see and trace their way backwards to the austere roots of Romanticism, that expression of modern society. Laugh on, then, and fritter away your time at your ease, you juvenile greybeards; and let us concern ourselves with our masters.

Among the ten works by David, the most important are *Marat*, *The Death of Socrates*, *Bonaparte on Mont St. Bernard*, and *Telemachus and Eucharis*.

The *divine* Marat,[2] with one hand hanging over the edge of the bath, limply holding its last pen, and his breast transfixed with the *sacrilegious* wound, has just breathed his last. On a green desk placed in front of him his other hand is still holding the treacherous letter: 'Citizen, my extreme misery suffices to give me a right to your benevolence.' The water in the bathtub is red with blood, the paper is blood-soaked; on the ground lies a great kitchen knife reeking with blood; on a wretched packing-case

[1] There is a curious point here. The French text reads 'une place de *sabouleux* à la cour des Miracles'. The 'cour des Miracles' was of course the Beggars' Quarter, as described by Hugo in *Notre Dame de Paris* (Bk. II, chap. 6): the word 'sabouleux' (italicized by Baudelaire) is an old beggars' slang term meaning a false epileptic who chewed soap (hence the derivation) to make his mouth froth; he then 'cured' himself with a remedy whose efficacy he thus demonstrated. The old English word 'cranke' (or 'counterfet cranke') which is used in the translation above occurs in Harman's dictionary of cant (1566); Harman has the following note: 'These that do counterfet the Cranke be yong knaves and yonge harlots, that deeply dissemble the falling sicknes'. I am indebted to my friend Felix Leakey for tracking down the French word, which occurs in none of the standard dictionaries.

[2] Brussels, Museum: see pl. 10.

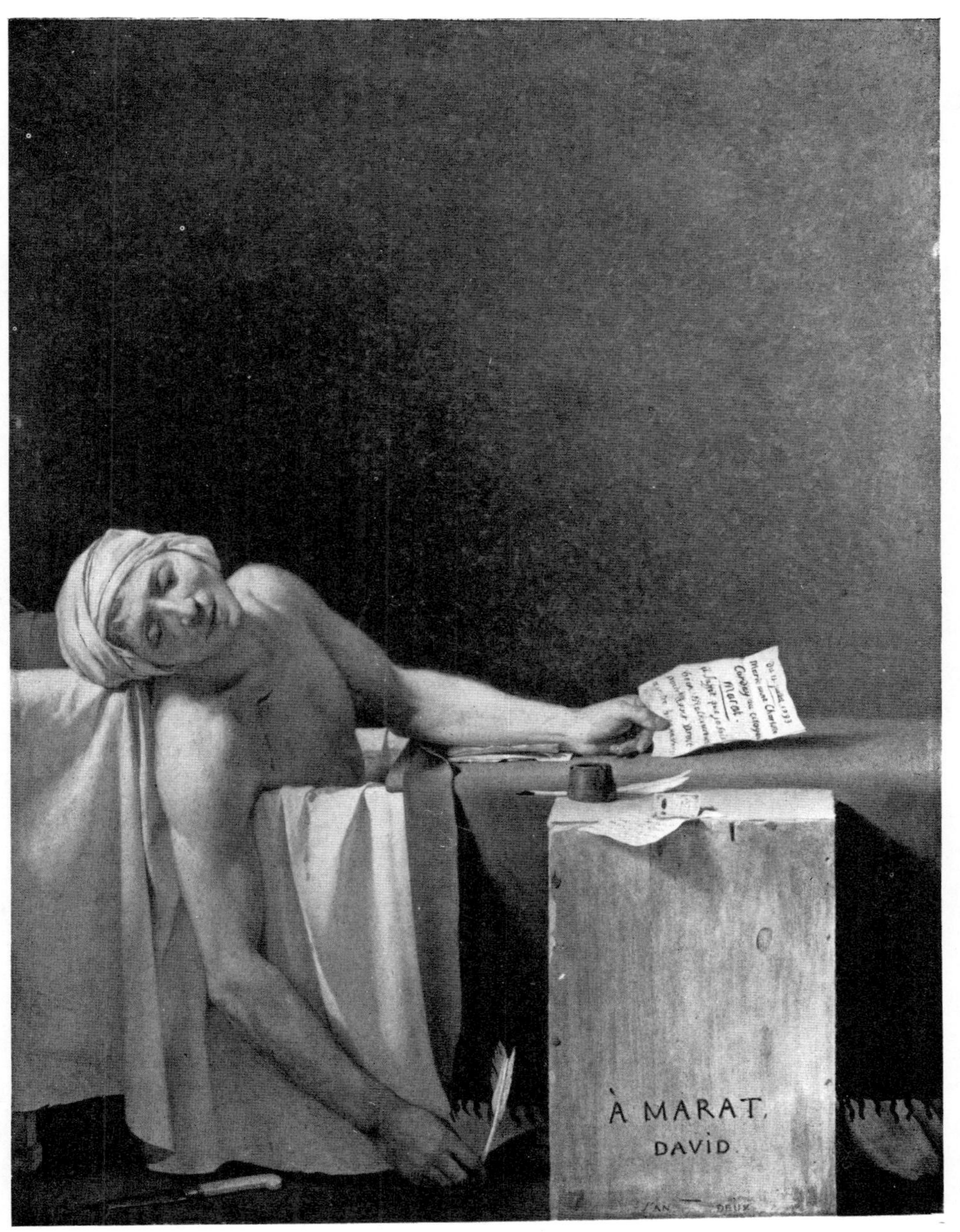

10. DAVID: *The Dead Marat*. Brussels, Musées Royaux.

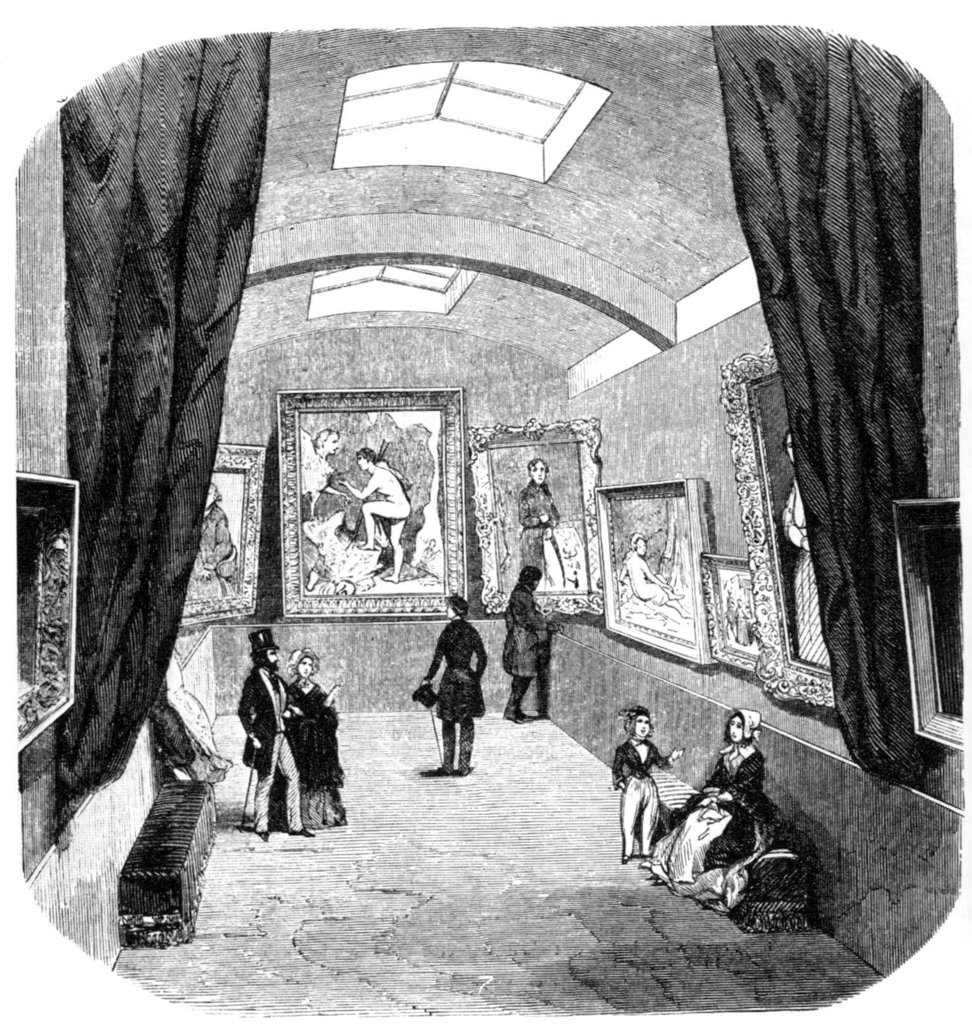

11. The Ingres Gallery at the Bazar Bonne-Nouvelle. Wood-engraving. 1846.

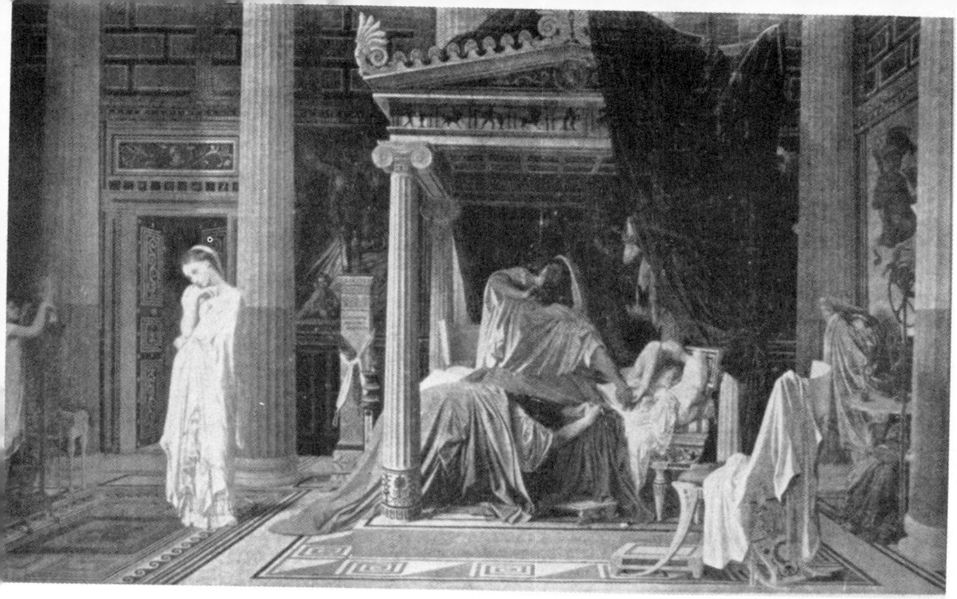

12. Ingres: *Stratonice*. Dated 1840. Chantilly, Musée Condé.

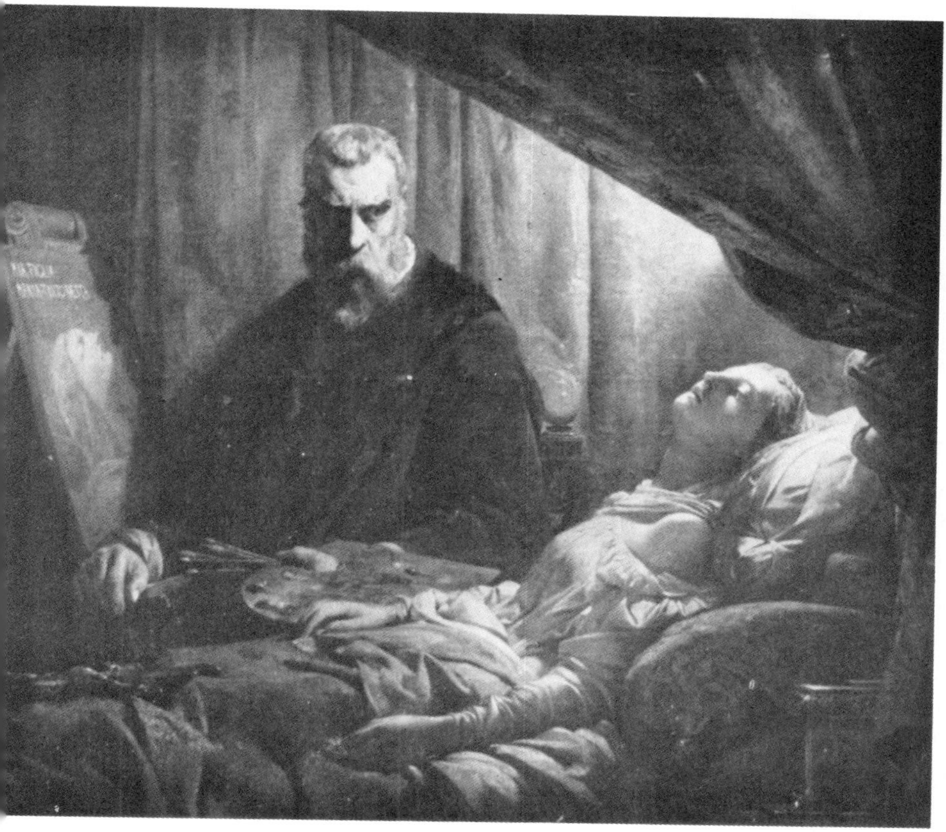

13. Cogniet: *Tintoretto Painting his Dead Daughter*. Bordeaux, Musée des Beaux-Arts.

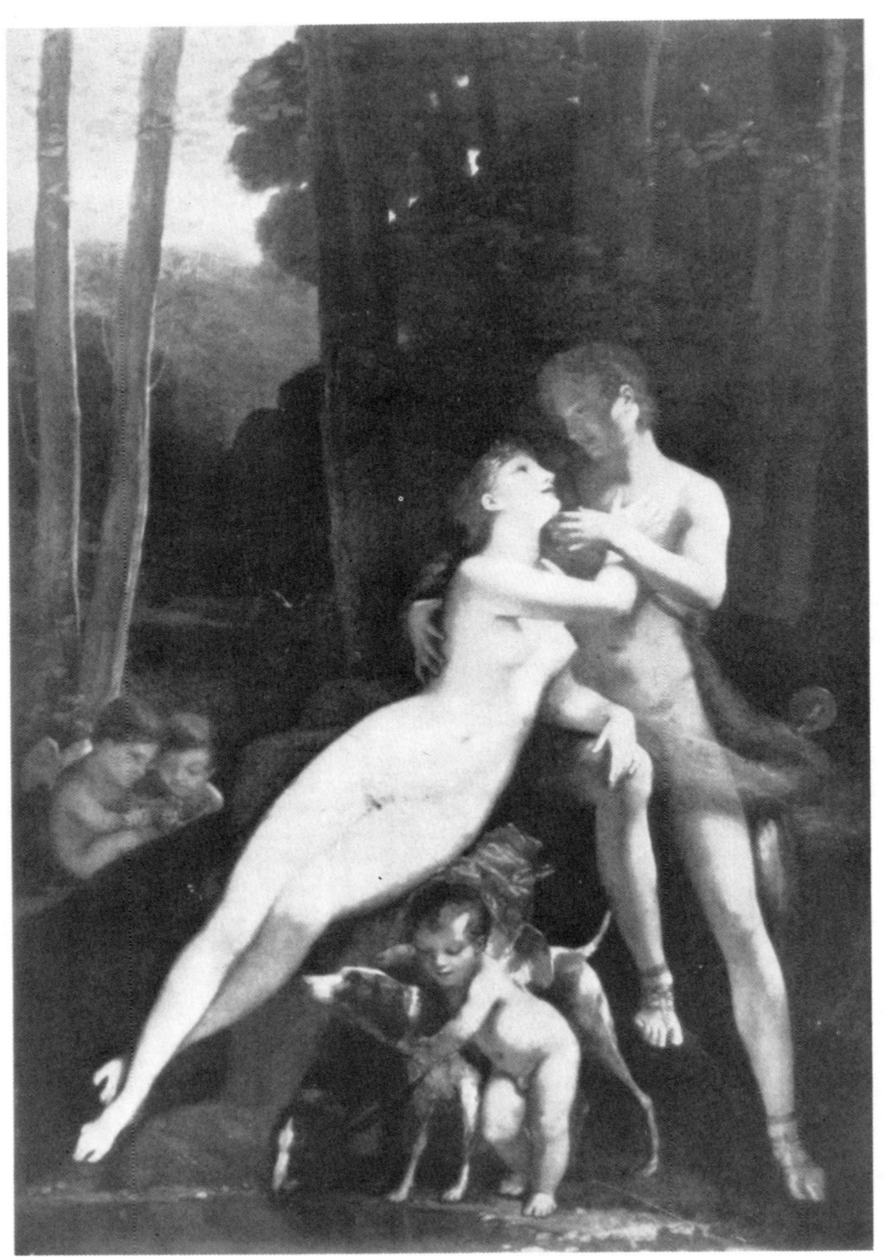

14. PRUD'HON: *Venus and Adonis*. Salon of 1812. London, Wallace Collection.

which comprised the working-furniture of the tireless journalist we read: 'A Marat, David.' All these details are as historical and real as a novel by Balzac; the drama is there, alive in all its pitiful horror, and by an uncanny stroke of brilliance, which makes this David's masterpiece and one of the great treasures of modern art, there is nothing trivial or ignoble about it. The most astonishing thing about this extraordinary poem is the fact that it is extremely rapidly painted, and when you think of the beauty of the design, this becomes quite staggering. It is the bread of the strong and the triumph of the spiritual; as cruel as nature, this picture has all the perfume of the ideal. Where now is that famous ugliness which holy Death has so swiftly wiped away with the tip of his wing? Henceforth Marat can challenge Apollo; Death has kissed him with his loving lips and he is at rest in the peace of his transfiguration. There is something at once both tender and poignant about this work; in the icy air of that room, on those chilly walls, about that cold and funereal bath, hovers a soul. May we have your leave, you politicians of all parties, and you too, wild liberals of 1845, to give way to emotion before David's masterpiece? This painting was a gift to a weeping country, and there is nothing dangerous about our tears.

Marat was paired at the Convention by *The Death of Lepelletier St. Fargeau*. This latter, however, has mysteriously vanished; the Deputy's family bought it, it is said, for 40,000 francs from David's heirs; we shall say no more of it, for fear of slandering people who must be presumed innocent.*

The Death of Socrates[1] is an admirable composition, known to all; but

* This picture was perhaps even more astonishing than the *Marat*. Lepelletier Saint-Fargeau was shown lying full-length on a mattress. Above him a mystic sword was pointing down vertically from the ceiling, at his head. On the sword was written: 'Pâris, garde du corps' (C.B.). See Cantinelli, *David*, 1930, pp. 38–39, and pl. XXXIV for a reproduction of a torn, and unique, impression of the engraving after this painting. A drawing by Anatole Devoge, showing the whole composition, is in the Dijon Museum (reproduced A. Humbert, *Louis David*, Editions Braun, 'Collection des Maîtres,' pl. 29). Both drawing and engraving make it clear that the sword was pointing not at the victim's head but at his side, where there is an open wound. It seems that Lepelletier's daughter, Mme de Mortefontaine, having reacted politically against her father, wished later to efface his memory. She bought the painting after David's death for 100,000 francs, according to the painter's grandson, not the 40,000 francs mentioned by Baudelaire. Lepeletier was assassinated on 20 January 1793, the eve of Louis XVI's execution, by Pâris, a member of the royal bodyguard.

[1] Paris, Louvre: reproduced Cantinelli, *op. cit.* pl. XVIII.

there is a commonplace look about it which puts one in mind of M. Duval-Lecamus the elder?[1] May David's shade forgive us!

The *Bonaparte on Mont St. Bernard*[2] is perhaps—along with the portrait by Gros, in his *Battle of Eylau*[3]—the solitary poetic and heroic Bonaparte owned by his country.

Telemachus and Eucharis[4] was painted in Belgium, during the great master's exile. This is a charming picture which, like *Paris and Helen*,[5] seems to be wanting to vie with the delicate and dream-like paintings of Guérin.

Of the two figures Telemachus is the more attractive, which leads one to suppose that the artist made use of a female model for his drawing.

Guérin is represented by two sketches, of which one, *The Death of Priam*,[6] is a superb thing. In it are to be found all the dramatic and almost fantasmagoric qualities of the author of *Theseus and Hippolytus*.

It is certain that Guérin was always much taken up with melodrama.

This sketch is based on Virgil's lines. There is Cassandra, with her hands bound, snatched from the Temple of Minerva, and the cruel Pyrrhus dragging the trembling old Priam by the hair and cutting his throat at the foot of the altar.—But why has it been so carefully hidden? Can it be that M. Cogniet, one of the organizers of this festival, bears a grudge against his venerable master?

Girodet's *Hippocrates refusing the Gifts of Artaxerxes* has returned to us from the Ecole de Médecine to display for our admiration its superb structure, its excellent finish and its spirited details. It is a curious thing, but this picture contains particular qualities and a multiplicity of intentions which remind one, in another system of execution, of the admirable canvases of M. Robert-Fleury. We should have liked, however, to have seen at this exhibition a few compositions which would have properly expressed the essentially poetic side of Girodet's talent (something like the *Endymion* or the *Atala*[7]). Girodet translated Anacreon, and his brush was always dipped in the most literary springs.

Baron Gérard was in the arts exactly what he was in his drawing-room,

[1] A pupil of David's.

[2] Versailles, Museum: reproduced Cantinelli, *op. cit.* pl. LX.

[3] Paris, Louvre.

[4] Present whereabouts unknown: Cantinelli, *op. cit.* cat. No. 147 (painted 1818).

[5] Paris, Louvre: reproduced Cantinelli, *op. cit.* pl. XX (detail).

[6] Angers, Museum.

[7] Both of these are in the Louvre.

the Amphitryon eager to please everyone; and it is this courtier-like eclecticism that was his undoing. David, Guérin and Girodet have stood firm, unshakeable and invulnerable relics of that great school, but Gérard has left behind him no more than the reputation of a delightful and highly witty man. Nevertheless it was he that proclaimed the arrival of Eugène Delacroix, saying 'A painter has been born to us! He is a man who runs along the rooftops'.

Gros and Géricault, without possessing the finesse, the delicacy, the sovereign reason or the harsh austerity of their predecessors, were nevertheless generous temperaments. There is a sketch by Gros at the exhibition, *King Lear and his Daughters*, which is a very arresting and strange; it reveals a fine imagination.

Next comes the delightful Prud'hon, whom some people go so far as to prefer to Correggio; Prud'hon, that amazing mixture, Prud'hon, that poet and painter who, in front of David, dreamt of colour! That soft, artful and almost invisible line which winds beneath his paint is a legitimate subject for surprise, especially when you consider his date.—For a long time to come our artists will have insufficiently well-tempered souls, so to speak, to attack the bitter joys of David and Girodet. The delicious caresses of Prud'hon will thus act as a preparation. We were particularly struck by a little picture, *Venus and Adonis*,[1] which will doubtless give M. Diaz something to think about.

In his special gallery[2] M. Ingres proudly displays eleven pictures; in other words, his entire life-work, or at least specimens from each period —in short, the whole Genesis of his genius. For a long time M. Ingres has refused to show at the Salon, and in our opinion he is right. His admirable talent is always more or less shouted down in the midst of those crushes in which the stunned and exhausted public wearily submits to the law of the loudest. M. Delacroix must have superhuman courage annually to brave so much paint-splashing. M. Ingres however, gifted with a patience no less great, if not with so generous a boldness, sat waiting his chance in his tent. Well, the chance has come, and he has made superb use of it. We have not the space, nor perhaps the command of language, to praise worthily his *Stratonice*,[3] which would have

[1] This was a study, whose present whereabouts is unknown, for the painting in the Wallace Collection; see pl. 14.

[2] See pl. 11.

[3] Chantilly, Musée Condé: see pl. 12.

astonished Poussin, his *Great Odalisque*,[1] by which Raphael would have been tormented, his *Little Odalisque*,[2] that delicious, odd fantasy which has not a single precedent among the old masters, and the portraits of M. Bertin,[3] M. Molé[4] and Mme d'Haussonville[5]—real portraits, in other words, ideal reconstructions of individuals. We think it well, however, to put right certain peculiar prejudices which are current on the score of M. Ingres among a certain section of the community whose ears are better endowed with memory than their eyes. It is agreed, or recognized, that M. Ingres's painting is *grey*.—Open your eyes, you nation of boobies, and tell us if you ever saw such dazzling, eye-catching painting, or even a greater elaboration of colour? In the second *Odalisque* this elaboration is excessive, but in spite of their multiplicity, the colours are all endowed with a particular distinction.—It is also generally agreed that M. Ingres is a great but clumsy draughtsman, quite ignorant of aerial perspective, and that his painting is as flat as a Chinese mosaic; to which we have nothing to say, except to compare his *Stratonice*, in which an enormous intricacy of tone and lighting-effects does nothing to upset the harmony, with the *Thamar*,[6] in which M. Horace Vernet has resolved an incredible problem—how to produce painting which is at once infinitely gaudy and infinitely indistinct and confused! We have never seen anything so chaotic. One of the things in our opinion that particularly distinguishes M. Ingres's talent is his love of women. His libertinism is serious and convinced. M. Ingres is never so happy nor so powerful as when his genius finds itself at grips with the charms of a young beauty. The muscles, the folds of the flesh, the shadowed dimples, the hilly undulations of the skin—nothing is overlooked. If the Island of Cythera were to commission a picture from M. Ingres, you can be very sure that it would not be laughing and frolicsome like Watteau's, but robust and nourishing like antique love.*

[1] Paris, Louvre: see pl. 29.
[2] The 'Odalisque with Slave', now in the Fogg Art Museum, Cambridge, Mass. (Wildenstein, *Ingres*, Phaidon Press, rev. edn., 1956, No. 228, fig. 149).
[3] Paris, Louvre: Wildenstein, *op. cit.* No. 208, pls. 88, 89.
[4] Private collection: Wildenstein, *op. cit.* No. 225, pls. 79–81.
[5] New York, Frick Collection: see pl. 31.
[6] Probably the *Thamar et Juda*, now in the Wallace Collection.
* M. Ingres's draughtsmanship reveals elaborations of a quite personal kind—extreme refinements, due perhaps to unusual working methods. We should not be surprised, for example, to find that in the *Odalisque* he had used a negress as model to emphasize more markedly certain bodily developments and attenuations. (C.B.)

It gave us great pleasure to see again the three little pictures by M. Delaroche, *Richelieu*, *Mazarin*[1] and *The Murder of the Duc de Guise*.[2] These are charming works in the middle reaches of talent and good taste. Why then has M. Delaroche succumbed to the disease of painting large pictures? Alas, they are always no more than just little ones—a drop of the pure essence in a barrel.

M. Cogniet has taken the best place in the gallery in which to hang his *Tintoretto*.[3]—M. Ary Scheffer is a man of outstanding talent, or rather a happy imagination, but he has changed his manner too often to possess a good one; he is a sentimental poet who soils canvases.

We saw nothing by M. Delacroix, which seems to us to be only one reason the more for speaking of him here.—On our honour, we naïvely believed that if the Commissioners had not asked the leader of the present-day school to take part in this artistic occasion, it was because, not understanding the mysterious kinship which binds him to the revolutionary school from which he emerged, they were chiefly concerned with unity and uniformity of aspect in their final result; and this we judged if not praiseworthy, at least pardonable. But not a bit of it. If there are no Delacroixs, it is because M. Delacroix is not a painter but a journalist; at least that was the answer given to one of our friends when he made it his business to ask for a little explanation on this matter. We have no desire to name the author of this witticism, sustained and supported as he was by a swarm of vulgar jibes which these gentlemen have permitted themselves at the expense of our great painter.—There is more in it for tears than for laughter.—Can it be that M. Cogniet, who has made such a good job of concealing his illustrious master, feared also to support his illustrious co-pupil? M. Dubufe[4] would have behaved better. Doubtless these gentlemen would deserve some respect because of their weakness, if they were not at the same time spiteful and envious.

Many a time we have heard young artists complaining of the Bourgeois, and depicting him as the enemy of everything great and beautiful.—This is a very false idea which it is time to pin down. If there is one thing a thousand times more dangerous than the Bourgeois, it is the Bourgeois-artist who was spiritually created to come between the public and the

[1] These two paintings are both in the Wallace Collection.

[2] Chantilly, Musée Condé.

[3] Bordeaux, Museum: see pl. 13.

[4] Cf. p. 18, above.

genius; he blocks one from the other. The Bourgeois, with few scientific notions, goes wherever he is pushed by the oracular voice of the Bourgeois-artist.—If he could be abolished, the grocer would carry M. Delacroix shoulder-high in triumph. The grocer is a great thing, a heavenly man whom we should respect, *homo bonae voluntatis*! Be very careful not to mock him for wanting to get out of his sphere and to aspire, excellent creature that he is, to the loftier regions. He wants to be moved, he wants to feel, to know, to dream as he loves; he wants to be complete; each day he asks you for his ration of art and poetry, and you snatch it from him. He lives on a diet of Cogniets, and this proves that his good-will is infinite. Put a masterpiece before him, and he will digest it and feel only the better as a result! [1]

[1] See the Introduction to the *Salon of 1846*, pp. 41–43, below.

THE SALON OF 1846

TO THE BOURGEOIS

YOU *are the majority—in number and intelligence; therefore you are the force—which is justice.*

Some are scholars, others are owners; a glorious day will come when the scholars shall be owners and the owners scholars. Then your power will be complete, and no man will protest against it.

Until that supreme harmony is achieved, it is just that those who are but owners should aspire to become scholars; for knowledge is no less of an enjoyment than ownership.

The government of the city is in your hands, and that is just, for you are the force. But you must also be capable of feeling beauty; for as not one of you today can do without power, so not one of you has the right to do without poetry.

You can live three days without bread—without poetry, never; and those of you who can say the contrary are mistaken; they are out of their minds.

The aristocrats of thought, the distributors of praise and blame, the monopolists of the things of the mind, have told you that you have no right to feel and to enjoy—they are Pharisees.

For you have in your hands the government of a city whose public is the public of the universe, and it is necessary that you should be worthy of that task.

Enjoyment is a science, and the exercise of the five senses calls for a particular initiation which only comes about through goodwill and need.

Very well, you need art.

Art is an infinitely precious good, a draught both refreshing and cheering which restores the stomach and the mind to the natural equilibrium of the ideal.

You understand its function, you gentlemen of the bourgeoisie—whether law-givers or businessmen—when the seventh or the eighth hour strikes and you bend your tired head towards the embers of your hearth or the cushions of your arm-chair.

That is the time when a keener desire and a more active reverie would refresh you after your daily labours.

But the monopolists have decided to keep the forbidden fruit of knowledge from you, because knowledge is their counter and their shop, and they are infinitely jealous of it. If they had merely denied you the power to create works of art or to understand the processes by which they are created, they would have asserted a truth at which you could not take offence, because public business and trade take up three quarters of your day. And as for your leisure hours, they should be used for enjoyment and pleasure.

But the monopolists have forbidden you even to enjoy, because you do not understand the technique of the arts, as you do those of the law and of business.

And yet it is just that if two-thirds of your time are devoted to knowledge, then the remaining third should be occupied by feeling—and it is by feeling alone that art is to be understood; and it is in this way that the equilibrium of your soul's forces will be established.

Truth, for all its multiplicity, is not two-faced; and just as in your politics you have increased both rights and benefits, so in the arts you have set up a greater and more abundant communion.

You, the bourgeois—be you king, law-giver, or business-man—have founded collections, museums and galleries. Some of those, which sixteen years ago were only open to the monopolists, have thrown wide their doors to the multitude.

You have combined together, you have formed companies and raised loans in order to realize the idea of the future in all its varied forms—political, industrial and artistic. In no noble enterprise have you ever left the initiative to the protesting and suffering minority,[1] *which anyway is the natural enemy of art.*

For to allow oneself to be outstripped in art and in politics is to commit suicide; and for a majority to commit suicide is impossible.

And what you have done for France, you have done for other countries too. The Spanish Museum[2] *is there to increase the volume of general ideas that you ought to possess about art; for you know perfectly well that just as a national museum is a kind of communion by whose gentle influence men's hearts are softened and their wills unbent, so a foreign museum is an international communion where two peoples, observing and studying one another more at their ease, can penetrate one another's mind and fraternize without discussion.*

You are the natural friends of the arts, because you are some of you rich men and the others scholars.

When you have given to society your knowledge, your industry, your labour and your money, you claim back your payment in enjoyments of the body, the reason and the imagination. If you recover the amount of enjoyments which is needed to establish the equilibrium of all parts of your being, then you are happy, satisfied and well-

[1] I.e. the Republicans.
[2] See p. 2.

disposed, as society will be satisfied, happy and well-disposed when it has found its own general and absolute equilibrium.

And so it is to you, the bourgeois, that this book is naturally dedicated; for any book which is not addressed to the majority—in number and intelligence—is a stupid book.

1st May 1846

BAUDELAIRE DUFAŸS

SALON DE 1846

Aux bourgeois. — A quoi bon la critique ?
Qu'est-ce que le romantisme ? — De la couleur.
E. Delacroix.
Des sujets amoureux et de Tassaert.
De quelques coloristes.
De l'idéal et du modèle. — De quelques dessinateurs.
Du portrait. — Du chic et du poncif.
Horace Vernet.
De l'éclectisme et du doute.
Ary Scheffer et les singes du sentiment.
De quelques douteurs.
Du paysage. — Pourquoi la sculpture est ennuyeuse.
Des écoles et des ouvriers.
De l'héroïsme de la vie moderne.

PARIS
MICHEL LÉVY FRÈRES, LIBRAIRES-ÉDITEURS
DES ŒUVRES D'ALEXANDRE DUMAS, FORMAT IN-18 ANGLAIS,
RUE VIVIENNE, 1.

1846

BAUDELAIRE'S 'SALON DE 1846': Title-page. London, British Museum. Baudelaire's mother was born Caroline Archimbault-Dufays, and his first works were published under the composite name 'Baudelaire Dufays'.

I. WHAT IS THE GOOD OF CRITICISM?

WHAT is the good?—A vast and terrible question-mark which seizes the critic by the throat from his very first step in the first chapter that he sits down to write.

At once the artist reproaches the critic with being unable to teach anything to the bourgeois, who wants neither to paint nor to write verses—nor even to art itself, since it is from the womb of art that criticism was born.

And yet how many artists today owe to the critics alone their sad little fame! It is there perhaps that the real reproach lies.

You will have seen a Gavarni which shows a painter bending over his canvas; behind him stands a grave, lean, stiff gentleman, in a white cravat holding his latest article in his hand. 'If art is noble, criticism is holy.'—'Who says that?'—'The critics!'[1] If the artist plays the leading role so easily, it is doubtless because his critic is of a type which we know so well.

Regarding technical means and processes taken from the works themselves,* the public and the artist will find nothing to learn here. Things like that are learnt in the studio, and the public is only concerned about the result.

I sincerely believe that the best criticism is that which is both amusing and poetic: not a cold, mathematical criticism which, on the pretext of explaining everything, has neither love nor hate, and voluntarily strips itself of every shred of temperament. But, seeing that a fine picture is nature reflected by an artist, the criticism which I approve will be that picture reflected by an intelligent and sensitive mind. Thus the best account of a picture may well be a sonnet or an elegy.

But this kind of criticism is destined for anthologies and readers of poetry. As for criticism properly so-called, I hope that the philosophers will understand what I am going to say. To be just, that is to say, to justify its existence, criticism should be partial, passionate and political, that is to say, written from an exclusive point of view, but a point of view that opens up the widest horizons.

[1] No. 4 of Gavarni's series of lithographs entitled *Leçons et Conseils*, published in *Le Charivari*, 27 November 1839. See pl. II.

* I know quite well that criticism today has other pretensions; that is why it will always recommend drawing to colourists, and colour to draughtsmen. Its taste is in the highest degree rational and sublime! (C.B.)

To extol line to the detriment of colour, or colour at the expense of line, is doubtless a point of view, but it is neither very broad nor very just, and it indicts its holder of a great ignorance of individual destinies.

You cannot know in what measure Nature has mingled the taste for line and the taste for colour in each mind, nor by what mysterious processes she manipulates that fusion whose result is a picture.

Thus a broader point of view will be an orderly individualism—that is, to require of the artist the quality of *naïveté* and the sincere expression of his temperament, aided by every means which his technique provides.* An artist without temperament is not worthy of painting pictures, and —as we are wearied of imitators and, above all, of eclectics—he would do better to enter the service of a painter of temperament, as a humble workman. I shall demonstrate this in one of my later chapters.[1]

The critic should arm himself from the start with a sure criterion, a criterion drawn from nature, and should then carry out his duty with passion; for a critic does not cease to be a man, and passion draws similar temperaments together and exalts the reason to fresh heights.

Stendhal has said somewhere: 'Painting is nothing but a construction in ethics!'[2] If you will understand the word 'ethics' in a more or less liberal sense, you can say as much of all the arts. And as the essence of the arts is always the expression of the beautiful through the feeling, the passion and the dreams of each man—that is to say a variety within a unity, or the various aspects of the absolute—so there is never a moment when criticism is not in contact with metaphysics.

As every age and every people has enjoyed the expression of its own beauty and ethos—and if, by *romanticism*, you are prepared to understand the most recent, the most modern expression of beauty—then, for the reasonable and passionate critic, the great artist will be he who will combine with the condition required above—that is, the quality of *naïveté*— the greatest possible amount of romanticism.

* With reference to the proper ordering of individualism, see the article on William Haussoullier, in the *Salon of 1845* (pp. 7–9). In spite of all the rebukes that I have suffered on this subject, I persist in my opinion; but it is necessary to understand the article. (C.B.)

[1] See pp. 113 ff.

[2] *Histoire de la Peinture en Italie*, chap. 156 (edition of 1859, p. 338, *n.* 2). Stendhal's phrase is 'de la morale construite', and he explains that he is using the past participle in the geometric sense.

II. WHAT IS ROMANTICISM?

FEW people today will want to give a real and positive meaning to this word; and yet will they dare assert that a whole generation would agree to join a battle lasting several years for the sake of a flag which was not also a symbol?

If you think back to the disturbances of those recent times, you will see that if but few romantics have survived, it is because few of them discovered romanticism, though all of them sought it sincerely and honestly.

Some applied themselves only to the choice of subjects; but they had not the temperament for their subjects. Others, still believing in a Catholic society, sought to reflect Catholicism in their works. But to call oneself a romantic and to look systematically at the past is to contradict oneself. Some blasphemed the Greeks and the Romans in the name of romanticism: but you can only make Romans and Greeks into romantics if you are one yourself. Many others have been misled by the idea of truth in art, and local colour. Realism had already existed for a long time when that great battle took place, and besides, to compose a tragedy or a picture to the requirements of M. Raoul Rochette is to expose yourself to a flat contradiction from the first comer if he is more learned than M. Raoul Rochette.[1]

Romanticism is precisely situated neither in choice of subjects nor in exact truth, but in a mode of feeling.

They looked for it outside themselves, but it was only to be found within.

For me, Romanticism is the most recent, the latest expression of the beautiful.

There are as many kinds of beauty as there are habitual ways of seeking happiness.*

This is clearly explained by the philosophy of progress; thus, as there have been as many ideals as there have been ways in which the peoples of the earth have understood ethics, love, religion, etc., so romanticism

[1] A well-known archaeologist (1789–1854), who held several important positions, and published many books on his subject.

* Stendhal. (C.B.) Baudelaire seems to have in mind a footnote in chap. 110 of the *Histoire de la Peinture en Italie*, where Stendhal wrote: 'La beauté est l'expression d'une certaine manière habituelle de chercher le bonheur . . .'.

will not consist in a perfect execution, but in a conception analogous to the ethical disposition of the age.

It is because some have located it in a perfection of technique that we have had the *rococo* of romanticism, without question the most intolerable of all forms.

Thus it is necessary, first and foremost, to get to know those aspects of nature and those human situations which the artists of the past have disdained or have not known.

To say the word Romanticism is to say modern art—that is, intimacy, spirituality, colour, aspiration towards the infinite, expressed by every means available to the arts.

Thence it follows that there is an obvious contradiction between romanticism and the works of its principal adherents.

Does it surprise you that colour should play such a very important part in modern art? Romanticism is a child of the North, and the North is all for colour; dreams and fairytales are born of the mist. England—that home of fanatical colourists, Flanders and half of France are all plunged in fog; Venice herself lies steeped in her lagoons. As for the painters of Spain, they are painters of contrast rather than colourists.

The South, in return, is all for nature; for there nature is so beautiful and bright that nothing is left for man to desire, and he can find nothing more beautiful to invent than what he sees. There art belongs to the open air: but several hundred leagues to the north you will find the deep dreams of the studio and the gaze of the fancy lost in horizons of grey.

The South is as brutal and positive as a sculptor even in his most delicate compositions; the North, suffering and restless, seeks comfort with the imagination, and if it turns to sculpture, it will more often be picturesque than classical.

Raphael, for all his purity, is but an earthly spirit ceaselessly investigating the solid; but that scoundrel Rembrandt is a sturdy idealist who makes us dream and guess at what lies beyond. The first composes creatures in a pristine and virginal state—Adam and Eve; but the second shakes his rags before our eyes and tells us of human sufferings.

And yet Rembrandt is not a pure colourist, but a harmonizer. How novel then would be the effect, and how matchless his romanticism, if a powerful colourist could realize our dearest dreams and feelings for us in a colour appropriate to their subjects!

But before passing on to an examination of the man who up to the present is the most worthy representative of romanticism, I should like to give you a series of reflections on colour, which will not be without use for the complete understanding of this little book.

III. ON COLOUR

LET us suppose a beautiful expanse of nature, where there is full licence for everything to be as green, red, dusty or iridescent as it wishes; where all things, variously coloured in accordance with their molecular structure, suffer continual alteration through the transposition of shadow and light; where the workings of latent heat allow no rest, but everything is in a state of perpetual vibration which causes lines to tremble and fulfils the law of eternal and universal movement. An immensity which is sometimes blue, and often green, extends to the confines of the sky; it is the sea. The trees are green, the grass and the moss are green; the tree-trunks are snaked with green, and the unripe stalks are green; green is nature's ground-bass, because green marries easily with all the other colours.* What strikes me first of all is that everywhere—whether it be poppies in the grass, pimpernels, parrots, etc.—red sings the glory of green; black (where it exists—a solitary and insignificant cipher) intercedes on behalf of blue or red. The blue—that is, the sky—is cut across with airy flecks of white or with grey masses, which pleasantly temper its bleak crudeness; and as the vaporous atmosphere of the season—winter or summer—bathes, softens or engulfs the contours, nature seems like a spinning-top which revolves so rapidly that it appears grey, although it embraces within itself the whole gamut of colours.

The sap rises, and as the principles mix, there is a flowering of *mixed tones*; trees, rocks and granite boulders gaze at themselves in the water and cast their *reflections* upon them; each transparent object picks up light and colour as it passes from nearby or afar. According as the daystar alters its position, tones change their values, but, always respecting their natural sympathies and antipathies, they continue to live in harmony by making reciprocal concessions. Shadows slowly shift, and colours are put to flight before them, or extinguished altogether, according as the light,

* Except for yellow and blue, its progenitors: but I am only speaking here of pure colours. For this rule cannot be applied to transcendent colourists who are thoroughly acquainted with the science of counterpoint. (C.B.)

itself shifting, may wish to bring fresh ones to life. Some colours cast back their reflections upon one another, and by modifying their own qualities with a *glaze* of transparent, borrowed qualities, they combine and recombine in an infinite series of melodious marriages which are thus made more easy for them. When the great brazier of the sun dips beneath the waters, fanfares of red surge forth on all sides; a harmony of blood flares up at the horizon, and green turns richly crimson. Soon vast blue shadows are rhythmically sweeping before them the host of orange and rose-pink tones which are like a faint and distant echo of the light. This great symphony of today, which is an eternal variation of the symphony of yesterday, this succession of melodies whose variety ever issues from the infinite, this complex hymn is called *colour*.

In colour are to be found harmony, melody and counterpoint.

If you will examine the detail within the detail in an object of medium dimensions—for example, a woman's hand, rosy, slender, with skin of the finest—you will see that there is perfect harmony between the green of the strong veins with which it is ridged and the ruby tints which mark the knuckles; pink nails stand out against the topmost joints, which are characterized by several grey and brown tones. As for the palm of the hand, the lifelines, which are pinker and more wine-coloured, are separated one from another by the system of green or blue veins which run across them. A study of the same object, carried out with a lens, will afford, within however small an area, a perfect harmony of grey, blue, brown, green, orange and white tones, warmed by a touch of yellow—a harmony which, when combined with shadows, produces the colourist's type of modelling, which is essentially different from that of the draughtsman, whose difficulties more or less boil down to the copying of a plaster cast.

Colour is thus the accord of two tones. Warmth and coldness of tone, in whose opposition all theory resides, cannot be defined in an absolute manner; they only exist in a relative sense.

The lens is the colourist's eye.

I do not wish to conclude from all this that a colourist should proceed by a minute study of the tones commingled in a very limited space. For if you admit that every molecule is endowed with its own particular tone, it would follow that matter should be infinitely divisible; and besides, as art is nothing but an abstraction and a sacrifice of detail to the whole, it is important to concern oneself above all with *masses*. I merely wished to prove that if the case were possible, any number of tones, so long as they were logically juxtaposed, would fuse naturally in accordance with the law which governs them.

Chemical affinities are the grounds whereby Nature cannot make mistakes in the arrangement of her tones; for with Nature, form and colour are one.

No more can the true colourist make mistakes; everything is allowed him, because from birth he knows the whole scale of tones, the force of tone, the results of mixtures and the whole science of counterpoint, and thus he can produce a harmony of twenty different reds.

This is so true that if an anti-colourist landowner took it into his head to repaint his property in some ridiculous manner and in a system of cacophonous colours, the thick and transparent varnish of the atmosphere and the learned eye of a Veronese between them would put the whole thing right and would produce a satisfying ensemble on canvas—conventional, no doubt, but logical.

This explains how a colourist can be paradoxical in his way of expressing colour, and how the study of nature often leads to a result quite different from nature.

The air plays such an important part in the theory of colour that if a landscape-painter were to paint the leaves of a tree just as he sees them, he would secure a false tone, considering that there is a much smaller expanse of air between the spectator and the picture than between the spectator and nature.

Falsifications are continually necessary, even in order to achieve a *trompe-l'oeil.*

Harmony is the basis of the theory of colour.

Melody is unity within colour, or overall colour.

Melody calls for a cadence; it is a whole, in which every effect contributes to the general effect.

Thus melody leaves a deep and lasting impression on the mind.

Most of our young colourists lack melody.

The right way to know if a picture is melodious is to look at it from far enough away to make it impossible to understand its subject or to distinguish its lines. If it is melodious, it already has a meaning and has already taken its place in your store of memories.

Style and feeling in colour come from choice, and choice comes from temperament.

Colours can be gay and playful, playful and sad, rich and playful, gay, rich and sad, commonplace and original.

Thus Veronese's colour is tranquil and gay. Delacroix's colour is often plaintive, and that of M. Catlin[1] is often terrible.

For a long time I lived opposite a drinking-shop which was crudely striped in red and green; it afforded my eyes a delicious pain.

I do not know if any *analogist* has ever established a complete scale of colours and feelings, but I remember a passage in Hoffmann which expresses my idea perfectly and which will appeal to all those who sincerely love nature: 'It is not only in dreams, or in that mild delirium which precedes sleep, but it is even awakened when I hear music—that perception of an analogy and an intimate connexion between colours, sounds and perfumes. It seems to me that all these things were created by one and the same ray of light, and that their combination must result in a wonderful concert of harmony. The smell of red and brown marigolds above all produces a magical effect on my being. It makes me fall into a deep reverie, in which I seem to hear the solemn, deep tones of the oboe in the distance.'*

It is often asked if the same man can be at once a great colourist and a great draughtsman.

Yes and no; for there are different kinds of drawing.

The quality of pure draughtsmanship consists above all in precision, and this precision excludes *touch*; but there are such things as happy touches, and the colourist who undertakes to express nature through colour would often lose more by suppressing his happy touches than by studying a greater austerity of drawing.

Certainly colour does not exclude great draughtsmanship—that of Veronese, for example, which proceeds above all by ensemble and by mass; but it does exclude the meticulous drawing of detail, the contour of the tiny fragment, where touch will always eat away line.

The love of air and the choice of subjects in movement call for the employment of flowing and fused lines.

Exclusive draughtsmen act in accordance with an inverse procedure which is yet analogous. With their eyes fixed upon tracking and surprising their line in its most secret convolutions, they have no time to see air

[1] On Catlin, see pp. 70–71.

* Kreisleriana. (C.B.). It is the third of the detached observations entitled *Höchst zerstreute Gedanken.*

and light—that is to say, the effects of these things—and they even compel themselves *not* to see them, in order to avoid offending the dogma of their school.

It is thus possible to be at once a colourist and a draughtsman, but only in a certain sense. Just as a draughtsman can be a colourist in his broad masses, so a colourist can be a draughtsman by means of a total logic in his linear ensemble; but one of these qualities always engulfs the detail of the other.

The draughtsmanship of colourists is like that of nature; their figures are naturally bounded by a harmonious collision of coloured masses.

Pure draughtsmen are philosophers and dialecticians.

Colourists are epic poets.

IV. EUGÈNE DELACROIX

ROMANTICISM and colour lead me straight to Eugène Delacroix. I do not know if he is proud of his title of 'romantic', but his place is here, because a long time ago—from his very first work, in fact—the majority of the public placed him at the head of the *modern* school.

As I enter upon this part of my work, my heart is full of a serene joy, and I am purposely selecting my newest pens, so great is my desire to be clear and limpid, so happy do I feel to be addressing my dearest and most sympathetic subject. But in order to make the conclusions of this chapter properly intelligible, I must first go back some little distance in the history of this period, and place before the eyes of the public certain documents of the case which have already been cited by earlier critics and historians, but which are necessary to complete my demonstration. Nevertheless, I do not think that true admirers of Eugène Delacroix will feel anything but a keen pleasure in re-reading an extract from the *Constitutionnel* of 1822, taken from the Salon of M. Thiers,[1] journalist.

> 'In my opinion no picture is a clearer revelation of future greatness than M. Delacroix's *Le Dante et Virgile aux Enfers*.[2] Here above all you can recognize the spurt of talent, that burst of dawning mastery which revives our hopes, already a trifle dashed by the too moderate worth of all the rest.

[1] Adolphe Thiers (1797–1877), later famous as statesman and historian, was at that time at the very outset of his career.

[2] In the Louvre; see pl. 33.

'Dante and Virgil are being ferried across the infernal stream by Charon; they cleave their way with difficulty through the mob which swarms round the barque in order to clamber aboard. Dante, pictured alive, bears the dreadful taint of the place: Virgil, crowned with gloomy laurel, wears the colours of death. The hapless throng, doomed eternally to crave the opposite bank, are clinging to the boat: one is clutching at it in vain, and, thrown backwards by his precipitate effort, plunges once more into the waters; another has hold, and is kicking back those who, like himself, are struggling to get on board; two others are gripping at the elusive timber with their teeth. There you have all the egoism of misery, the despair of Hell. In a subject which borders so closely on exaggeration, you will yet find a severity of taste, a propriety of setting, so to say, which enhances the design, though stern judges—*in this case ill-advised*—might perhaps criticize it for a lack of nobility. It is painted with a broad, firm, brush, and its colour is simple and vigorous, if a trifle raw.

'Apart from that poetic imagination which is common both to painter and writer, the author of this picture has another, *artistic* imagination, which one might almost call 'the graphic imagination',[1] and which is quite different from the first. He throws his figures on to the canvas, he groups and bends them at will, with the boldness of Michelangelo and the abundance of Rubens. Some strange recollection of the great masters seized hold of me at the sight of this picture; once more I found that power—wild, ardent, but natural—which yields without effort to its own impulse. . . .

'I do not believe that I am mistaken when I say that M. Delacroix has been given genius. Let him advance with assurance, let him devote himself to immense tasks, an indispensable condition of talent; and let him take still further confidence when I say that the opinion which I am expressing here is shared by one of the great masters of the school.'[2]

A. T. . . rs

These enthusiastic paragraphs are truly staggering, as much for their precocity as for their boldness. If, as is to be presumed, the editor of the

[1] *L'imagination du dessin.*

[2] According to Silvestre (*Histoire des artistes vivants*, 1856, p. 62), this was Gérard.

journal had pretensions himself as a connoisseur of painting, the young Thiers must have struck him as a trifle mad.

To obtain a proper idea of the profound confusion into which the picture of Dante and Virgil must have thrown contemporary minds—of the amazement, the dumbfoundedness, the rage, the shouts of praise and of abuse, the enthusiasm and the peals of offensive laughter which beset this fine picture (a true signal of revolution)—you must remember that in the studio of M. Guérin (a man of great worth, but a despot and absolutist, like his master David) there was only a small group of pariahs who devoted themselves in secret to the old masters and who dared shyly to conspire beneath the wing of Raphael and Michelangelo. There was as yet no question of Rubens.

M. Guérin, who was harsh and severe towards his young pupil, only looked at the picture because of the clamour that raged around it.

Géricault, who was back from Italy (where he was said to have renounced several of his almost original qualities before the great frescoes of Rome and Florence) complimented the new and still bashful painter so warmly that he was almost overcome.[1]

It was in front of this painting, or, some time afterwards, in front of the *Pestiférés de Scio*,* that Gérard himself, who, as it seems, was more a wit than a painter, cried 'A painter has just been revealed to us, but he is a man who runs along the roof-tops!'—To run along the roof-tops you need a firm step and an eye illumined by an interior light.

Let glory and justice be accorded to MM. Thiers and Gérard!

It is doubtless a lengthy interval that separates the *Dante and Virgil* from the paintings in the Palais Bourbon[2]; but the biography of Eugène Delacroix is poor in incident. For a man like this, endowed with such courage and such passion, the most interesting struggles are those which he has to maintain against himself; horizons need not be vast for battles to be important, and the most curious events and revolutions take place beneath the firmament of the skull, in the close and mysterious laboratory of the brain.

Now that the man had been duly revealed and was continuing to

[1] Géricault is elsewhere recorded as saying that it was a picture that he would have been glad to have signed himself.

* I write *pestiférés* instead of *massacres* in order to explain to the critics those flesh-tones to which they have so often and so stupidly objected. (C.B.) The picture is now in the Louvre. It was painted in 1824. Reproduced *Painter of Modern Life*, pl. 26.

[2] On which Delacroix was still engaged in 1846.

reveal himself more and more (in the allegorical picture *La Grèce*,[1] *Sardanapalus*,[2] *La Liberté*,[3] etc.), and now that the contagion of the new gospel was spreading from day to day, even academic disdain found itself forced to take this new genius into account. One fine day M. Sosthène de La Rochefoucauld, then *Directeur des Beaux-Arts*, sent for Eugène Delacroix, and, after lavishing compliments upon him, told him that it was vexing that a man of so rich an imagination and so fine a talent, a man, moreover, to whom the government was favourably disposed, should not be prepared to add a little water to his wine; he asked him once and for all if it would not be possible for him to modify his manner. Eugène Delacroix, vastly surprised at this quaint condition and these ministerial counsels, replied with almost a parody of rage that evidently if he painted thus, it was because he had to and because he could not paint otherwise. He fell into complete disgrace and was cut off from any kind of official work for seven years. He had to wait for 1830. Meanwhile M. Thiers had written a new and very lofty article in *Le Globe*.[4]

A journey to Morocco[5] seems to have left a deep impression on his mind; there he could study at leisure both man and woman in their independence and native originality of movement, and could comprehend antique beauty in the sight of a race pure of all base-breeding and adorned with health and the free development of its muscles. The composition of *The Women of Algiers*[6] and a mass of sketches probably date from this period.

Up to the present, Eugène Delacroix has met with injustice. Criticism, for him, has been bitter and ignorant; with one or two noble exceptions, even the praises of his admirers must often have seemed offensive to him. Generally speaking, and for most people, to mention Eugène Delacroix is to throw into their minds goodness knows what vague ideas of ill-directed fire, of turbulence, of hazardous inspiration, of chaos, even; and for those gentlemen who form the majority of the public, pure chance, that loyal and obliging servant of genius, plays an important part in his happiest compositions. In that unhappy period of revolution of which I was speaking a moment ago, and whose numerous errors I

[1] Painted in 1827: first exhibited the following year, and now in the Bordeaux Museum.

[2] Painted in 1827, and now in the Louvre; reproduced *Journal*, pl. 8.

[3] Painted in 1830, and now in the Louvre; reproduced *Journal*, pl. 13.

[4] On the Salon of 1824. [5] In 1832.

[6] Painted in 1834, and now in the Louvre. See pl. 34.

have recorded, people used often to compare Eugène Delacroix to Victor Hugo. They had their romantic poet; they needed their painter. This necessity of going to any length to find counterparts and analogues in the different arts often results in strange blunders; and this one proves once again how little people knew what they were about. Without any doubt the comparison must have seemed a painful one to Eugène Delacroix, if not to both of them; for if my definition of romanticism (intimacy, spirituality, and the rest) places Delacroix at its head, it naturally excludes M. Victor Hugo. The parallel has endured in the banal realm of accepted ideas, and these two preconceptions still encumber many feeble brains. Let us be done with these rhetorical ineptitudes once and for all. I beg all those who have felt the need to create some kind of aesthetic for their own use and to deduce causes from their results, to make a careful comparison between the productions of these two artists.

M. Victor Hugo, whose nobility and majesty I certainly have no wish to belittle, is a workman far more adroit than inventive, a labourer much more correct than *creative*. Delacroix is sometimes clumsy, but he is essentially creative. In all his pictures, both lyric and dramatic, M. Victor Hugo lets one see a system of uniform alignment and contrasts. With him even eccentricity takes symmetrical forms. He is in complete possession of, and coldly employs, all the modulations of rhyme, all the resources of antithesis and all the tricks of apposition. He is a composer of the decadence or transition, who handles his tools with a truly admirable and curious dexterity. M. Hugo was by nature an academician even before he was born, and if we were still living in the time of fabulous marvels, I would be prepared to believe that often, as he passed before their wrathful sanctuary, the green lions of the Institut would murmur to him in prophetic tones, 'Thou shalt enter these portals.'

For Delacroix justice is more sluggish. His works, on the contrary, are poems—and great poems, *naïvely** conceived and executed with the usual insolence of genius. In the works of the former there is nothing left to guess at, for he takes so much pleasure in exhibiting his skill that he omits not one blade of grass nor even the reflection of a street lamp. The latter in his work throws open immense vistas to the most adventurous

* By the *naïveté* of the genius you must understand a complete knowledge of technique combined with the *γνῶθι σεαυτόν* of the Greeks, but with knowledge modestly surrendering the leading role to temperament (C.B.). The word *naïveté*, used in this special sense, is one of the keywords of this *Salon*.

imaginations. The first enjoys a certain calmness, let us rather say a certain detached egoism, which causes an unusual coldness and moderation to hover above his poetry—qualities which the dogged and melancholy passion of the second, at grips with the obstinacies of his craft, does not always permit him to retain. One starts with detail, the other with an intimate understanding of his subject; from which it follows that one only captures the skin, while the other tears out the entrails. Too earth-bound, too attentive to the superficies of nature, M. Victor Hugo has become a painter in poetry; Delacroix, always respectful of his ideal, is often, without knowing it, a poet in painting.

As for the second preconception, the preconception of pure chance, it has no more substance than the first. Nothing is sillier or more impertinent than to talk to a great artist, and one as learned and as thoughtful as Delacroix, about the obligations which he may owe to the god of chance. It quite simply makes one shrug one's shoulders in pity. There is no pure chance in art, any more than in mechanics. A happy invention is the simple consequence of a sound train of reasoning whose intermediate deductions one may perhaps have skipped, just as a fault is the consequence of a faulty principle. A picture is a machine, all of whose systems of construction are intelligible to the practised eye; in which everything justifies its existence, if the picture is a good one; where one tone is always planned to make the most of another; and where an occasional fault in drawing is sometimes necessary, so as to avoid sacrificing something more important.

This intervention of chance in the business of Delacroix's painting is all the more improbable since he is one of those rare beings who remain original after having drunk deep of all the true wells, and whose indomitable individuality has borne and shaken off the yokes of all the great masters in turn. Not a few of you would be quite astonished to see one of his studies after Raphael—patient and laborious masterpieces of imitation; and few people today remember his lithographs after medals and engraved gems.[1]

Here are a few lines from Heinrich Heine which explain Delacroix's method rather well—a method which, like that of all robustly-framed beings, is the result of his temperament:

> 'In artistic matters, I am a supernaturalist. I believe that the artist cannot find all his forms in nature, but that the most remarkable are

[1] Delacroix made six such lithographs in 1825.

revealed to him in his soul, like the innate symbology of innate ideas, and at the same instant. A modern professor of aesthetics, the author of *Recherches sur l'Italie*,[1] has tried to restore to honour the old principle of the *imitation of nature*, and to maintain that the plastic artist should find all his forms in nature. The professor, in thus setting forth his ultimate principle of the plastic arts, had only forgotten one of those arts, but one of the most fundamental—I mean architecture. A belated attempt has now been made to trace back the forms of architecture to the leafy branches of the forest and the rocks of the grotto; and yet these forms were nowhere to be found in external nature, but rather in the soul of man.'[2]

Now this is the principle from which Delacroix sets out—that a picture should first and foremost reproduce the intimate thought of the artist, who dominates the model as the creator dominates his creation; and from this principle there emerges a second which seems at first sight to contradict it—namely that the artist must be meticulously careful concerning his material means of execution. He professes a fanatical regard for the cleanliness of his tools and the preparation of the elements of his work. In fact, since painting is an art of deep ratiocination, and one that demands an immediate contention between a host of different qualities, it is important that the hand should encounter the least possible number of obstacles when it gets down to business, and that it should accomplish the divine orders of the brain with a slavish alacrity; otherwise the ideal will escape.

The process of conception of this great artist is no less slow, serious and conscientious than his execution is nimble. This moreover is a quality which he shares with the painter whom public opinion has set at the opposite pole from him—I mean M. Ingres. But travail is by no means the same thing as childbirth, and these great princes of painting, though endowed with a seeming indolence, exhibit a marvellous agility in covering a canvas. *St Symphorian*[3] was entirely re-painted several times, and at the outset it contained far fewer figures.

Nature, for Eugène Delacroix, is a vast dictionary whose leaves he

[1] The reference is to Carl Friedrich von Rumohr (1785–1843); his book, *Italienische Forschungen*, was published in three volumes between 1827 and 1831.

[2] From Heine's Salon of 1831, which was published in a French translation in his *De la France*, 1833.

[3] Ingres's *St. Symphorian* was commissioned for Autun cathedral in 1824; it was not completed until ten years later.

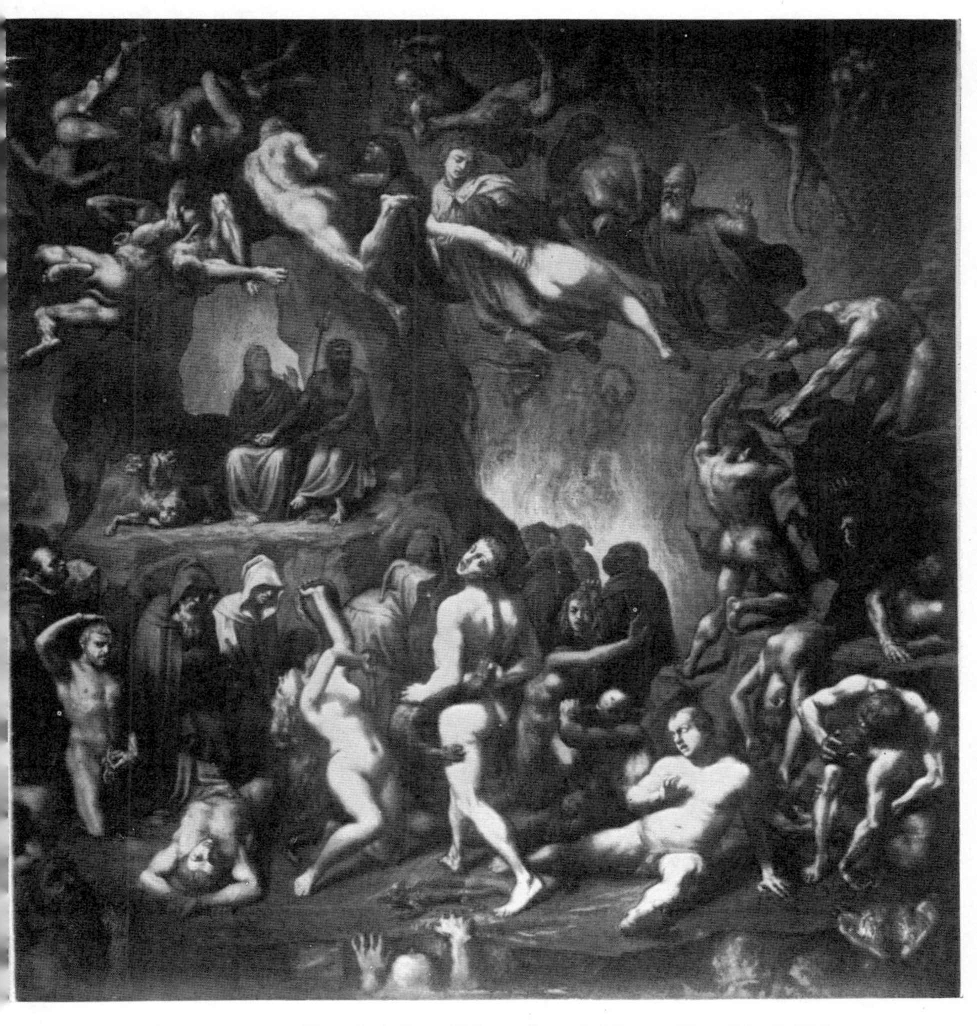

15. CHENAVARD: *Dante's Inferno*. Salon of 1846. Montpellier, Musée Fabre.

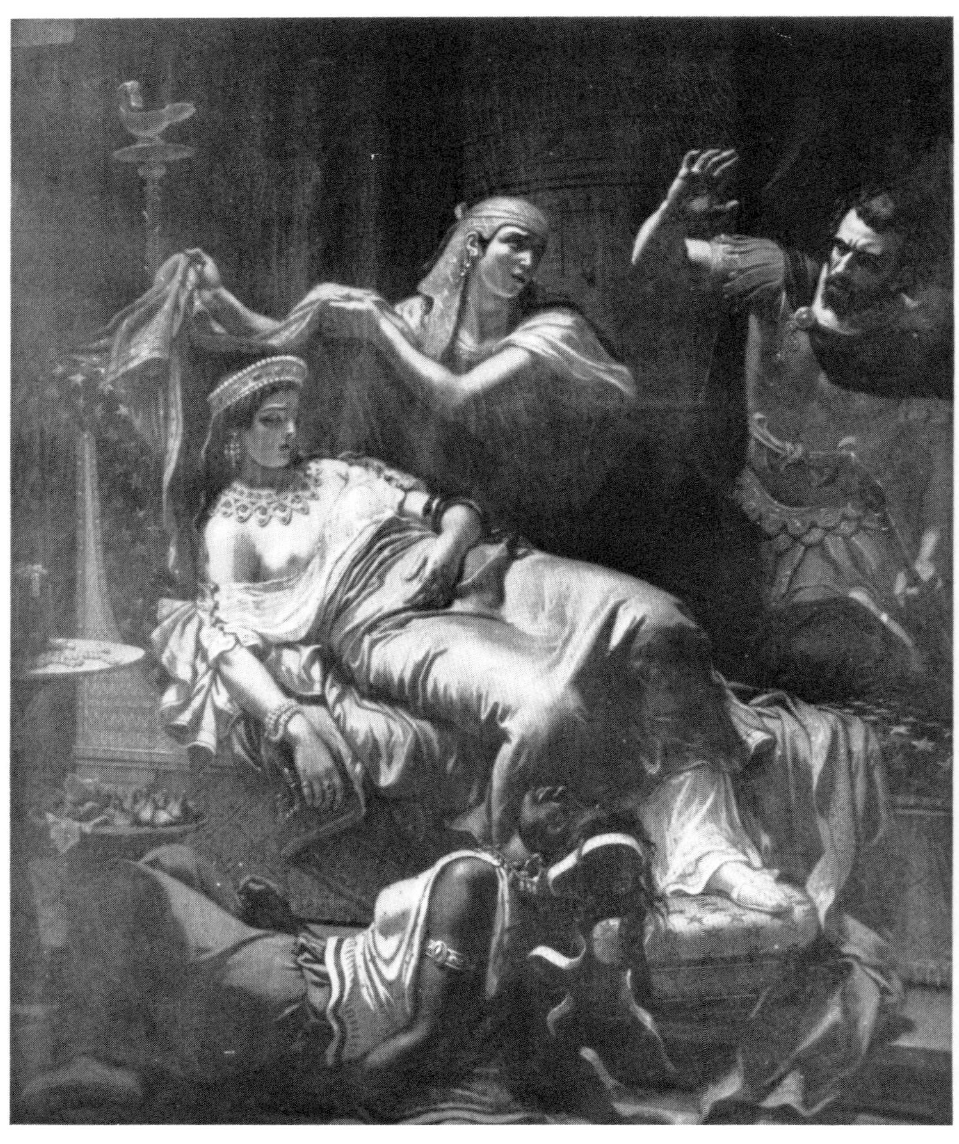

16. Lassale-Bordes: *The Death of Cleopatra*. Salon of 1846. Autun, Musée Municipal.

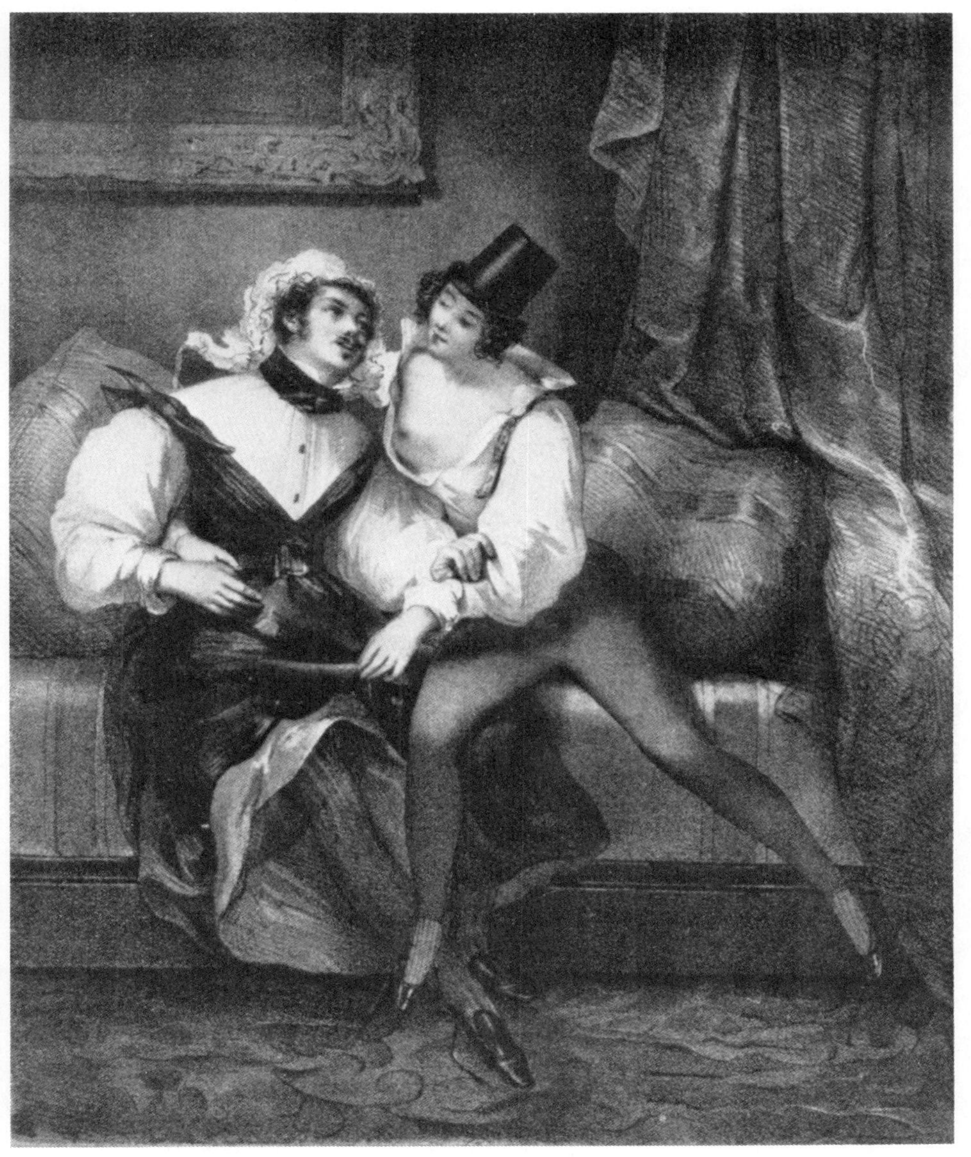

17. TASSAERT: *'Don't Play the Heartless One!'* Lithograph. Paris, Bibliothèque Nationale.

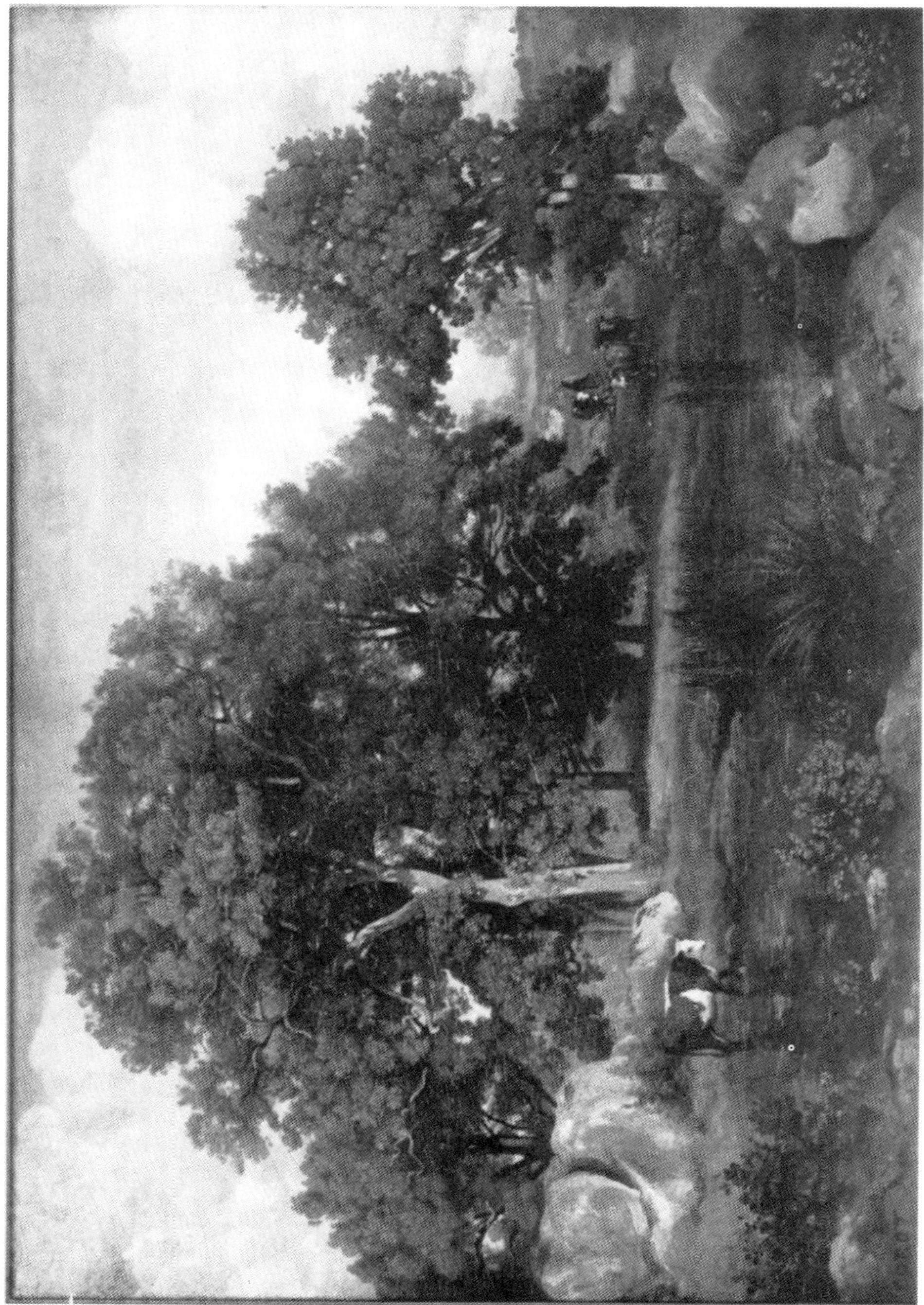

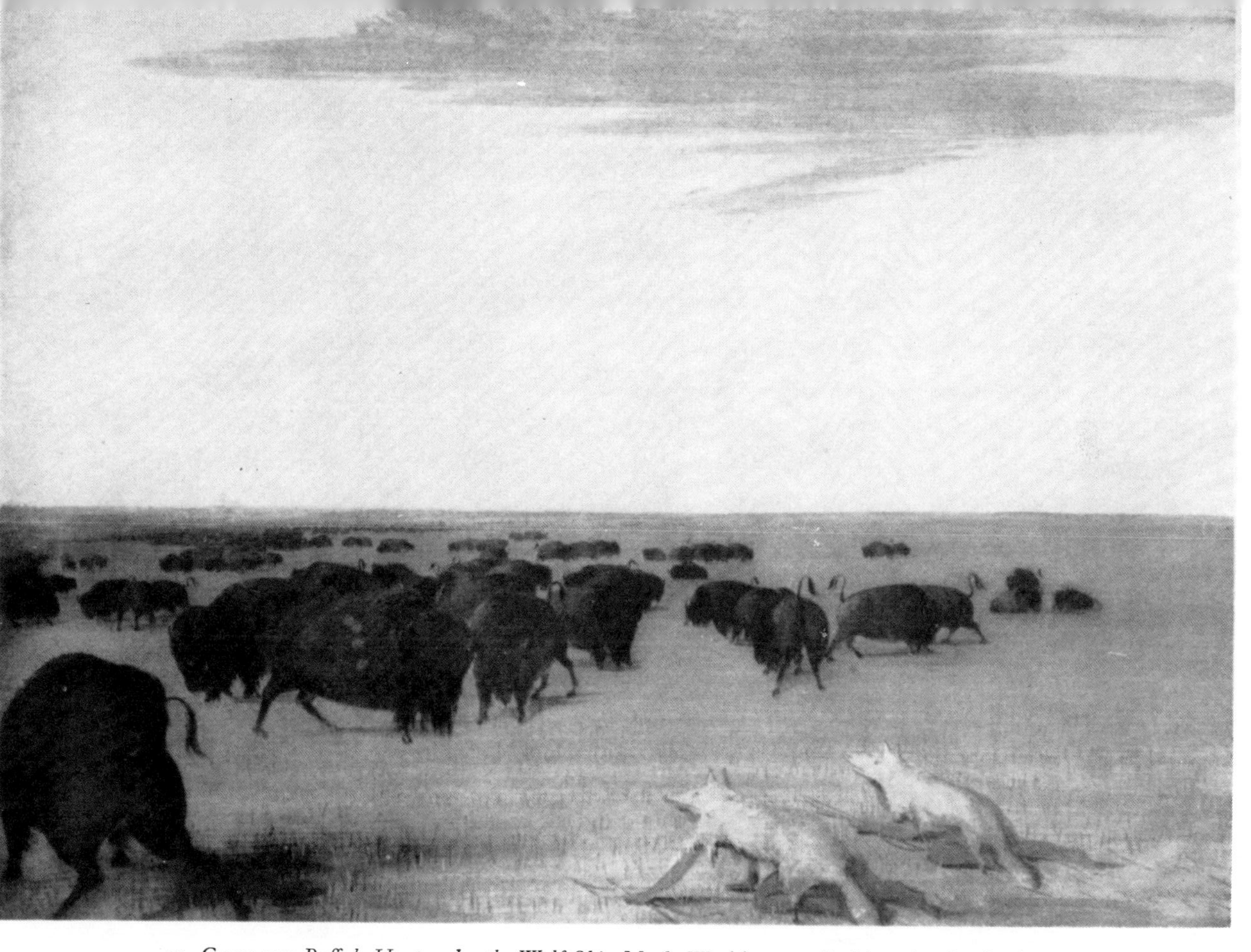

19. Catlin: *Buffalo-Hunt under the Wolf-Skin Mask*. Washington, Smithsonian Institution.

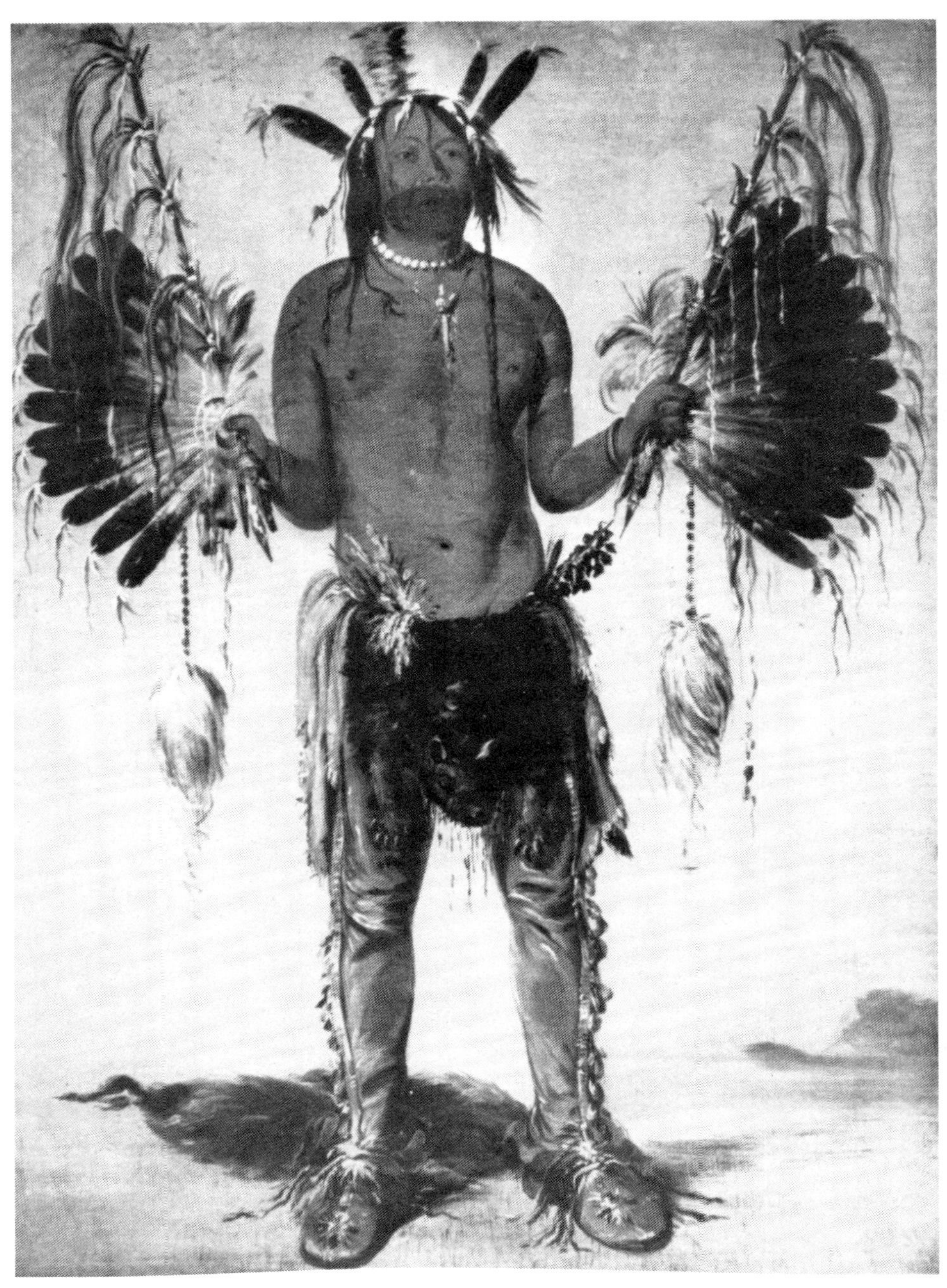

20. CATLIN: *Mah-to-he-ha, the Old Bear*. Washington, Smithsonian Institution.

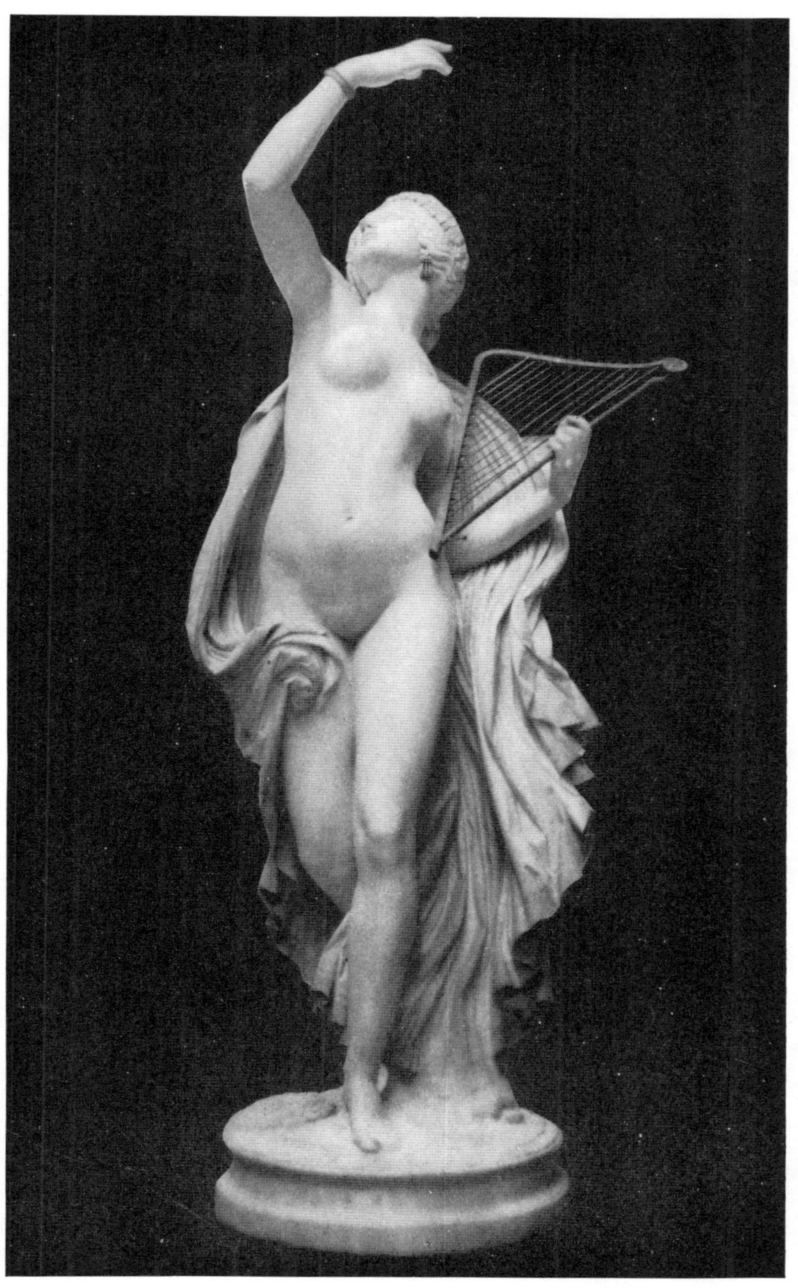

21. PRADIER: *The Frivolous Muse*. Marble. Salon of 1846.
Nîmes, Musée des Beaux-Arts.

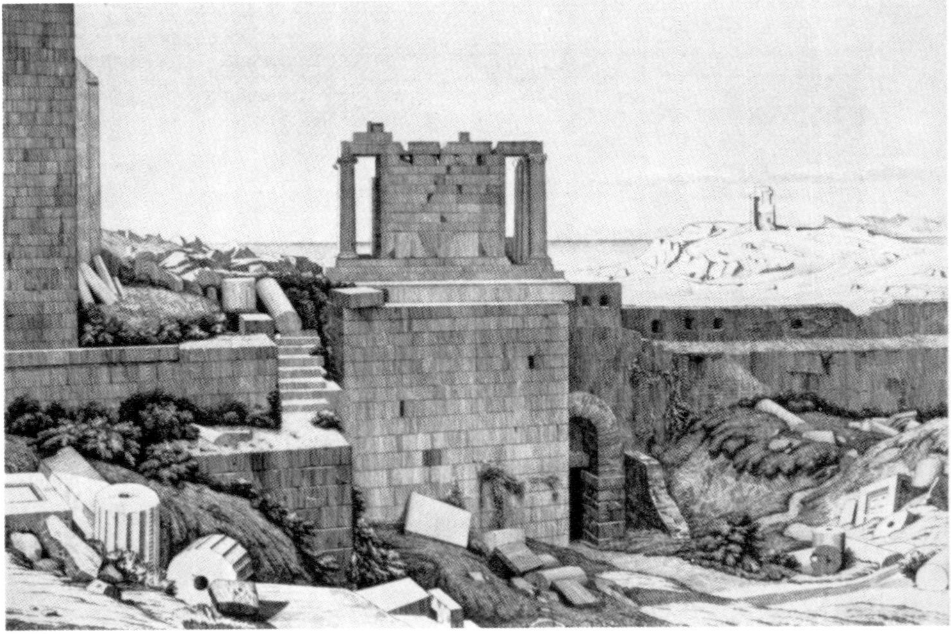

22. ALIGNY: *The Acropolis, Athens*. Etching. Salon of 1846. London, Victoria and Albert Museum.

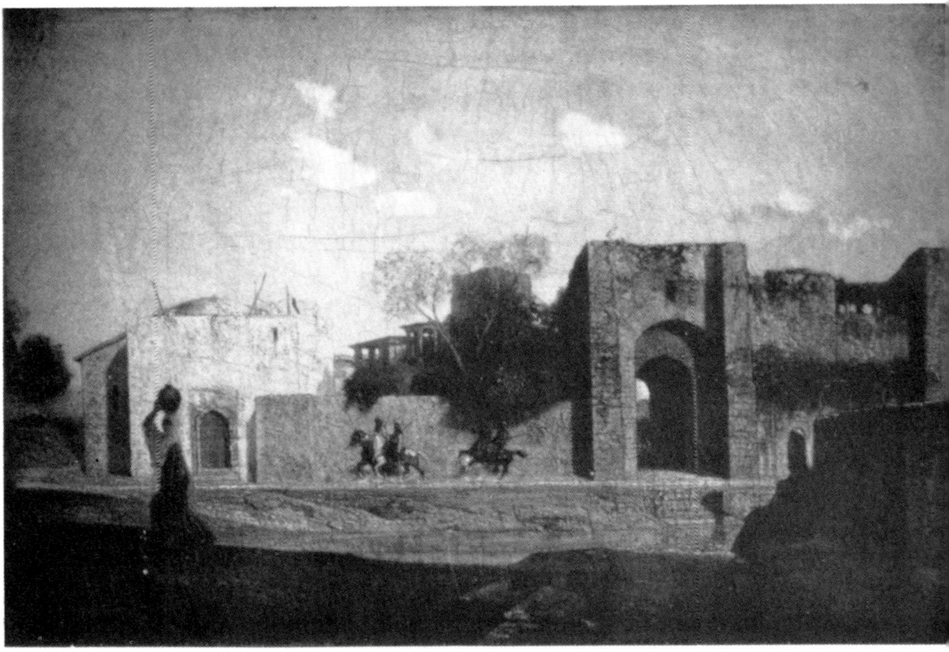

23. DECAMPS: *Turkish Landscape*. Salon of 1846. Amsterdam, Fodor Museum.

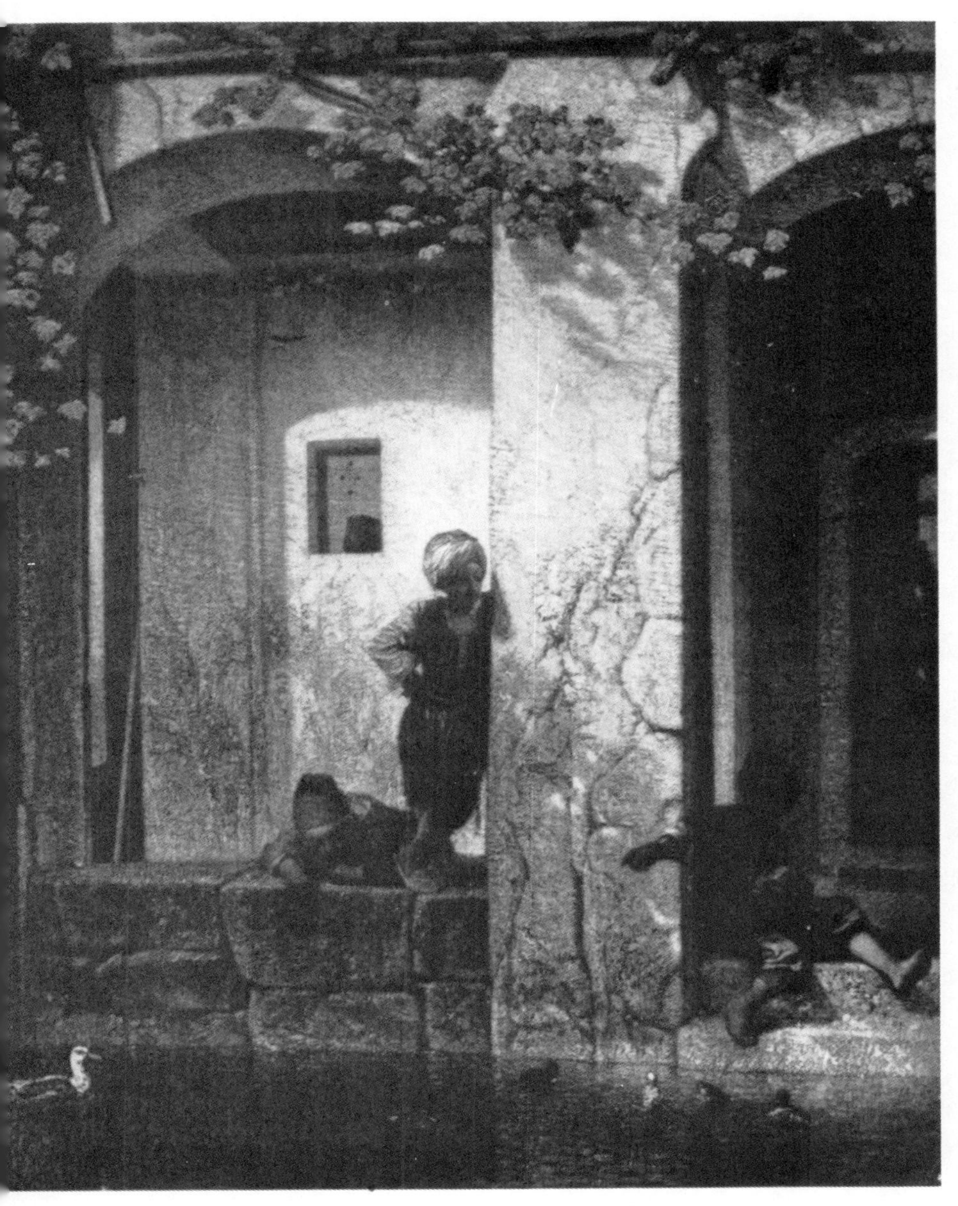

24. Decamps: *Souvenir of Turkey in Asia.* Salon of 1846. Chantilly, Musée Condé.

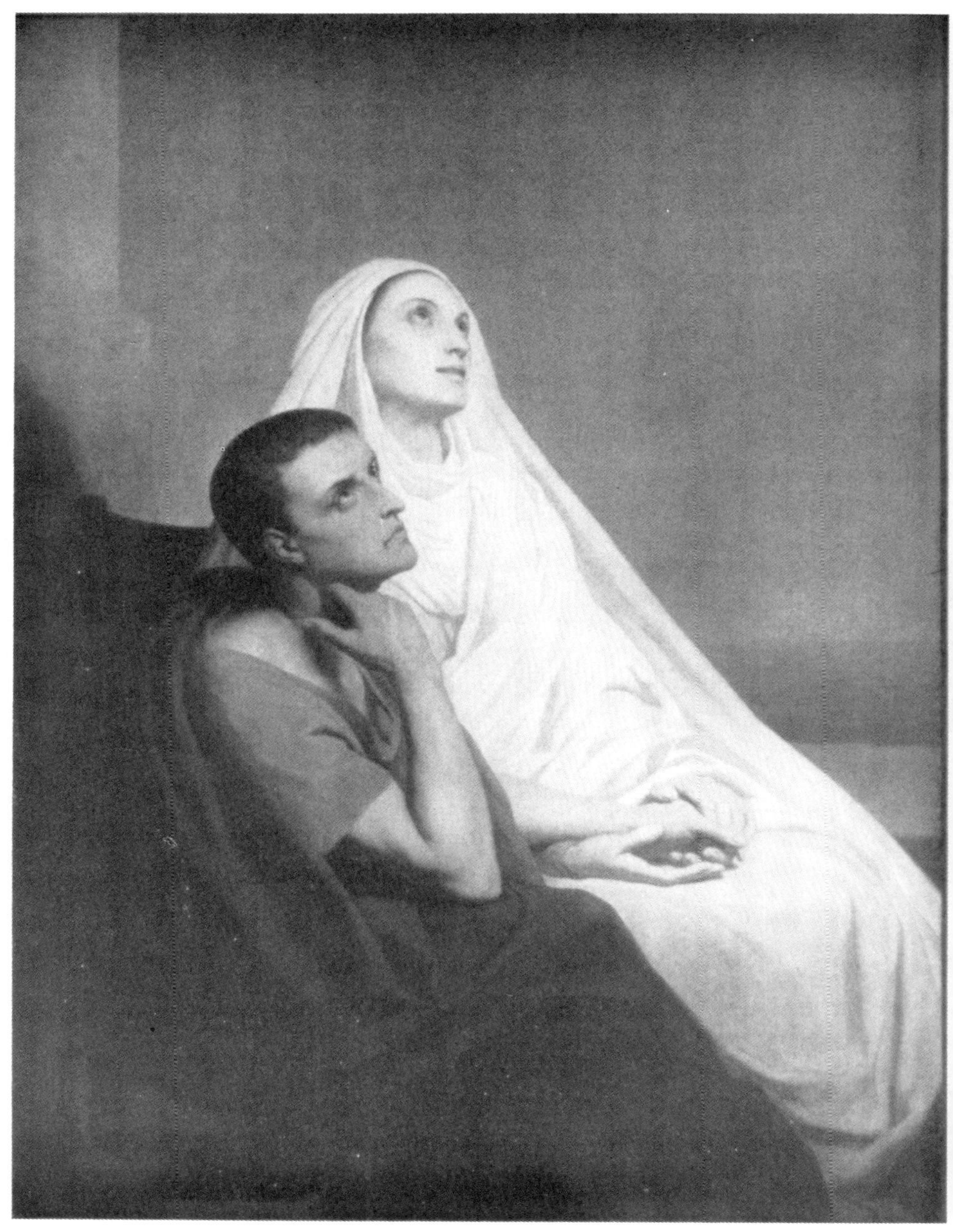

25. Ary Scheffer: *St. Augustine and St. Monica*. Salon of 1846 (later version). London, National Gallery.

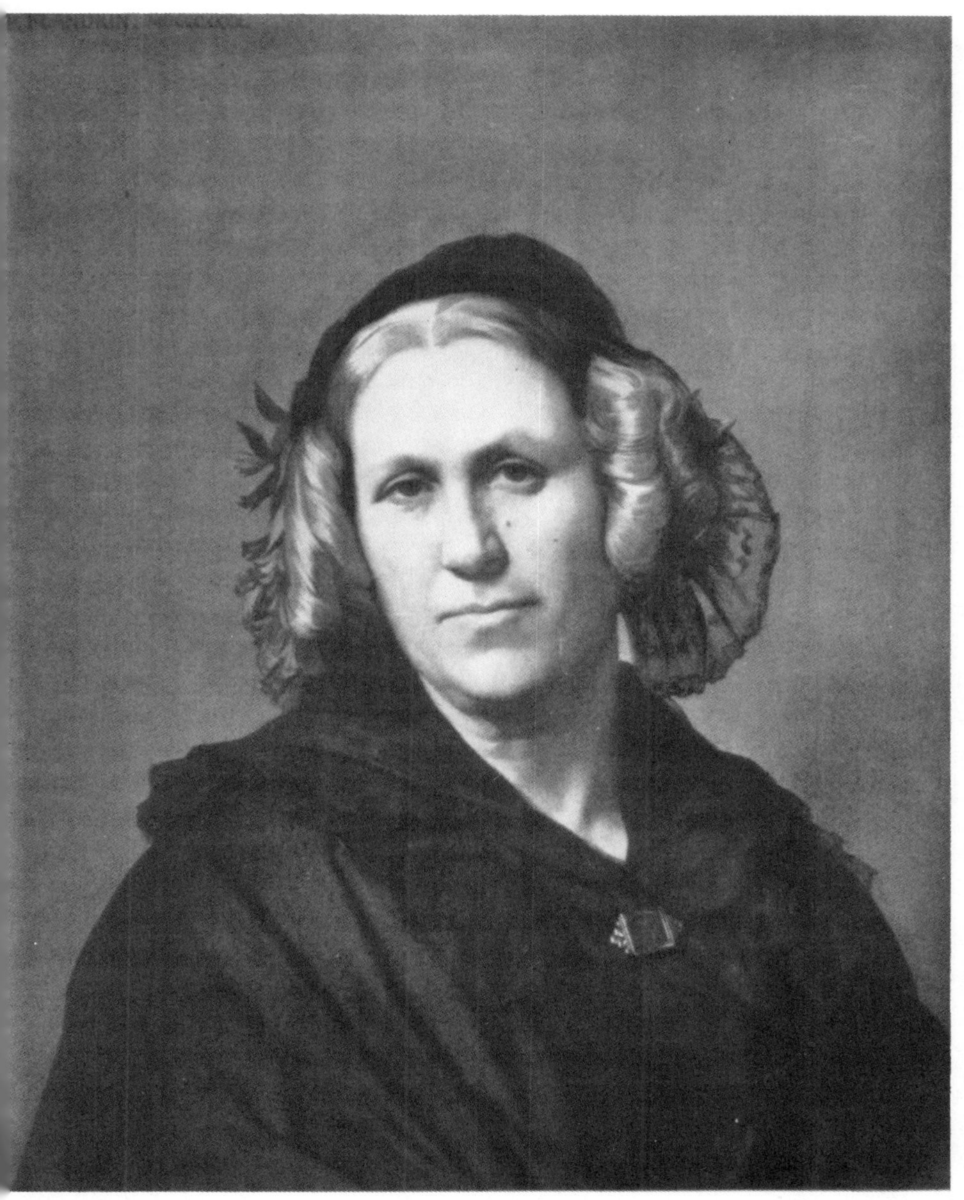

26. HIPPOLYTE FLANDRIN: *Portrait of Mme Vinet*. Dated 1840. Paris, Musée du Louvre.

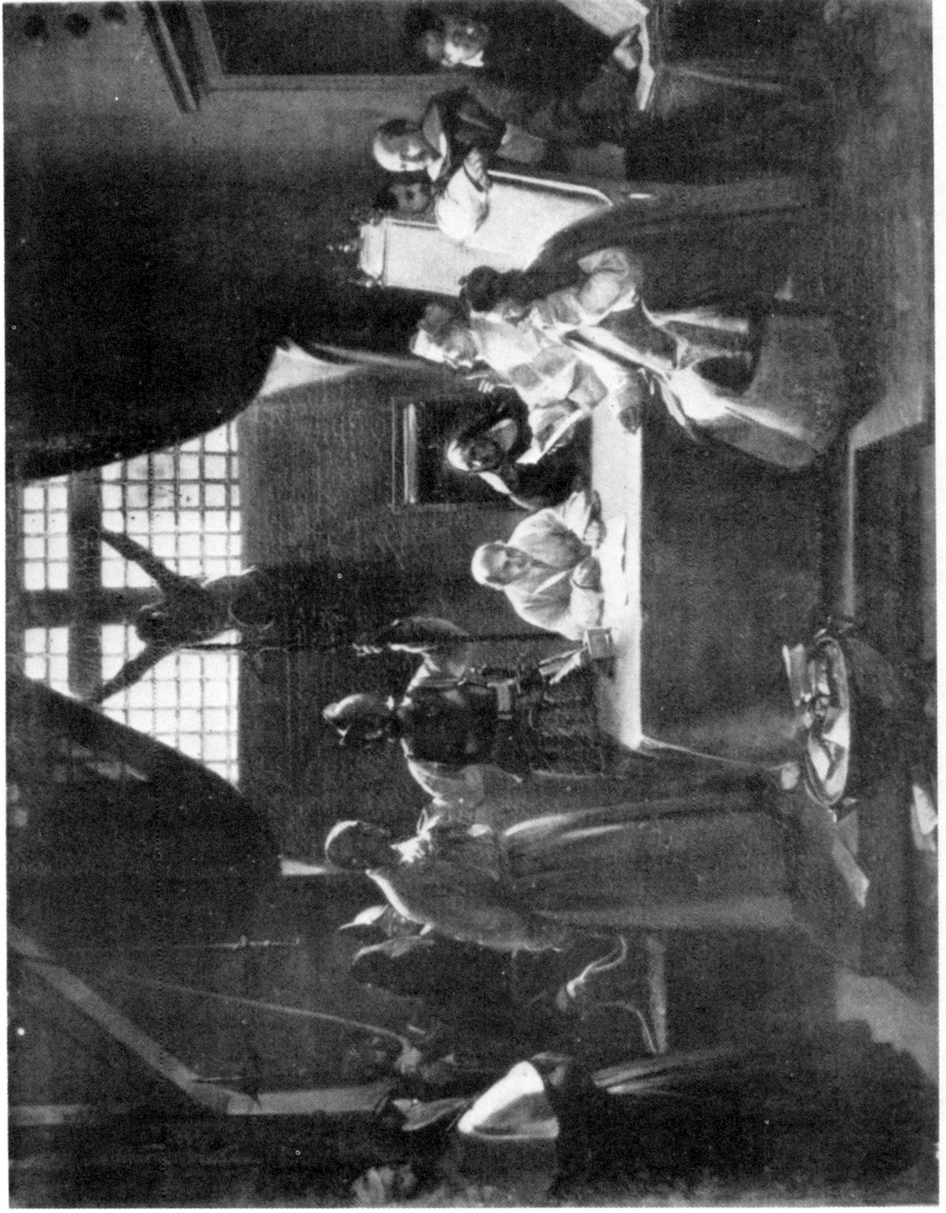

turns and consults with a sure and searching eye; and his painting which issues above all from the memory, speaks above all to the memory. The effect produced upon the spectator's soul is analogous to the artist's means. A picture by Delacroix—*Dante and Virgil*, for example—always leaves a deep impression whose intensity increases with distance. Ceaselessly sacrificing detail to whole, and hesitating to impair the vitality of his thought by the drudgery of a neater and more calligraphic execution, he rejoices in the full use of an inalienable originality, which is his searching intimacy with the subject.

The employment of a dominant note can only rightfully take place at the expense of the rest. An excessive taste makes sacrifices necessary, and masterpieces are never anything but varied extracts from nature. That is the reason why it is necessary to submit to the consequences of a grand passion (whatever it may be), to accept the destiny of a talent, and not to try and bargain with genius. This is a thing never dreamt of by those people who have jeered so much at Delacroix's draughtsmanship—particularly the sculptors, men more partial and purblind than they have a right to be, whose judgement is worth no more than half that of an architect, at the most. Sculpture, to which colour is impossible and movement difficult, has nothing to discuss with an artist whose chief preoccupations are movement, colour and atmosphere. These three elements necessarily demand a somewhat undecided contour, light and floating lines, and boldness of touch. Delacroix is the only artist today whose originality has not been invaded by the tyrannical system of straight lines; his figures are always restless and his draperies fluttering. From Delacroix's point of view the line does not exist; for, however tenuous it may be, a teasing geometrician may always suppose it thick enough to contain a thousand others: and for colourists, who seek to imitate the eternal throbbings of nature, lines are never anything else but the intimate fusion of two colours, as in the rainbow.

Moreover there are several kinds of drawings, as there are of colour: the exact or silly, the physiognomic and the imaginative.

The first is negative, incorrect by sheer force of reality, natural but absurd; the second is a naturalistic, but idealized draughtsmanship—the draughtsmanship of a genius who knows how to choose, arrange, correct, rebuke, and guess at nature; lastly the third, which is the noblest and strangest, and can afford to neglect nature—it realizes *another* nature, analogous to the mind and the temperament of the artist.

Physiognomic drawing is generally the domain of the fanatical, like M. Ingres; creative drawing is the privilege of genius.*

The great quality of the drawing of supreme artists is truth of movement; and Delacroix never violates this natural law.

But let us pass on to an examination of still more general qualities. Now one of the principal characteristics of the great painter is his universality. Take an epic poet, Homer or Dante, for example: he can write an idyll, a narrative, a speech, a description, an ode, etc., all equally well.

In the same way, if Rubens paints fruit, he will paint finer fruit than any specialist that you care to name.

Eugène Delacroix is universal. He has painted genre-pictures full of intimacy, and historical pictures full of grandeur. He alone, perhaps, in our unbelieving age has conceived religious paintings which were neither empty and cold, like competition works, nor pedantic, mystical or neo-Christian, like the works of all those philosophers of art who make religion into an archaistic science, and who believe that not until they have made themselves masters of the traditions and symbology of the early church, can they strike and sound the chords of religion.

This is easy to understand if you are prepared to consider that Delacroix, like all the great masters, is an admirable mixture of science—that is to say, he is a complete painter—and of *naïveté*—that is to say, he is a complete man. Go to St. Louis au Marais[1] and look at his *Pietà*, in which the majestic Queen of Sorrows is holding the body of her dead Son on her knees, with her two arms extended horizontally in an access of despair, a mother's paroxysm of grief. One of the two figures, who is supporting and soothing her anguish, is sobbing like the most pitiful characters in his *Hamlet*—a work with which, moreover, this painting has no little affinity. Of the two holy women, the first, still decked with jewels and tokens of luxury, is crouching convulsively on the ground; the other, fair and golden-haired, sinks more feebly beneath the enormous weight of her despair.

The group is spread out and disposed entirely against a background of a dark, uniform green which suggests a tempest-ridden sea no less than massed boulders. This background is fantastic in its simplicity, for, like Michelangelo, Eugène Delacroix seems to have suppressed the access-

* This is what M. Thiers called 'l'imagination du dessin' (C.B.). See p. 53.

1 Baudelaire is mistaken here. Delacroix's *Pietà* was painted (in 1844) for the church of Saint-Denis-du-Saint-Sacrement, Paris, where it is now to be seen.

ories in order not to damage the clarity of his idea. This masterpiece leaves a deep furrow of melancholy upon the mind. But this was not the first time that he had tackled religious subjects. His *Agony in the Garden*[1] and his *St. Sebastian*[2] had already testified to the seriousness and deep sincerity with which he can stamp them.

But to explain what I declared a moment ago—that only Delacroix knows how to paint religious subjects—I would have the spectator note that if his most interesting pictures are nearly always those whose subjects he chooses himself—namely, subjects of fantasy—nevertheless the grave sadness of his talent is perfectly suited to our religion which is itself profoundly sad—a religion of universal anguish, and one which, because of its very catholicity, grants full liberty to the individual and asks no better than to be celebrated in each man's own language—so long as he knows anguish and is a painter.

I remember a friend of mine—a lad of some merit, too, and an already fashionable colourist; one of those precocious young men who give promise all their lives, and who is far more academic than he himself believes—I remember him calling this 'a cannibal's painting'.

It is perfectly true that our young friend will look in vain among the niceties of a loaded palette, or in the dictionary of rules, for a blood-soaked and savage desolation such as this, which is only just offset by the sombre green of hope.

This terrible hymn to anguish affected his classical imagination in just the same way as the formidable wines of Anjou, Auvergne or the Rhine affect a stomach which is used to the pale violets of Médoc.

So much for universality of feeling—and now for universality of knowledge!

It is a long time since our painters *unlearnt*, so to speak, the genre called 'decoration'. The *Hemicycle*[3] at the Beaux-Arts is a puerile, clumsy work whose intentions contradict one another; it is hardly more than a collection of historical portraits. The *Plafond d'Homère*[4] is a fine picture which makes a bad ceiling. Most of the chapels executed in recent times and

[1] Exhibited in 1827, and now in the church of Saint-Paul-Saint-Louis.

[2] Painted in 1836 and bought for the church of Nantua.

[3] Painted by Paul Delaroche, 1838–41. It represents the most celebrated artists of all nations, up to the end of the seventeenth century.

[4] Painted by Ingres in 1827 for the ceiling in one of the galleries of the Louvre. It was removed in 1855 in order to be shown at the *Exposition Universelle*, and some years later was replaced by a copy. The original now hangs as a picture in the Louvre. See pl. 32.

distributed among the pupils of Ingres were done according to the methods of the Italian primitives—that is, they aim at achieving unity by the suppression of effects of light and by a vast system of softened colourings. This method, which is doubtless more reasonable, nevertheless evades the difficulties. Under Louis XIV, XV and XVI, painters produced decorations of dazzling brilliance, but they lacked unity in colour and composition.

Eugène Delacroix had decorations to paint, and he solved the great problem. He discovered pictorial unity without doing hurt to his trade as a colourist.

We have the Palais Bourbon[1] to bear witess to this extraordinary *tour de force*. There the light is dispensed economically, and it spreads evenly across all the figures, without tyrannically catching the eye.

The circular ceiling in the library of the Luxembourg[2] is a still more astonishing work, in which the painter has arrived not only at an even blander and more unified effect, while suppressing nothing of the qualities of colour and light which are the characteristic feature of all his pictures—but he has gone further and revealed himself in an altogether new guise: Delacroix the landscape-painter!

Instead of painting Apollo and the Muses, the invariable decoration for a library, Eugène Delacroix has yielded to his irresistible taste for Dante, whom Shakespeare alone, perhaps, can challenge in his mind, and he has chosen the passage where Dante and Virgil meet with the principal poets of antiquity in a mysterious place:

> We ceased not to go, though he was speaking; but passed the wood meanwhile, the wood, I say, of crowded spirits. Our way was not yet far since my slumber, when I saw a fire which conquered a hemisphere of the darkness. We were still a little distant from it; yet not so distant that I did not in part discern what honourable people occupied that place.
>
> 'O thou that honourest every science and art; who are these, who have such honour that it separates them from the manner of the rest?'
>
> And he to me: 'The honoured name, which glorifies them in that life of thine, gains favour in Heaven which thus advances them.'

[1] Delacroix made twenty allegorical paintings for the library of the *Chambre des Députés* between 1838 and 1847.

[2] Delacroix was nearing the end of his work at the Luxembourg at the time that this was written.

Meanwhile a voice was heard by me: 'Honour the great Poet! His shade returns that was departed.'

After the voice had paused and was silent, I saw four great shadows come to us; they had an aspect neither sad nor joyful.

The good Master began to speak: 'Mark him with that sword in hand, who comes before the three as their lord: that is Homer, the sovereign poet; the next who comes is Horace the satirist; Ovid is the third, and the last is Lucan. Because each agrees with me in the name which the one voice sounded, they do me honour; and therein they do well.'

Thus I saw assembled the goodly school of that lord of highest song, who like an eagle soars above the rest. After they had talked a space together, they turned to me with a sign of salutation; and my Master smiled thereat. And greatly more besides they honoured me; for they made me of their number, so that I was a sixth amid such intelligences.[1]

I shall not pay Eugène Delacroix the insult of an exaggerated panegyric for having so successfully mastered the concavity of his canvas, or for having placed his figures upright upon it. His talent is above these things. I am concentrating above all upon the *spirit* of this painting. It is impossible to express in prose all the blessed calm which it breathes, and the deep harmony which imbues its atmosphere. It makes you think of the most luxuriant pages of *Télémaque*, and brings to life all the memories which the mind has ever gathered from tales of Elysium. From the point of view at which I took up my position a short while ago, the landscape, which is nevertheless no more than an accessory—such is the universality of the great masters!—is a thing of the greatest importance. This circular landscape, which embraces an enormous area, is painted with the assurance of a history-painter, and with the delicacy and love of a painter of landscape. Clumps of laurel and considerable patches of shade dissect it harmoniously; pools of gentle, uniform sunlight slumber on the greensward; mountains, blue or forest-girt, form a perfect horizon *for the eyes' pleasure*.[2] The sky is blue and white—an amazing thing with Delacroix; the clouds, which are spun and drawn out in different directions, like a

[1] Dante, *Inferno*, canto iv. lines 64 ff.

[2] The phrase italicized (by Baudelaire) is an exact verbal echo from Fénelon's description of Calypso's island (*Télémaque*, Bk. 1).

piece of gauze being rent, are of a wonderful airiness; and the deep and luminous vault of the sky recedes to a prodigious height. Even Bonington's water colours are less transparent.

This masterpiece, which, in my opinion, is superior to the finest of Veronese, needs a great tranquillity of mind and a very gentle light to be properly comprehended. Unfortunately the brilliant daylight which will burst through the great window of the façade, as soon as it is cleared of its tarpaulins and scaffolding, will make this task more difficult.

Delacroix's pictures this year are *The Abduction of Rebecca* taken from *Ivanhoe*, the *Farewell of Romeo and Juliet*, *Marguerite in Church* and *A Lion* in water-colour.

The admirable thing about *The Abduction of Rebecca*[1] is the perfect ordering of its colours, which are intense, close-packed, serried and logical; the result of this is a thrilling effect. With almost all painters who are not colourists, you will always be noticing vacuums, that is to say great holes, produced by tones which are below the level of the rest, so to speak. Delacroix's painting is like nature; it has a horror of a vacuum.

Romeo and Juliet[2] are shown on the balcony, in the morning's cold radiance, holding one another devoutly clasped by the waist. In the violence of this farewell embrace, Juliet, with her hands laid on the shoulders of her lover, is throwing back her head as though to draw breath, or in a movement of pride and joyful passion. This unwonted attitude—for almost all painters glue their lovers' lips together—is nevertheless perfectly natural; this vigorous movement of the neck is typical of dogs and cats in the thrill of a caress. The scene, with the romantic landscape which completes it, is enveloped in the purplish mists of the dawn.

The general success which this picture has achieved, and the interest which it inspires, only go to show what I have already said elsewhere—that Delacroix is *popular*, whatever the painters may say; and that it will be enough not to keep the public away from his works for him to be as much so as inferior painters are.

Marguerite in Church[3] belongs to that already numerous class of charming genre-pictures, by which Delacroix seems to be wanting to explain his lithographs,[4] which have been so bitterly criticized.

[1] In the Metropolitan Museum, New York; reproduced *Journal*, pl. 39.

[2] See pl. 37.

[3] Reproduced Escholier, vol. II, facing p. 308.

[4] Delacroix's *Faust* lithographs were first published in book form in 1828. Goethe had seen some of them two years before, and spoke of them with great admiration to

The water-colour *Lion* has a special merit for me, quite apart from its beauty of drawing and attitude; this is because it is painted with a great simplicity. Water-colour is restricted here to its own modest role; it makes no attempt to rival oil-paint in stature.

To complete this analysis, it only remains for me to note one last quality in Delacroix—but the most remarkable quality of all, and that which makes him the true painter of the nineteenth century; it is the unique and persistent melancholy with which all his works are imbued, and which is revealed in his choice of subject, in the expression of his faces, in gesture and in style of colour. Delacroix has a fondness for Dante and Shakespeare, two other great painters of human anguish: he knows them through and through, and is able to translate them freely. As you look through the succession of his pictures, you might think that you were assisting at the celebration of some dolorous mystery: *Dante and Virgil*, *The Massacre at Chios*, *Sardanapalus*, *Christ in the Garden of Olives*, *St. Sebastian*, *Medea*,[1] *The Shipwreck of Don Juan*,[2] and the *Hamlet*,[3] which was so much mocked at and so misunderstood. In several of them, by some strange and recurring accident, you will find one figure which is more stricken, more crushed than the others; a figure in which all the surrounding anguish is epitomized—for example, the kneeling woman, with her hair cast down, in the foreground of the *Crusaders at Constantinople*,[4] or the old woman, so wrinkled and forlorn, in *The Massacre at Chios*. This aura of melancholy surrounds even the *Women of Algiers*,[5] that most engaging and showy of his pictures. That little poem of an interior, all silence and repose, and crammed with rich stuffs and knick-knacks of the toilet, seems somehow to exhale the heady scent of a bordello, which quickly enough guides our thoughts towards the fathomless limbo of sadness. Generally speaking he does not paint pretty women—not at any rate from the point of view of the fashionable world. Almost all of them are sick, and gleaming with a sort of interior beauty. He expresses physical force not by bulk of muscle, but by nervous tension. He is

Eckermann (see *Conversations of Goethe with Eckermann*, Everyman edn., pp. 135–6). Between 1834 and 1843 Delacroix made sixteen lithographs of scenes from *Hamlet*.

[1] Painted in 1838, and now in the Lille Museum.

[2] Painted in 1841, and now in the Louvre; reproduced *Journal*, pl. 30.

[3] Delacroix painted several versions of *Hamlet and the Gravedigger*: that of 1839 is in the Louvre; see pl. 36.

[4] Painted in 1840, and now in the Louvre; reproduced *Journal*, pl. 25.

[5] Painted in 1834, and now in the Louvre; see pl. 34.

unrivalled at expressing not merely suffering, but above all *moral* suffering—and here lies the prodigious mystery of his painting! This lofty and serious melancholy of his shines with a gloomy brilliance, even in his colour, which is broad, simple and abundant in harmonious masses, like that of all the great colourists; and yet it is as plaintive and deep-toned as a melody by Weber.[1]

Each one of the old masters has his kingdom, his prerogative, which he is often constrained to share with illustrious rivals. Thus Raphael has form, Rubens and Veronese colour, Rubens and Michelangelo the 'graphic imagination'. There remained one province of the empire in which Rembrandt alone had carried out a few raids; I mean drama, natural and living drama, the drama of terror and melancholy, expressed often through colour, but always through gesture.

In the matter of sublime gestures, Delacroix's only rivals are outside his art. I know of scarcely any others but Frédérick Lemaître[2] and Macready.[3]

It is because of this entirely modern and novel quality that Delacroix is the latest expression of progress in art. Heir to the great tradition—that is, to breadth, nobility and magnificence in composition—and a worthy successor of the old masters, he has even surpassed them in his command of anguish, passion and gesture! It is really this fact that establishes the importance of his greatness. Suppose, indeed, that the baggage of one of the illustrious departed were to go astray; he will almost always have his counterpart, who will be able to explain him and disclose his secret to the historian's scrutiny. But take away Delacroix, and the great chain of history is broken and slips to the ground.

In an article which must seem more like a prophecy than a critique, what is the object of isolating faults of detail and microscopic blemishes? The whole is so fine that I have not the heart. Besides it is such an easy thing to do, and so many others have done it! Is it not a pleasant change to view people from their good side? M. Delacroix's defects are at

[1] The simile recurs in the stanza devoted to Delacroix in Baudelaire's poem *Les Phares*. See pp. 141–2, where Baudelaire analyses this stanza.

[2] Frédérick Lemaître (1800–76) was one of the great French actors of the Romantic generation. He made his first great success as Robert Macaire in *L'Auberge des Adrets* (1823), and later created the title-rôle in Victor Hugo's *Ruy Blas*.

[3] William Charles Macready (1793–1873), the notable English tragedian of the same generation as Edmund Kean. His grand, impassioned style greatly impressed the French when he acted in Paris in 1828 (twice) and again in 1844.

times so obvious that they strike the least trained eye. You have only to open at random the first paper that comes your way, and you will find that they have long followed the opposite method from mine, in persistently not seeing the glorious qualities which constitute his originality. Need I remind you that great geniuses never make mistakes by halves, and that they have the privilege of enormity in every direction?

Among Delacroix's pupils there are some who have happily appropriated whatever elements of his talent could be captured—that is, certain parts of his method—and who have already earned themselves something of a reputation. Nevertheless their colour has, generally speaking, this flaw—that it scarcely aims above picturesqueness and 'effect'; the ideal is in no sense their domain, although they readily dispense with nature, without having earned the right to do so by dint of their master's intrepid studies.

This year we must regret the absence of M. Planet, whose *Sainte Thérèse*[1] attracted the eyes of the connoisseurs at the last Salon—and of M. Riesener, who has often given us broadly-coloured pictures, and by whom you can see some good ceilings at the Chambre des Pairs—and see them with pleasure, too, in spite of the terrible proximity of Delacroix.

M. Léger Chérelle has sent *Le Martyre de Sainte Irène*.[2] The composition consists of a single figure and a pike, which makes a somewhat unpleasant effect. Nevertheless the colour and the modelling of the torso are generally good. But I rather think that M. Léger Chérelle had already shown the public this picture before, with some minor variations.

A somewhat surprising feature of *La Mort de Cléopâtre*,[3] by M. Lassale-Bordes, is that the artist does not seem to be uniquely preoccupied with colour; and this is perhaps a merit. Its tints are, so to speak, equivocal, and this sourness of taste is not without its charms.

Cleopatra is dying, on her throne, while Octavius's envoy stoops forward to gaze at her. One of her handmaidens has just expired at her feet. The composition does not lack majesty, and the painting has been

[1] See pp. 5–16.
[2] The note in the Salon catalogue runs as follows: 'Cette vierge, ayant caché les livres saints, contre les ordres de l'empereur Dioclétien, fut mise en prison et percée d'une flèche' (Vies des Saints).
[3] Now in the Autun Museum; see pl. 16.

executed with quite a daring simplicity; Cleopatra's head is beautiful, and the negress's green and pink attire contrasts happily with the colour of her skin. This huge picture has been successfully carried through with no regard for imitation, and it certainly contains something to please and attract the unattached *flâneur*.

V. ON EROTIC SUBJECTS IN ART, AND ON M. TASSAERT

HAS IT ever been your experience, as it has mine, that after spending long hours turning over a collection of bawdy prints, you fall into a great spell of melancholy? And have you ever asked yourself the reason for the charm sometimes to be found in rummaging among these annals of lubricity, which are buried in libraries or lost in dealers' portfolios—and sometimes also for the ill-humour which they cause you? It is a mixture of pleasure and pain, a vinegar for which the lips are always athirst! The pleasure lies in your seeing represented in all its forms that most important of natural feelings—and the anger in often finding it so badly copied or so stupidly slandered. Whether it has been by the fireside during the endless winter evenings, or in a corner of a dealer's shop, in the dog-days when the hours hang heavy, the sight of such drawings has often put my mind into enormous drifts of reverie, in much the same way as an obscene book sweeps us towards the mystical oceans of the deep. Many times, when faced with these countless samples of the universal feeling, I have found myself wishing that the poet, the connoisseur and the philosopher could grant themselves the enjoyment of a Museum of Love, where there would be a place for everything, from *St. Teresa*'s undirected affections down to the serious debaucheries of the ages of ennui. No doubt an immense distance separates *Le Départ pour l'île de Cythère*[1] from the miserable daubs which hang above a cracked pot and a rickety side-table in a harlot's room; but with a subject of such importance, nothing should be neglected. Besides, all things are sanctified by genius, and if these subjects were treated with the necessary care and reflection, they would in no wise be soiled by that revolting obscenity, which is bravado rather than truth.

[1] By Watteau.

Let not the moralist be too alarmed! I shall know how to keep the proper bounds, and besides, my dream is limited to a wish for this immense poem of love as sketched by only the purest hands—by Ingres, Watteau, Rubens, Delacroix! The playful and elegant princesses of Watteau beside the grave and composed Venuses of M. Ingres, the resplendent pearls of Rubens and Jordaens and the sad beauties of Delacroix, just as one can imagine them—great, pale women, drowned in satin.*

And so, to give complete reassurance to the reader's startled modesty, let me say that I should class among erotic subjects not only all pictures which are especially concerned with love, but also any picture which suggests love, be it only a portrait.**

In this immense museum I envisage the beauty and the love of all climes, expressed by the leading artists—from the mad, scatter-brained *merveilleuses* which Watteau *fils*[1] has bequeathed us in his fashion engravings, down to Rembrandt's Venuses who are having their nails done and their hair combed with great boxwood combs, just like simple mortals.

Subjects of this nature are so important a thing that there is no artist, small or great, who has not devoted himself to them, secretly or in public, from Giulio Romano to Devéria and Gavarni.

In general their great defect is a lack of sincerity and *naïveté*. I remember, however, a lithograph[2] which expresses one of the great truths of wanton love—though unhappily without too much refinement. A young man, disguised as a woman, and his mistress, dressed as a man, are seated side by side on a sofa—the sofa which you know so well, the sofa of the furnished lodgings and the private apartment. The young woman is trying to lift her lover's skirt.*** In the ideal museum of which I was

* I have been told that many years ago Delacroix made a whole mass of marvellous studies of women in the most voluptuous attitudes, for his *Sardanapalus*. (C.B.)

** M. Ingres's *Grande* and *Petite Odalisque* are two pictures of our times which are essentially concerned with love, and are admirable, moreover. (C.B.) The *Grande Odalisque* is in the Louvre (see pl. 29): the *Petite Odalisque* is presumably the *Odalisque with Slave*, in the Fogg Art Museum, Cambridge, Mass.

[1] François Watteau (de Lille) (1758–1823), son of Louis Watteau and nephew of Antoine Watteau.

[2] One of the series 'Les Amants et les Epoux' by Tassaert. The lady's words are 'Ne fais donc pas la cruelle!' See pl. 17.

*** 'Sedebant in fornicibus pueri puellaeve sub titulis et lychnis, illi faemineo compti mundo sub stola, hae parum comptae sub puerorum veste, ore ad puerilem formam composito. Alter veniebat sexus sub altero sexu. *Corruperat omnis caro viam suam.*'

speaking, this lewd sheet would be counterbalanced by many others in which love would only appear in its most refined forms.

These reflections have occurred to me in connection with two pictures by M. Tassaert—*Erigone* and *Le Marchand d'esclaves*.

M. Tassaert, of whom I made the grave mistake of not saying enough last year, is a painter of the greatest merit, and one whose talent would be most happily applied to erotic subjects.

Erigone is half recumbent upon a mound overshadowed with vines—in a provocative pose, with one leg almost bent back, the other stretched out, and the body thrust forward; the drawing is fine, and the lines sinuous and expertly organized. Nevertheless I would criticize M. Tassaert, who is a colourist, for having painted this torso in too uniform a tone.

The other picture represents a market of women awaiting buyers. These are true women, civilized women, whose feet have felt the rubbing of shoes; they are a little common, a little too pink perhaps, but a silly, sensual Turk is going to buy them as superfine beauties. The one who is seen from behind, and whose buttocks are enveloped in a transparent gauze, still wears upon her head a milliner's hat, a hat bought in the Rue Vivienne or at the Temple. The poor girl has doubtless been carried off by pirates!

The colour of this picture is remarkable in the extreme for its delicacy and transparency of tone. One would imagine that M. Tassaert has been studying Delacroix's manner; nevertheless he has managed to retain a colour of his own.

He is an outstanding artist, whom only the *flâneurs* appreciate and whom the public does not know well enough; his talent has never ceased growing, and when you think of whence he started, and where he has arrived, there is reason to look forward to ravishing things from him in the future.

VI. ON SOME COLOURISTS

THERE are two curiosities of a certain importance at the Salon. These are the portraits of *Petit Loup* and of *Graisse du dos de buffle* by M. Catlin,

Meursius. (C.B.) This passage is quoted from Nicolas Chorier's *Aloysiae Sygeae satira sotadica de arcanis Amoris et Veneris* (1658), which purported to be Meursius's Latin version of a Spanish original.

the impresario of the red-skins.[1] When M. Catlin came to Paris, with his Museum and his Ioways, the word went round that he was a good fellow who could neither paint nor draw, and that if he had produced some tolerable studies, it was thanks only to his courage and his patience. Was this an innocent trick of M. Catlin's, or a blunder on the part of the journalists? For today it is established that M. Catlin can paint and draw very well indeed. These two portraits would be enough to prove it to me if I could not call to mind many other specimens equally fine. I had been particularly struck by the transparency and lightness of his skies.

M. Catlin has captured the proud, free character and the noble expression of these splendid fellows in a masterly way; the structure of their heads is wonderfully well understood. With their fine attitudes and their ease of movement, these savages make antique sculpture comprehensible. Turning to his colour, I find in it an element of mystery which delights me more than I can say. Red, the colour of blood, the colour of life, flowed so abundantly in his gloomy Museum that it was like an intoxication; and the landscapes—wooded mountains, vast savannahs, deserted rivers—were monotously, eternally green. Once again I find Red (so inscrutable and dense a colour, and harder to penetrate than a serpent's eye)—and Green (the colour of Nature, calm, gay and smiling)—singing their melodious antiphon in the very faces of these two heroes.—There is no doubt that all their tattooing and pigmentations had been done in accordance with the harmonious systems of nature.

I believe that what has led the public and the journalists into error with regard to M. Catlin is the fact that his painting has nothing to do with that *brash* style, to which all our young men have so accustomed us that it has become the *classic* style of our time.

[1] George Catlin (1796–1872), the American artist, spent eight years with Indian tribes residing in United States, British and Mexican territories, between 1829 and 1837. During this period he painted some five hundred portraits and other pictures of Red Indians. During 1838 and 1839 he toured his collection in the United States, and then brought it to London, where he established himself at 6 Waterloo Place. In 1845 he visited Paris, bringing with him not only his paintings but several live Indians as well. One of these was *Shon-ta-yi-ga*, or *Little Wolf*, whose portrait Baudelaire mentions here. See Alfred Delvau's *Lions du Jour* (1867), and also Catlin's own *Descriptive Catalogue*, published by himself in London in 1848; it contains appreciations from the American, English and French press.

Catlin's collection is now in the care of the Smithsonian Institution, Washington; a small selection was brought to Europe and exhibited in 1954. See pls. 19–20.

Last year I already entered my protest against that unanimous *De profundis*—against that conspiracy of ingratitude—concerning the brothers Devéria. This year has proved me right. Many a precocious name which has been substituted for theirs is not yet worth as much. M. Achille Devéria has attracted special attention at this year's Salon by a picture, *Le Repos de la Sainte Famille*,[1] which not only retains all of that grace peculiar to these charming brother-geniuses, but which also recalls the solid qualities of the older schools of painting—minor schools, perhaps, which do not precisely sweep the board either by their drawing or their colour, but which, nevertheless, by their sense of order and of sound tradition are placed well above the extravagances proper to transitional ages. In the great battle of Romanticism, the Devéria brothers were members of the sacred band of the colourists; and thus their place was marked out here. The composition of M. Achille Devéria's picture is excellent, and, over and above this, the eye is struck by its soft and harmonious appearance.

M. Boissard, whose beginnings were also brilliant and full of promise, is one of those excellent artists who have taken their nourishment from the old masters; his *Madeleine au désert* is good and sound in colour—except for the flesh-tones which are a trifle dingy. The pose is a happy one.

In this interminable Salon, where differences have been more than ever wiped out, and where everyone can draw and paint a little, but not enough to deserve even to be classed, it is a great joy to meet a frank and true painter like M. Debon. Perhaps his *Concert dans l'atelier*[2] is a little too *artistic* a picture—Valentin, Jordaens and several others have their part in it; but at least it is fine, healthy painting, which marks its author as a man who is perfectly sure of himself.

M. Duveau has sent *Le Lendemain d'une tempête*. I do not know if he has it in him to become a frank colourist, but some parts of his picture give hopes of it. At first sight you search your memory for some historical scene which it can represent; for in fact the English are almost alone in daring to paint genre-pictures of such vast proportions. Nevertheless it is well organized and in general seems well designed. The tonality, which is a little too uniform and offends the eye at first, is doubtless based on an effect of nature, all of whose features appear singularly crude in colour after being washed by the rains.

[1] Reproduced *Illustr.* vol. VII (1846), p. 56.

[2] Reproduced *Illustr.* vol. VII (1846). p. 121.

M. Laemlein's *Charité*[1] is a charming woman with a whole bunch of little brats of all countries—white, yellow, black, and so on—held by the hand or carried at the breast. Certainly M. Laemlein has a feeling for good colour. If his picture contains one great fault, it is that the little Chinaman is so pretty, and his garment so delightful to the eye, that he practically monopolizes the spectator's attention. This little mandarin never stops trotting through the memory, and he will cause many people to forget all the rest.

M. Decamps is one of those who, for many years now, have tyrannically possessed the public's interest; and nothing could be more legitimate.

This artist, who is gifted with a marvellous capacity for analysis, used often to achieve powerfully effective results by means of a happy conflict of little tricks. If he shirked linear detail too much, often contenting himself with movement and general contour, and if his drawing used occasionally to verge upon the *chic*, nevertheless his meticulous taste for Nature, studied above all in her effects of light, always kept him safe and sustained him on a superior plane.

If M. Decamps was not precisely a draughtsman in the generally accepted sense of the word, nevertheless, in his own way and in a particular fashion, he was one. No one has seen large figures from his pencil; but certainly the drawing—that is to say, the *build*—of his little manikins was brought out and realized with remarkable boldness and felicity. Their bodily nature and habits were always clearly revealed; for M. Decamps can make a figure intelligible in a few lines. His sketches were diverting and profoundly comical. It was the draughtsmanship of a wit, almost of a caricaturist; for he possessed an extraordinary geniality, or mocking fancy, which was a perfect match for the ironies of nature; and so his figures were always posed, draped or dressed in accordance with the truth and with the eternal proprieties and habits of their persons. If there was a certain immobility in his drawing, this was by no means unpleasing, and actually put the seal upon his orientalism. Normally he took his models in repose; and when they were shown running, they often reminded you of frozen shadows or of silhouettes suddenly halted in their course; they ran as though they were part of a bas-relief. But it was colour that was his strong suit, his great and unique affair. Now M. Delacroix is without doubt a great colourist; but he is not a

[1] Laemlein made a lithograph also of this subject.

fanatical one. He has many other concerns, and the scale of his canvases demands it. But for M. Decamps colour was the great thing; it was, so to speak, his favourite mode of thought. His splendid and radiant colour had, what is more, a style very much of its own. It was, to use words borrowed from the moral order, both sanguinary and mordant. The most appetizing dishes, the most thoughtfully prepared kickshaws, the most piquantly seasoned products of the kitchen, had less relish and tang, and exhaled less fierce ecstasy upon the nose and the palate of the epicure than M. Decamps's pictures possessed for the lover of painting. Their strangeness of aspect halted you, held you captive and inspired you with an irresistible curiosity. Perhaps this had something to do with the unusual and meticulous methods which the artist often employs—for he *lucubrates* his painting, they say, with the tireless will of an alchemist. So sudden and so novel was the impression that it produced upon the mind of the spectator at that time, that it was difficult to conceive its ancestry, or to decide who had fathered this singular artist, and from what studio this solitary and original talent had emerged. Certainly a hundred years from now historians will have trouble in identifying M. Decamps's master. Sometimes he seemed to stem from the boldest colourists of the old Flemish school, but he had more style than they, and he grouped his figures more harmoniously; sometimes the splendour and the triviality of Rembrandt were his keen preoccupation; at other times his skies would suggest a loving memory of the skies of Claude. For M. Decamps was a landscape-painter too, and, what is more, a landscape-painter of the greatest merit. But his landscapes and his figures formed a single whole and helped one another mutually; one had no more importance than the other, for with him nothing was an accessory—so curiously wrought was every part of his canvas, and to such an extent was each detail planned to contribute to the total effect! Nothing was unnecessary—not even the rat swimming across a tank in one or other of his Turkish pictures—a picture all lethargy and fatalism; nor even the birds of prey which hover in the background of that masterpiece entitled *Le Supplice des Crochets*.

At that time the sun and light played a great part in M. Decamps's painting. No one studied atmospheric effects with so much care. The weirdest and most improbable tricks of shadow and light pleased him more than anything. In a picture by M. Decamps the sun seemed really to scorch the white walls and the chalky sands; every coloured object had a keen and lively transparency. The waters were of untold depth; the great shadows which used to cut across the flanks of his houses or to sleep stretched out upon the ground or the water had the languor and sweet drowsiness of shadows beyond description. And in the midst of this fascinating décor, you would find little figures bestirring themselves or dreaming—a complete little world in all its native and comic truth.

Yes, M. Decamps's pictures were full of poetry, and often of reverie; but what others, like Delacroix, would achieve by great draughtsmanship, by an original choice of model or by broad and flowing colour, M. Decamps achieved by intimacy of detail. The only criticism, in fact, which you could make, was that he was too concerned with the material execution of objects; his houses were made of true plaster and true wood, his walls were made of true lime-mortar; and in front of these masterpieces, the heart was often saddened by a painful idea of the time and the trouble which had been devoted to their making. How much finer they would have been if executed less artfully!

Last year, when M. Decamps took up a pencil and thought fit to challenge Raphael and Poussin, the enthusiastic *flâneurs* of both parties—men whose hearts embrace the whole world, but who are quite content with things as the Almighty has designed them, and who, all of them, adored M. Decamps as one of the rarest products of creation—these men said amongst themselves: 'If Raphael prevents Decamps from sleeping, then it's no more Decampses for us! who will do them now—? Alas! it will be MM. Guignet[1] and Chacaton.'

All the same, M. Decamps has reappeared this year with some Turkish things, some landscapes, some genre-pictures, and an *Effet de Pluie*.[2] But you have to look for them; they no longer strike the eye at once.

M. Decamps, who is so good at giving us the sun, has failed, however, with the rain; besides, he has given his ducks a slab of stone to swim on, etc. His *Ecole turque*, nevertheless, is more like his best pictures; there they all are, those lovely children whom we know so well, and that luminous, dust-charged atmosphere of a room which the sun is trying to enter bodily.

It seems to me so easy to console ourselves with the magnificent

[1] See p. 23.

[2] Of Decamps's four exhibits this year, one, the *Souvenir de la Turquie d'Asie* (catalogued as *Enfants turcs auprès d'une fontaine*, and incorrectly assigned to 1839) is in the Musée Condé, Chantilly; the others are in the Fodor Museum, Amsterdam. See pls. 23–24.

Decampses which already adorn our galleries, that I do not want to analyse the faults of these ones. It would be a senseless task, and besides everyone will do it very well for himself without any help from me.

Amongst the paintings by M. Penguilly-l'Haridon,[1] which are all good pieces of workmanship—little pictures, broadly, yet finely painted—there is one that especially stands out and attracts the eye: *Pierrot présente à l'assemblée ses compagnons Arlequin et Polichinelle.*[2]

Pierrot, with one eye open and the other closed, and that crafty air which is traditional, is presenting Harlequin to the public; Harlequin advances with sweeping and obsequious gestures, and with one leg gallantly pointed in front of him. Punchinello follows him, with swimming head, fatuous glance, and his poor little legs in great big sabots. A ridiculous face, with a huge nose, huge spectacles and a huge curled moustache, appears between two curtains. The colour of the whole thing is pleasing—both simple and fine—and the three characters stand out perfectly against a grey background. But the thrilling effect of this picture is less the result of its general appearance than of its composition, which is excessively simple. The figure of Punchinello, which is essentially comic, reminds us of the English *Punch*, who is usually shown touching the end of his nose with his index finger, to express his pride in it, or his vexation. I would, however, criticize M. Penguilly for not having taken his type from Deburau,[3] who is the true Pierrot of today—the Pierrot of modern history—and should therefore have his place in any painted harlequinade.

Now here is another fantasy, which is very much less adroit and less learned, and whose beauty is all the greater in that it is perhaps involuntary; I refer to M. Manzoni's *La Rixe des mendiants*. I have never seen anything so poetically brutal, even in the most Flemish of orgies. Here, under six heads, are the different reactions of the visitor who passes in front of this picture: 1. Lively curiosity. 2. 'How shocking!' 3. 'It's badly painted, but the composition is unusual and does not lack charm' 4. 'It's not so badly painted as we thought at first.' 5. 'Let's have another look at this picture.' And 6. A lasting memory.

It has a ferocity and a brutality of manner which suit the subject rather

[1] At one time Baudelaire considered him as a possible illustrator for the *Fleurs du Mal.*

[2] This painting was Lot 59 at the Moreau-Nélaton sale, Paris, 11 May 1900; its present whereabouts is unknown.

[3] Jean-Gaspard Deburau, the famous French pantomimist, died this year.

well and put us in mind of Goya's violent sketches. These, in fact, are the most ruffianly countenances that you could wish to see: it is a weird conglomeration of battered hats, wooden legs, broken glasses, befuddled topers; lust, ferocity and drunkenness are shaking their rags.

The ruddy beauty who is kindling the desires of these gentlemen is a fine stroke of the brush, and well formed to please the connoisseurs. I have rarely seen anything so comic as that poor wretch up against a wall, whom his neighbour has victoriously nailed with a pitchfork.

The second picture, *L'Assassinat nocturne*, has a less strange look. Its colour is dim and commonplace, and the fantastic ingredient is confined to the manner in which the scene is represented. A beggar is brandishing a knife in the face of a miserable fellow whose pockets are being ransacked and who is half dead from fear. Those white dominoes, in the form of gigantic noses, are very droll and give the most singular stamp to this scene of terror.

M. Villa-Amil has painted the throne-room in Madrid. At first sight, you might say that it was very simply executed; but if you look at it with more care, you will recognize a lot of cleverness in the organization and in the general colouring of this decorative picture. It is less fine in tone, perhaps, but it is firmer in colour than the pictures of the same type for which M. Roberts[1] has a liking. If it has a fault, it is that the ceiling looks less like a ceiling than a real sky.

MM. Wattier and Pérèse generally treat almost similar subjects—fair ladies wearing old-fashioned costumes, in parks, beneath ancient shades. What distinguishes M. Pérèse is that he paints with much more simplicity, and his name does not compel him to ape Watteau. But in spite of the studied delicacy of M. Wattier's figures, M. Pérèse is his superior in invention. You might say that there is the same difference between their works as between the mincing gallantry of the age of Louis XV and the honest gallantry of the age of Louis XIII.

The school of Couture—since we must call it by its name—has given us much too much this year.

M. Diaz de la Peña,[2] who is, in little, the extreme representative of this *little* school, sets out from the principle that a palette is a picture. As for overall harmony, M. Diaz thinks that you will invariably find it. Of

[1] Presumably David Roberts, R.A., who is chiefly remembered for his Spanish scenes.

[2] Diaz had eight paintings at the Salon this year, of which Baudelaire mentions the names of two. Another, entitled *Orientale*, is reproduced *Illustr.* vol. VII (1846), p. 136.

draughtsmanship—the draughtsmanship of movement, the draughtsmanship of the colourists—there is no question; the limbs of all his little figures behave for all the world like bundles of rags, or like arms and legs scattered in a railway accident. I would far rather have a kaleidoscope; at least it does not presume to give us *Les Délaissées* or *Le Jardin des amours*—it provides designs for shawls and carpets, and its role is a modest one. It is true that M. Diaz is a colourist; but enlarge his frame by a foot, and his strength will fail him, because he does not recognize the necessity for *general* colour. That is why his pictures leave no memory behind them.

But each man has his allotted part, you say. Great painting is not made for everyone, by any means. A fine dinner contains both hors-d'oeuvres and main courses. Would you dare to sneer at the Arles sausages, the pimentoes, the anchovies, the *aioli*, and the rest?—Appetizing hors-d'oeuvres?, I reply. Not a bit of it. These things are bonbons and nauseating sweetmeats. Who would want to feed on dessert? You hardly do more than just touch it when you are pleased with your dinner.

M. Célestin Nanteuil knows how to place a brush-stroke, but he does not know how to fix the proportions and the harmony of a picture.

M. Verdier paints well enough, but fundamentally I believe him to be an enemy of thought.

M. Muller, the man of the *Sylphes*, the great connoisseur of poetic subjects—of subjects streaming with poetry—has painted a picture which he calls *Primavera*. People who do not know Italian will think that this word means *Decameron*.

M. Faustin Besson's colour loses much by being no longer dappled and befogged by the windows of Deforge's shop.[1]

M. Fontaine is obviously a serious-minded man; he has given us M. de Béranger surrounded by youngsters of both sexes, whom he is initiating into the mysteries of Couture's manner.

And what great mysteries they are! A pink or peach-coloured light, and a green shadow—that's all there is to it! The terrible thing about this painting is that it forces itself upon the eye; you notice it from a great distance.

Without a doubt the most unfortunate of all these gentlemen is M. Couture himself, who throughout plays the interesting role of victim. An imitator is a babbler who gives away secrets.

[1] In the Boulevard Montmartre.

In the various specialities of Bas-Breton, Catalan, Swiss, Norman subjects and the rest, MM. Armand and Adolphe Leleux are outstripped by M. Guillemin, who is inferior to M. Hédouin, who himself yields the palm to M. Haffner.

Several times I have heard this peculiar criticism directed at the MM. Leleux—that whether they were supposed to be Swiss, Spanish or Breton, all their characters seemed to come from Brittany.

M. Hédouin is certainly a commendable painter, who possesses a firm touch and understands colour; no doubt he will succeed in establishing his own particular originality.

As for M. Haffner, I owe him a grudge for once having painted a portrait in a superbly romantic style, and for having painted no more like it.[1] I believed that he was a great artist, rich in poetry and, above all, in invention, a portraitist of the front rank, who came out with an occasional daub in his spare time; but it seems that he is no more than just a painter.

VII. ON THE IDEAL AND THE MODEL

SINCE colour is the most natural and the most *visible* thing, the party of the colourists is the most numerous and the most important. But analysis, which facilitates the artist's means of execution, has divided nature into colour and line; and before I proceed to an examination of the men who form the second party, I think that it would be well if I explained some of the principles by which they are guided—sometimes even without their knowing it.

The title of this chapter is a contradiction, or rather an agreement of contraries; for the drawing of a great draughtsman ought to epitomize both things—the ideal and the model.

Colour is composed of coloured masses which are made up of an infinite number of tones, which, through harmony, become a unity; in the same way, Line, which also has its masses and its generalizations, can be subdivided into a profusion of particular lines, of which each one is a feature of the model.

[1] The portrait was at the Salon of the previous year: see p. 19. This year Haffner exhibited three landscapes only, of which one is reproduced *Illustr.* vol. VII (1846), p. 185.

The circumference of a circle—the ideal of the curved line—may be compared with an analogous figure, composed of an infinite number of straight lines which have to fuse with it, the inside angles becoming more and more obtuse.

But since there is no such thing as a perfect circumference, the absolute ideal is a piece of nonsense. By his exclusive taste for simplicity, the idiotic artist is led to a perpetual imitation of the same type. But poets, artists, and the whole human race would be miserable indeed if the ideal—that absurdity, that impossibility—were ever discovered. If that happened, what would everyone do with his poor *ego*—with his crooked line?

I have already observed that memory is the great criterion of art; art is a kind of mnemotechny of the beautiful. Now exact imitation spoils a memory. There are some wretched painters for whom the least wart is a stroke of luck; not only is there no fear of their forgetting it, but they find it necessary to paint it four times as large as life. And thus they are the despair of lovers—and when a people commissions a portrait of its king, it is nothing less than a lover.

A memory is equally thwarted by too much particularization as by too much generalization. I prefer the *Antinous* to the *Apollo Belvedere* or to the *Gladiator*, because the *Antinous* is the ideal of the charming Antinous himself.

Although the universal principle is one, Nature presents us with nothing absolute, nothing even complete*; I see only individuals. Every animal of a similar species differs in some respect from its neighbour, and among the thousands of fruits that the same tree can produce, it is impossible to find two that are identical, for if so, they would be one and the same; and duality, which is the contradiction of unity, is also its consequence.** But it is in the human race above all that we see the most appalling capacity for variety. Without counting the major types which nature has distributed over the globe, every day I see passing beneath my window a certain number of Kalmouks, Osages, Indians, Chinamen and Ancient Greeks, all more or less Parisianized. Each individual is a unique harmony; for you must often have had the surprising experience of turning back at the sound of a known voice and finding

* Nothing absolute;—thus the geometric ideal is the worst of idiocies. Nothing complete;—thus everything has to be completed, and every ideal recaptured. (C.B.)

** I say *contradiction*, and not *contrary*; for contradiction is an invention of man's. (C.B.)

yourself face to face with a complete stranger—the living reminder of someone else endowed with a similar voice and similar gestures. This is so true that Lavater has established a nomenclature of noses and mouths which agree together, and he has pointed out several errors of this kind in the old masters, who have been known to clothe religious or historical characters in forms which are contrary to their proper natures. It is possible that Lavater was mistaken in detail; but he had the basic idea. Such and such a hand demands such and such a foot; each epidermis produces its own hair. Thus each individual has his ideal.

I am not claiming that there are as many fundamental ideals as there are individuals, for the mould gives several impressions; but in the painter's soul there are just as many ideals as individuals, because a portrait is *a model complicated by an artist.*

Thus that ideal is not that vague thing—that boring and impalpable dream—which we see floating on the ceilings of academies; an ideal is an individual put right by an individual, reconstructed and restored by brush or chisel to the dazzling truth of its native harmony.

The first quality of a draughtsman is therefore a slow and sincere study of his model. Not only must the artist have a profound intuition of the character of his model; but further, he must generalize a little, he must deliberately exaggerate some of the details, in order to intensify a physiognomy and make its expression more clear.

It is curious to note that, when guided by this principle—namely, that the sublime ought to avoid details—art finds the way of self-perfection leading back towards its childhood. For the first artists also used not to express details. The great difference, however, is that, in doing the arms and the legs of their figures like drainpipes, it was not *they* who were avoiding the details, but the details which were avoiding *them*; for in order to choose, you have first to possess.

Drawing is a struggle between nature and the artist, in which the artist will triumph the more easily as he has a better understanding of the intentions of nature. For him it is not a matter of copying, but of interpreting in a simpler and more luminous language.

The introduction of the portrait—that is to say, of the idealized model—into historical, religious or imaginative subjects necessitates at the outset an exquisite choice of model, and is certainly capable of rejuvenating and revitalizing modern painting, which, like all our arts, is too inclined to be satisfied with the imitation of the old masters.

Everything else that I might say on the subject of ideals seems to me to be contained in a chapter of Stendhal, whose title is as clear as it is insolent:

'How are we to go one better than Raphael?'

'In the affecting scenes brought about by the passions, the great painter of modern times—if ever he appears—will give to each one of his characters *an ideal beauty, derived from a temperament* which is constituted to feel the effect of that passion with the utmost vividness.

Werther will not be indifferently sanguine or melancholic, nor Lovelace phlegmatic or bilious. Neither good Doctor Primrose nor gentle Cassio will have a bilious temperament; this is reserved for Shylock the Jew, for dark Iago, for Lady Macbeth, for Richard III. The pure and lovely Imogen will be a trifle phlegmatic.

The artist's first observations led him to fashion the *Apollo Belvedere*. But will he restrict himself to coldly producing copies of the Apollo every time that he wishes to represent a young and handsome god? No, he will set a link between the action and the type of beauty. Apollo delivering the Earth from the serpent Python will be more robust; Apollo paying court to Daphne will be more delicate of feature.'*

VIII. SOME DRAUGHTSMEN

IN THE preceding chapter I said nothing at all about imaginative or creative draughtsmanship, because in general this is the prerogative of the colourists. Michelangelo, who, from a certain point of view, is the inventor of the ideal among the moderns, is the only man to have possessed the 'graphic' imagination in its supreme degree without being a colourist. Pure draughtsmen are naturalists endowed with excellent perception; but they draw by the light of reason, whereas colourists—that is, *great* colourists—draw by the light of temperament, almost without knowing it. Their method is analogous to nature; they draw because they colour, whereas pure draughtsmen, if they wanted to be logical and true to their profession of faith, would content themselves with a black pencil. Nevertheless they devote themselves to colour with an unimaginable enthusiasm, taking no notice at all of the contradictions involved.

* Stendhal, *Histoire de la Peinture en Italie*, chap. 101. This was printed in 1817. (C.B.)

They start by delimiting their forms in a cruel and absolute manner, and then they proceed to fill up the spaces. This double method ceaselessly thwarts their efforts, and gives to all their productions a strange element of bitterness, toil and contention. Their works are an eternal piece of litigation, an exhausting dualism. A draughtsman is a would-be colourist.

This is so true that M. Ingres, the most illustrious representative of the naturalistic school of draughtsmanship, is forever in pursuit of colour. What admirable and unfortunate obstinacy! It is the eternal story of people wanting to trade a reputation which they have earned for one which they cannot win. M. Ingres adores colour, like a fashionable milliner. It is at once a pain and a pleasure to observe the efforts which he makes in choosing and coupling his tones. The result—which is not always discordant, but is nevertheless bitter and violent—is often pleasing to corrupt poets; but even so, when they have allowed their tired minds a long spell of amusement in the midst of these dangerous struggles, they feel an absolute need to come to rest upon a Velasquez or a Lawrence.

If M. Ingres occupies the most important place after Eugène Delacroix, it is because of that entirely personal draughtsmanship whose mysteries I was analysing a moment ago, and with which he has achieved the best epitome to date of the ideal and the model. M. Ingres draws admirably well, and he draws rapidly. In his sketches he attains the ideal quite naturally. His drawing is often only lightly charged and does not contain many strokes; but each one realizes an important contour. But now take a look at the drawings of all those *artisans* of painting—many of them his pupils; they start by rendering the minute details, and it is for this reason that they enchant the vulgar, which will only open its eye for what is *little*, in whatever genre.

In a certain sense M. Ingres draws better than Raphael, the popular king of draughtsmen. Raphael decorated immense walls: but he would not have done the portrait of your mother, your friend or your mistress so well as Ingres. The daring of this man is all his own, and it is combined with cunning in such a way that he shirks no sort of ugliness or oddity. Did he stop at M. Molé's frock-coat[1] or Cherubini's *carrick*? And did he not put a blind man, a one-eyed and a one-armed man, and a hunchback into the *Plafond d'Homère*[2]—a work which, more than any

[1] Now in a private collection (Wildenstein 225). [2] See p. 61.

other, aspires towards the ideal? Nature repays him handsomely for this pagan adoration. He could make a sublime thing even of Mayeux.[1]

The beautiful *Muse de Cherubini*[2] is still a portrait. If M. Ingres, who lacks the 'graphic' imagination, does not know how to make pictures—at least, on a large scale—it is nevertheless just to say that his portraits are *almost* pictures—that is, intimate poems.

His is a grudging, cruel, refractory and suffering talent—a singular mixture of contrary qualities, all placed to the credit of Nature, and one whose strangeness is not among its least charms. He is Flemish in his execution, an individualist and a naturalist in his drawing, antique by his sympathies and an idealist by reason.

To reconcile so many contraries is no meagre task; and so it is not without reason that, in order to display the sacred mysteries of his draughtsmanship, he has adopted an artificial system of lighting which serves to render his thought more clear—something similar to the sort of twilight in which a still-sleepy Nature has a wan and raw appearance and in which the countryside reveals itself in a fantastic and striking guise.

A rather distinctive fact about M. Ingres's talent, and one which I believe has been overlooked, is that he is happier in dealing with female subjects. He depicts them as he sees them, for it would appear that he loves them too much to wish to change them; he fastens upon their slightest beauties with the keenness of a surgeon, he follows the gentlest sinuosities of their line with the humble devotion of a lover. His *Angélique*,[3] his two *Odalisques* and his portrait of Mme d'Haussonville[4] are works of a deeply sensuous rapture. But we are never allowed to see any of these things except in a light which is almost frightening—it is neither the golden atmosphere in which the fields of the ideal lie bathed, nor yet the tranquil and measured light of the sublunar regions.

The works of M. Ingres are the result of an excessive attentiveness, and they demand an equal attentiveness in order to be understood. Born of suffering, they beget suffering. As I explained above, this is due to the fact that his method is not one and simple, but rather consists in the use of a succession of methods.

[1] A grotesque hunchback invented by the caricaturist Traviès and much used by him and others in the 1830s. See *Painter of Modern Life*, pp. 185–6.

[2] In the Louvre (Wildenstein 236); see pl. 30.

[3] I.e. *Roger et Angélique* (1819), in the Louvre (Wildenstein 124).

[4] In the Frick Collection, New York (Wildenstein 248); see pl. 31.

Around M. Ingres, whose teaching has a strange austerity which inspires fanaticism, there is a small group of artists, of whom the best-known are MM. Flandrin, Lehmann and Amaury-Duval.

But what an immense distance separates the master from his pupils! M. Ingres remains alone in his school. His method is the result of his nature, and however weird and uncompromising it may be, it is frank and, so to speak, involuntary. Passionately in love with the antique and with his model, and a respectful servant of nature, he paints portraits which can rival the best sculptures of the Romans. These gentlemen, however, have coldly, deliberately and pedantically chosen the unpleasing and unpopular part of his genius to translate into a system; it is their pedantry that pre-eminently distinguishes them. Curiosity and erudition are what they have seen and studied in their master. Hence their pursuit of leanness and pallor, and all the rest of those ridiculous conventions which they have adopted without examination or good faith. They have plunged deep, very deep, into the past, just in order to copy its deplorable mistakes with a puerile servility; they have deliberately discarded all the means of successful execution which the experience of the ages had made available to them. People still remember *La Fille de Jephté pleurant sa virginité*[1]; but those excessive elongations of hands and feet, those exaggerated ovals of heads, all those ridiculous affectations—conventions and habits of the brush which have a tolerable resemblance to the *chic*—are singular faults in an ardent worshipper of form. Since his portrait of the Princess Belgiojoso, M. Lehmann has never ceased painting abnormally big eyes, in which the pupil swims like an oyster in a soup-tureen. This year he has sent some portraits and some other pictures. The pictures are *Les Océanides*, *Hamlet* and *Ophelia*. *Les Océanides* is a sort of Flaxman, and its general aspect is so ugly that it kills any desire to examine the design. In the portraits of *Hamlet* and *Ophelia*[2] there are visible pretensions to *colour*—the great hobby-horse of this school! But this unfortunate imitation of colour is as saddening and distressing to me as a copy of a Veronese or a Rubens made by an inhabitant of the moon. As for their physical and spiritual deportment, these two figures reminded me of the bombast of the actors at the old Bobino, when they used to play melodramas there. Without a doubt Hamlet's hand is fine;

[1] Exhibited by Henri Lehmann at the Salon of 1836.

[2] Both reproduced *Illustr.* vol. VII (1846), p. 184, and the *Illustrated London News*, 23 May 1846.

but a well-executed hand does not make a draughtsman—that would really be asking too much of *detail*, even for an Ingrist!

I think that Mme Calamatta also belongs to the party of the enemies of the sun; but sometimes her pictures are quite happily composed, and they have a little of that air of authority which women—even the most literary of them, and the real *artists*—find it less easy to borrow from men than their absurdities.

M. Janmot has done a *Station—Le Christ portant sa Croix*—whose composition has some character and gravity, but whose colour, being no longer mysterious, or rather *mystical*, as in his last works, is unhappily reminiscent of the colour of all possible *Stations*. As you look at this crude and glossy picture, it is only too easy to guess that M. Janmot comes from Lyons. In fact this is just the kind of painting which suits that city of cash-tills—that city of bigotry and punctilio, where everything, down to religion, has to have the calligraphic neatness of an account-book.[1]

The names of M. Curzon and M. Brillouin have already often been linked in the public mind, although at the start they gave promise of more originality. This year M. Brillouin—*A quoi rêvent les jeunes filles*[2]—has stepped out of himself, and M. Curzon has been content to do Brillouins. Their tendency reminds one of the school of Metz[3]—a literary, mystical and *Germanic* school. M. Curzon, who often paints fine, generously-coloured landscapes, could interpret Hoffmann in a less erudite, a less conventional way. But although he is obviously a man of wit—his choice of subjects is enough to prove it—you feel that the Hoffmannesque afflatus has passed nowhere near him.[4] The old-fashioned style of the German artists bears no resemblance to the style of this great poet, whose compositions have a very much more modern and more romantic character. The artist has vainly tried to obviate this capital defect by choosing the least fantastic of all the stories, *Master Martin and his Apprentices*, of which Hoffmann himself said: 'It is the most mediocre of my works; there is not a shred of the terrible or the grotesque in it,

[1] The Lyons school of painting was particularly deplored by Baudelaire. See p. 27, above.

[2] Under this main title, Brillouin exhibited four drawings, with individual titles such as 'Les présents de l'étranger' and 'Le retour du bien-aimé.'

[3] See p. 28, above.

[4] Curzon exhibited five drawings illustrating Hoffmann's *Meister Martin*; five such drawings are now in the Poitiers Museum.

and these are the two most important arrows in my quiver!' But in spite of that, even in *Master Martin* Hoffmann's lines are more floating and his atmosphere more supernatural than M. Curzon has made them.

Properly speaking M. Vidal's place is not here at all, for he is not a true draughtsman. Nevertheless the moment is not too badly chosen, for he has several of the ridiculous fads of the Ingrists—that is to say, a fanatical regard for the *little* and the *pretty*, and an enthusiasm for beautiful paper and fine canvases. All this has nothing to do with the sense of order with which a strong and vigorous mind is ruled and girt, nor yet with the adequate neatness of a man of good sense; it is neatness run mad.

The preconception about Vidal[1] began, I think, three or four years ago. Even so, at that time his drawings were less pedantic and less mannered than they are today.

This morning I was reading an article by M. Théophile Gautier,[2] in which he sang the praises of M. Vidal for being able to interpret modern beauty. I do not know why M. Gautier has donned the uniform of the 'good-natured man' this year; for he has praised everyone, and there is no wretched dauber whose pictures he has not catalogued. Can it be perchance that the hour of the Academy—that solemn and soporific hour—has struck for him, if he is already so well-mannered? and has literary prosperity such disastrous results that the public is forced to call us to order by rubbing our noses in our original certificates of romanticism? Nature has endowed M. Gautier with an excellent, broad and poetic mind. Everyone knows what fierce admiration he has always evinced for sincere and generous works. What potion can the painters have poured into his wine this year? or what rose-tinted spectacles has he selected with which to go to work?

So M. Vidal understands modern beauty, does he? Come now! Thanks to nature, our women have not so much wit or sophistication; but they are infinitely more romantic. Look at nature, sir. A man does not arm himself with wit and with meticulously sharpened pencils in order to *paint*! for some critics rank you—I really do not know why—among the noble family of painters. It is no use you calling your women *Fatinitza*,[3]

[1] See p. 28.

[2] In *La Presse*, 7 April 1846. Gautier's praise of Ary Scheffer in this article must have especially disgusted Baudelaire: see p. 99.

[3] Salon of 1845.

Stella, Vanessa, Saison des Roses[1]—a bunch of names for cosmetics; you will not produce poetic women that way. You once set yourself the task of expressing the idea of *Self-love*[2]—a great and fine idea, a supremely feminine idea—but you quite failed to interpret the sharp element of greed and the magnificent egoism of the subject. You never rose above puerile obscurity.

Nevertheless all these affectations will pass away like rancid unguents. A ray of sunshine is enough to bring out all their stench. I would rather leave Time to do its work than waste my own in expounding all the poverties of this sorry genre.

IX. ON PORTRAITURE

THERE are two ways of understanding portraiture—either as history or as fiction.

The first is to set forth the contours and the modelling of the subject faithfully, severely and minutely; this does not however exclude idealization, which, for enlightened naturalists, will consist in choosing the sitter's most characteristic attitude—the attitude which best expresses his habits of mind. Further, one must know how to give a reasonable exaggeration to each important detail—to lay stress on everything which is naturally salient, marked and essential, and to disregard (or to fuse with the whole) everything which is insignificant or which is the effect of some accidental blemish.

The masters of the 'historical' school are David and Ingres, and its best manifestations are the portraits by David which were to be seen at the Bonne Nouvelle exhibition,[3] and those of M. Ingres, such as M. Bertin and Cherubini.[4]

The second method, which is the special province of the colourists, is to transform the portrait into a picture—a poem with all its accessories, a poem full of space and reverie. This is a more difficult art, because it is a more ambitious one. The artist has to be able to immerse a head in the soft haze of a warm atmosphere, or to make it emerge from depths of

[1] Salon of 1846.

[2] Salon of 1845: reproduced *Illustr.* vol. v (1845), p. 152.

[3] This exhibition took place in January 1846. See pp. 33–40, above.

[4] Ingres's portraits of M. Bertin (1832) and of Cherubini (1841) are in the Louvre (Wildenstein 208 and 236).

gloom. Here the imagination has a greater part to play, and yet, just as it often happens that fiction is truer than history, so it can happen that a model is more clearly realized by the abundant and flowing brush of a colourist than by the draughtsman's pencil.

The masters of the 'fictional', or 'romantic', school are Rembrandt, Reynolds and Lawrence. Well-known examples are *La Dame au chapeau de paille*[1] and *Master Lambton*.[2]

A characteristic excellence of MM. Flandrin, Amaury-Duval and Lehmann is the truth and subtlety of their modelling. The detail is well grasped and executed easily and all in one breath, so to speak; nevertheless their portraits are often vitiated by a pretentious and clumsy affectation. Their immoderate taste for *distinction* never ceases to trip them up. We know with what an admirable simplicity of mind they seek after *distinguished* tones—that is to say, tones which, if intensified, would scream at one another like the devil and holy water, or like marble and vinegar; but since these are excessively etiolated and given in homoeopathic doses, their effect is one of surprise rather than of pain; and that is their great triumph!

The *distinction* in their draughtsmanship consists in their sharing the prejudices of certain modish ladies, who have a smattering of debased literature and a horror of little eyes, large feet, large hands, little brows and cheeks glowing with joy and health—all of which can be extremely beautiful.

This pedantry in colour and draughtsmanship does constant injury to the works of these gentlemen, however estimable they may be in other respects. Thus, while I was contemplating M. Amaury-Duval's *blue* portrait (and the same applies to many other portraits of Ingresque, or *Ingrized*, women), some strange association of ideas brought to mind the following wise words of the dog Berganza,[3] who used to run away from *blue-stockings* as ardently as these gentlemen seek them out:

'Have you never found Corinne[4] quite impossible? . . . At the idea of seeing her come near me, in flesh and blood, I used to feel an almost

[1] It is not quite clear to which straw-hatted lady Baudelaire refers: Crépet suggests a portrait of the Countess Spencer by Reynolds, but several others of Reynolds's portraits (e.g. *Nelly O'Brien*, in the Wallace Collection) fit the description.

[2] Lawrence's *Master Lambton* was shown in Paris in 1827.

[3] The reference is to Hoffmann's *Nachricht von den neuesten Schicksalen des Hundes Berganza*. Hoffmann had taken over the character of the speaking dog Berganza from a story by Cervantes.

[4] The heroine of Mme de Staël's novel of that name.

physical oppression, and found myself quite incapable of preserving my serenity and freedom of mind in her presence . . . . Whatever the beauty of her arms or her hand, I could never have endured her caresses without feeling slightly sick—without a kind of internal shudder which tends to take away my appetite. . . . Of course I am only speaking here in my canine capacity!'

I have had the same sensation as the witty Berganza in front of nearly all the portraits of women—whether old or new ones—by MM. Flandrin, Lehmann and Amaury-Duval; and this in spite of the beautiful hands (really well-painted, too) which they know how to give them, and in spite of the flattering elegance of certain details. If Dulcinea del Toboso herself were to pass through the studio of these gentlemen, she would emerge as pellucid and prim as an elegy, after a slimming diet of aesthetic tea and aesthetic butter.

M. Ingres, however—and this must be repeated over and over again—M. Ingres, the great master, understands things in quite another way.

In the sphere of portraiture understood according to the second method, MM. Dubufe the elder, Winterhalter, Lépaulle and Mme Frédérique O'Connell, given a sincerer taste for nature and a solider colour, might have won a justifiable reputation.

M. Dubufe is destined to retain the privilege of elegance in portraiture for a long time yet; his natural and almost poetic taste successfully conceals his innumerable faults.

It is worth observing that the people who hurl the word 'bourgeois' so frequently at M. Dubufe are the very ones who have allowed themselves to be enchanted by M. Pérignon's wooden heads.[1] How much one would have forgiven M. Delaroche if it had been possible to foresee the Pérignon factory!

M. Winterhalter is really on the decline. M. Lépaulle is still the same, now and again an excellent painter, but always devoid of taste and good sense. Charming eyes and mouths, well executed arms—and *toilettes* calculated to send decent people running!

Mme O'Connell knows how to paint with freedom and rapidity; but her colour lacks firmness. That is the unhappy fault of English painting, which is transparent to excess and is always characterized by too great a fluidity.[2]

[1] See p. 19.

[2] In spite of her name, Mme O'Connell was born German.

An excellent example of the kind of portrait whose essence I was attempting to define a moment ago is that portrait of a woman by M. Haffner—drenched in grey and radiating mystery—which led the connoisseurs at the last Salon to entertain such high hopes; but M. Haffner had not yet become a genre-painter, seeking to fuse and to reconcile Diaz, Decamps and Troyon.

You would suppose that Mlle E. Gautier was seeking to modify her manner a little. She is wrong to do so.

MM. Tissier and J. Guignet have preserved their touch and their colour, which are both firm and solid. Generally speaking there is this excellent quality about their portraits, that they are above all pleasant to look at—that is the first impression, and the most important.

M. Victor Robert, the creator of a vast allegory of Europe,[1] is certainly a good painter, gifted with a firm hand. But an artist who undertakes the portrait of a famous man ought not to be content to achieve a merely felicitous paint-surface; for he is also painting the portrait of a mind. M. Granier de Cassagnac[2] is much uglier, or, if you prefer it, much more handsome. To start with he has a broader nose, and his mouth, which is mobile and sensitive, has a slyness and a delicacy which the painter has missed. M. Granier de Cassagnac seems somehow smaller and more athletic—down to his very brow. The present pose is theatrical rather than expressive of the genuine force which characterizes the man. It gives no hint of that challenging and martial bearing with which he attacks life and all its problems. It is enough to have seen him suddenly thunder forth his passions, with leaps and starts of pen and chair—it is enough simply to have read them in the paper—to realize that the whole man is not here. The copy of *Le Globe*, which recedes into the shadow, is a complete absurdity—surely it ought to have been in full view, if it had to be there at all!

I have always had the notion that M. Boulanger would have made an excellent engraver; he is a simple workman, quite devoid of invention, who gains much by working on someone else's model. His romantic pictures are bad, but his portraits are good—clear, solid, easily and simply painted. And the curious thing is that they often have the look of those excellent engravings after the portraits of Van Dyck. They have the dense shadows and the bright highlights of vigorous etchings. Each

[1] Exhibited at the Salon of 1845. See pp. 14–15.

[2] Editor of *Le Globe*.

time that M. Boulanger has tried to rise higher, he has fallen into bathos. I believe him to be a man of honest, calm and sound intelligence, whom only the exaggerated praises of the poets could have led astray.

What am I to say of M. L. Cogniet, that amiable eclectic, that painter of such sincerity and of so restless an intelligence that, in order to paint M. Granet's[1] portrait properly, he has had the idea of using the colour proper to M. Granet's own pictures—which is generally black, as we have all known for a long time?

Mme de Mirbel is the only artist who knows how to thread her way through the difficult problem of taste and truth. It is because of this special sincerity, and also because of their enchanting appearance, that her miniatures have all the importance of serious painting.

X. THE 'CHIC' AND THE 'PONCIF'

THE WORD 'chic'—a dreadful word of modern invention, which I do not even know how to spell correctly,* but which I am obliged to use, because it has been sanctioned by artists in order to describe a modern monstrosity—the word 'chic' means a total neglect of the model and of nature. The 'chic' is an abuse of the memory; moreover it is a manual, rather than an intellectual, memory that it abuses—for there are artists who are gifted with a profound memory for characters and forms—Delacroix or Daumier, for example—and who have nothing to do with it.

The 'chic' may be compared with the work of those writing-masters who, with an elegant hand and a pen shaped for italic or running script, can shut their eyes and boldly trace a head of Christ or Napoleon's hat, in the form of a flourish.

The meaning of the word 'poncif'[2] has much in common with that of the word 'chic'. Nevertheless it applies more particularly to attitudes and to the expressions of the head.

Rage can be 'poncif', and so can astonishment—for example, the kind of astonishment expressed by a horizontal arm with the thumb splayed out.

There are certain beings and things, in life and nature, which are 'poncif'—that is to say, which are an epitome of the vulgar and banal

[1] Now in the Musée Granet, Aix-en-Provence.

* Somewhere or other Balzac spells it 'chique'. (C.B.)

[2] The word is a slang derivation from 'poncer', 'to pounce', in the technical sense of transferring, and then of multiplying and perhaps vulgarizing, a design.

ideas which are commonly held about those beings and those things; great artists, therefore, have a horror of them.

Everything that is conventional and traditional owes something to the 'chic' and the 'poncif'.

When a singer places his hand upon his heart, this commonly means 'I shall love her always!' If he clenches his fists and scowls at the boards or at the prompter, it means 'Death to him, the traitor!' That is the 'poncif' for you.

XI. M. HORACE VERNET

SUCH ARE the stern principles which guide this eminently *national* artist in his quest for beauty—this artist whose compositions decorate the poor peasant's cottage no less than the carefree student's garret, the salon of the meanest bordello as often as the palaces of our kings. I am quite aware that this man is a Frenchman, and that a Frenchman in France is a holy and sacred thing—even abroad I am told that this is so; but it is for that very reason that I hate him.

In its most widely accepted sense, the word 'Frenchman' means *vaudevilliste*,[1] and the word 'vaudevilliste' means a man whose head swims at the thought of Michelangelo, and whom Delacroix strikes into a brutish stupor, just as certain animals are struck by thunder. Everything that towers or plunges, above or below him, causes him prudently to take to his heels. The sublime always affects him like a riot, and he only opens his Molière in fear and trembling—because someone has persuaded him that Molière is an amusing author.

Therefore all respectable folk in France (excepting M. Horace Vernet) hate the Frenchman. It is not ideas that this restless people wants, but facts, historical reports, topical rhymes, and *Le Moniteur*.[2] That is all: abstractions, never! The Frenchman has done great things, but almost by mistake. He has been *caused* to do them.

M. Horace Vernet[3] is a soldier who practises painting. Now I hate an art which is improvised to the roll of the drum, I hate canvases splashed

[1] The literal, unsarcastic meaning of the word is a writer of *vaudevilles*, i.e. light theatrical entertainments interspersed with catchy, popular songs.

[2] *Le Moniteur universel*, founded 1789, and until 1869 the official government organ.

[3] This year Horace Vernet exhibited a characteristically enormous picture (roughly 15 × 30 feet) of the Battle of Isly. It is now in the Versailles Museum.

over at the gallop, I hate painting manufactured to the sound of pistol-shots, since I hate the army, the police-force—everything, in fact, that trails its noisy arms in a peaceful place. This immense popularity—which, however, will endure no longer than war itself, and will decline in proportion as the peoples of the world contrive other joys for themselves—this popularity, do I call it?—this *vox populi, vox Dei* for me is like a physical oppression.

I hate this man because his pictures have nothing whatever to do with painting (I would prefer to call them a kind of brisk and frequent masturbation in paint, a kind of itching on the French skin), just as I hate another such great man,[1] whose solemn hypocrisy has given him dreams of the consulate, and who has repaid the people's love with nothing more substantial than bad verses—verses which have nothing to do with poetry, but are ruptured and ill-composed, full of barbarities and solecisms, but also of civic virtue and patriotism.

I hate him because he was born under a lucky star,* and because for him art is a simple and easy matter. Nevertheless he is the chronicler of your National glory, and that is the great thing. But what, I ask you, can that matter to the enthusiastic traveller, to the cosmopolitan spirit who prefers beauty to glory?

To define M. Horace Vernet as clearly as possible, he is the absolute antithesis of the artist: he substitutes *chic* for drawing, cacophony for colour and episodes for unity; he paints Meissoniers as big as houses.

Furthermore, in order to fulfil his official mission, M. Horace Vernet is gifted with two outstanding qualities—the one of deficiency, the other of excess; for he lacks all passion, and has a memory like an almanach!**

[1] The reference is to Béranger.

* (Literally 'with a caul on his head', Fr. *coiffé*). An expression of M. Marc Fournier's, which is applicable to almost all our fashionable novelists and historians, who are hardly more than literary journalists, like M. Horace Vernet. (C.B.). Marc Fournier (b. 1818) was a popular playwright.

** 'True memory, considered from a philosophical point of view, consists, I think, in nothing else but a very lively and easily-roused imagination, which is consequently given to reinforcing each of its sensations by evoking scenes from the past, and endowing them, as if by magic, with the life and character which are proper to each of them—at least I have heard this theory upheld by one of my past teachers who had a prodigious memory, although he could not carry a single date or proper name in his head. My teacher was right, and in this matter there is, no doubt, a difference between sayings or utterances which have embedded themselves deep in the soul and whose intimate and mysterious meaning has been grasped, and words which have merely been learnt by heart.' Hoffmann (C.B.)

Who knows better than he the correct number of buttons on each uniform, or the anatomy of a gaiter or a boot which is the worse for innumerable days' marching, or the exact spot on a soldier's gear where the copper of his small arms deposits its verdigris? Therefore what a vast public he has, and what bliss he affords them! He has, in fact, as many different publics as it takes trades to manufacture uniforms, shakos, swords, muskets and cannons! Imagine all those honourable guilds mustered in front of a Horace Vernet by their common love of glory! What a sight!

One day I remember twitting some Germans with their taste for Scribe[1] and Horace Vernet. They answered, 'We have a deep admiration for Horace Vernet as being the most complete representative of his age.' Well said!

The tale is told that one day M. Horace Vernet went to see Peter Cornelius.[2] He overwhelmed him with compliments, but had to wait a long time to be repaid; for Peter Cornelius congratulated him only once during the whole interview—and that was on the quantity of champagne that he was able to consume without suffering ill effects! True or false, the story has all the ring of poetic truth.

And now tell me again that the Germans are a simple-minded people!

Many people who believe in the oblique approach when it comes to a critical drubbing, and who have no more love than I for M. Horace Vernet, will blame me for being clumsy in my attack. But there can be no imprudence in being brutal and going straight to the point when in every sentence the 'I' stands for a 'we'—a vast, but silent and invisible 'we', a whole new generation which hates war and national follies; 'we', a generation full of health because it is young, a generation which is already elbowing its way to the front and working up into a good position—serious, derisive and menacing!*

[1] Eugène Scribe (1791–1861), the popular dramatist of the mid-nineteenth century.

[2] Peter Cornelius (1783–1867), chiefly noted for his revival of fresco. From 1824 he was director of the Munich Academy.

* Thus there is not one of M. Horace Vernet's canvases before which it would not be appropriate to sing:

Vous n'avez qu'un temps à vivre,
Amis, passez-le gaiement.

The gaiety is essentially French. (C.B.)

These lines are by the eighteenth-century French general, the comte de Bonneval.

MM. Granet and Alfred Dedreux are two more vignette-makers and great adorers of the 'chic'. But they apply their capacities of improvisation to very different genres—M. Granet[1] to the sphere of religion, and M. Dedreux[2] to that of smart life. The first does monks, and the second horses; the first is dark in colour, the second is bright and dazzling. M. Alfred Dedreux has two excellent qualities; he knows how to paint, and his works have the fresh and vivid appearance of theatrical decors. One would suppose that he is more concerned with nature in those subjects which form his speciality; for his studies of running hounds are more convincing and more solid than the rest. There is a touch of the comic, however, in his hunting-scenes; each one of those all-important hounds could gobble up four horses. They remind one of those famous sheep in Jouvenet's *Vendeurs du Temple*,[3] which quite swamp the figure of Christ.

XII. ON ECLECTICISM AND DOUBT

As you see, we are now in the hospital of painting. We are probing its sores and its sicknesses; and this is by no means among the least strange or contagious of them.

In the present age, just as in ages past, today no less than yesterday, the strong and vigorous divide between them the various territories of art, each according to his tastes and his temperament, and there they labour in full freedom, following the fatal law of propensities. Some gather an easy and abundant harvest in the golden, autumnal vineyards of colour; others toil patiently and laboriously to drive the deep furrow of drawing. Each of these men knows quite well that his monarchy involves a sacrifice, and that it is on this condition alone that he can reign securely up to his limiting frontiers. Each of them has a banner to his crown, and the words inscribed upon that banner are clear for all the world to read. Not one of their number has doubts of his monarchy, and it is in this unshakeable conviction that their serene glory resides.

M. Horace Vernet himself, that odious representative of the 'chic', has

[1] All of Granet's eight pictures at this Salon had religious subjects.

[2] One of Dedreux's pictures, entitled *Chasse au faucon*, reproduced *Illustr.* vol. VII (1846), p. 57.

[3] One of the four pictures which Jean-Baptiste Jouvenet (1644–1717) painted for the church of Saint-Martin-des-Champs; it is now in the Lyons Museum, and a replica is in the Louvre.

at least the merit of not being a *doubter*. He is a man of a happy and playful disposition, who inhabits an artificial country where the actors and the scenery are all made of the same pasteboard; yet he reigns as master in his kingdom of pantomine and parade.

Doubt, which today is the principal cause of all morbid affections in the moral world, and whose ravages are now greater than ever before, is itself dependent upon higher causes which I shall analyse in my penultimate chapter, entitled *On Schools and Journeymen*. And Doubt begat Eclecticism; for the doubters had a genuine will for salvation.

Eclecticism has at all periods and places held itself superior to past doctrines, because, coming last on to the scene, it finds the remotest horizons already open to it; but this *impartiality* only goes to prove the impotence of the eclectics. People who are so lavish with their time for reflection are not complete men: they lack the element of passion.

It has never occurred to the eclectics that man's attention is the more intense as it is restricted and limits its own field of observation. It is a question of grasp all, lose all.

It is in the arts, above all, that eclecticism has had the most manifest and palpable consequences, because if art is to be profound, it must aim at constant idealization, which is not to be achieved except in virtue of sacrifice—an involuntary sacrifice.

No matter how clever he may be, an eclectic is but a feeble man; for he is a man without love. Therefore he has no ideal, no *parti pris*; neither star nor compass. He mixes four different systems, which only results in an effect of darkness—a negation.

An eclectic is a ship which tries to sail before all four winds at once.

However great its defects, a work conceived from an exclusive point of view will always have a great attraction for temperaments analogous to that of the artist.

An eclectic's work leaves no memory behind it.

The eclectic does not know that the first business of an artist is to protest against Nature by putting Man in her place. This protest is not made coldly and calculatedly, like a decree or a rhetorical exercise; it is spontaneous and urgent, like vice, passion or appetite. Thus an eclectic is no man.

Doubt has led certain artists to beg the aid of all the other arts. Experiment with contradictory means, the encroachment of one art upon another, the importation of poetry, wit and sentiment into painting—all these modern miseries are vices peculiar to the eclectics.

XIII. ON M. ARY SCHEFFER AND THE APES OF SENTIMENT

M. ARY SCHEFFER is a disastrous example of this method—if an absence of method can so be called.

After imitating Delacroix, after aping the colourists and draughtsmen of the French school, and the neo-Christian school of Overbeck,[1] it dawned upon M. Ary Scheffer—a little late, no doubt—that he was not a painter born. From that moment he was obliged to turn to other shifts; and he decided to ask help and protection from poetry.

It was a ridiculous blunder, for two reasons. First of all, poetry is not the painter's immediate aim: when poetry happens to be mixed with painting, the resulting work cannot but be more valuable; but poetry is unable to disguise the shortcomings of a work. To make a deliberate point of looking for poetry during the conception of a picture is the surest means of not finding it. It must come without the artist's knowledge. It is the result of the art of painting itself; for it lies in the spectator's soul, and it is the mark of genius to awaken it there. Painting is only interesting in virtue of colour and form; it is no more like poetry than poetry is like painting—than the extent, I mean, to which poetry is able to awaken ideas of painting in the reader.

In the second place—and this is a consequence of these last observations—it should be noticed that great artists, whose instinct always guides them aright, have taken only the most highly coloured and clearly visual subjects from the poets. Thus they prefer Shakespeare to Ariosto.

And now, to choose a striking example of M. Ary Scheffer's ineptitude, let us examine the subject of his painting entitled *St. Augustine and St. Monica*.[2] An honest painter of the Spanish School, with his double piety —artistic and religious—would simply and sincerely have done his best to paint the general idea which he had formed of the two saints. But put all that out of your mind; here the vital thing is to express the following passage—with brushes and colour: 'We did betwixt ourselves seek at

[1] Friedrich Overbeck (1789–1869), leader of the 'Nazarenes'. From 1810 he worked in Rome.

[2] The Salon of 1846 was the last at which Ary Scheffer exhibited. The painting of St. Augustine and his mother proved, however, to be one of his most popular works, and he painted at least four replicas; one is in the National Gallery, one in the Louvre and one in the Dordrecht Museum. See pl. 25.

that Present Truth (which Thou art) in what manner the eternal life of the saints was to be, which eye hath not seen, nor ear heard, nor hath it entered into the heart of man.'[1] It is the very height of absurdity. It is like watching a dancer execute a mathematical figure!

Formerly M. Ary Scheffer enjoyed the public's favour; in his *poetical* pictures, people rediscovered their dearest memories of the great poets—and that was enough for them. The transient vogue for M. Ary Scheffer was in fact a homage to the memory of Goethe.[2] But our artists—even those of them who are only gifted with a moderate originality—have for a long time been showing the public samples of real painting, executed with a sure hand and according to the simplest rules of art. And so, little by little the public has grown sick of *invisible* painting, and today, where M. Ary Scheffer is concerned, its favour has turned to harshness and ingratitude. How like all publics! But upon my word, they are quite right!

Moreover this kind of painting is so wretched, so dismal, so blurred and so muddy that many people have taken M. Ary Scheffer's pictures for those of M. Henri Scheffer,[3] another artistic Girondist. In my opinion, they are more like pictures by M. Delaroche which have been left out in a heavy rainstorm.

A simple method of learning an artist's range is to examine his public. Eugène Delacroix has the painters and the poets on his side; M. Decamps has the painters; M. Horace Vernet has the garrisons, and M. Ary Scheffer those aesthetic ladies who revenge themselves on the curse of their sex by indulging in religious music.*

The apes of sentiment are, generally speaking, bad artists. If it were otherwise, they would do something other than sentimentalize. The best of them are those whose understanding does not go beyond the *pretty*.

As feeling or sentiment, like fashion, is an infinitely variable and multiple thing, there are apes of sentiment of different orders.

The ape of sentiment relies above all on the catalogue. It should be

[1] St. Augustine's *Confessions*, Bk. IX, chap. 10.

[2] A reference to Gautier's Salon in *La Presse*, in which he wrote that Marguerite belonged to Scheffer almost as much as to Goethe himself.

[3] Ary Scheffer's younger brother.

* To those who must sometimes have been shocked by my pious wrath, I would recommend the reading of Diderot's *Salons*. Among other examples of properly bestowed charity, they will find that that great philosopher, when speaking of a painter who had been recommended to him because he had many mouths to feed, observed that either pictures or families would have to be abolished. (C.B.)

noted, however, that the picture's title never tells its subject—and this is particularly true with those artists who, by an engaging fusion of horrors, mix sentiment with wit. In this way, by extending the method, it will be possible to achieve the *sentimental rebus*.[1]

For example, you find in the catalogue something called *Pauvre Fileuse!*[2] Well, it is quite possible that the picture may represent a female silkworm, or a caterpillar, squashed by a child. This is an age without pity!

Aujourd'hui and *Demain*.[3] What can that be? Perhaps a white flag—and a tricolour? or perhaps a deputy in his moment of triumph—and the same deputy after being sent packing? But no; it is a young maiden, promoted to the status of street-walker, playing with roses and jewels; and then the same girl, crippled and emaciated, suffering the consequences of her indiscretions in the gutter.

L'Indiscret.[4] I beg of you to look for this one. It represents a gentleman surprising a couple of blushing damsels with a naughty picture-book. This picture comes into the Louis XV class of sentimental genre, which began, I believe, to slip into the Salon in the wake of *La Permission de dix heures*.[5] Quite a different order of sentiments is involved, here as you can see; these ones are less *mystical*.

In general, sentimental genre-pictures are taken from the latest poems of some blue-stocking or other—that is the melancholy and misty kind; or else they are a pictorial translation of the outcries of the poor against the rich—the protesting kind; or else they are borrowed from the wisdom of the nations—the witty kind; and sometimes from the works of M. Bouilly[6] or of Bernardin de Saint-Pierre[7]—the moralizing kind.

Here are a few more examples of the same genre: *L'Amour à la campagne*—happiness, calm and repose; and *L'Amour à la ville*[8]—shouts, disorder, upturned chairs and books. It is a metaphysic within the reach of the simple.

[1] Baudelaire returns to the subject of titles in the *Salon of 1859*: see pp. 172 ff.
[2] By Mme Céleste Pensotti.
[3] By Charles Landelle.
[4] By H.-G. Schlésinger.
[5] By Eugène Giraud, exh. at the Salon of 1839.
[6] Jean-Nicolas Bouilly (1763–1842), playwright.
[7] The author of *Paul et Virginie*.
[8] Compte Calix exhibited *L'Amour au château* and *L'Amour à la chaumière* (both reproduced *Illustr.*, Vol. VII (1846), p. 89): Pierre Cottin exhibited *L'Amour à la ville*, an engraving after Guillemin.

La Vie d'une jeune fille en quatre compartiments.[1] A warning to those who have a bent for motherhood!

L'Aumône d'une vierge folle.[2] The crazed old creature is giving a copper, earned by the sweat of her brow, to the beggar who mounts eternal guard at the door of Félix, the pastry-cook.[3] Inside, the rich of the day are gorging themselves on sweetmeats. This one evidently derives from literature of the *Marion Delorme*[4] persuasion, which consists of preaching the virtues of whores and assassins.

How witty the French are, and what pains they take in order to delude themselves! Books, pictures, drawing-room ballads, nothing is without its use, no means is neglected by this charming people when it is a question of throwing dust in their own eyes.

XIV. ON SOME DOUBTERS

DOUBT assumes a whole host of forms; it is a Proteus which often does not recognize its own face. And so there is infinite variety among doubters, and I am obliged now to bundle together several individuals who have nothing in common beyond the absence of any substantial individuality.

Some of them are serious-minded and full of great goodwill. These ones deserve our pity.

There is M. Papety, for instance, who at the time of his return from Rome was regarded as a colourist by some people (chiefly his friends). This year he has sent a picture entitled *Solon dictant ses lois*,[5] which is shockingly unpleasant to look at.—Perhaps it is because it hangs too high for its details to be properly visible, that it reminds one of the ridiculous tail-end of the Imperial School.

For two years running now M. Papety has sent entirely different-looking pictures to the same Salon.

[1] Charles Richard's picture was in fact in *five* divisions: 'le rendezvous: le bal: le luxe: la misère: Saint-Lazare.'

[2] This was perhaps A. Béranger's *La Charité*.

[3] No. 42, rue Vivienne.

[4] Victor Hugo's play about the famous courtesan of the seventeenth century was produced in 1831.

[5] According to the Salon catalogue, this painting was commissioned by the Ministry of the Interior. Dominique Papety was for a while one of Chenavard's assistants.

M. Glaize is compromising his early success by giving us works both vulgar in style and muddled in composition. Every time that he has to do anything else but a study of a woman, he gets lost. M. Glaize believes that you become a colourist by the exclusive choice of certain hues. Window-dressers' assistants and theatrical costumiers, too, have a taste for rich hues; but that does not make a taste for harmony.

In *Le Sang de Vénus*,[1] the Venus is a pretty and delicate figure, with a good suggestion of movement; but the nymph who crouches in front of her is an appalling example of the *poncif*.

M. Matout is liable to the same criticism on the score of colour. Furthermore, an artist who formerly took his bow as a draughtsman, and who used to devote his mind above all to the compound harmony of lines, should avoid giving a figure improbable movements of the neck and arm. Even if nature demands it, the artist who is an idealist, and who wishes to be true to his principles, should not comply.

M. Chenavard is an eminently learned and hardworking artist, whose *Martyre de St. Polycarpe*, painted in collaboration with M. Comairas, attracted attention several years ago. This picture bespoke a real grasp of the science of composition and a thorough connoisseurship of all the Italian masters. This year M. Chenavard has given further proof of taste in his choice of subject, and of cleverness in his drawing.[2] But when you are contending with Michelangelo, would it not be fitting to outdo him in *colour*, at least?

M. Guignet always carries two men about in his head—Salvator Rosa and M. Decamps. M. Salvator Guignet paints in sepia; M. Guignet Decamps is an entity weakened by duality. *Les Condottières après un pillage*[3] is painted in the first manner; *Xerxès* verges upon the second. Nevertheless this picture is well enough composed, were it not for a

[1] In the Montpellier Museum.

[2] This painting, entitled *L'Enfer de Dante*, is now in the Montpellier Museum. Chenavard was a high-minded and socially-conscious painter—Silvestre called him 'un orateur en peinture'—whose subdued colour often approached *grisaille*. His *Martyrdom of St. Polycarp*, mentioned here, was exhibited at the 1841 Salon, and then placed in the church of Argenton-sur-Creuse (Indre). Comairas was also one of his assistants in a later project, entitled *Palingénésie Universelle*, for a series of *grisailles* to decorate the interior of the Pantheon: after three years the work had to be abandoned when the Pantheon was returned to the Church, in 1851. For a painter who came from Lyons, Baudelaire treats Chenavard with surprising respect. He was a close friend of Delacroix. See pl. 15; and the article 'Philosophic Art', in *Painter of Modern Life*, pp. 204–212.

[3] Reproduced *Illustr.*, vol. VII (1846), p. 221.

taste for erudition and connoisseurship, which amuses and fascinates the spectator, and deflects his attention from the principal idea; the same thing was wrong with his *Pharaons*.[1]

MM. Brune and Gigoux are already established names. But even at his best period, M. Gigoux hardly produced anything more than vast vignettes. After numerous setbacks, he has at last shown us a picture which, if not very original, is at least quite well *built*. *Le Mariage de la Sainte Vierge* looks like a work by one of those countless masters of the Florentine decadence, supposing him to have become suddenly preoccupied with colour. M. Brune puts one in mind of the Carracci and the eclectic painters of the second epoch; a solid manner, but little or no soul—no great faults, but no great quality.

If there are some doubters who excite interest, there are also some grotesque ones, whom the public meets again each year with that wicked delight characteristic of bored *flâneurs* for whom excessive ugliness always secures a few moments' distraction.

The coldly frivolous M. Bard seems to be really and truly succumbing beneath the burden which he has imposed upon himself. He returns from time to time, however, to his natural manner—which is the same as everybody else's. I have been told that the author of *La Barque de Caron* was a pupil of M. Horace Vernet.

M. Biard[2] is a universal man. This would seem to indicate that he has not the least doubt in the world, and that no one on earth is surer of his ground. Nevertheless I ask you to observe that amidst all this appalling lumber—history-pictures, travel-pictures, sentimental pictures, epigrammatic pictures—one genre is neglected. M. Biard has flinched before the religious picture. He is not yet sufficiently convinced of his powers.

XV. ON LANDSCAPE

IN LANDSCAPE, as in portraiture and history-painting, it is possible to establish classifications based on the different methods used; thus there are landscape-colourists, landscape-draughtsmen, and imaginative landscapists; there are naturalists who idealize without knowing it, and partisans of the 'poncif', who devote themselves to a weird and peculiar genre called *historical* landscape.

[1] At the 1845 Salon: see p. 23 and pl. 3.

[2] Of Biard's eight exhibits, three are reproduced *Illustr.*, vol. VII (1846), pp. 152–3.

At the time of the romantic revolution, the landscape-painters, following the example of the most celebrated Flemish masters, devoted themselves exclusively to the study of nature; it was this that was their salvation and gave a particular lustre to the modern school of landscape. The essence of their talent lay in an eternal adoration of visible creation, under all its aspects and in all its details.

Others, more philosophic and more dialectical, concentrated chiefly on style—that is to say, on the harmony of the principal lines, and on the architecture of nature.

As for the landscape of fantasy, which is the expression of man's dreaming, or the egoism of man substituted for nature, it was little cultivated. This curious genre, of which the best examples are offered by Rembrandt, Rubens, Watteau and a handful of English illustrated annuals, and which is itself a small-scale counterpart of the magnificent stage décors at the Opera, represents our natural need for the marvellous. It is the 'graphic imagination' imported into landscape. Fabulous gardens, limitless horizons, streams more limpid than in nature, and flowing in defiance of the laws of topography, gigantic boulders constructed according to ideal proportions, mists floating like a dream—the landscape of fantasy, in short, has had but few enthusiastic followers among us, either because it was a somewhat un-French fruit, or because our school of landscape needed before all else to reinvigorate itself at purely natural springs.

As for historical landscape, over which I want to say a few words in the manner of a requiem-mass, it is neither free fantasy, nor has it any connection with the admirable slavishness of the naturalists; it is ethics applied to nature.

What a contradiction, and what a monstrosity! Nature has no other ethics but the brute facts, because Nature is her own ethics; nevertheless we are asked to believe that she must be reconstructed and set in order according to sounder and purer rules—rules which are not to be found in simple enthusiasm for the ideal, but in esoteric codes which the adepts reveal to no one.

Thus, Tragedy—that genre forgotten of men, of which it is only at the Comédie Française (the most deserted theatre in the universe) that one can find a few samples[1]—the art of Tragedy, I say, consists in cutting out certain eternal patterns (for example, patterns of love, hate, filial piety,

[1] Baudelaire's remark is somewhat reminiscent of what Heine had to say some ten years before, in his *Letters on the French Stage*. Heine wrote: 'I frequented the Théâtre-

ambition, etc.), and after suspending them on wires, in making them walk, bow, sit down and speak, according to a sacred and mysterious ceremonial. Never, even by dint of using mallet and wedge, will you cause an idea of the infinite degrees of variety to penetrate the skull of a tragic poet, and even if you beat or kill him, you will not persuade him that there must be different sorts of morality too. Have you ever seen tragic persons eat or drink? It is obvious that these people have invented their own moral system to fit their natural needs, and that they have created their own temperament, whereas the majority of mankind have to *submit* to theirs. I once heard a poet-in-ordinary to the Comédie Française say that Balzac's novels wrung his heart with pain and disgust; that, as far as he was concerned, he could not conceive of lovers existing on anything else but the scent of flowers and the tear-drops of the dawn. It seems to me that it is time the government took a hand; for if men of letters, who each have their own labours and their own dreams, and for whom there is no such thing as Sunday—if men of letters can escape the risk of tragedy quite naturally, there are nevertheless a certain number of people who have been persuaded that the Comédie Française is the sanctuary of art, and whose admirable goodwill is cheated one day in every seven. Is it reasonable to allow some of our citizens to besot themselves and to contract false ideas? But it seems that tragedy and historical landscape are stronger than the gods themselves.

So now you understand what is meant by a good tragic landscape. It is an arrangement of master-patterns of trees, fountains, tombs and funerary urns. The dogs are cut out on some sort of historical dog-pattern; a historical shepherd could never allow himself any others, on pain of disgrace. Every *immoral* tree that has allowed itself to grow up on its own, and in its own way, is, of necessity, cut down: every toad- or tadpole-pond is pitilessly buried beneath the earth. And if ever a historical landscape-painter feels remorse for some natural peccadillo or other, he imagines his Hell in the guise of a *real* landscape, a pure sky, a free and rich vegetation; a savannah, for example, or a virgin forest.

MM. Paul Flandrin, Desgoffe, Chevandier and Teytaud are the men who have undertaken the glorious task of struggling against the taste of a nation.

Français very little. That house has for me something of the mournfulness of the desert. There the spectres of the old tragedies reappear, with dagger and poisoned cup in their wan hands . . .'

I do not know what is the origin of historical landscape. It certainly cannot have sprung from Poussin, for in comparison with these gentlemen, he is a depraved and perverted spirit.

MM. Aligny, Corot and Cabat are much concerned with style. But what, with M. Aligny, is a violent and philosophic dogma, is an instinctive habit and a natural turn of mind with M. Corot. Unfortunately he has only sent one landscape this year; it represents cows coming to drink at a pool in the forest of Fontainebleau.[1] M. Corot is a harmonist rather than a colourist; and it is their very simplicity of colour, combined with their complete lack of pedantry, that gives such enchantment to his compositions. Almost all his works have the particular gift of unity, which is one of the requirements of the memory.

M. Aligny has etched some very beautiful views of Corinth and Athens which perfectly express the preconceived idea of these places. M. Aligny's serious and idealistic talent has found a most suitable subject in these harmonious poems of stone, and his method of translating them on to copper suits him no less well.[2]

M. Cabat has completely deserted the path on which he had won himself such a great reputation. Without ever being a party to the *bravura* peculiar to certain naturalistic landscape-painters, he was formerly very much more brilliant and very much more *naïf*. He is truly mistaken in no longer putting his trust in nature, as he used to do. He is a man whose talent is too great for any of his compositions to lack a special distinction; but this latter-day Jansenism, this retrenchment of means, this deliberate self-privation cannot add to his glory.[3]

In general the influence of Ingrism cannot possibly produce satisfactory results in landscape. Line and style are no substitutes for light, shadow, reflections and the *colouring* atmosphere—all of which play too great a part in the poetry of Nature to allow her to submit to this method.

The members of the opposite party, the naturalists and the colourists, are much more popular and have made much more of a mark. Their main qualities are a rich and abundant colour, transparent and luminous skies, and a special kind of sincerity which makes them accept everything

[1] Entitled *Vue prise dans la forêt de Fontainbleau*: now in the Boston Museum; see pl. 18.

[2] The previous year Aligny had published a set of ten *Vues des sites les plus célèbres de la Grèce Antique, dessinées sur nature et gravées par Théodore Aligny*. To judge by a remark in Thoré's *Salon de 1846* (edn. of 1868, p. 371), it was eight of these etchings that Aligny exhibited this year. See pl. 22.

[3] Of Cabat's two exhibits, that entitled *Le Repos* is in the Louvain Museum.

that nature gives. It is a pity that some of them, like M. Troyon,[1] take too much delight in the tight-rope tricks of their brush; these devices, known in advance, acquired with much trouble, and monotonously triumphant, sometimes intrigue the spectator more than the landscape itself. In these circumstances, it may even happen that a surprise pupil, like M. Charles Le Roux,[2] will push still further the limits of boldness and security; for there is only one inimitable thing, and that is natural simplicity.

M. Coignard has sent a large and fairly well-constructed landscape which has much attracted the public eye; it has a number of cows in the foreground, and in the background the skirts of a forest. The cows are beautiful and well-painted, and the picture looks well as a whole; but I do not think that the trees are vigorous enough to support such a sky. This suggests that if you took away the cows, the landscape would become very unsightly.

M. Français is one of our most distinguished landscape-painters. He knows how to study nature, and how to blend with it a romantic perfume of the purest essence. His *Etude de Saint-Cloud* is a charming thing and full of taste, except for M. Meissonier's *fleas* which are a fault of taste.[3] They attract the attention too much, and they amuse the blockheads. Nevertheless they are done with that particular sort of perfection which this artist puts into all his little things.*

Unfortunately M. Flers has only sent pastels. His own loss is equal to that of the public.

M. Héroult is one of those who are particularly obsessed with light and atmosphere. He is very good at rendering clear, smiling skies, and floating mists shot through with a ray of sunlight. He is no stranger to

[1] Of Troyon's four exhibits, that entitled *Vallée de Chevreuse* is reproduced *Illustr.*, vol. VII (1846), p. 187.
[2] Le Roux was a pupil of Corot's.
[3] Français's *Etude de Saint-Cloud*, with figures by Meissonier, was in the Pourtalès collection. His *Effet de soleil couchant,* also exhibited, is in the Musée Fabre, Montpellier.

* At last I have found a man who has contrived to express his admiration for this artist's works in the most judicious fashion and with an enthusiasm just like my own. It is M. Hippolyte Babou. I think, as he does, that they should all be hung along the *flies* of the Gymnase. '*Geneviève* or *La Jalousie paternelle* is a ravishing little Meissonier which M. Scribe has hung up on the flies of the Gymnase': *Courrier français*, in the *feuilleton* of 6 April. This strikes me as so sublime that I take it that MM. Scribe, Meissonier and Babou cannot but gain all three by my quoting it here. (C.B.) It was Hippolyte Babou (1824–78) who later suggested the title 'Les Fleurs du Mal' to Baudelaire. On Scribe, see note on p. 95.

the special poetry of the northern countries. But his colour, which is a little too soft and fluid, smacks of the methods of water-colour; and if he has been able to avoid the heroics of the other landscape-painters, he does not always possess a sufficient firmness of touch.

As a rule MM. Joyant, Chacaton, Lottier and Borget go to distant lands in search of their subjects, and their pictures have the charm of an evening with a travel-book.

I have nothing against specialization; but I would not have anyone abuse it to the extent of M. Joyant, who has never set foot outside the Piazza San Marco and has never crossed to the Lido.[1] If M. Joyant's speciality attracts the eye more than the next man's, it is doubtless because of the monotonous perfection which he brings to it and which results always from the same tricks. It seems to me that M. Joyant has never been able to move onwards.

M. Borget, however, has crossed the frontiers of China, and has brought us landscapes from Mexico, Peru and India. Without being a painter of the first rank, he has brilliant and fluent colour, and his tones are fresh and pure. With a little less art, and if he could concern himself less with other landscape-painters and could paint more as a simple traveller, M. Borget would perhaps obtain more interesting results.

M. Chacaton, who has devoted himself exclusively to the Orient, has for a long time been one of our cleverest painters. His pictures are bright and smiling. Unfortunately they almost always suggest paintings by Decamps or Marilhat, bleached, and reduced in size.

M. Lottier, instead of looking for the grey and misty effects of the warm climates, loves to bring out their harshness and their fiery dazzle. The truth of these sun-swamped panoramas is marvellously brutal. You would think that they had been done with a colour-daguerreotype.

There is one man who, more than all of these, and more even than the most celebrated absentees, seems to me to fulfil the conditions of beauty in landscape: he is a man but little known to the multitude, for past setbacks and underhand plotting have combined together to keep him away from the Salon. You will already have guessed that I am referring

[1] Nevertheless the painting by Joyant reproduced in *l'Illustration* this year (vol. VII, p. 89) represented *Le Pont Saint-Bénezet, Avignon*. His other two pictures were of Venetian subjects.

to M. Rousseau[1]—and it seems to me to be high time that he took his bow once again before a public which, thanks to the efforts of other painters, has gradually become familiar with new aspects of landscape.

It is as difficult to interpret M. Rousseau's talent in words as it is to interpret that of Delacroix, with whom he has other affinities also. M. Rousseau is a northern landscape-painter. His painting breathes a great sigh of melancholy. He loves nature in her *bluish* moments—twilight effects—strange and moisture-laden sunsets—massive, breeze-haunted shades—great plays of light and shadow. His colour is magnificent, but not dazzling. The fleecy softness of his skies is incomparable. Think of certain landscapes by Rubens and Rembrandt; add a few memories of English painting, and assume a deep and serious love of nature dominating and ordering it all—and then perhaps you will be able to form some idea of the magic of his pictures. Like Delacroix, he adds much of his soul to the mixture; he is a naturalist, ceaselessly swept towards the ideal.

M. Gudin[2] is increasingly compromising his reputation. The more the public sees good painting, the more it parts company from even the most popular artists if they cannot offer it the same amount of pleasure. For me, M. Gudin comes into the class of people who stop their wounds with artificial flesh; of bad singers of whom it is said that they are great actors; and of *poetic* painters.

M. Jules Noël has produced a really beautiful marine-painting, of a fine, clear colour, bright and luminous.[3] A huge *felucca*, with its strange shapes and colours, is lying at anchor in some great harbour, bathed in all the shifting light of the Orient. A little too much *colouring*, perhaps, and not enough unity? But M. Jules Noël certainly has too much talent not to have still more, and he is doubtless one of those who impose a daily amount of progress upon themselves.—Furthermore the success achieved by this canvas proves that the public of today is ready to extend a warm welcome to all newcomers, in all the genres.

[1] Although he had had a moderate success at the Salon in the early 1830s, Théodore Rousseau's landscapes were consistently rejected from 1838 until 1849. He was nicknamed 'Le Grand Refusé'.

[2] Gudin's thirteen exhibits this year ranged from landscapes to sea-battles.

[3] Repro. *Illustr.*, vol. VII (1846), p. 120.

M. Kiorboë is one of those sumptuous painters of old who knew so well how to decorate their noble dining-rooms, which one imagines full of heroic and ravenous huntsmen. M. Kiorboë's painting has joyfulness and power, and his colour is fluent and harmonious. The drama of his *Wolf Trap*,[1] however, is not quite easy enough to follow, perhaps because the trap itself is partly in the shadow. The hindquarters of the dog which is falling back with a yelp are not vigorously enough painted.

M. Saint-Jean,[2] who, I am told, is the delight and the glory of the city of Lyons, will never achieve more than a moderate success in a country of painters. That excessive minuteness of his is intolerably pedantic. Whenever anyone talks to you of the *naïveté* of a painter from Lyons, do not believe a word of it. For a long time now the overall colour of M. Saint-Jean's pictures has been the yellow of urine. You might imagine that he had never seen real fruit, and that he does not care a scrap, because he can do them very nicely by mechanical means. Not only do natural fruits look quite different, but they are less finished and less highly wrought than these.

It is quite a different matter with M. Arondel,[3] whose chief merit is a real artlessness. Therefore his painting contains several obvious blemishes; but the felicitous passages are entirely successful. Some other parts are too dark, and you might suppose that, while painting, this artist fails to take into account all the necessary accidents of the Salon—the adjacent paintings, the distance from the spectator, and the modification which distance causes in the mutual effect of tones. Besides, it is not enough to paint well. The famous Flemish painters all knew how to dispose of their dead game and how to go on worrying at it for ages, just as one worries at a model; the point was to discover felicitous lines, and rich and clear tonal harmonies.

M. P. Rousseau, whose dazzling and colourful pictures have received such widespread notice, is making serious progress. He was already an excellent painter, it is true; but now he is looking at nature more attentively and he is striving to bring out her particularity of feature.[4] The other day at Durand-Ruel's[5] I saw some ducks by M. Rousseau; they were wonderfully beautiful, and really behaved and acted like ducks.

[1] The correct title of Kiorboë's painting was *Un renard au piège, trouvé par des chiens de bergers*. [2] Saint-Jean specialized as a flower-and-fruit painter. [3] See p. 27.
[4] P. Rousseau's *Le chat et le vieux rat* was reproduced *Illustr.*, vol. VII (1846), p. 88.
[5] The well-known dealer.

XVI. WHY SCULPTURE IS TIRESOME

THE ORIGIN of sculpture is lost in the mists of time; thus it is a *Carib* art.

We find, in fact, that all races bring real skill to the carving of fetishes long before they embark upon the art of painting, which is an art involving profound thought and one whose very enjoyment demands a particular initiation.

Sculpture comes much closer to nature, and that is why even today our peasants, who are enchanted by the sight of an ingeniously-turned fragment of wood or stone, will nevertheless remain unmoved in front of the most beautiful painting. Here we have a singular mystery which is quite beyond human solving.

Sculpture has several disadvantages which are a necessary consequence of its means and materials. Though as brutal and positive as nature herself, it has at the same time a certain vagueness and ambiguity, because it exhibits too many surfaces at once. It is in vain that the sculptor forces himself to take up a unique paint of view, for the spectator who moves around the figure can choose a hundred different points of view, except for the right one, and it often happens that a chance trick of the light, an effect of the lamp, may discover a beauty which is not at all the one the artist had in mind—and this is a humiliating thing for him. A picture, however, is only what it means to be; there is no other way of looking at it than on its own terms. Painting has but one point of view; it is exclusive and absolute, and therefore the painter's expression is much more forceful.

That is why it is as difficult to be a connoisseur of sculpture as it is to be a bad sculptor. I have heard the sculptor Préault[1] say, 'I am a connoisseur of Michelangelo, of Jean Goujon, of Germain Pilon; but of *sculpture* I am a complete ignoramus.' It is obvious that he meant the sculpture of the sculpturizers—in other words, of the Caribs.

Once out of the primitive era, sculpture, in its most magnificent development, is nothing else but a *complementary* art. It is no longer a question of skilfully carving portable figures, but of becoming a humble associate of painting and architecture, and of serving their intentions. Cathedrals soar up into the sky and load their thousand echoing chasms with

[1] Like Théodore Rousseau, Auguste Préault was systematically refused by the Salon juries from the early 1830s until 1848. He was the Romantic sculptor *par excellence*, and was as well known for his wit as for his statuary.

sculptures, which form but one flesh and body with the edifice itself: please note that I am speaking of *painted* sculptures, whose pure and simple colours, arranged in accordance with a special scale, harmonize with the rest and complete the poetic effect of the whole. Versailles shelters her race of statues beneath leafy shades which serve them as background, or under arbours of living waters which shower upon them the thousand diamonds of the light. At all great periods, sculpture is a complement; at the beginning and at the end, it is an isolated art.

As soon as sculpture consents to be seen close at hand, there are no childish trivialities which the sculptor will not dare, and which triumphantly outrun the fetish and the calumet. When it has become a drawing-room or a bedroom art, it is the cue for the Caribs of lace (like M. Gayrard), or for the Caribs of the wrinkle, the hair and the wart (like M. David[1]) to put in an appearance.

Next we have the Caribs of the andiron, the clock and the writing-desk, etc., like M. Cumberworth, whose *Marie* is a maid-of-all-work, employed at the Louvre and at Susse's, as a statue or a candelabra[2]; or like M. Feuchère, who possesses the gift of a universality which takes one's breath away; colossal figures, match-boxes, goldsmiths' motifs, busts and bas-reliefs—he is capable of anything. The bust which he has done this year of a very well-known actor[3] is no better a likeness than last year's; they are never more than rough approximations. Last year's bust resembled Jesus Christ, and this year's, which is dry and mean-looking, in no way conveys the original, angular, sardonic and shifting physiognomy of the model. Nevertheless you should not suppose that these people lack knowledge. They are as learned as academicians —or as *vaudevillistes*; they make free with all periods and all genres; they have plumbed the depth of all the schools. They would he happy to convert even the tombs of St. Denis into cigar- or shawl-boxes, and every Florentine bronze into a threepenny bit. If you want the fullest information concerning the principles of this frivolous and trifling school, you should apply to M. Klagmann,[4] who is, I think, the master of this whole vast workshop.

[1] I.e. David d'Angers.

[2] The catalogue makes it clear that Cumberworth's *Marie* was the negress slave in Bernardin de Saint-Pierre's *Paul et Virginie*. Cumberworth was regularly employed by Susse frères, the dealers in decorative sculpture.

[3] J.-F.-S. Provost; the bust is now at the Comédie Française.

[4] Klagmann's plaster statue was entitled *Une petite fille effeuillant une rose*.

An excellent proof of the pitiable state of sculpture today is the fact that M. Pradier[1] is its king. Admittedly this artist knows how to do flesh, and he has his particular refinements of the chisel; but he has neither the imagination necessary for great compositions, nor the 'graphic imagination'. His talent is cold and academic. He has spent his life fattening up a small stock of antique torsos and equipping them with the coiffures of kept women. His *Poésie Légère*[2] seems all the colder as it is the more mannered; its execution is not as opulent as in the sculptor's former works, and, seen from behind, it looks hideous. Besides this, he has done two bronzes —*Anacréon* and *La Sagesse*—which are impudent imitations of the antique and show clearly that without this noble crutch M. Pradier would stumble at every step.

The bust is a genre which demands less imagination and capacities less lofty—though no less delicate—than sculpture on the grand scale. It is a more intimate and more restricted art, whose successes are less public. As in the portrait done according to the manner of the naturalists, it is necessary to have a perfect grasp of the model's essential nature, and to express its poetic quality; for there are few models who completely lack poetry. Almost all of M. Dantan's busts[3] are done according to the best doctrines. They all have a particular distinction, and their detail does not exclude breadth and ease of execution.

M. Lenglet's chief fault,[4] on the contrary, is a certain timidity, a childishness, an excess of sincerity in his execution, which gives an appearance of dryness to his work; but, on the other hand, no one could give a truer and more authentic character to a human face. This little bust—stocky, grave and frowning—has the magnificent character of the best work of the Romans—an idealization discovered in nature herself. Another distinguishing quality of antique portraiture which I noticed in M. Lenglet's bust is a profound concentration of attention.

XVII. ON SCHOOLS AND JOURNEYMEN

If ever your idler's curiosity has landed you in a street brawl, perhaps you will have felt the same delight as I have often felt to see a protector

[1] Pradier has been described as the Romantic sculptor of the 'juste-milieu'.

[2] In the Nîmes Museum; See pl. 21.

[3] This is presumably Antoine-Laurent Dantan (1798–1878), though his younger brother Jean Pierre Dantan (1800–69) also exhibited at this Salon.

[4] This was Lenglet's first Salon.

of the public slumbers—a policeman or a municipal guard (the real army)—thumping a republican. And if so, like me, you will have said in your heart: 'Thump on, thump a little harder, thump again, beloved constable! for at this supreme thumping, I adore thee and judge thee the equal of Jupiter, the great dealer of justice! The man whom thou thumpest is an enemy of roses and of perfumes, and a maniac for *utensils*. He is the enemy of Watteau, the enemy of Raphael, the bitter enemy of luxury, of the fine arts and of literature, a sworn iconoclast and butcher of Venus and Apollo! He is no longer willing to help with the public roses and perfumes, as a humble and anonymous journeyman. He wants to be *free*, poor fool; but he is incapable of founding a factory for *new* flowers and *new* scents. Thump him devoutly across the shoulder-blades, the anarchist!'*

In the same way philosophers and critics should pitilessly thump *artistic* apes—emancipated journeymen who hate the force and the sovereignty of genius.

Compare the present age with past ages. On leaving the Salon or some newly-decorated church, go and rest your eyes in a museum of old masters. And then analyse the differences.

In the one, all is turbulence, a hurly-burly of styles and colours, a cacophony of tones, enormous trivialities, platitudes of gesture and pose, nobility 'by numbers', clichés of all kinds—and all this clearly manifested not only by different pictures in juxtaposition, but even within one and the same picture. In short, there is a complete absence of unity, whose only result is a terrible weariness for the mind and the eyes.

In the other place you are immediately struck by that feeling of reverence which causes children to doff their hats and which catches at your soul in the way that the dust of vaults and tombs catches your throat. But this is by no means the mere effect of yellow varnish or the grime of ages: it is the effect of unity, of profound unity. For a great Venetian painting clashes less with a Giulio Romano beside it than a group of our pictures—and I do not mean the worst of them—clash amongst themselves.

A magnificence of costume, a nobility of movement—a nobility often mannered, yet grand and stately—and an absence of little tricks and

* I often hear people complaining about the theatre of today; it lacks originality, they say, because there are no longer any types. But the Republican? what about *him*? Is he not an essential for any comedy that aims at being gay? and in him have we not a successor to the role of Marquis? (C.B.)

contradictory tactics—these are qualities which are all implied in the phrase 'the great tradition'.

Then you had schools of painting; *now* you have emancipated journeymen.

There were still schools under Louis XV; there was one under the Empire—a school—that is, a faith—that is, the impossibility of doubt. There you had pupils united by common principles, obedient to the rule of a powerful leader, and helping him in all his undertakings.

Doubt, or the absence of faith and of *naïveté*, is a vice peculiar to this age, for today no one is obedient, and *naïveté*, which means the dominion of temperament within manner, is a divine privilege which almost all are without.

Few men have a right to rule, for few men have an overruling passion.

And as everyone today wants to rule, no one knows how to govern himself.

Now that everyone is abandoned to his own devices, a master has many unknown pupils for whom he is not responsible, and his blind and involuntary dominion extends well beyond his studio, as far as regions where his thought cannot be understood.

Those who are nearer to the word and the idiom of the master preserve the purity of his doctrine, and by obedience and tradition they do what the master does by the fatality of his nature.

But outside of this family-circle there is a vast population of mediocrities—apes of different and mixed breeds, a floating race of half-castes who each day move from one country to another, taking away from each the customs which suit them, and seeking to make a personality for themselves by a system of contradictory borrowings.

There are people who will steal a fragment from a picture by Rembrandt, and without modifying it, without digesting it, without even finding the glue to stick it on with, will incorporate it into a work composed from an entirely different point of view.

There are some who change from white to black in a day: yesterday, colourists in the 'chic' manner, colourists with neither love nor originality—tomorrow, sacrilegious imitators of M. Ingres, but without discovering any more taste or faith.

The sort of man who today comes into the class of the apes—even the cleverest apes—is not, and never will be, anything but a mediocre painter. There was a time when he would have made an excellent journeyman: but now he is lost, for himself and for all mankind.

That is why it would have been more in the interest of their own salvation, and even of their happiness, if the lukewarm had been subjected to the lash of a vigorous faith. For strong men are rare, and today you have to be a Delacroix or an Ingres if you are to come to the surface and be seen amid the chaos of an exhausting and sterile freedom.

The apes are the republicans of art, and the present state of painting is the result of an anarchic freedom which glorifies the individual, however feeble he may be, to the detriment of communities—that is to say, of schools.

In schools, which are nothing else but organizations of inventive force, those individuals who are truly worthy of the name absorb the weak. And that is justice, for an abundant production is only a mind equipped with the power of a thousand arms.

This glorification of the individual has necessitated the infinite division of the territory of art. The absolute and divergent liberty of each man, the division of effort and the disjunction of the human will have led to this weakness, this doubt and this poverty of invention. A few sublime and long-suffering eccentrics are a poor compensation for this swarming chaos of mediocrity. Individuality—that little *place of one's own* —has devoured collective originality. And just as a well known chapter of a romantic novel[1] has shown that the printed book has killed the monument of stone, so it is fair to say that, for the time being, it is the painter that has killed the art of painting.

XVIII. ON THE HEROISM OF MODERN LIFE

Many people will attribute the present decadence in painting to our decadence in behaviour.* This dogma of the studios, which has gained currency among the public, is a poor excuse of the artists. For they had a vested interest in ceaselessly depicting the past; it is an easier task, and one that could be turned to good account by the lazy.

It is true that the great tradition has been lost, and that the new one is not yet established.

[1] Victor Hugo, *Notre-Dame de Paris*, Bk. V, chap. ii, 'Ceci tuera cela'.

* These two types of decadence must not be confused; one has regard to the public and its feelings, the other concerns the studios alone. (C.B.)

But what *was* this great tradition, if not a habitual, everyday idealization of ancient life—a robust and martial form of life, a state of readiness on the part of each individual, which gave him a habit of gravity in his movements, and of majesty, or violence, in his attitudes? To this should be added a public splendour which found its reflection in private life. Ancient life was a great *parade*. It ministered above all to the pleasure of the eye, and this day-to-day paganism has marvellously served the arts.

Before trying to distinguish the epic side of modern life, and before bringing examples to prove that our age is no less fertile in sublime themes than past ages, we may assert that since all centuries and all peoples have had their own form of beauty, so inevitably we have ours. That is in the order of things.

All forms of beauty, like all possible phenomena, contain an element of the eternal and an element of the transitory—of the absolute and of the particular. Absolute and eternal beauty does not exist, or rather it is only an abstraction skimmed from the general surface of different beauties. The particular element in each manifestation comes from the emotions: and just as we have our own particular emotions, so we have our own beauty.

Except for Hercules on Mount Oeta, Cato of Utica and Cleopatra (whose suicides are not *modern* suicides*) ,what suicides do you find represented in the old masters? You will search in vain among pagan existences—existences dedicated to appetite—for the suicide of Jean-Jacques,[1] or even the weird and marvellous suicide of Rafael de Valentin.[2]

As for the garb, the outer husk, of the modern hero, although the time is past when every little artist dressed up as a grand panjandrum and smoked pipes as long as duck-rifles, nevertheless the studios and the world at large are still full of people who would like to poeticize *Antony* with a Greek cloak and a parti-coloured vesture.[3]

* The first killed himself because he could no longer endure his burning shirt; the second, because there was nothing more that he could do for the cause of liberty; and the voluptuous queen, because she had lost both her throne and her lover. But none of them destroyed himself in order to change skins through metempsychosis. (C.B.)

[1] Rousseau. The belief that he committed suicide is now considered to be without foundation.

[2] The hero of Balzac's *La Peau de Chagrin*.

[3] Dumas the elder's prose-drama *Antony* was produced in 1831. The central character became a powerful hero-figure of the times, and young men who cast themselves for this rôle in real life were popularly known as 'Antonys'.

But all the same, has not this much-abused garb its own beauty and its native charm? Is it not the necessary garb of our suffering age, which wears the symbol of a perpetual mourning even upon its thin black shoulders? Note, too, that the dress-coat and the frock-coat not only possess their political beauty, which is an expression of universal equality, but also their poetic beauty, which is an expression of the public soul—an immense cortège of undertaker's mutes (mutes in love, political mutes, bourgeois mutes . . .). We are each of us celebrating some funeral.

A uniform livery of affliction bears witness to equality; and as for the eccentrics, whose violent and contrasting colours used easily to betray them to the eye, today they are satisfied with slight nuances in design in cut, much more than in colour. Look at those grinning creases which play like serpents around mortified flesh—have they not their own mysterious grace?

Although M. Eugène Lami[1] and M. Gavarni[2] are not geniuses of the highest order, they have understood all this very well—the former, the poet of official dandyism, the latter the poet of a raffish and reach-me-down dandyism! The reader who turns again to M. Jules Barbey d'Aurevilly's book on Dandyism[3] will see clearly that it is a modern thing, resulting from causes entirely new.

Let not the tribe of colourists be too indignant. For if it is more difficult, their task is thereby only the more glorious. Great colourists know how to create colour with a black coat, a white cravat and a grey background.

But to return to our principal and essential problem, which is to discover whether we possess a specific beauty, intrinsic to our new emotions, I observe that the majority of artists who have attacked modern life have contented themselves with public and official subjects—with our victories and our political heroism. Even so, they do it with an ill grace, and only because they are commissioned by the government which pays them. However there are private subjects which are very much more heroic than these.

The pageant of fashionable life and the thousands of floating existences—criminals and kept women—which drift about in the underworld of a

[1] Lami exhibited an oil-painting, *La reine Victoria dans le Salon de famille au château d'Eu, le 3 Septembre 1843*, and a water-colour, *Le grand bal masqué de l'Opéra*.

[2] See *Painter of Modern Life*, pp. 182–3.

[3] Barbey d'Aurevilly's *Du Dandysme et de Georges Brummell* had been published the previous year.

great city; the *Gazette des Tribunaux* and the *Moniteur* all prove to us that we have only to open our eyes to recognize our heroism.

Suppose that a minister, baited by the opposition's impertinent questioning, has given expression once and for all—with that proud and sovereign eloquence which is proper to him—to his scorn and disgust for all ignorant and mischief-making oppositions. The same evening you will hear the following words buzzing round you on the Boulevard des Italiens: 'Were you in the Chamber today? and did you see the minister? Good Heavens, how handsome he was! I have never seen such scorn!'

So there *are* such things as modern beauty and modern heroism!

And a little later;—'I hear that K.— or F. —has been commissioned to do a medal on the subject; but he won't know how to do it—he has no understanding for these things.'

So artists can be more, or less, fitted to understand modern beauty!

Or again: 'The sublime rascal! Even Byron's pirates have less nobility and scorn. Would you believe it—he jostled the Abbé Montès aside, and literally *fell* upon the guillotine, shouting: 'Leave me my courage intact!'

This last sentence alludes to the grave-side braggadocio of a criminal —a great *protestant*, robust of body and mind, whose fierce courage was unabashed in the face of the very engine of death![1]

All these words that fall from your lips bear witness to your belief in a new and special beauty, which is neither that of Achilles nor yet of Agamemnon.

The life of our city is rich in poetic and marvellous subjects. We are enveloped and steeped as though in an atmosphere of the marvellous; but we do not notice it.

The *nude*—that darling of the artists, that necessary element of success— is just as frequent and necessary today as it was in the life of the ancients; in bed, for example, or in the bath, or in the anatomy theatre. The themes and resources of painting are equally abundant and varied; but there is a new element—modern beauty.

For the heroes of the Iliad are but pigmies compared to you, Vautrin, Rastignac and Birotteau![2]—and you, Fontanarès,[3] who dared not

[1] The reference is to Lacenaire (1800–36), deserter, murderer and rebel, whose career became a Romantic symbol for the revolt against society. The Abbé Montès was senior chaplain at the prison of La Grande Roquette.

[2] Well known characters from Balzac's novels.

[3] The hero of Balzac's play *Les ressources de Quinola* (1842), which was set in the sixteenth century—the period of doublet and hose.

publicly declaim your sorrows in the funereal and tortured frock-coat which we all wear today!—and you, Honoré de Balzac, you the most heroic, the most extraordinary, the most romantic and the most poetic of all the characters that you have produced from your womb![1]

[1] A few months before, Baudelaire had published a satirical article at Balzac's expense, entitled *Comment on paie ses dettes quand on a du génie*. There occurred here a passage strikingly similar in form, but with a marked difference of epithet: 'lui [Balzac] le personnage le plus cocasse, le plus intéressant, et le plus vaniteux des personnages de la *Comédie humaine*, lui, cet original aussi insupportable dans la vie que délicieux dans ses écrits, ce gros enfant bouffé de génie et de vanité . . .

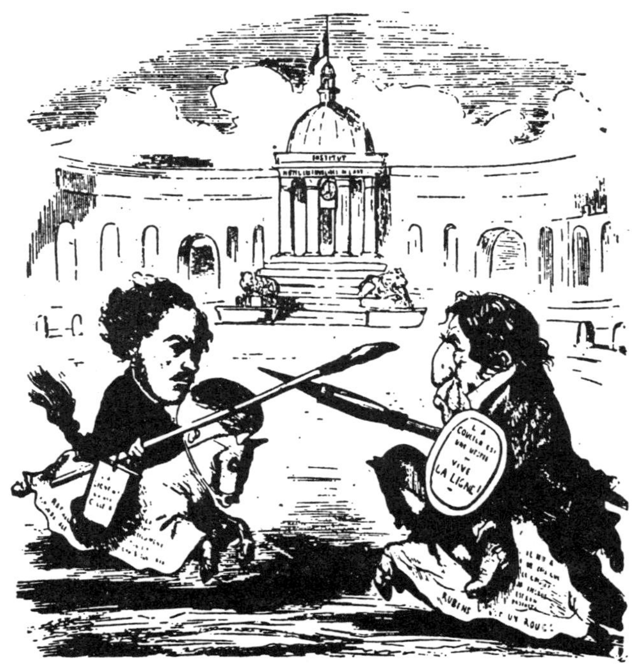

Ingres v. Delacroix, with the *Institute* in the background.
From a contemporary Caricature.

THE EXPOSITION UNIVERSELLE 1855

I. CRITICAL METHOD—ON THE MODERN IDEA OF PROGRESS AS APPLIED TO THE FINE ARTS—ON THE SHIFT OF VITALITY

THERE can be few occupations so interesting, so attractive, so full of surprises and revelations for a critic, a dreamer whose mind is given to generalization as well as to the study of details—or, to put it even better, to the idea of an universal order and hierarchy—as a comparison of the nations and their respective products. When I say 'hierarchy', I have no wish to assert the supremacy of any one nation over another. Although Nature contains certain plants which are more or less holy, certain forms more or less spiritual, certain animals more or less sacred; and although, following the promptings of the immense universal analogy, it is legitimate for us to conclude that certain nations (vast animals, whose organisms are adequate to their surroundings) have been prepared and educated by Providence for a determined goal—a goal more or less lofty, more or less near to Heaven;—nevertheless all I wish to do here is to assert their *equal* utility in the eyes of Him who is indefinable, and the miraculous way in which they come to one another's aid in the harmony of the universe.

Any reader who has been at all accustomed by solitude (far better than by books) to these vast contemplations will already have guessed the point that I am wanting to make; and, to cut across the periphrastics and hesitations of Style with a question which is almost equivalent to a formula, I will put it thus to any honest man, always provided that he has thought and travelled a little. Let him imagine a modern Winckelmann (we are full of them; the nation overflows with them; they are the idols of the lazy). What would *he* say, if faced with a product of China—something weird, strange, distorted in form, intense in colour and sometimes delicate to the point of evanescence? And yet such a thing is a specimen of universal beauty; but in order for it to be understood, it is necessary for the critic, for the spectator, to work a transformation in himself which partakes of the nature of a mystery—it is necessary for him, by means of a phenomenon of the will acting upon the imagination, to learn of himself to participate in the surroundings which have given birth to this singular flowering. Few men have the divine grace of cosmopolitanism in its entirety; but all can acquire it in different degrees. The best endowed in this respect are those solitary wanderers who have lived for years in the heart of forests, in the midst of illimitable prairies, with no other companion but their gun—contemplating, dissecting, writing. No scholastic veil, no university paradox, no academic utopia has intervened between them and the complex truth. They know the admirable, eternal and inevitable relationship between form and function. Such people do not criticize; they contemplate, they study.

If, instead of a pedagogue, I were to take a man of the world, an intelligent being, and transport him to a faraway country, I feel sure that, while the shocks and surprises of disembarkation might be great, and the business of habituation more or less long and laborious, nevertheless sooner or later his sympathy would be so keen, so penetrating, that it would create in him a whole new world of ideas, which would form an integral part of himself and would accompany him, in the form of memories, to the day of his death.[1] Those curiously-shaped buildings, which at first provoke his academic eye (all peoples are academic when they judge others, and barbaric when they are themselves judged); those plants and trees, which are disquieting for a mind filled with memories of its native land; those men and women, whose muscles do not pulse to they classic rhythms of his country, whose gait is not measured according to the accustomed beat, and whose gaze is not directed with the same magnetic power; those perfumes, which are no longer the perfumes of his mother's boudoir; those mysterious flowers, whose deep colour forces an entrance into his eye, while his glance is teased by their shape; those fruits, whose taste deludes and deranges the senses, and reveals to the palate ideas which belong to the sense of smell;—all that world of new harmonies will enter slowly into him, will patiently penetrate him, like the vapours of a perfumed Turkish bath; all that undreamt-of

[1] Baudelaire was doubtless thinking of his own experience, and of that of Delacroix and Decamps (both of whom had made early journeys, to Morocco and Turkey respectively, and had been indelibly affected by them). The 'journey to the Orient' was a classic Romantic experience.

vitality will be added to his own vitality; several thousands of ideas and sensations will enrich his earthly dictionary, and it is even possible that, going a step too far and transforming justice into revolt, he will do like the converted Sicambrian[1] and burn what he had formerly adored—and adore what he had formerly burnt.

Or take one of those modern 'aesthetic pundits', as Heinrich Heine[2] calls them—Heine, that delightful creature, who would be a genius if he turned more often towards the divine. What would *he* say? what, I repeat, would *he* write if faced with such unfamiliar phenomena? The crazy doctrinaire of Beauty would rave, no doubt; locked up within the blinding fortress of his system, he would blaspheme both life and nature; and under the influence of his fanaticism, be it Greek, Italian or Parisian, he would prohibit that insolent race from enjoying, from dreaming or from thinking in any other ways but his very own. O ink-smudged science, bastard taste, more barbarous than the barbarians themselves! you that have forgotten the colour of the sky, the movement and the smell of animality! you whose wizened fingers, paralysed by the pen, can no longer run with agility up and down the immense keyboard of the universal *correspondences*[3]!

Like all my friends I have tried more than once to lock myself up within a system in order to preach there at my ease. But a system is a kind of damnation which forces one to a perpetual recantation; it is always necessary to be inventing a new one, and the drudgery involved is a cruel punishment. Now my system was always beautiful, spacious, vast, convenient, neat and, above all, water-tight; at least so it seemed to me. But always some spontaneous, unexpected product of universal vitality would come to give the lie to my childish and superannuated wisdom—that lamentable child of Utopia! It was no good shifting or stretching my criterion—it always lagged behind universal man, and never stopped chasing after multiform and multi-coloured Beauty as it moved in the infinite spirals of life. Condemned unremittingly to the humiliation of a new conversion, I took a great decision. To escape from the horror of these philosophical apostasies, I haughtily resigned myself to modesty; I became content to *feel*; I returned to seek refuge in impeccable *naïveté*. I humbly beg pardon of the academics of all kinds who occupy the various

[1] I.e. Clovis. [2] In his *Salon* of 1831.

[3] Miss Gilman (p. 113) points out that this is the first time that Baudelaire uses this important word in its full sense.

workrooms of our artistic factory. But it is *there* that my philosophic conscience has found its rest; and at least I can declare—in so far as any man can answer for his virtues—that my mind now rejoices in a more abundant impartiality.

Anyone can easily understand that if those whose business it is to express beauty were to conform to the rules of the pundits, beauty itself would disappear from the earth, since all types, all ideas and all sensations would be fused in a vast, impersonal and monotonous unity, as immense as boredom or total negation. Variety, the *sine qua non* of life, would be effaced from life. So true is it that in the multiple productions of art there is an element of the ever-new which will eternally elude the rules and analyses of the school! That shock of surprise, which is one of the great joys produced by art and literature, is due to this very variety of types and sensations. The *aesthetic pundit*—a kind of mandarin-tyrant—always puts me in mind of a godless man who substitutes himself for God.

With all due respect to the over-proud sophists who have taken their wisdom from books, I shall go even further, and however delicate and difficult of expression my idea may be, I do not despair of succeeding. *The Beautiful is always strange.*[1] I do not mean that it is coldly, deliberately strange, for in that case it would be a monstrosity that had jumped the rails of life. I mean that it always contains a touch of strangeness, of simple, unpremeditated and unconscious strangeness, and that it is this touch of strangeness that gives it its particular quality as Beauty. It is its endorsement, so to speak—its mathematical characteristic. Reverse the proposition, and try to imagine a *commonplace Beauty*! Now how could this necessary, irreducible and infinitely varied strangeness, depending upon the environment, the climate, the manners, the race, the religion and the temperament of the artist—how could it ever be controlled, amended and corrected by Utopian rules conceived in some little scientific temple or other on this planet, without mortal danger to art itself? This dash of strangeness, which constitutes and defines individuality (without which there can be no Beauty), plays in art the role of taste and of seasoning in cooking (may the exactness of this comparison excuse its triviality!), since, setting aside their utility or the quantity of nutritive

[1] Cf. Poe, who quotes Bacon: ' "There is no exquisite beauty," says Bacon, Lord Verulam, speaking truly of all the forms and *genera* of beauty, "without some *strangeness* in the proportion." ' (*Ligeia*, and elsewhere.)

substance which they contain, the only way in which dishes differ from one another is in the *idea* which they reveal to the palate.

Therefore, in the glorious task of analysing this fine exhibition, so varied in its elements, so disturbing in its variety, and so baffling for the pedagogues, I shall endeavour to steer clear of all kind of pedantry. Others enough will speak the jargon of the studio and will exhibit *themselves* to the detriment of the *pictures*. In many cases erudition seems to me to be a childish thing and but little revealing of its true nature. I would find it only too easy to discourse subtly upon symmetrical or balanced composition, upon tonal equipoise, upon warmth and coldness of tone, etc. O Vanity! I choose instead to speak in the name of feeling, of morality and of pleasure. And I hope that a few people who are learned without pedantry will find my *ignorance* to their liking.

The story is told of Balzac (and who would not listen with respect to any anecdote, no matter how trivial, concerning that great genius?) that one day he found himself in front of a beautiful picture—a melancholy winter-scene, heavy with hoar-frost and thinly sprinkled with cottages and mean-looking peasants; and that after gazing at a little house from which a thin wisp of smoke was rising, 'How beautiful it is!', he cried. 'But what are they doing in that cottage? What are their thoughts? what are their sorrows? has it been a good harvest? *No doubt they have bills to pay*?'

Laugh if you will at M. de Balzac. I do not know the name of the painter whose honour it was to set the great novelist's soul a-quiver with anxiety and conjecture; but I think that in his way, with his delectable *naïveté*, he has given us an excellent lesson in criticism. You will often find me appraising a picture exclusively for the sum of ideas or of dreams that it suggests to my mind.

Painting is an evocation, a magical operation (if only we could consult the hearts of children on the subject!), and when the evoked character, when the reanimated idea has stood forth and looked us in the face, we have no right—at least it would be the acme of imbecility!—to discuss the magician's formulae of evocation. I know of no problem more mortifying for pedants and philosophizers than to attempt to discover in virtue of what law it is that artists who are the most opposed in their method can evoke the same ideas and stir up analogous feelings within us.

There is yet another, and very fashionable, error which I am anxious to avoid like the very devil. I refer to the idea of 'progress'. This gloomy beacon,[1] invention of present-day philosophizing, licensed without guarantee of Nature or of God—this modern lantern throws a stream of darkness upon all the objects of knowledge; liberty melts away, discipline vanishes. Anyone who wants to see his way clear through history must first and foremost extinguish this treacherous aid. This grotesque idea, which has flowered upon the rotten soil of modern fatuity, has discharged each man from his duty, has delivered each soul from its responsibility and has released the will from all the bonds imposed upon it by the love of the Beautiful. And if this disastrous folly lasts for long, the dwindling races of the earth will fall into the drivelling slumber of decrepitude upon the pillow of their destiny. Such an infatuation is the symptom of an already too obvious decadence.

Take any good Frenchman who reads *his* newspaper each day in *his* taproom, and ask him what he understands by 'progress'. He will answer that it is steam, electricity and gas—miracles unknown to the Romans—whose discovery bears full witness to our superiority over the ancients. Such is the darkness that has gathered in that unhappy brain, and so weird is the confusion of the material and the spiritual orders that prevails therein! The poor man has become so Americanized by zoöcratic and industrial philosophers that he has lost all notion of the differences which characterize the phenomena of the physical and the moral world—of the natural and the supernatural.[2]

If a nation understands the issues of morality with a greater refinement than they were understood in the previous century, then you have progress; that is clear enough. If this year an artist produces a work which gives evidence of greater knowledge or imaginative force than he showed last year, it is certain that he has made progress. If provisions are cheaper and of better quality today than they were yesterday, that is an indisputable example of progress in the material order. But where, I

[1] The whole passage from the words 'This gloomy beacon' (*Ce fanal obscur . . .*) down to 'its own eternal despair' (*son éternel désespoir*) was absent from the text as printed in *Le Pays*.

[2] See *Fusées* XXII: 'La mécanique nous aura tellement américanisés, le progrès aura si bien atrophié en nous toute la partie spirituelle, que rien parmi les rêveries sanguinaires, sacrilèges ou antinaturelles des utopistes ne pourra être comparé à ses résultats positifs. . . .' See also Andrew Lang's *Letters to Dead Authors* (1886), p. 148: '. . . By this time, of course, you [Poe] have made the acquaintance of your translator, M. Charles Baudelaire, who so strenuously shared your views about Mr. Emerson and the Transcendentalists, and who so energetically resisted all those ideas of "progress" which "came from Hell or Boston".'

ask you, is the guarantee that this progress will continue overnight? For that is how the disciples of the philosophers of steam and sulphur-matches understand it; progress only appears to them in the form of an unending series. But where *is* that guarantee? It does not exist, I tell you, except in your credulity and your fatuity.

I leave on one side the question of deciding whether, by continually refining humanity in proportion to the new enjoyments which it offers, indefinite progress would not be its most cruel and ingenious torture; whether, proceeding as it does by a stubborn negation of itself, it would not turn out to be a perpetually renewed form of suicide, and whether, shut up in the fiery circle of divine logic, it would not be like the scorpion which stings itself with its own terrible tail—progress, that eternal desideratum which is its own eternal despair!

Transported into the sphere of the imagination—and there have been hotheads, fanatics of logic who have attempted to do so—the idea of progress takes the stage with a gigantic absurdity, a grotesqueness which reaches nightmare heights. The theory can no longer be upheld. The facts are too palpable, too well known. They mock at sophistry and confront it without flinching. In the poetic and artistic order, the true prophets are seldom preceded by forerunners. Every efflorescence is spontaneous, individual. Was Signorelli really the begetter of Michelangelo? Did Perugino contain Raphael? The artist stems only from himself. His own works are the only promises that he makes to the coming centuries. He stands security only for himself. He dies childless. He has been his own king, his own priest, his own God. It is in prodigies like this that the famous and violent formula of Pierre Leroux finds its true application.[1]

It is just the same with the nations that joyfully and successfully cultivate the arts of the imagination. Present prosperity is no more than a temporary and alas! a very short-termed guarantee. There was a time when the dawn broke in the east; then the light moved towards the south, and now it streams forth from the west. It is true that France, by reason of her central position in the civilized world, seems to be summoned to gather to herself all the ideas, all the poetic products of her neighbours and to return them to other peoples, marvellously worked upon and embroidered. But it must never be forgotten that nations, those vast collective beings, are subject to the same laws as individuals. They have

[1] This sentence did not occur in the text as printed in *Le Pays*. Crépet relates it to a passage in Pierre Leroux's *La Grève de Samarez*, which was not published until 1863.

their childhood, in which they utter their first stammering cries and gradually grow in strength and size. They have their youth and maturity, the period of sound and courageous works. Finally they have their old age, when they fall asleep upon their piled-up riches. It often happens that it is the root principle itself that has constituted their strength, and the process of development that has brought with it their decadence—above all when that root principle, which was formerly quickened by an all-conquering enthusiasm, has become for the majority a kind of routine. Then, as I half suggested a moment ago, the vital spirit shifts and goes to visit other races and other lands. But it must not be thought that the newcomers inherit lock, stock and barrel from their predecessors or that they receive from them a ready-made body of doctrine. It often happens (as happened in the Middle Ages) that all being lost, all has to be re-fashioned.

Anyone who visited the *Exposition Universelle* with the preconceived idea of finding the children of Leonardo, Raphael and Michelangelo among the Italians, the spirit of Dürer among the Germans, or the soul of Zurbaran and Velasquez among the Spaniards, would be preparing himself for a needless shock. I have neither the time, nor perhaps sufficient knowledge, to investigate what are the laws which shift artistic vitality, or to discover why it is that God dispossesses the nations sometimes for a while only, and sometimes for ever; I content myself with noting a very frequent occurrence in history. We are living in an age in which it is necessary to go on repeating certain platitudes—in an arrogant age which believes itself to be above the misadventures of Greece and Rome.

The English section of the exhibition is very fine, most uncommonly fine, and worthy of a long and patient study. I had wanted to begin with a glorification of our neighbours, of that nation so admirably rich in poets and novelists, of the nation of Shakespeare, Crabbe, Byron, Maturin and Godwin; of the fellow-citizens of Reynolds, Hogarth and Gainsborough. But I want to study them further. I have an excellent excuse. It is only out of extreme politeness that I am putting off such a pleasurable task. I am biding my time in order to do better.[1]

[1] There is no evidence that Baudelaire's article on the English painters was ever written. But the passage devoted to English painters in the *Salon de 1859* (see pp. 145–6, below) was clearly based on notes and studies made at this time.

I begin therefore with an easier undertaking. I propose to make a rapid study of the principal masters of the French School, and to analyse the elements of progress or the seeds of dissolution that it contains within it.

II. INGRES

THE FRENCH SECTION of this Exhibition is at once so vast and is in general made up of such familiar items—quite enough of whose bloom has already been rubbed off by the artistic curiosity of the metropolis—that the duty of criticism should be to seek to penetrate deep into the temperament and activating motives of each artist, rather than to attempt to analyse and describe each work minutely.

When David, that icy star, rose above the horizon of art, with Guérin and Girodet (his historical satellites, who might be called the *dialecticians* of the party), a great revolution took place. Without analysing here the goal which they pursued; without endorsing its legitimacy or considering whether they did not overshoot it, let us state quite simply that they had a goal, a great goal which consisted in reaction against an excess of gay and charming frivolities, and which I want neither to appraise nor to define; further, that they fixed this goal steadfastly before their eyes, and that they marched by the light of their artificial sun with a frankness, a resolution and an *esprit de corps* worthy of true party-men. When the harsh idea softened and became tender beneath the brush of Gros, the cause was already lost.

I remember most distinctly the prodigious reverence which in the days of our childhood surrounded all those unintentionally fantastic figures, all those academic spectres—those elongated human freaks, those grave and lanky Adonises, those prudishly chaste and classically voluptuous women (the former shielding their modesty beneath antique swords, the latter behind pedantically transparent draperies)—believe me, I could not look at them without a kind of religious awe. And the whole of that truly extra-natural world was forever moving about, or rather *posing*, beneath a greenish light, a fantastic parody of the real sun. But these masters, who were once overpraised and today are over-scorned, had the great merit—if you will not concern yourself too much with their eccentric methods and systems—of bringing back the taste for heroism into the French character. That endless contemplation of Greek and Roman history could not, after all, but have a salutary, Stoic influence; but they were not always quite so Greek and Roman as they wished to appear. David, it is true, never ceased to be heroic—David the inflexible, the despotic evangelist. But as for Guérin and Girodet, it would not be hard to find in them a few slight specks of corruption, one or two amusing and sinister symptoms of future Romanticism—so dedicated were they, like their prophet, to the spirit of melodrama. Does it not seem to you that Guérin's *Dido* [1]—so affectedly and theatrically adorned, so languorously stretched out in the setting sun, like an indolent Creole woman—reveals more kinship with the first visions of Chateaubriand than with the conceptions of Virgil, and that her moist eye, bathed in the misty vapours of a Keepsake, almost looks forward to certain of Balzac's Parisian heroines? As for Girodet's *Atala*,[2] whatever certain ageing wags may think of it, as drama it is far superior to a whole crowd of unmentionable modern insipidities.

But today we are faced with a man of an immense and incontestable renown, whose work is very much more difficult to understand and to explain. A moment ago, in connection with those illustrious unfortunates, I was irreverently bold enough to utter the word 'freakish'. No one, then, could object if, in order to explain the sensation of certain sorts of artistic temperament when placed in contact with the works of M. Ingres, I say that they feel themselves face to face with a *freakishness* far more complex and mysterious than that of the masters of the Republican and Imperial school—whence, nevertheless, it took its point of departure.

Before broaching the subject more seriously, I am anxious to record a first impression which has been felt by many people and which they will inevitably remember the moment that they enter the sanctuary consecrated to the works of M. Ingres. This impression, which is hard to define—and which partakes, in unknown quantities, of uneasiness, boredom and fear—reminds one vaguely and involuntarily of the feelings of faintness induced by the rarefied air, the physical atmosphere, of a chemistry laboratory, or by the awareness that one is in the presence of an unearthly order of being; let me say, rather, of an order of being which *imitates* the unearthly—of an *automatic* population, whose too palpable and visible extraneity would make our senses swim. It is no longer that childlike reverence of which I spoke a moment ago—that reverence

[1] Exhibited at the 1817 Salon; now in the Louvre.

[2] Exhibited at the 1808 Salon; now in the Louvre.

which possessed us in front of the *Sabines*,[1] and of *The Dead Marat*[2]—in front of the *Déluge*[3] or the melodramatic *Brutus*.[1] It is a powerful sensation, it is true—why deny M. Ingres's power?—but of an inferior, an almost morbid variety. We might almost call it a negative sensation, if the phrase were admissible. In fact, as must be owned right away, this famous, and in his own way revolutionary, painter has merits—charms, even—which are so indisputable (and whose origin I shall shortly analyse) that it would be absurd not to record at this point a gap, a deficiency, a shrinkage in his stock of spiritual faculties. The Imagination, which sustained his great predecessors, lost though they were amid their academic gymnastics—the Imagination, that Queen of the Faculties, has vanished.

No more imagination: therefore no more movement. I do not propose to push irreverence and ill-will to the lengths of saying that this is an act of resignation on the part of M. Ingres; I have sufficient insight into his character to hold that with him it is an heroic immolation, a sacrifice upon the altar of those faculties which he sincerely considers as nobler and more important.

However enormous a paradox it may seem, it is in this particular that he comes near to a young painter whose remarkable début[4] took place recently with all the violence of an armed revolt. I refer of course to M. Courbet, who also is a mighty workman, a man of fierce and indomitable will; and the results that he has achieved—results that for certain minds have already more charm than those of the great master of the Raphaelesque tradition, owing doubtless to their positive solidity and their unabashed indelicacy[5]—have just the same peculiarity, in that they also reveal a dissenting spirit, a massacrer of faculties. Politics and literature, no less, produce robust temperaments like these—protestants, anti-supernaturalists, whose sole justification is a spirit of reaction which is sometimes salutary. The providence which presides over the affairs of painting gives them as confederates all those whom the ideas of the prevailing opposition have worn down or oppressed. But the difference is that the heroic sacrifice offered by M. Ingres in honour of the idea and

[1] By David; now in the Louvre.
[2] By David; now in the Brussels Museum. See pl. 10.
[3] By Girodet; now in the Louvre.
[4] Courbet held an exhibition of his own simultaneously with the *Exposition Universelle*.
[5] Such paintings as the *Baigneuses* (1853) had already caused some scandal.

the tradition of Raphaelesque Beauty is performed by M. Courbet on behalf of external, positive and immediate Nature. In their war against the imagination they are obedient to different motives; but their two opposing varieties of fanaticism lead them to the same immolation.

And now, to resume the regular course of our analysis, let us ask what is M. Ingres's goal. It is certainly not the translation of sentiments, emotions, or variations of those emotions and sentiments; no more is it the representation of great historical scenes (in spite of its Italianate, its over-Italianate, beauties, his picture of St. Symphorian,[1] which is Italianized down to the very congestion of its figures, does nothing to reveal the sublime glory of a Christian victim, nor the bestiality, at once savage and indifferent, of the orthodox heathen). What then is M. Ingres seeking? What are his dreams? What has he come into this world to say? What new appendix is he bringing to the gospel of Painting?

I would be inclined to believe that his ideal is a sort of ideal composed half of good health and half of a calm which amounts almost to indifference—something analogous to the antique ideal, to which he has added the frills and furbelows of modern art. It is just this coupling which often gives his works their singular charm. Thus smitten with an ideal which is an enticingly adulterous union between Raphael's calm solidity and the gewgaws of a *petite-maîtresse*, M. Ingres might be expected to succeed above all in portraiture; and in fact it is precisely in this genre that he has achieved his greatest and his most legitimate successes. But he is far from being one of those painters-by-the-hour, one of those routine portrait-factories to which a common lout can go, purse in hand, to demand the reproduction of his unseemly person. M. Ingres *chooses* his models, and it must be admitted that he brings a wonderful discernment to his choice of those that are best suited to exploit his special kind of talent. Beautiful women, rich and generous natures, embodiments of calm and flourishing health—here lies his triumph and his joy!

But at this point a question arises which has been a thousand times debated, and which is still worth returning to. What is the quality of M. Ingres's drawing? Is it of a superior order? is it absolutely *intelligent*? Anyone who has made a comparison of the graphic styles of the leading masters will understand me when I say that M. Ingres's drawing is the drawing of a man with a system. He holds that nature ought to be corrected, improved; he believes that a happily-contrived and agreeable

[1] In Autun Cathedral (Wildenstein 212).

artifice, which ministers to the eye's pleasure, is not only a right but a duty. Formerly it was said that nature must be interpreted and translated as a whole and in her total logic; but in the works of the present master, sleight-of-hand, trickery and violence are common occurrences, and sometimes downright deception and sharp-practice. Here we find an army of too-uniformly tapered fingers whose narrow extremities cramp the nails, such as a Lavater, on inspection of that ample bosom, that muscular forearm, that somewhat virile frame, would have expected to be square-tipped—indicative of a mind given to masculine pursuits, to the symmetry and disciplines of art. Here again we find a sensitive face and shoulders of a simple elegance associated with arms too robust, too full of a Raphaelesque opulence. But Raphael loved stout arms, and the first thing required was to obey and to please the master. Elsewhere we shall find a navel which has strayed in the direction of the ribs, or a breast which points too much towards the armpit; and in one place—a thing less pardonable, for generally these various conjuring-tricks have a more or less plausible excuse, and one that can always be easily traced to his immoderate appetite for *style*—in one place, I say, we are utterly baffled by an egregious leg, thin as a lath, with neither muscles nor contours, and without even a fold at the knee-joint (*Jupiter and Antiope* [1]).

Let us note further that, carried away as he is by this almost morbid preoccupation with *style*, our painter often does away with his modelling, or reduces it to the point of invisibility, hoping thus to give more importance to the contour, so that his figures look like the most correct of paper-patterns, inflated in a soft, lifeless manner, and one quite alien to the human organism. Sometimes it happens that the eye falls upon charming details, irreproachably alive; but at once the wicked notion flashes across the mind, that it is not M. Ingres who has been seeking nature, but Nature that has *ravished* M. Ingres—that that high and mighty dame has overpowered him by her irresistible ascendency.

From all that goes before, the reader will easily understand that M. Ingres may be considered as a man endowed with lofty qualities, an eloquent amateur of beauty, but quite devoid of that energy of temperament which constitutes the fatality of genius. His dominant preoccupations are his taste for the antique and his respect for the School. His admiration, on the whole, is fairly easily bestowed, and his character is somewhat eclectic, like all men who are lacking in fatality. And so we

[1] Now in the Louvre (Wildenstein 265).

see him wandering from archaism to archaism; Titian (*The Sistine Chapel* [1]), the Renaissance enamellers (*Venus Anadyomene* [2]), Poussin and the Carracci (*Venus* and *Antiope*), Raphael (*St. Symphorian*), the German primitives (all those little things in an anecdotal, picture-book style), antique bric-à-brac and the chequered colouring of Persian and Chinese art (the small *Odalisque* [3]), are forever disputing for his preference. The love and influence of antiquity make themselves felt throughout his work; but it often seems to me that M. Ingres is to antiquity what the transitory caprices of good taste are to the natural good manners which spring from the dignity and charity of the individual.

It is above all in the *Apotheosis of the Emperor Napoleon* [4]—the picture that has been lent from the Hôtel de Ville—that M. Ingres has let his taste for the Etruscans be revealed. And yet, great simplifiers as they were, even the Etruscans never pushed simplification to the lengths of not harnessing their horses to their chariots! But these supernatural horses of M. Ingres (what, by the way, are they made of, these horses that seem to be of some polished, solid substance, like the wooden horse that captured the city of Troy?)—can it be that they are endowed with some magnetic force, that they are able to drag the car behind them with neither traces nor harness? As for the figure of the emperor himself, I feel bound to say that it gave me no hint of that epic and fatal beauty with which his contemporaries and historians generally endowed him; and further, that it distresses me not to see the outward and legendary characteristics of great men preserved, and that the populace, agreeing with me in this, can hardly imagine its favourite hero except in his official, ceremonial robes, or in that historic iron-grey cloak, which, with all due deference to the fanatical amateurs of Style, would do nothing to mar a modern apotheosis.

But there is a more serious criticism to be made of this work. The cardinal feature of an apotheosis ought to be its supernatural feeling, a power of ascent towards loftier regions, an impulse, an irresistible surge towards Heaven, the goal of every human aspiration and classic abode

[1] Now in the Louvre (Wildenstein 131).
[2] Now in the Musée Condé, Chantilly (Wildenstein 257).
[3] Presumably the *Odalisque with Slave*, which was exhibited at the *Exposition Universelle*, and is now in the Fogg Art Museum, Cambridge, Mass. (Wildenstein 228).
[4] Painted for the ceiling of the Salon de l'Empereur in the Hôtel de Ville. It was completed at the end of 1853, and destroyed by fire in 1871 (Wildenstein 270). There is a sketch for it at the Musée Carnavalet, Paris (Wildenstein 271). See pl. 28.

of all great men. Well, *this* apotheosis, or rather this *equipage*, is falling—falling with a speed proportionate to its weight. The horses are dragging the chariot earthwards. The whole thing, like a fully-ballasted balloon without gas, is inevitably going to smash itself to bits on the surface of the globe.

As for his *Joan of Arc*,[1] a picture whose most obvious distinction is an inordinate technical pedantry—I do not trust myself to speak of it. However lacking in sympathy towards M. Ingres I may have appeared in the eyes of his fanatical admirers, I prefer to believe that the loftiest talent always reserves certain rights to make mistakes. Here, as in the *Apotheosis*, there is a total absence of sentiment and supernaturalism. We look in vain for that noble virgin who, according to the promises of the good M. Delécluze, was to avenge herself, and us, upon the scurrilous attacks of Voltaire. To sum up, and setting aside his erudition and his intolerant and almost wanton taste for beauty, I believe that the faculty which has made M. Ingres what he is—the mighty, the indisputable, the absolute despot—is the power of his will, or rather an immense abuse of that power. On the whole, what he is now he has been from the very start. And thanks to that vital energy which he possesses, he will remain the same to the end. As he has not progressed, he will not grow old. His over-passionate admirers will always be what they were—in love to the point of blindness; and nothing will change in France—not even the eccentric habit of taking over from a great artist those odd qualities which can only belong to him; and of imitating the inimitable.

A thousand lucky circumstances have combined in the establishment of this formidable renown. He has commanded the respect of polite society by his ostentatious love of antiquity and the great tradition. The eccentric, the *blasé* and the thousand fastidious spirits who are always looking for something new, even if it has a bitter taste—all these he has pleased by his *oddness*. But his good, or at all events his *engaging*, qualities have produced a lamentable effect in the crowd of his imitators; and this is a fact that I shall have more than one opportunity of demonstrating.

III. EUGÈNE DELACROIX

MM. Eugène Delacroix and Ingres share between them the support and the antipathy of the public. It is a long time since popular

[1] Now in the Louvre (Wildenstein 273).

opinion first drew a cordon round them, like a pair of wrestlers. But without giving our acceptance to this childish and vulgar love of antithesis, we must nevertheless begin by an examination of these two French masters, since around and below them are grouped and ranged almost all the individuals who go to make up our artistic company.

Faced with thirty-five pictures by M. Delacroix, the first idea to take possession of the spectator is the idea of a well-filled life, of a stubborn and unremitting love of art. Which of these pictures is the finest?—it is impossible to say. Which the most interesting?—one hesitates. Here and there one seems to detect instances of progress; but if some of the more recent pictures show that certain important qualities have been pushed to their extreme limits, it is humbling for the impartial critic to have to recognize that from his earliest productions, from his very youth (*Dante and Virgil* dates from 1822) M. Delacroix has possessed greatness. At times perhaps he has been more subtle, at times more curious, at times more painterly—but he has never ceased to be great.

In[1] the presence of a destiny so nobly and so happily fulfilled, a destiny blessed by nature and consummated by the most admirable power of will, I am conscious of some lines by one of our great poets, ceaselessly echoing in my mind:

Il naît sous le soleil de nobles créatures
Unissant ici-bas tout ce qu'on peut rêver;
Corps de fer, coeurs de flamme, admirables natures!

Dieu semble les produire afin de se prouver;
Il prend, pour les pétrir, une argile plus douce,
Et souvent passe un siècle à les parachever.

Il met comme un sculpteur, l'empreinte de son pouce
Sur leurs fronts rayonnants de la gloire des cieux,
Et l'ardente auréole en gerbes d'or y pousse.

Ces hommes-là s'en vont, calmes et radieux,
Sans quitter un instant leur pose solennelle,
Avec l'oeil immobile et le maintien des dieux.

. . . .

[1] The following paragraph, with Gautier's poem and the sentence which rounds it off, were not in the text as printed in 1855.

Ne leur donnez qu'un jour ou donnez-leur cent ans,
L'orage ou le repos, la palette ou le glaive:
Il mèneront à bout leurs destins éclatants.

Leur existence étrange est le réel du rêve;
Ils exécuteront votre plan idéal,
Comme un maître savant le croquis d'un élève.

Vos désirs inconnus, sous l'arceau triomphal,
Dont votre esprit en songe arrondissait la voûte,
Passent assis en croupe au dos de leur cheval.

. . . .

De ceux-là chaque peuple en compte cinq ou six,
Cinq ou six, tout au plus, dans les siècles prospères,
Types toujours vivants dont on fait des récits.[1]

Théophile Gautier calls this a '*Compensation*'.[2] And could not M. Delacroix fill up the vacant spaces of a whole century entirely on his own?

Never was an artist more attacked, more held up to ridicule, or more thwarted. But what care we for the hesitations of governments (I speak of some years ago), the scoldings of a few bourgeois salons, the spiteful tracts of a smoking-room academy or two, or the pedantry of domino-players? *Probatum est*, the matter has been settled once and for all, the result is before our eyes in its manifest, immense and blazing truth.

M. Delacroix has practised every genre; his imagination and his learning have ranged over every inch of the territory of painting. He has

[1] 'Noble creatures are sometimes born under the sun; earthly epitomes of all that one dreams of—bodies of iron, hearts of flame, glorious spirits. God seems to produce them so as to prove Himself; He takes a softer clay to mould them, and often spends a century in bringing them to perfection. Like a sculptor, He places the print of His thumb on their brows, which shine with the glory of the heavens; their fiery haloes burgeon in rays of gold.

Calm or radiant they go their way, never for a moment abandoning their solemn gait, with the motionless eye and the bearing of the gods. . . . Give them but one day, or give them a hundred years, tumult or tranquillity, the palette or the sword: they will fulfil their shining destinies. Their strange existence is the reality of the dream; they will carry out your ideal plan, as a clever master carries out a pupil's sketch. Through the triumphal arch which you have built in dreams, your unknown desires will ride behind them on their steeds. . . . Of such men each nation can count five or six at the most, in prosperous ages, ever-living symbols of which legends are made.'

[2] From *La Comédie de la Mort* (1838).

painted charming little pictures, filled with depth and intimate feeling—and with what a loving sensitivity has he painted them! He has glorified the walls of our palaces: he has filled our museums with enormous compositions.

This year he has most rightfully availed himself of the opportunity of showing a fairly considerable portion of his life's work, and thus of making us reconsider, so to speak, the documents of the case. The collection has been most discerningly assembled, so as to provide us with a set of varied and decisive samples of his mind and his talent.

We start with *Dante and Virgil*,[1] that young man's picture which was a revolution in itself, and in which one figure (the upturned male torso) was for long falsely attributed to Géricault. Among the big pictures, we may perhaps be allowed to hesitate between the *Justice of Trajan*[2] and the *Taking of Constantinople by the Crusaders*.[1] The former is such a marvellously luminous picture, so airy, so full of tumult and splendour! How handsome the Emperor! how turbulent the crowd as it twists round the columns or moves along with the procession! how dramatic the weeping widow! This is the picture that was immortalized some years ago by the egregious M. Karr[3] and his little jokes about *pink horses*—as if some horses were not slightly pink, and as if in any case a painter had not a perfect right to do them that way if he wished!

But quite apart from its subject-matter, what makes the second picture so deeply moving is its tempestuous and gloomy harmony. What a sky, and what a sea! All is tumult and tranquillity, as in the aftermath of a great event. The city, ranged behind the Crusaders who have just passed through it, stretches back into the distance with a miraculous truth. And everywhere the fluttering and waving of flags, unfurling and snapping their bright folds in the transparent atmosphere! Everywhere the restless, stirring crowd, the tumult of arms, the ceremonial splendour of the clothes, and a rhetorical truth of gesture amid the great occasions of life! These two pictures are of an essentially Shakespearian beauty. For after Shakespeare, no one has excelled like Delacroix in fusing a mysterious unity of drama and reverie.

The public will renew acquaintance with all those pictures of stormy memory which were in themselves revolts, struggles and triumphs: the

[1] Now in the Louvre.

[2] Now in the Rouen Museum; reproduced *Journal*, pl. 27.

[3] Alphonse Karr (1808–90), novelist, journalist and occasional art-critic.

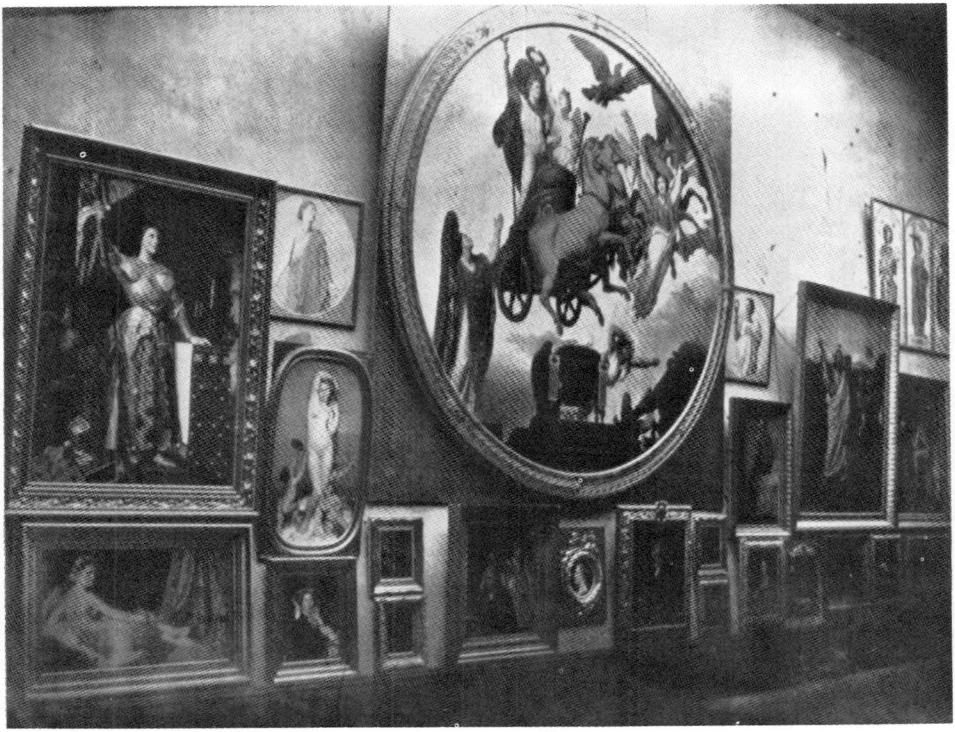

28. The Ingres Gallery at the Exposition Universelle, 1855. Contemporary photograph. London, Victoria and Albert Museum.

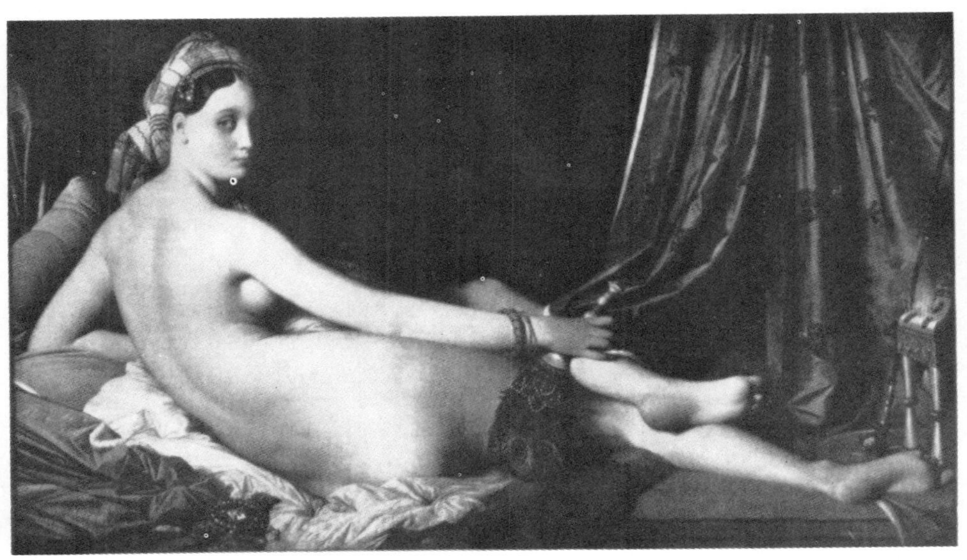

29. INGRES: *The 'Grande Odalisque'*. Dated 1814. Paris, Musée du Louvre.

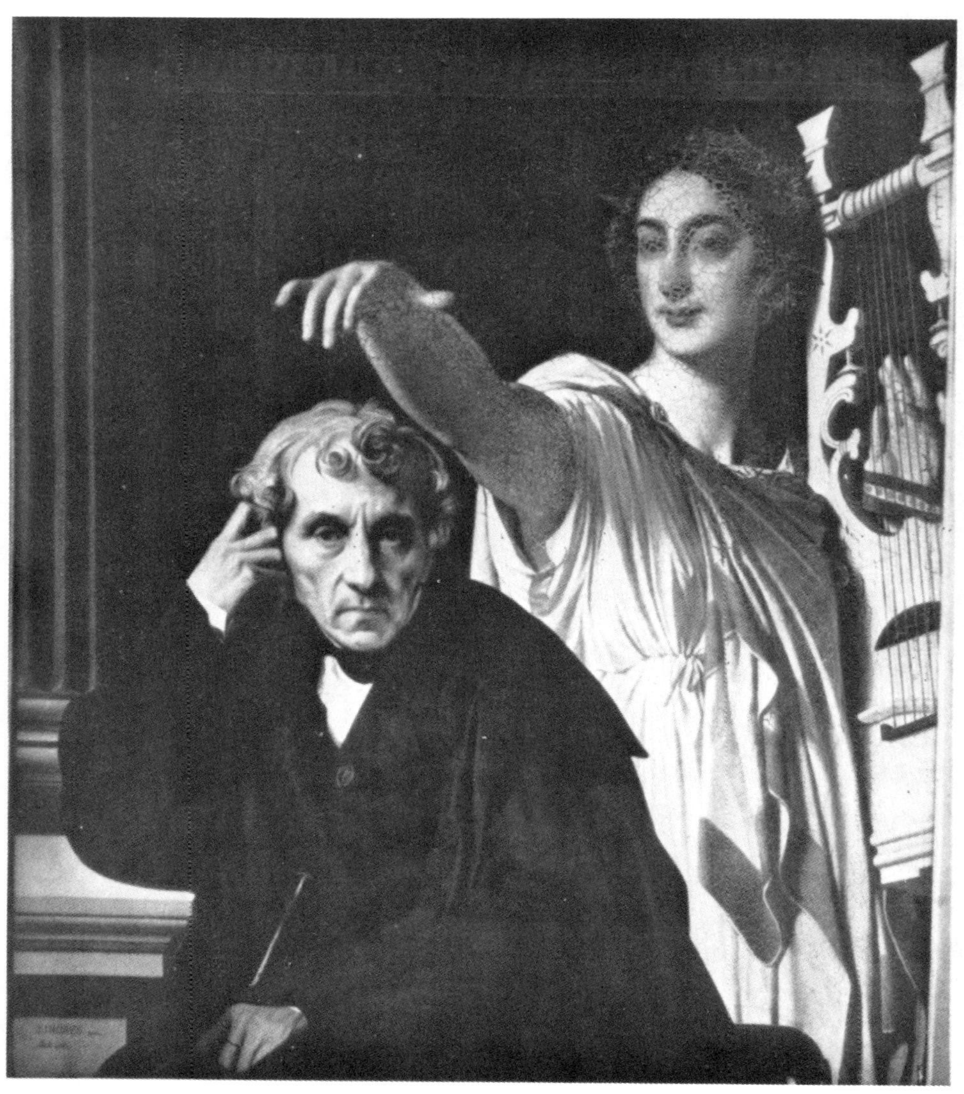

30. INGRES: *Cherubini and his Muse*. Dated 1842. Paris, Musée du Louvre.

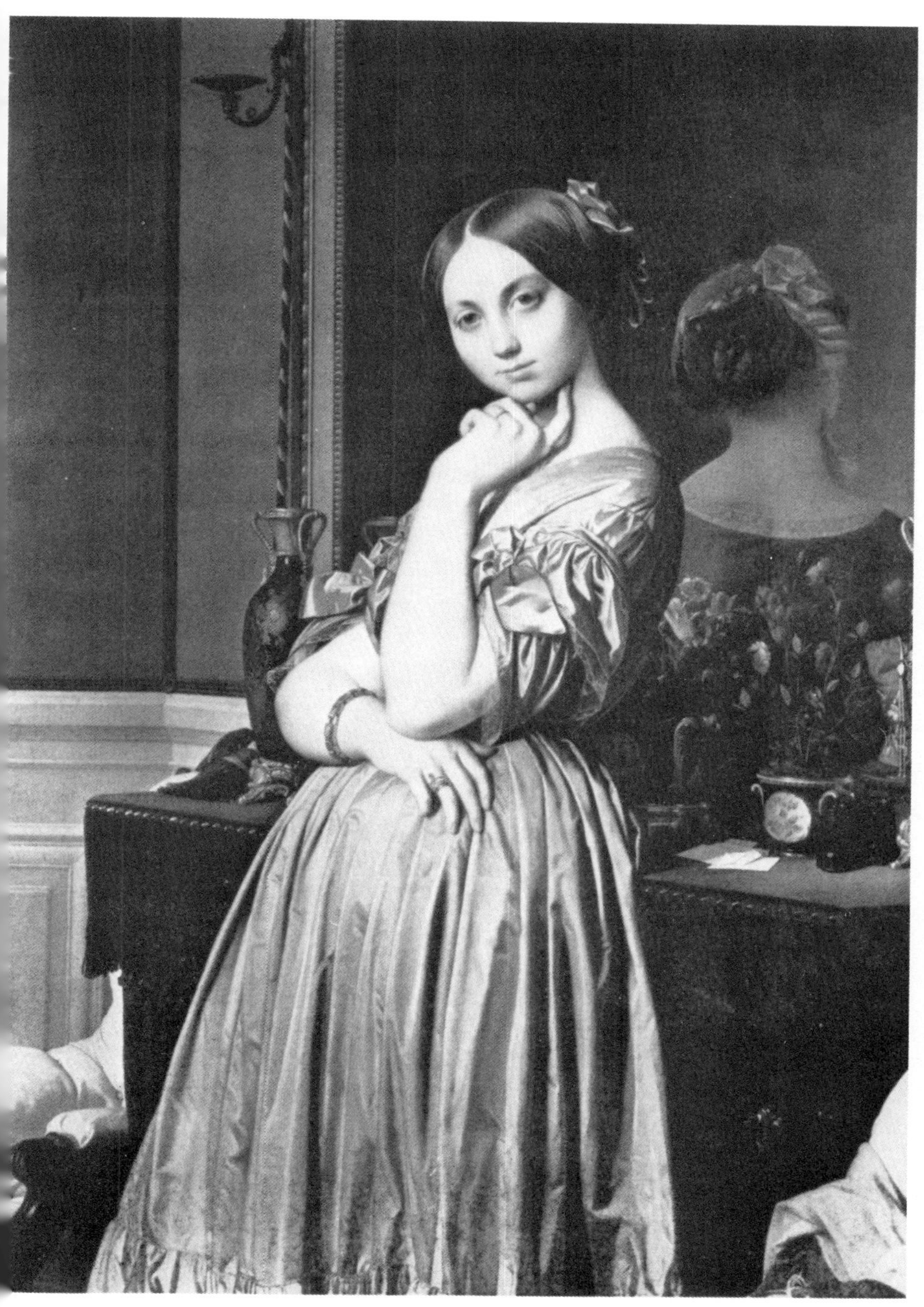

31. INGRES: *The Comtesse d'Haussonville*. Dated 1845. New York, Frick Collection.

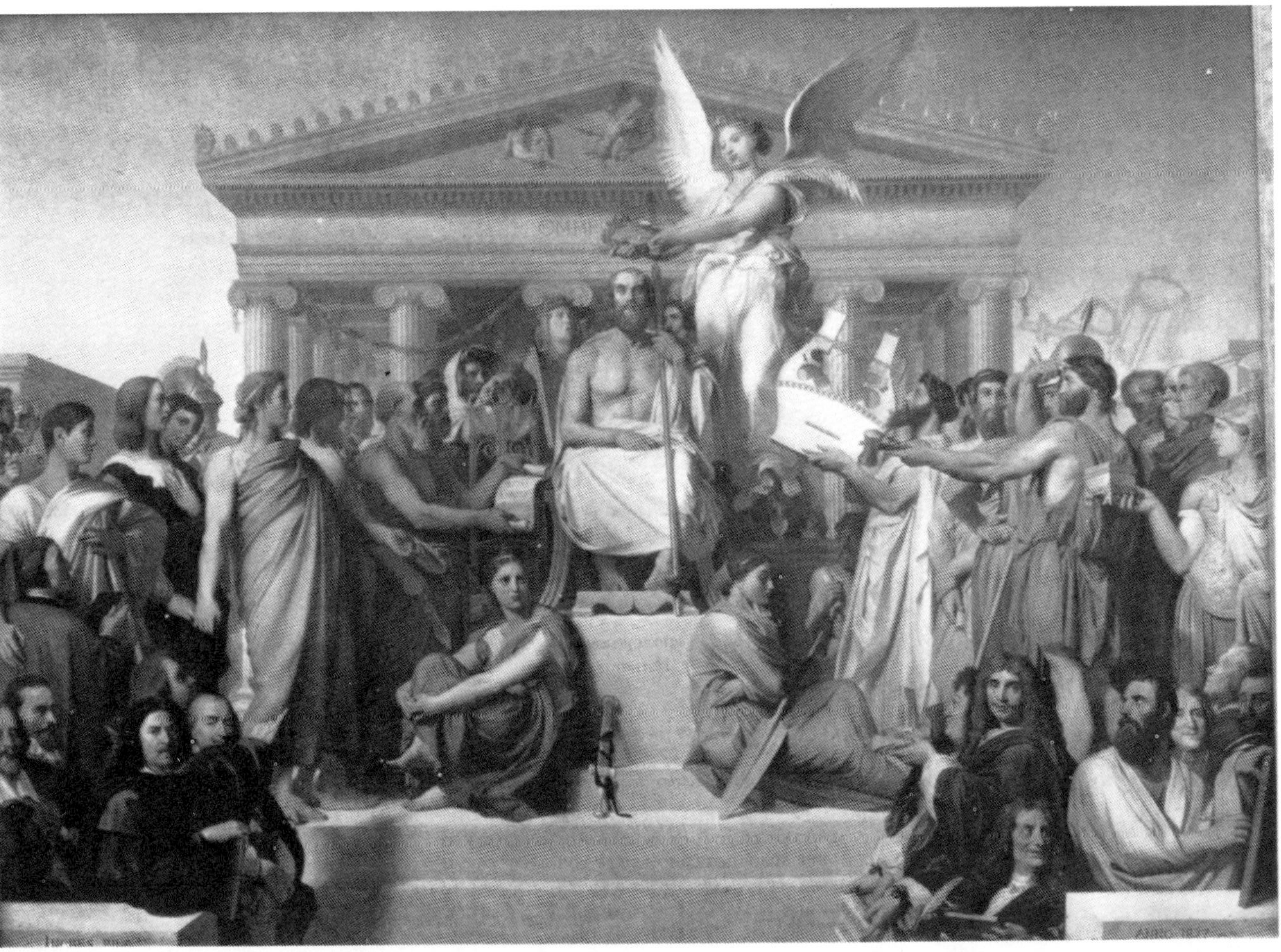
ΟΜΗΡ
ANNO 1827

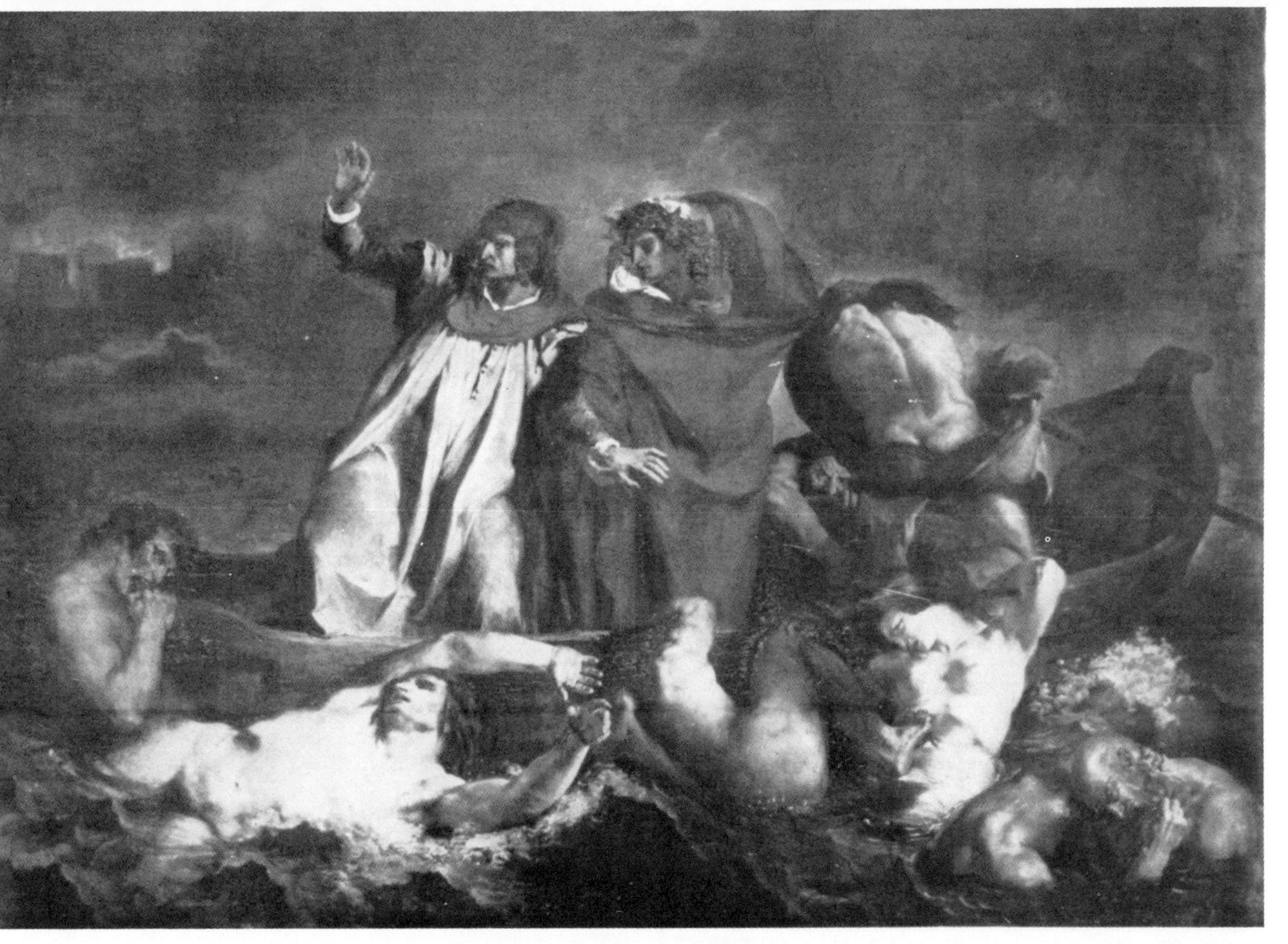

33. Delacroix: *Dante and Virgil*. Salon of 1822. Paris, Musée du Louvre.

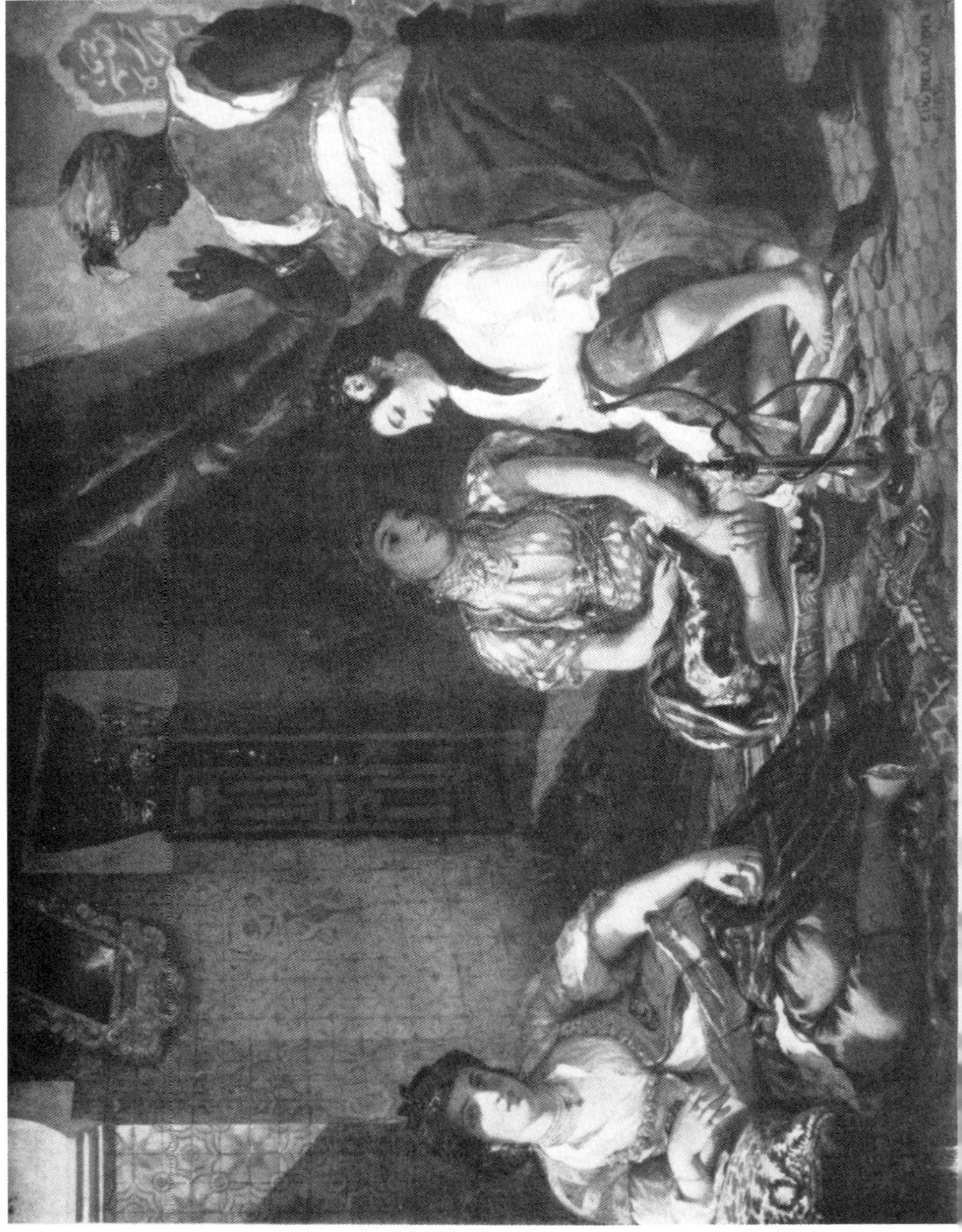

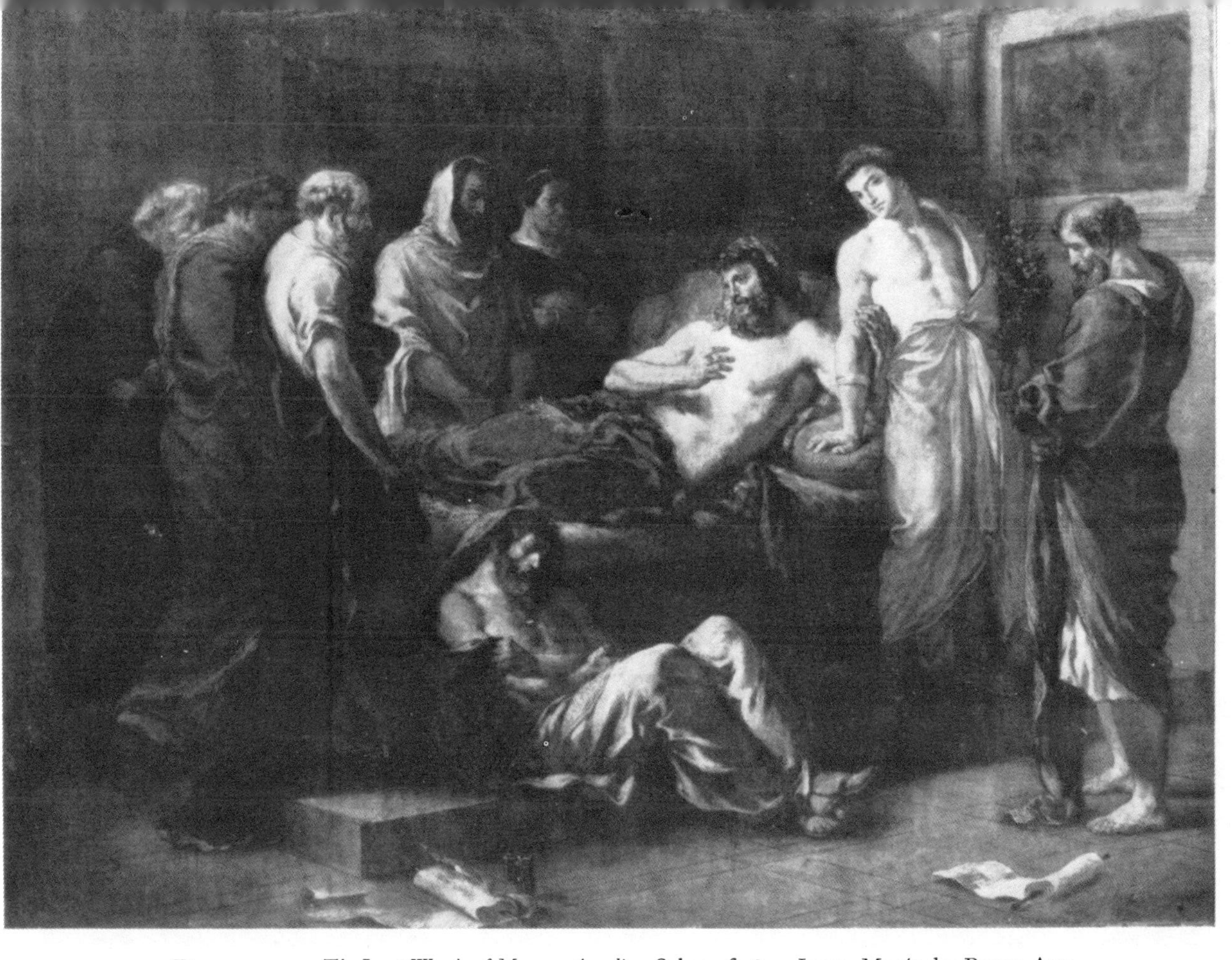

35. DELACROIX: *The Last Words of Marcus Aurelius*. Salon of 1845. Lyon, Musée des Beaux-Arts.

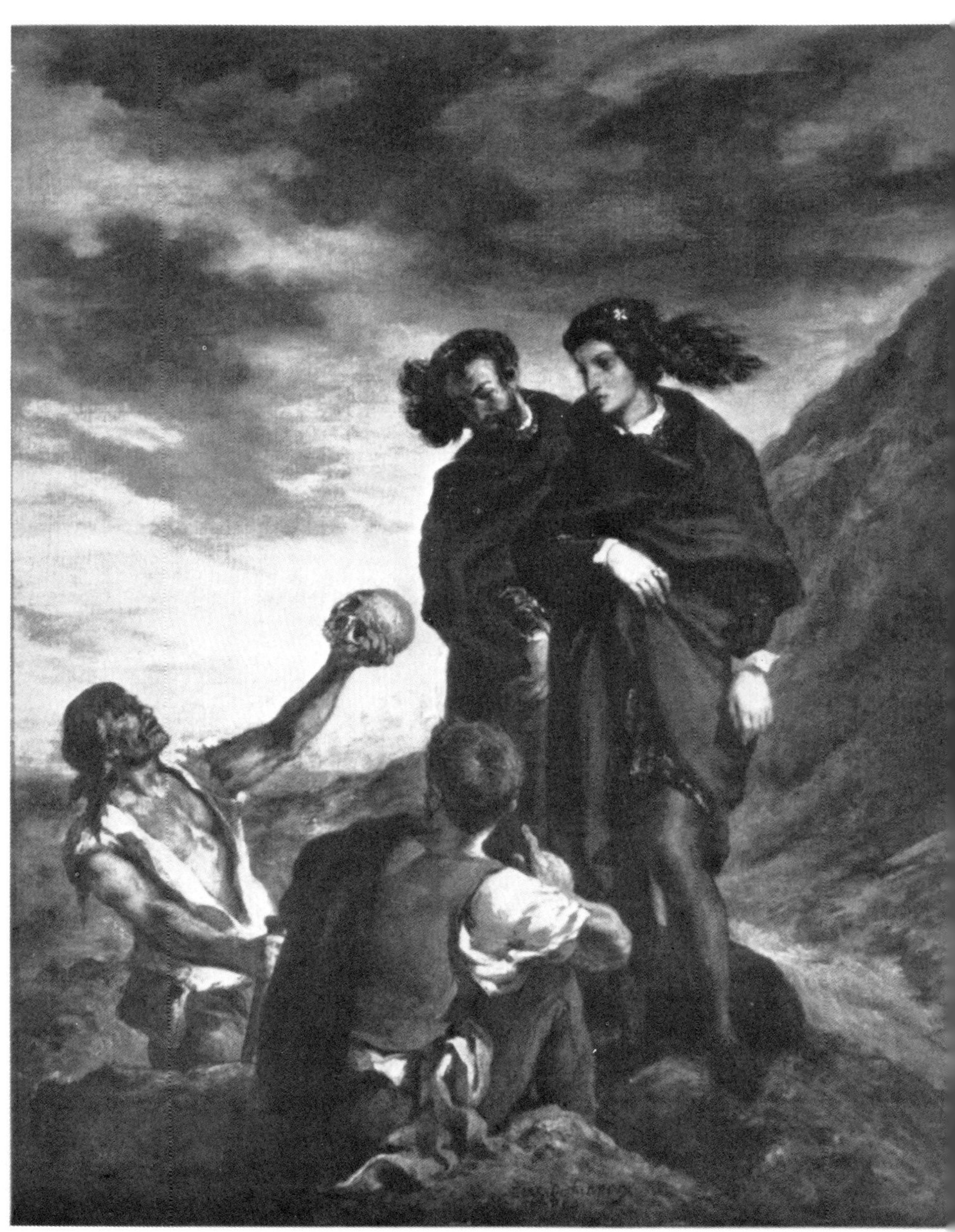

36. DELACROIX: *Hamlet and the Gravedigger*. Salon of 1839. Paris, Musée du Louvre.

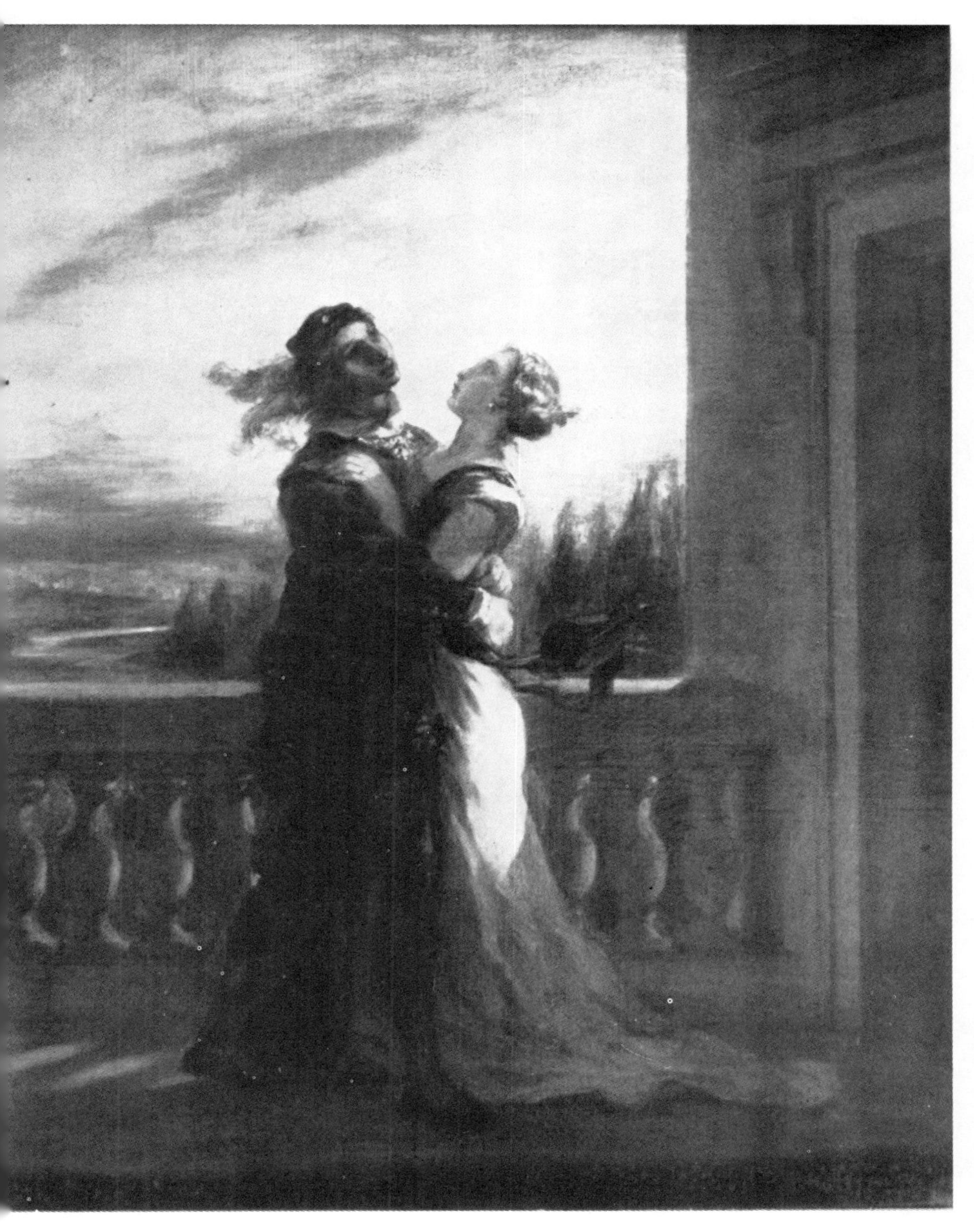

37. DELACROIX: *Romeo and Juliet*. Salon of 1846. Basle, Dr. Robert von Hirsch.

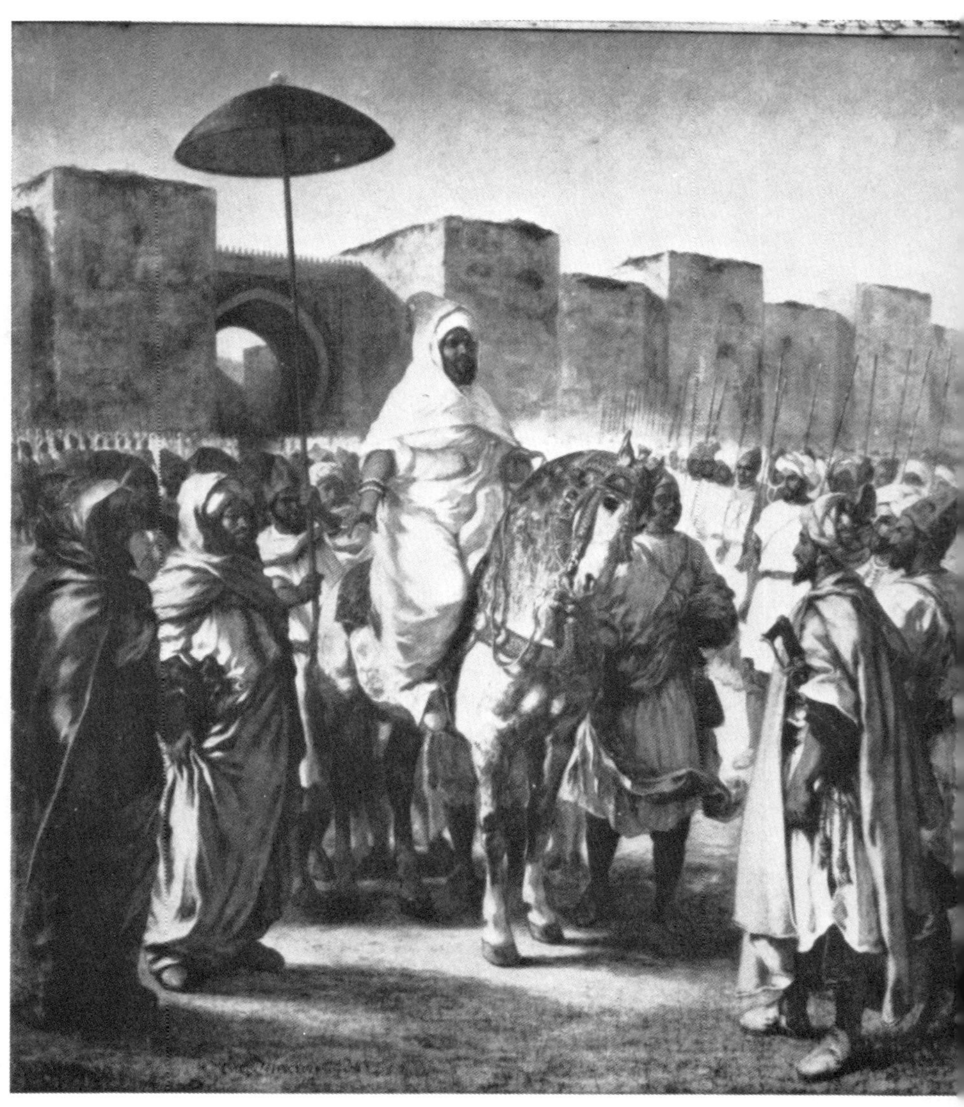

38. Delacroix: *The Sultan of Morocco with his Bodyguard*. Salon of 1845. Toulouse, Musée des Augustins.

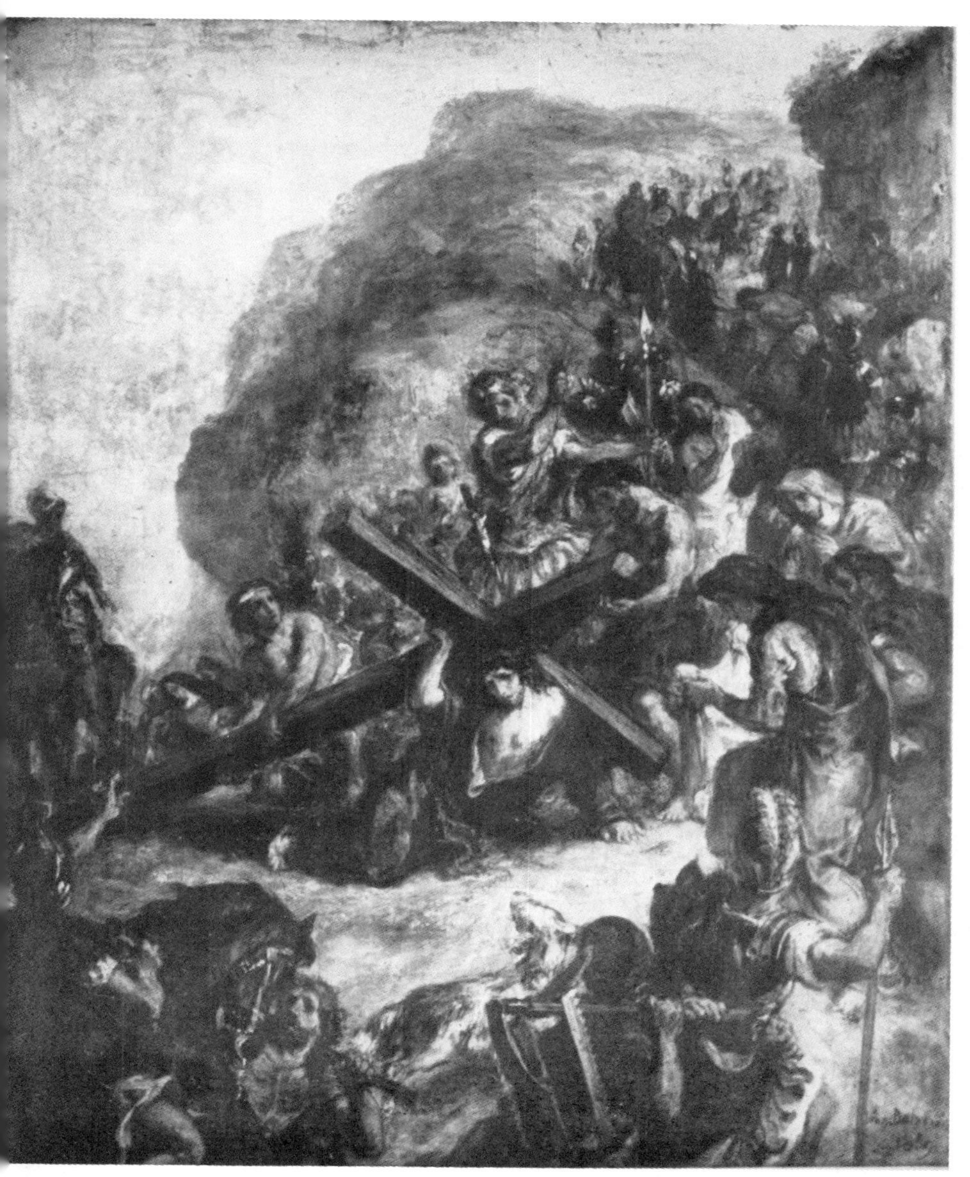

39. DELACROIX: *The Ascent to Calvary*. Salon of 1859. Metz, Musée Central.

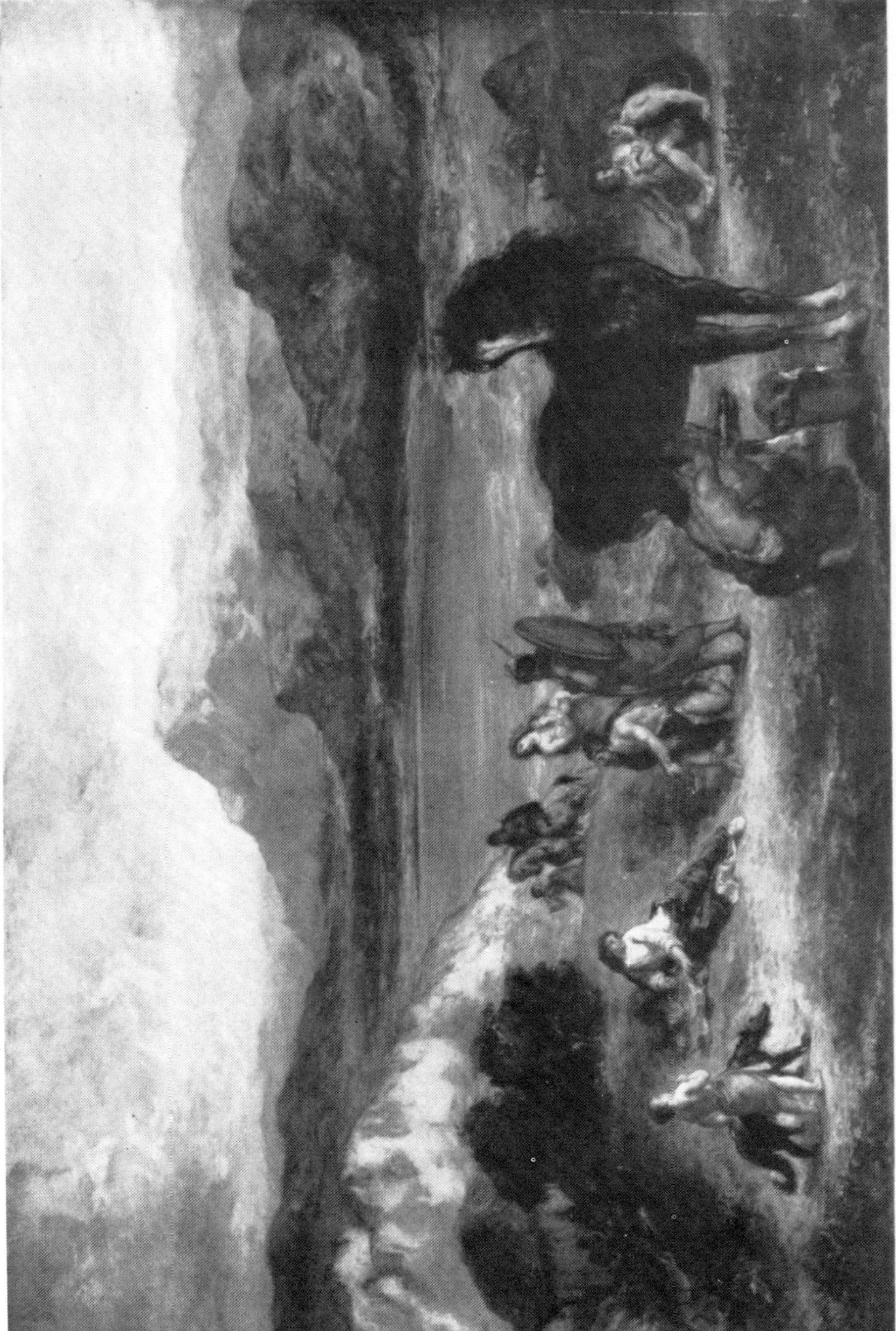

Doge Marino Faliero [1] (Salon of 1827. It is curious to note that *Justinian drafting his Laws* [2] and the *Christ in the Garden of Olives* [3] are of the same year); the *Bishop of Liège*,[4] that admirable translation of Walter Scott, all crowd, bustle and light; the *Massacre at Chios* ;[4] the *Prisoner of Chillon* ;[4] the *Tasso in Prison* ;[5] the *Jewish Wedding* ;[4] the *Convulsionaries of Tangier*,[6] etc. But how is one to define that charming class of picture, such as the *Hamlet in the Graveyard Scene*,[4] and the *Farewell of Romeo and Juliet*,[7] which are so deeply moving and attractive that once it has bathed in their little worlds of melancholy, the eye can no longer escape them, and the mind is forever in their thrall?

Et le tableau quitté nous *tourmente et* nous *suit*.[8]

But this is not the Hamlet which Rouvière [9] showed us recently, and with such brilliant success—the sour, unhappy, violent Hamlet, driving his restlessness to the pitch of frenzy. There you have the romantic *strangeness* of the great tragedian; but Delacroix, more faithful perhaps to his text, has shown us a delicate and pallid Hamlet, a Hamlet with white, feminine hands, a refined, soft and somewhat irresolute nature, and an almost colourless eye.

Here too is the famous upturned head of the Magdalen,[10] with her strange, mysterious smile, and so supernaturally beautiful that you cannot tell whether she has been transfigured by death or beautified by the spasms of divine love.

On the subject of the *Romeo and Juliet* I have an observation to make which I believe to be of no little importance. I have heard so much fun made of the *ugliness* of Delacroix's women—though without being able to understand that kind of fun—that I welcome the opportunity of

[1] Now in the Wallace Collection; reproduced *Journal*, pl. 7.

[2] Burnt in 1871.

[3] Church of Saint-Paul-Saint-Louis.

[4] Now in the Louvre.

[5] Private collection, England.

[6] Now in the collection of Mrs Jerome Hill, New York.

[7] See pl. 56.

[8] 'And once left, the picture torments and follows us.' From the *Terza Rima* in Gautier's *Comédie de la mort*.

[9] The actor Philibert Rouvière had played the part of Hamlet at the Théâtre Historique, December 1847, in Dumas and Meurice's version of the play. Baudelaire, published an enthusiastic article on Rouvière in 1855 (reprinted in *L'Art Romantique*). Manet's *L'Acteur Tragique* represents Rouvière as Hamlet.

[10] 1845 Salon: see pp. 3–4. above.

protesting against this misguided notion, which was shared, I understand, by M. Victor Hugo. You will remember how, in the high summer of Romanticism, he deplored the fact that the man who enjoyed a parallel glory to his own in the eyes of the public should commit such monstrous errors in respect of beauty. He went so far as to liken Delacroix's women to *frogs*. But M. Victor Hugo is a great *sculptural* poet whose eye is closed to spirituality.

I am sorry that the *Sardanapalus* [1] has not reappeared this year, for there you would have seen some very beautiful women, bright and shining and pink—to the best of my recollection. And Sardanapalus himself was beautiful as a woman. Generally speaking, Delacroix's women may be divided into two classes. Those of the first class, who present no difficulties to the understanding and are often mythological, are of necessity beautiful (for example the recumbent nymph, seen from behind, in the ceiling of the Galerie d'Apollon [2]). They are rich, robust, opulent, abundant women, and are endowed with a wonderful transparency of flesh and superb heads of hair.

But the others, who are sometimes historical women (like the *Cleopatra* [3] looking at the asp), but are more often women of fancy, of *genre*—Marguerites, Ophelias, even Blessed Virgins or Magdalens—these I would be inclined to call 'women in intimacy'. Their eyes seem heavy with some painful secret which cannot be buried in the grave of secrecy. Their pallor is like a revelation of their internal struggles. Whether they owe their distinction to the fascination of crime or to the odour of sanctity, and whether their gestures are languid or violent, these women, sick at heart or in mind, have in their eyes the leaden hues of fever, or the strange, abnormal sparkle of their malady—and, in their glance, the intensity of a supernatural vision.

But always, and in spite of everything, these are distinguished, essentially *distinguished* women; and if I am to put the whole thing in a nutshell, I would say that M. Delacroix seems to me to be of all artists the best equipped to express modern woman, and, above all, modern woman in her heroic manifestation, in the divine or the infernal interpretation of the word. These women even have the physical beauty of today, that

[1] Now in the Louvre; reproduced *Journal*, pl. 8, and (detail) *Painter of Modern Life*, pl. 27.

[2] In the Louvre; sketch reproduced *Journal*, pl. 33.

[3] In a private collection, Switzerland.

air of reverie (for all the fullness of their breasts), with their slightly narrow ribs, their broad hips and their charming limbs.

Some of these paintings are new and unknown to the public; such are the *Two Foscari*,[1] the *Arab Family*,[2] the *Lion Hunt*[3] and a *Head of an Old Woman*[4] (a portrait by M. Delacroix is a rarity). These different paintings serve to demonstrate the prodigious sureness which the master has achieved. The *Lion Hunt* is a veritable *explosion* of colour (the word is intended in its good sense). Never can colours more beautiful or more intense have penetrated to the soul through the channel of the eyes!

The minute and careful examination of these pictures can only reinforce certain irrefutable truths suggested by a first rapid and generalized glance. First of all it is to be noted—and this is very important—that even at a distance too great for the spectator to be able to analyse or even to comprehend its subject-matter, a picture by Delacroix will already have produced a rich, joyful or melancholy impression upon the soul. It almost seems as though this kind of painting, like a magician or a hypnotist, can project its thought at a distance. This curious phenomenon results from the colourist's special power, from the perfect concord of his tones and from the harmony, which is pre-established in the painter's brain, between colour and subject-matter. If the reader will pardon me a stratagem of language in order to express an idea of some subtlety, it seems to me that M. Delacroix's colour *thinks for itself*, independently of the objects which it clothes. Further, these wonderful *chords* of colour often give one ideas of melody and harmony, and the impression that one takes away from his pictures is often, as it were, a musical one. A[5] poet has attempted to express these subtle sensations in some lines whose sincerity must excuse their singularity:

Delacroix, lac de sang, hanté des mauvais anges,
Ombragé par un bois de sapins toujours vert,
Où, sous un ciel chagrin, des fanfares étranges
Passent comme un soupir étouffé de Weber.[6]

[1] Now at the Musée Condé, Chantilly.
[2] In a private collection, Paris.
[3] Now in the Bordeaux Museum; reproduced *Journal*, pl. 55.
[4] In a private collection, France.
[5] The passage from this sentence down to the end of the paragraph was not in the text as printed in 1855.
[6] From *Les Phares* (*Les Fleurs du Mal*, VI), which was not published until 1857.

Lac de sang (lake of blood)—the colour red; *hanté des mauvais anges* (haunted by bad angels)—supernaturalism; *un bois toujours vert* (an evergreen wood)—the colour green, the complementary of red; *un ciel chagrin* (a sullen sky)—the turbulent, stormy backgrounds of his pictures; *les fanfares et Weber* (fanfares, and Weber)—ideas of romantic music awakened by the harmonies of his colour.

Of Delacroix's drawing, which has been so absurdly and so banally criticized, what am I to say, except that it is one of those elementary truths which are completely misunderstood? What am I to say, except that a good drawing is not a hard, cruel, despotic and rigid line, imprisoning a form like a strait-jacket? that drawing should be like nature, alive and in motion? that simplification in drawing is a monstrosity, like tragedy in the world of the theatre, and that nature presents us with an infinite series of curved, receding and crooked lines, following an impeccable law of generation, in which parallelism is always vague and sinuous, and concavities and convexities correspond with and pursue one another? and, last of all, that M. Delacroix admirably satisfies all these conditions, and that even though his drawing may admit of occasional weaknesses or excesses, it has at least the enormous merit of being a constant and effective protest against the barbarous invasion of the straight line—that tragic, systematic line whose present ravages in painting and in sculpture are already enormous?

Another very great and far-reaching quality of M. Delacroix's talent, and one which makes him the painter beloved of the poets, is that he is essentially literary. Not only has his art ranged—and successfully ranged—over the field of the great literatures of the world; not only has it translated, and been the companion of, Ariosto, Byron, Dante, Scott and Shakespeare, but it has the power of revealing ideas of a loftier, a subtler and a deeper order than the art of the majority of modern painters. And rest assured that it is never by means of a mere feint, by a trifle or a trick of the brush, that M. Delacroix achieves this prodigious result; rather is it by means of the total effect, the profound and perfect harmony between his colour, his subject-matter and his drawing, and the dramatic gesticulation of his figures.

Edgar Poe has it somewhere [1] that the effect of opium upon the senses is to invest the whole of nature with a supernatural intensity of interest, which gives to every object a deeper, a more wilful, a more despotic

[1] In *A Tale of the Ragged Mountains.*

meaning. Without having recourse to opium, who has not known those miraculous moments—veritable feast-days of the brain—when the senses are keener and sensations more ringing, when the firmament of a more transparent blue plunges headlong into an abyss more infinite, when sounds chime like music, when colours speak, and scents tell of whole worlds of ideas? Very well then, M. Delacroix's painting seems to me to *translate* those fine days of the soul. It is invested with intensity, and splendour is its special privilege. Like nature apprehended through extra-sensitive nerves, it reveals what lies beyond nature.

How will M. Delacroix stand with Posterity? what will that righter of wrongs have to say of him? He has now reached a point in his career at which it is already easy to give the answer without finding too many to contradict one. Like us, Posterity will say that he was an unique meeting-place of the most astonishing faculties; that like Rembrandt he had a sense of intimacy and a profoundly magical quality, like Rubens and Lebrun a feeling for decoration and combination, like Veronese an enchanted sense of colour, etc.; but that he also had a quality all his own, a quality indefinable but itself defining the melancholy and the passion of his age—something quite new, which has made him an unique artist, without ancestry, without precedent, and probably without a successor—a link so precious that it could in no wise be replaced; and that by destroying it—if such a thing were possible—a whole world of ideas and sensations would be destroyed, and too great a gap would be blasted in the chain of history.

THE SALON OF 1859

LETTERS TO THE EDITOR OF THE REVUE FRANÇAISE

I. THE MODERN ARTIST

My dear M—, when you did me the honour of asking for an analysis of the Salon, you said, 'Be brief; do not write a catalogue, but a general impression, something like the account of a rapid philosophical walk through the galleries'. Very well, you shall have your wish; not because your programme accords (as it does) with my own conception of that tiresome kind of article called a 'Salon'; nor because your method is easier than the other—it is not, for brevity always demands more effort than diffuseness; but simply because, above all in the present instance, there is no other possible way. Certainly I should have been more seriously embarrassed if I had found myself lost in a forest of originality, if the modern French temperament, suddenly modified, purified, and rejuvenated, had put forth flowers so vigorous and of a scent so varied as to command irrepressible wonder, to provoke floods of praise—a garrulous admiration—or to necessitate a whole series of new categories in the language of criticism. But there is nothing of all that, fortunately (for me). No explosions; not a single unknown genius. The thoughts suggested by the sight of this Salon are of so simple, so traditional, so classic an order, that a few pages will doubtless be sufficient to develop them. Do not be surprised, then, if banality in the painter should have given rise to the *commonplace* in your writer. Besides, you will be no whit the loser; for is there anything (I am delighted to record that you share my opinion in this)—is there anything in the world more charming, more fruitful, of a nature more positively *exciting*, than the commonplace?

Before I begin, allow me to express a regret, which I believe will be but seldom expressed. We had been told that we should have some guests to receive—guests, however, who are not exactly unknown to us, for the exhibition in the Avenue Montaigne [1] has already introduced to the

[1] The *Exposition Universelle* of 1855. At the end of his first article on that exhibition, Baudelaire had announced his intention of writing an article on the contemporary English school (see p. 128, above).

Parisian public several of those charming artists of whom it has been for too long ignorant. I was thus looking forward with the greatest pleasure to re-establishing my acquaintance with Leslie,[1] that rich, naïf and noble *humourist*, one of the most emphatic expressions of the British mind; with the two Hunts,[2] the one a stubborn naturalist, and the other the passionate and self-willed creator of Pre-Raphaelitism; with the bold compositions of Maclise,[3] no less impetuous than sure of himself; with Millais,[4] that poet of meticulous detail; with J. Chalon,[5] that mixture of Claude and Watteau, chronicler of charming *fêtes champêtres* in great Italian parks; with Grant, that natural heir of Reynolds; with Hook,[6] who knows how to flood his *Venetian dreams* with a magic light; with that curious Paton,[7] who brings back Fuseli to mind and embroiders his graceful, pantheistic chaos with the patience of another age; with Cattermole, the history-painter in water-colour, and with that other astonishing artist whose name escapes me, a visionary architect, who builds on paper cities whose bridges have elephants for supports, allowing gigantic three-masters in full sail to pass between their countless, colossal limbs.[8] A special place had even been set aside for these devotees of the imagination and of exotic colour, for these favourites of the fantastic muse; but alas, for reasons which I do not know and whose explanation cannot, I think, find a place in your journal, my hopes were disappointed. And so farewell, you tragic passions—gesticulations *à la* Kean or Macready; you charming, intimate glimpses of the *home*; you splendours of the Orient, reflected in the poetic mirror of the English mind; you Scottish verdures, magical visions of freshness, receding depths in water-colours as vast as

[1] Leslie's pictures at the *Exposition Universelle* had included *Uncle Toby and the Widow Wadman* (now in the Victoria and Albert Museum) and *Sancho Panza and the Duchess* (National Gallery). The word 'humourist' is Baudelaire's own.

[2] W. H. Hunt had 11 water-colours, and Holman Hunt had *The Light of the World*, *Strayed Sheep* (Tate Gallery), and *Claudio and Isabella*.

[3] Maclise's two exhibits were *Merry Christmas in the Baron's Hall*, and *Ordeal by Touch*.

[4] Millais had *The Order of Release*, *The Return of the Dove to the Ark*, and *Ophelia*.

[5] J. J. Chalon had *A Summer's Day*: Morning, Afternoon and Evening.

[6] J. C. Hook had one Venetian painting.

[7] Noel Paton had *Oberon and Titania* (National Gallery of Scotland).

[8] In Baudelaire's article on Gautier, where the greater part of this paragraph also occurs, the names of Cockerell or Kendall are suggested here. From Adolphe Lance's *Compte-rendu* of the architectural exhibits at the exhibition (pp. 56 ff.), it is quite clear that H. E. Kendall, jun., is the 'visionary architect' in question. See F. W. Leakey's 'Baudelaire et Kendall', in the *Revue de littérature comparée*, Jan.-Mar. 1956.

stage-decorations, although so small—we shall not gaze upon you, this time at least. Were you so badly received then the first time, you eager representatives of the imagination and of the most precious powers of the soul? and do you consider us unworthy of understanding you?

And so, my dear M—, we shall content ourselves with France, of necessity. And believe me, it would give me immense pleasure to adopt a lyrical tone in speaking of the artists of my own country; but unhappily, however little practised a critic's mind may be, patriotism does not play an absolutely tyrannical role therein, and we have some humiliating admissions to make. The first time that I set foot in the Salon, I met on the staircase one of the most subtle and best-regarded of our critics, and to my first question—to the natural question that I put to him—he replied, 'Flat, mediocre; I have seldom seen so dismal a Salon.' He was both right and wrong. An exhibition which contains numerous works by Delacroix, Penguilly, Fromentin, cannot be dismal; but from the point of view of a general inspection, I saw that he was in the right. It cannot be doubted that at all times mediocrity has dominated; but that it should be more than ever on the throne, that its encumbrance should have turned into an absolute triumph—it is this fact that is as true as it is distressing. After having passed my eyes for some time over so many successfully-completed platitudes, so much carefully-laboured drivel, so much cleverly-constructed stupidity and falseness, I was led by the natural course of my reflections to consider the artist in times past and to place him face to face with the artist of the present: and then, at the end of these discouraging reflections, that terrible and eternal question-mark inevitably reared its head, as it always does. It would seem that littleness, puerility, incuriosity and the leaden calm of fatuity have taken the place of ardour, nobility and turbulent ambition, no less in the fine arts than in literature; and that for the moment nothing gives us reason to hope for any spiritual flowering as abundant as that of the Restoration. (And believe me, I am not alone in being oppressed by these bitter reflections; I will prove it to you in good time). I therefore asked myself the following questions: What *was* he, then—the artist of former times (Lebrun, or David for example)? Lebrun was all erudition, imagination, knowledge of the past, and love of grandeur; and David, that colossus slandered by pigmies—did not he also embody love of the past and love of grandeur combined with erudition? But what of the artist today—that ancient brother to the poet? To answer that question properly, my dear M—, one must not shrink from being too stern. A scandalous favouritism sometimes demands an equivalent response. Despite his lack of merit, the artist is today, and for many years has been, nothing but a *spoiled child*. How many honours, how much money has been showered upon men without soul and without education! I am certainly far from advocating the introduction into an art of means which are alien to it; and yet, to quote an example, I cannot prevent myself from feeling sympathetic towards an artist such as Chenavard, who is always agreeable in the way that books are agreeable, and graceful even when he is dull and pompous. What do I care that he is the butt of every dauber's jokes? At least with him I am sure that I can have a conversation about Virgil or about Plato. Préault has a charming talent, an instinctive taste which hurls him upon the beautiful like a hunting animal upon its natural prey. Daumier is gifted with a radiant good sense which colours all his conversation. Ricard, in spite of the dazzle and elusiveness of his talk, never fails to let one see that he knows, and has compared, a great deal. It is unnecessary, I think, to speak of the conversation of Eugène Delacroix, which is an admirable mixture of philosophical solidity, of lively wit and of blazing enthusiasm. But apart from these, I cannot think of any other artist who is worthy to converse with a philosopher or a poet. Apart from them, you will hardly find anything but *spoiled children*. I beg and implore you to tell me in what salon, in what tavern, in what social or intimate gathering you have heard a single witty remark uttered by a *spoiled child*—a profound, brilliant, or acute remark, to make one ponder or dream—in short, a *suggestive* remark? If such a remark has been thrown out, it may not indeed have been by a politician or a philosopher, but by someone of an outlandish profession, a hunter, a sailor or a taxidermist; but by an artist, a *spoiled child*, never.

The *spoiled child* has inherited privileges, once legitimate, from his predecessors. The enthusiasm which greeted David, Guérin, Girodet, Gros, Delacroix and Bonington, still sheds its charitable light upon his sorry person; and while good poets and vigorous historians make their living with extreme difficulty, the besotted business-man pays magnificently for the indecent little fooleries of the *spoiled child*. Please do not misunderstand me; if this goodwill were bestowed upon men of merit, I should not complain. When a singer or a dancer has reached the summit of her art, I am not one of those who envy her the fortune which she has gained by the labours and the risks of every day. I should be afraid of falling into the vice of the late Girardin,[1] of sophistical memory, who one day rebuked Théophile Gautier for rating his imagination at a much higher value than the services of a *sous-préfet*. It was, if you remember, on one of those ill-omened days when the terrified public heard him speaking Latin: *pecudesque locutae*! No, I am not as unjust as all that; but it is a good thing to raise the voice and to cry shame on contemporary folly when, at the same time that a ravishing picture by Delacroix had difficulty in finding a buyer at 1,000 francs, the practically-invisible figures of Meissonier fetched ten or twenty times as much. But those happy times have passed; we have fallen even lower, and M. Meissonier, who, in spite of all his merits, had the misfortune of introducing and popularizing the taste for littleness, is a veritable giant compared with today's toy-makers.

Discredit of the imagination, disdain of the great, love—no, this is too fine a word—exclusive *practice*, rather, of technique,—such, I believe, are the principal reasons for the artist's degradation. The more imagination one has, the better will be the technique needed to accompany it in its adventures and to overcome the difficulties which it avidly courts. And the better one's technique, the less should one make a virtue of it and display it, so that the imagination may be allowed to burn with its full brilliance. This is the counsel of wisdom; and wisdom says also: 'He who possesses no more than technical skill is but a beast, and the imagination which attempts to do without it is insane.' But, for all their simplicity, these things are both above and below the modern artist. A concierge's daughter says to herself: 'I shall go to the Conservatoire, I shall make my début at the Comédie Française, I shall declaim the lines of Corneille until I am classed above those who have been declaiming them for years.' And she does as she has said. She is very classically monotonous, and very classically boring and ignorant; but she has succeeded in what was very easy, that is to say, in winning, by her patience, the privileges of a *sociétaire*. And the *spoiled child*, the modern painter, says to himself: 'What is imagination? A danger and a toil. What is reading and contemplation of the past? Waste of time. I shall be classical, not like Bertin[2] (for the classical changes its place and its name), but like. . . . Troyon, for example.' And he does as he has said. He paints on and on; he stops up his soul and continues to paint, until at last he becomes like

[1] The journalist and politician Girardin was a particular *bête noire* of Baudelaire's.

[2] Victor Bertin, a pupil of P.-H. Valenciennes, the neo-classic landscape-painter.

the artist of the moment, and by his stupidity and his skill he earns the acclaim and the money of the public. The imitator of the imitator finds his own imitators, and in this way each pursues his dream of greatness, better and better stopping up his soul and above all *reading nothing*, not even *The Perfect Cook*, which at any rate would have been able to open up for him a career of greater glory, if less profit. When he is thoroughly master of the art of sauces, of patinas, of glazes, of scumbles, of gravies, of stews (I speak of painting), the *spoiled child* strikes proud attitudes and repeats with more conviction than ever that nothing else is necessary.

There was once a German peasant who went to a painter and said to him: '*Sir*, I want you to paint my portrait. You will show me sitting at the front door of my farm-house, in the great armchair which I inherited from my father. Beside me you will paint my wife with her distaff, and behind us my daughters passing to and fro, preparing the family supper. By the avenue to the left come those of my sons who are returning from the fields after having herded the cattle to their byres; others, with my grandsons, are bringing back waggons laden with hay. While I am watching this scene, I beg you not to forget the puffs of smoke from my pipe, which are shot through by the rays of the setting sun. I should like the spectator to *hear* the sound of the Angelus which is ringing from the nearby churchtower. That is where we were all married, both the fathers and the sons. It is important that you should paint the *air of satisfaction* which I enjoy at this moment of the day, when at one and the same time I contemplate *my family and my riches increased by the labours of a day*!' [1]

Three cheers for that peasant! Without for a moment suspecting it, he understood painting. Love of his profession had heightened his *imagination*. But which of our fashionable painters would be worthy of executing this portrait? Which of them can claim that his imagination has reached such a level?

II. THE MODERN PUBLIC AND PHOTOGRAPHY

MY DEAR M—, if I had time to divert you, it would be the easiest thing in the world, merely by flicking through the catalogue and making an

[1] The above paragraph seems to be an imitation and development of a passage in Diderot's *Essai sur la peinture*; the passage is quoted in Crépet's edition of *Curiosités esthétiques* (p. 489).

extract of all the ridiculous titles and preposterous subjects which are intended to attract our eyes. There's our famous Gallic wit for you! To seek to astonish by means which are alien to the art in question is the great standby of men who are not *natural* painters. Sometimes even—but always in France—this vice infects men who are not altogether devoid of talent and who debase it in this way with an adulterous mixture. I could parade before your eyes the comic title (in the manner of the *vaudevillistes*), the sentimental title (which lacks only an exclamation-mark), the punning title, the profound and philosophical title, the false or trick title, of the type of '*Brutus, lâche César*!' 'O faithless generation!', said Our Lord. 'How long shall I be with you? how long shall I suffer you?' This generation, in fact, both artists and public, has so little faith in painting that it spends its time in seeking to disguise it, to wrap it up in sugar pills like an unpleasant medicine; and what sugar, Great Heavens! I will instance two titles of pictures, which however I have not seen. The first is *Amour et Gibelotte*! [1] Doesn't that immediately whet the appetite of your curiosity? 'Love and Rabbit-stew!' Let me try and make an intimate combination of these two ideas, the idea of love and the idea of a rabbit skinned and made into a stew. I can hardly suppose that the painter's imagination can have gone so far as to fit a quiver, a pair of wings and an eye-bandage upon the corpse of a domestic animal; the allegory would be really too obscure. I imagine rather that the title has been invented upon the recipe of *Misanthropie et Repentir*.[2] The true title would thus be *Lovers eating a Rabbit-Stew*. Now you will ask, are they young or old, a labourer and a working-girl, or perhaps a retired veteran and a waif, in some dusty bower? I really ought to have seen the picture!—Next we have *Monarchique, catholique et soldat*! [3] Here is one in the noble, the *crusader* style, like *Itinéraire de Paris à Jérusalem* (forgive me, Chateaubriand! but the most noble peal of bells can become a means of caricature, and the political utterances of the leader of an empire can be turned into a dauber's squibs). This picture can only represent one character doing three things *at once*—fighting in battle, making his communion and assisting at the *petit lever* of Louis XIV. Or could it be a

[1] By Ernest Seigneurgens.

[2] The French translation of Kotzebue's play *Menschenhass und Reue* (1789), in which a wife's infidelity occasions a husband's misanthropy, which leads to repentance and a happy ending.

[3] By Joseph Gouézou.

warrior tattooed with *fleurs de lys* and devotional images? But what is the good of perplexing ourselves further? Let us simply say that this is a false and sterile method of attracting attention. What is even more deplorable is that the picture may perhaps be a good one, however odd this may seem. And the same with *Amour et Gibelotte*. Did I not catch sight of an excellent little group of sculpture whose number I had unfortunately not noted, and when I wanted to know the subject I re-read the catalogue four times—but to no avail! At last you kindly informed me that it was called *Toujours et Jamais*.[1] I felt truly sorry to see a man of real talent uselessly cultivating the art of the rebus.

I beg your forgiveness for having amused myself a little while in the manner of the lighter journals. But however frivolous the matter may seem to you, if you look carefully you will find that it contains a deplorable symptom. To sum up in a style of paradox, I will ask you, and those of my friends who are more learned than I in the history of art, if the taste for the asinine and the taste for the witty (which is really the same thing) have always existed; if *Appartement à Louer*[2] and other far-fetched conceptions have appeared in all ages, in order to provoke the same popular enthusiasm; if the Venice of Veronese and Bassano was afflicted by these pictorial anagrams, and if the eyes of Giulio Romano, of Michelangelo, and of Bandinelli were alarmed by similar monstrosities; I ask, in a word, if M. Biard is eternal and omnipresent, like God. I do not believe so; I regard these horrors as a special grace bestowed upon the French nation. It is true that her artists infect her with the taste for them; that, once infected, she demands to have her needs satisfied is no less true; for if the artist makes the public stupid, the public pays him back in kind. They are two correlative terms which act upon one another with an equal power. And so let us marvel at the momentum with which we plunge into the track of progress (by progress I mean the progressive domination of matter), and at the miraculous everyday diffusion of the common run of skill—of something which can be acquired by patience alone.

For us the natural painter, like the natural poet, is almost a monster. The exclusive taste for the True (so noble a thing when it is limited to its proper applications) oppresses and stifles the taste of the Beautiful. Where one should see nothing but Beauty (I mean in a beautiful painting,

[1] By Emile Hébert. See pp. 211–2, below.

[2] By F.-A. Biard; one of the great successes of the 1844 Salon.

and you can easily guess what is in my mind), our public looks only for Truth. The people are not artists, not naturally artists; philosophers perhaps, moralists, engineers, connoisseurs of instructive anecdotes, whatever you like, but never spontaneously artists. They feel, or rather they judge, in stages, analytically. Other more fortunate peoples feel immediately, all at once, synthetically.

I was speaking just now of artists who seek to astonish the public. The desire to astonish and to be astonished is very proper. 'It is a happiness to wonder'; but also 'it is a happiness to dream'.[1] The whole question, then, if you insist that I confer upon you the title of artist or of connoisseur of the fine arts, is to know by what processes you wish to create or to feel wonder. Because the Beautiful is *always* wonderful, it would be absurd to suppose that what is wonderful is *always* beautiful. Now our public, which is singularly incapable of feeling the happiness of dreaming or of marvelling (a sign of its meanness of soul), wishes to be made to wonder by means which are alien to art, and its obedient artists bow to its taste; they try to strike, to surprise, to stupefy it by means of unworthy tricks, because they know that it is incapable of ecstasy in front of the natural devices of true art.

During this lamentable period, a new industry arose which contributed not a little to confirm stupidity in its faith and to ruin whatever might remain of the divine in the French mind. The idolatrous mob demanded an ideal worthy of itself and appropriate to its nature—that is perfectly understood. In matters of painting and sculpture, the present-day *Credo* of the sophisticated, above all in France (and I do not think that anyone at all would dare to state the contrary), is this: 'I believe in Nature, and I believe only in Nature (there are good reasons for that). I believe that Art is, and cannot be other than, the exact reproduction of Nature (a timid and dissident sect would wish to exclude the more repellent objects of nature, such as skeletons or chamber-pots). Thus an industry that could give us a result identical to Nature would be the absolute of art.' A revengeful God has given ear to the prayers of this multitude. Daguerre was his Messiah. And now the faithful says to himself: 'Since Photography gives us every guarantee of exactitude that we could desire (they really believe that, the mad fools!), then Photography and Art are the same thing.' From that moment our squalid society rushed, Narcissus to a man, to gaze at its trivial image on a scrap of

[1] Quoted from Poe, *Morella*.

metal. A madness, an extraordinary fanaticism took possession of all these new sun-worshippers. Strange abominations took form. By bringing together a group of male and female clowns, got up like butchers and laundry-maids at a carnival, and by begging these *heroes* to be so kind as to hold their chance grimaces for the time necessary for the performance, the operator flattered himself that he was reproducing tragic or elegant scenes from ancient history. Some democratic writer ought to have seen here a cheap method of disseminating a loathing for history and for painting among the people, thus committing a double sacrilege and insulting at one and the same time the divine art of painting and the noble art of the actor. A little later a thousand hungry eyes were bending over the peepholes of the stereoscope, as though they were the attic-windows of the infinite. The love of pornography, which is no less deep-rooted in the natural heart of man than the love of himself, was not to let slip so fine an opportunity of self-satisfaction. And do not imagine that it was only children on their way back from school who took pleasure in these follies; the world was infatuated with them. I was once present when some friends were discreetly concealing some such pictures from a beautiful woman, a woman of high society, not of mine—they were taking upon themselves some feeling of delicacy in her presence; but 'No,' she cried. 'Give them to me! Nothing is too much for me.' I swear that I heard that; but who will believe me? 'You can see that they are great ladies,' said Alexandre Dumas. 'There are some still greater!,' said Cazotte.[1]

As the photographic industry was the refuge of every would-be painter, every painter too ill-endowed or too lazy to complete his studies, this universal infatuation bore not only the mark of a blindness, an imbecility, but had also the air of a vengeance. I do not believe, or at least I do not wish to believe, in the absolute success of such a brutish conspiracy, in which, as in all others, one finds both fools and knaves; but I am convinced that the ill-applied developments of photography, like all other purely material developments of progress, have contributed much to the impoverishment of the French artistic genius, which is already so scarce. In vain may our modern Fatuity roar, belch forth all

[1] The first remark is taken from Dumas's play *La Tour de Nesle* (Act I, sc. 9); the second from Gérard de Nerval's preface to Cazotte's *Le Diable amoureux*. The somewhat complicated point of the joke is explained by Crépet in his note on this passage (*Curiosités esthétiques*, p. 490).

the rumbling wind of its rotund stomach, spew out all the undigested sophisms with which recent philosophy has stuffed it from top to bottom; it is nonetheless obvious that this industry, by invading the territories of art, has become art's most mortal enemy, and that the confusion of their several functions prevents any of them from being properly fulfilled. Poetry and progress are like two ambitious men who hate one another with an instinctive hatred, and when they meet upon the same road, one of them has to give place. If photography is allowed to supplement art in some of its functions, it will soon have supplanted or corrupted it altogether, thanks to the stupidity of the multitude which is its natural ally. It is time, then, for it to return to its true duty, which is to be the servant of the sciences and arts—but the very humble servant, like printing or shorthand, which have neither created nor supplemented literature. Let it hasten to enrich the tourist's album and restore to his eye the precision which his memory may lack; let it adorn the naturalist's library, and enlarge microscopic animals; let it even provide information to corroborate the astronomer's hypotheses; in short, let it be the secretary and clerk of whoever needs an absolute factual exactitude in his profession—up to that point nothing could be better. Let it rescue from oblivion those tumbling ruins, those books, prints and manuscripts which time is devouring, precious things whose form is dissolving and which demand a place in the archives of our memory—it will be thanked and applauded. But if it be allowed to encroach upon the domain of the impalpable and the imaginary, upon anything whose value depends solely upon the addition of something of a man's soul, then it will be so much the worse for us!

I know very well that some people will retort, 'The disease which you have just been diagnosing is a disease of imbeciles. What man worthy of the name of artist, and what true connoisseur, has ever confused art with industry?'. I know it; and yet I will ask them in my turn if they believe in the contagion of good and evil, in the action of the mass on individuals, and in the involuntary, forced obedience of the individual to the mass. It is an incontestable, an irresistible law that the artist should act upon the public, and that the public should react upon the artist; and besides, those terrible witnesses, the facts, are easy to study; the disaster is verifiable. Each day art further diminishes its self-respect by bowing down before external reality; each day the painter becomes more and more given to painting not what he dreams but what he sees. Nevertheless *it is a happiness to dream*, and it used to be a glory to express what one dreamt. But I ask you! does the painter still know this happiness?

Could you find an honest observer to declare that the invasion of photography and the great industrial madness of our times have no part at all in this deplorable result? Are we to suppose that a people whose eyes are growing used to considering the results of a material science as though they were the products of the beautiful, will not in the course of time have singularly diminished its faculties of judging and of feeling what are among the most ethereal and immaterial aspects of creation?

III. THE QUEEN OF THE FACULTIES

IN RECENT YEARS we have heard it said in a thousand different ways, 'Copy nature; just copy nature. There is no greater delight, no finer triumph than an excellent copy of nature.' And this doctrine (the enemy of art) was alleged to apply not only to painting but to all the arts, even to the novel and to poetry. To these doctrinaires, who were so completely satisfied by Nature, a man of imagination would certainly have had the right to reply: 'I consider it useless and tedious to represent what *exists*, because nothing that *exists* satisfies me. Nature is ugly, and I prefer the monsters of my fancy to what is positively trivial.' And yet it would have been more philosophical to ask the doctrinaires in question first of all whether they were quite certain of the existence of external nature, or (if this question might seem too well calculated to pander to their sarcasm) whether they were quite certain of knowing *all nature*, that is, all that is contained in nature. A 'yes' would have been the most boastful and extravagant of answers. So far as I have been able to understand its singular and humiliating incoherences, the doctrine meant —at least I do it the honour of believing that it meant: The artist, the true artist, the true poet, should only paint in accordance with what he sees and with what he feels. He must be *really* faithful to his own nature. He must avoid like the plague borrowing the eyes and the feelings of another man, however great that man may be; for then his productions would be lies in relation to himself, and not *realities*. But if these pedants of whom I am speaking (for there is a pedantry even among the mean-spirited) and who have representatives everywhere (for their theory flatters impotence no less than laziness)—if these pedants, I say, did not wish the matter to be understood in this way, let us simply believe that they meant to say, 'We have no imagination, and we decree that no one else is to have any.'

How mysterious is Imagination, that Queen of the Faculties! It touches all the others; it rouses them and sends them into combat. At times it resembles them to the point of confusion, and yet it is always itself, and those men who are not quickened thereby are easily recognizable by some strange curse which withers their productions like the fig-tree in the Gospel.

It is both analysis and synthesis; and yet men who are clever at analysis and sufficiently quick at summing up, can be devoid of imagination. It is that, and it is not entirely that. It is sensitivity, and yet there are people who are very sensitive, too sensitive perhaps, who have none of it. It is Imagination that first taught man the moral meaning of colour, of contour, of sound and of scent. In the beginning of the world it created analogy and metaphor. It decomposes all creation, and with the raw materials accumulated and disposed in accordance with rules whose origins one cannot find save in the furthest depths of the soul, it creates a new world, it produces the sensation of newness. As it has created the world (so much can be said, I think, even in a religious sense), it is proper that it should govern it. What would be said of a warrior without imagination? that he might make an excellent soldier, but that if he is put in command of an army, he will make no conquests. The case could be compared to that of a poet or a novelist who took away the command of his faculties from the imagination to give it, for example, to his knowledge of language or to his observation of facts. What would be said of a diplomat without imagination? that he may have an excellent knowledge of the history of treaties and alliances in the past, but that he will never guess the treaties and alliances held in store by the future. Of a scholar without imagination? that he has learnt everything that, having been taught, could be learnt, but that he will never discover any laws that have not yet been guessed at. Imagination is the queen of truth, and the *possible* is one of the provinces of truth. It has a positive relationship with the infinite.

Without imagination, all the faculties, however sound or sharpened they may be, are as though they did not exist, whereas a weakness in some of the secondary faculties, so long as they are excited by a vigorous imagination, is a secondary misfortune. None of them can do without it, but the lack of some of them can be made up by it. Often when our other faculties only find what they are seeking after successive trials of several different methods which are ill-adapted to the nature of things, imagination steps in, and proudly and simply guesses the answer. Finally, it plays a powerful role even in ethical matters; for—allow me to go so far and to ask, What is virtue without imagination? You might as well speak of virtue without pity, virtue without Heaven—it is a hard, cruel, sterilizing thing, which in some countries has become bigotry and in others protestantism.

In spite of all the magnificent privileges that I attribute to the imagination, I will not pay your readers the insult of explaining to them that the more it is helped in its work, the more powerful it is, and that there is nothing more formidable in our battles with the ideal than a fine imagination disposing of an immense armoury of observed fact. Nevertheless, to return to what I was saying a moment ago concerning the prerogative of making up deficiencies, which the imagination owes to its divine origin, I should like to quote you an example, a tiny example, which I hope you will not scorn. Do you think that the author of *Antony*, of *Count Hermann*, and of *Monte Cristo*, is a scholar? I imagine not. Do you suppose that he has steeped himself in the practice of the arts and has made a patient study of them? Of course not. I should even imagine that to do so would be antipathetic to his nature. Very well then, *he* is an example to prove that the imagination, although unassisted by practice or by acquaintance with technical terms, is nevertheless incapable of producing heretical nonsense in a matter which is, for the most important part, within its province. Not long ago I was in a train and I was pondering over the article which I am now writing: I was considering above all that singular reversal of values which has permitted (in a century, I grant you, in which, for man's chastening, everything has been permitted him) a disdain of the most honourable and the most useful of the moral faculties. And then I saw lying on a nearby cushion a forgotten copy of the *Indépendance Belge*. Alexandre Dumas had taken over this year's account of the works in the Salon.[1] This circumstance aroused my curiosity. You can guess my delight when I discovered my reflections amply verified by an example thrown in my way by chance.

[1] Dumas's articles on this Salon were collected and published as *L'art et les artistes contemporains au Salon de 1859*.

What a fine subject for surprise! you will say—that this man, who seems to represent universal vitality, should pronounce a magnificent eulogy on a period when life overflowed; that the creator of the romantic drama should raise his voice, which I assure you did not lack grandeur, and should sing the praises of that happy time when at the side of the new school of literature there flourished a new school of painting—Delacroix, the Devéria brothers, Boulanger, Poterlet, Bonington, etc.: —that is exactly what you would expect! *Laudator temporis acti*! But that he should pay a witty tribute to Delacroix, that he should succinctly explain the nature of his opponents' madness, and that he should go even further and point out the sins of the best of the most recently celebrated painters; that he, Alexandre Dumas, so reckless and fluent a writer, should demonstrate so well, for example, that Troyon has no genius, and should even analyse what he lacks in order to simulate genius—tell me, my friend, do you find *that* so simple? All this, of course, was written in that loose dramatic style which he has gradually adopted in talking to his innumerable audience; and yet, what grace, what swiftness in the expression of truth! You will already have finished my argument for me: If Alexandre Dumas, who is no scholar, had not been lucky enough to possess a rich imagination, he would only have spoken nonsense; as it is, he has spoken sound sense, and he has spoken it well, because imagination, one must conclude, thanks to its *supplementing* nature, embraces also the critical spirit.

There remains yet one device for my adversary; it is to declare that Alexandre Dumas is not the author of his *Salon*. But this insult is such an old one, and this device so stale, that it should be thrown to the old-clothes-fanciers, to journalistic hacks and penny-a-liners. If they have not already picked it up, they will do so.

We shall shortly be embarking upon a more intimate examination of the functions of this *cardinal* faculty (does not its richness put you in mind of ecclesiastical crimson?). I shall simply tell you what I learnt from the lips of a master[1]; and just as at that time I used to verify his simple precepts by reference to every picture that came under my eyes—with all the delight of a man who is educating himself—so we, in our turn, shall be able to apply them in succession, like touch-stones, to several of our painters.

[1] I.e. Delacroix.

IV. THE GOVERNANCE OF THE IMAGINATION

YESTERDAY evening I sent you the last pages of my letter, in which I wrote, not without a certain diffidence: '*Since Imagination created the world, it is Imagination that governs it.*' Afterwards, as I was turning the pages of *The Night Side of Nature*,[1] I came across this passage, which I quote simply because it is a paraphrase and justification of the line which was worrying me: '*By imagination, I do not simply mean to convey the common notion implied by that much abused word, which is only* fancy, *but the* constructive *imagination, which is a much higher function, and which, in as much as man is made in the likeness of God, bears a distant relation to that sublime power by which the Creator projects, creates, and upholds his universe.*' I feel no shame—on the contrary, I am very happy—to have coincided with the excellent Mrs. Crowe on this point; I have always admired and envied her capacity for *belief*, which is as fully developed as is that of *doubt* in others.

I said that a long time ago I had heard a man who was a true scholar and deeply learned in his art, expressing the most spacious and yet the simplest of ideas on this subject. When I met him for the first time, I possessed no other experience but that which results from a consuming love, nor any other power of reasoning but instinct. It is true that this love and this instinct were passably lively; for even in my extreme youth my eyes had never been able to drink their fill of painted or sculpted images, and I think that worlds could have come to an end, *impavidum ferient*, before I had become an iconoclast. Obviously he wished to show the greatest indulgence and kindness to me; for we talked from the very beginning of *commonplaces*—that is to say, of the vastest and most profound questions. About nature, for example: 'Nature is but a dictionary,' he kept on repeating. Properly to understand the extent of meaning implied in this sentence, you should consider the numerous ordinary usages of a dictionary. In it you look for the meaning of words, their genealogy and their etymology—in brief, you extract from it all the elements that compose a sentence or a narrative: but no one has ever thought of his dictionary as a *composition*, in the poetic sense of the word. Painters who are obedient to the imagination seek in their dictionary for

[1] On Mrs. Crowe's *The Night Side of Nature* (London 1848), see Gilman, pp. 128 ff. and notes.

the elements which suit with their conception; in adjusting those elements, however, with more or less of art, they confer upon them a totally new physiognomy. But those who have no imagination just copy the dictionary. The result is a great vice, the vice of banality, to which those painters are particularly prone whose speciality brings them closer to external nature—landscape-painters, for example, who generally consider it a triumph if they contrive not to show their personalities. By dint of contemplating, they forget to feel and to think.

For this great painter, however, no element of art, of which one man takes this and another that as the most important, was—I should rather say, is—anything but the humblest servant of a unique and superior faculty.

If a very neat execution is called for, that is so that the language of the dream may be translated as neatly as possible; if it should be very rapid, that is lest anything may be lost of the extraordinary vividness which accompanied its conception; if the artist's attention should even be directed to something so humble as the material cleanliness of his tools, that is easily intelligible, seeing that every precaution must be taken to make his execution both deft and unerring.

With such a method, which is essentially logical, all the figures, their relative disposition, the landscape or interior which provides them with horizon or background, their garments—everything, in fact, must serve to illuminate the idea which gave them birth, must carry its original warmth, its livery, so to speak. Just as a dream inhabits its own proper atmosphere, so a conception which has become a composition needs to move within a coloured setting which is peculiar to itself. Obviously a particular tone is allotted to whichever part of a picture is to become the key and to govern the others. Everyone knows that yellow, orange and red inspire and express the ideas of joy, richness, glory and love: but there are thousands of different yellow or red atmospheres, and all the other colours will be affected logically and to a proportionate degree by the atmosphere which dominates. In certain of its aspects the art of the colourist has an evident affinity with mathematics and music. And yet its most delicate operations are performed by means of a sentiment or perception to which long practice has given an unqualifiable sureness. We can see that this great law of overall harmony condemns many instances of dazzling or raw colour, even in the work of the most illustrious painters. There are paintings by Rubens which not only make one think of a coloured firework, but of several fireworks set off on the same platform. It is obvious that the larger a picture, the broader must be its *touch*; but it is better that individual strokes should not be materially fused, for they will fuse naturally at a distance determined by the law of sympathy which has brought them together. Colour will thus achieve a greater energy and freshness.

A good picture, which is a faithful equivalent of the dream which has begotten it, should be brought into being like a world. Just as the creation, as we see it, is the result of several creations in which the preceding ones are always completed by the following, so a harmoniously-conducted picture consists of a series of pictures superimposed on one another, each new layer conferring greater reality upon the dream, and raising it by one degree towards perfection. On the other hand I remember having seen in the studios of Paul Delaroche and Horace Vernet huge pictures, not sketched but actually begun—that is to say, with certain passages completely finished, while others were only indicated with a black or a white outline. You might compare this kind of work to a piece of purely manual labour—so much space to be covered in a given time—or to a long road divided into a great number of stages. As soon as each stage is reached, it is finished with, and when the whole road has been run, the artist is delivered of his picture.

It is clear that all these rules are more or less modifiable, in accordance with the varying temperaments of artists. Nevertheless I am convinced that what I have just described is the surest method for men of a rich imagination. Consequently, if an artist's divergences from the method in question are too great, there is evidence that an abnormal and undue importance is being set upon some secondary element of art.

I have no fear that anyone may consider it absurd to suppose a single education to be applicable to a crowd of different individuals. For it is obvious that systems of rhetoric or prosody are no arbitrarily invented tyrannies, but rather they are collections of rules demanded by the very constitution of the spiritual being. And systems of prosody and rhetoric have never yet prevented originality from clearly emerging. The contrary—namely that they have assisted the birth of originality—would be infinitely more true.

To be brief, I must pass over a whole crowd of corollaries resulting from my principal formula, in which is contained, so to speak, the entire formulary of the true aesthetic, and which may be expressed thus: The whole visible universe is but a storehouse of images and signs to which the imagination will give a relative place and value; it is a sort of pasture which the imagination must digest and transform. All the faculties of the human soul must be subordinated to the imagination, which puts them in requisition all at once. Just as a good knowledge of the dictionary does not necessarily imply a knowledge of the art of composition, and just as the art of composition does not itself imply a *universal* imagination, in the same way a *good* painter need not be a *great* painter. But a great painter is perforce a good painter, because a universal imagination embraces the understanding of all means of expression and the desire to acquire them.

As a result of the ideas which I have just been making as clear as I have been able (but there are still so many things that I should have mentioned, particularly concerning the concordant aspects of all the arts, and their similarities in method), it is clear that the vast family of artists—that is to say, of men who have devoted themselves to artistic expression—can be divided into two quite distinct camps. There are those who call themselves 'realists'—a word with a double meaning, whose sense has not been properly defined, and so, in order the better to characterize their error, I propose to call them 'positivists'; and *they* say, 'I want to represent things as they are, or rather as they would be, supposing that I did not exist.' In other words, the universe without man. The others however—the 'imaginatives'—say, 'I want to illuminate things with my mind, and to project their reflection upon other minds.' Although these two absolutely contrary methods could magnify or diminish any subject, from a religious scene to the most modest landscape, nevertheless the man of imagination has generally tended to express himself in religious paintings and in fantasy, while landscape and the type of painting called 'genre' would appear to offer enormous opportunities to those whose minds are lazy and excitable only with difficulty.

But besides the imaginatives and the self-styled realists, there is a third class of painters who are timid and servile, and who place all their pride at the disposal of a code of false dignity. While one group believes that it is copying nature, and another is seeking to paint its own soul, these men conform to a purely conventional set of rules—rules entirely arbitrary, not derived from the human soul, but simply imposed by the routine of a celebrated studio. In this very numerous but very boring class we include the false amateurs of the antique, the false amateurs of style—in short, all those men who by their impotence have elevated the 'poncif' to the honours of the grand style.

V. RELIGION, HISTORY, FANTASY

AT EVERY fresh exhibition, the critics observe that religious painting is more and more deficient. I do not know if they are correct so far as numbers are concerned; but certainly they make no mistake as to quality. Religious writers, like socialist writers, naturally tend to make beauty dependent upon belief, and more than one religious writer has attributed to a simple lack of faith this difficulty in giving expression to the things of faith. This error could be philosophically demonstrated if the facts did not show us sufficient proof to the contrary, and if the history of painting did not offer us the example of impious and atheistical artists producing excellent religious works. Let us simply say then that since religion is the highest *fiction* of the human mind (I am purposely speaking as an atheistic professor of the fine arts would speak, and nothing of what I say should be inferred as arguing against my own faith), it will require the most vigorous imagination and the most concentrated efforts from those who devote themselves to the expression of its acts and its sentiments. In the same way the character of Polyeuctes demands from the poet and the actor a spiritual ascent and an enthusiasm far more lively than those demanded by some vulgar character in love with a vulgar earthly creature, or even than a purely political hero. The only concession that one can reasonably make to those who hold to the theory of faith as the unique source of religious inspiration, is that at the moment of executing his work the poet, the actor and the artist must believe in the reality of what he is representing, fired as he is by necessity. Thus it is that art is the only spiritual sphere in which man can say, 'I shall believe if I wish, and if I do not wish, I shall not believe.' The cruel and humiliating maxim, *Spiritus flat ubi vult*, loses its credit in matters of art.

I do not know if MM. Legros and Amand Gautier have faith as the Church understands it, but certainly, in composing each of them an excellent devotional work, they have had sufficient faith for the object in view. They have proved that even in the nineteenth century an artist can produce a good religious picture, provided that his imagination is fit to rise so far. Although the more important paintings of Eugène Delacroix are calling us and demanding our attention, I have nevertheless thought it right, my dear M—, to start off with two names but little, if at all, known. To the natural scent of the forgotten or unfamiliar flower is added the paradoxical scent of its own obscurity, and its positive value is enhanced for us by the joy of having discovered it. Perhaps I am wrong to be totally ignorant of M. Legros, but I will admit that I had never before seen a work signed with his name. The first time that I noticed his picture, I was with our common friend Monsieur C—, whose attention I drew to this humble and penetrating work. He could not deny its singular merits; but his eyes, being in love with elegant and worldly beauties, like those of a good connoisseur, were a little disconcerted by its *rustic* aspect—by this little community, clothed in corduroy, cotton and home-spun, which the evening *Angelus* [1] assembles within the nave of the church of one of our great cities —these simple people with their sabots and their umbrellas, all bowed with work, wrinkled with age and their skin parched by the flame of sorrow. He was evidently subject to that national mood, that fear above all of being made a dupe, which was most cruelly mocked by the French writer who was himself most singularly obsessed by it.[2] Nevertheless the mind of the true critic, like that of the true poet, should be open to every beauty; it is as easy for him to take delight in the dazzling grandeur of Caesar in triumph as in the grandeur of a poor suburbanite on his knees in the presence of his God. See how the artist has realized and recaptured for us all those feelings of refreshment which dwell beneath the roof of the Catholic church—the humility which rejoices in itself, the confidence of the poor in the justice of God, and the hope of succour, even if it does not mean the forgetting of present misfortunes! That the vulgar trappings of his subject do no injury to its moral grandeur, but that, on the contrary, this triviality is like a seasoning for its charity and tenderness, only goes to prove that M. Legros is a man of vigorous mind. By a mysterious association of ideas which subtle wits will understand, the grotesquely attired child who is awkwardly twisting his cap in the temple of God made me think of Sterne's donkey

[1] Formerly in the collection of Mr. Asa Lingard. See pl. 42.

[2] Probably Stendhal, though Crépet, in his note on this passage, suggests the possibility that Mérimée may be intended.

and the macaroons. The donkey's comic appearance while eating a cake does nothing to diminish the feeling of compassion that we feel when we see the miserable slave of the farm receiving a few dainties at the hand of a philosopher. In the same way this poor man's child is all embarrassment, and trembles as he tastes the celestial sweets. I forgot to mention that the execution of this pious work is of a remarkable solidity; the somewhat dull colour and the minuteness of the details are in harmony with the eternally *precious* character of devotion. Monsieur C—pointed out to me that the background does not recede sufficiently [1] and that the figures seem to be stuck somewhat flatly on to the decoration which surrounds them. But I own that this fault, by recalling the burning *naïveté* of the primitives, was for me but an added charm. In a work less intimate and less penetrating, it would not have been acceptable.

M. Amand Gautier is the author of a work which had already struck the eye of the critics several years ago—a remarkable work, which was rejected, I believe, by the jury, but which can be studied today in the window of one of the principal picture-dealers of the city. It represents the courtyard of an asylum for female lunatics—a subject which he treated not according to the philosophic, Germanic method (that of Kaulbach for example, which makes one think of the categories of Aristotle), but with the dramatic feeling of the French, combined with a faithful and intelligent amount of observation. The painter's friends claim that everything in the work—heads, gestures and physiognomies—was minutely exact, and copied from nature. I do not agree, first because I detected symptoms to the contrary in the organization of the picture, and then because what is positively and universally exact is never admirable. This year M. Amand Gautier has exhibited a single work which bears the simple title, *Les Sœurs de Charité*.[2] It requires a true mastery to distil the tender poetry contained in those long uniform garments, in those rigid head-dresses and those attitudes as modest and serious as the religious life itself. Everything in M. Gautier's picture contributes to the development of the central thought; those long white walls, those trees correctly set in line, that façade which is simple to a degree of poverty,

[1] According to Pennell (*Life of Whistler*, 1908, vol. 1, p. 77), Seymour Haden, the original owner of the picture, also noticed a fault of perspective here. He found this so irritating that finally he corrected it himself, to the great annoyance of Legros, who stole the picture back in order to restore it to its original state.

[2] Now in the Lille Museum; see pl. 43.

those upright attitudes, lacking all feminine coquetry, that whole sex subdued to discipline like a soldier, its face gleaming sadly with the rosy pallor of consecrated virginity—all these things give us a sensation of the eternal, of the invariable, of duty pleasurable in all its monotony. While studying this canvas, which is painted with a touch as broad and simple as its subject, I felt that curious impression which is produced by certain paintings of Lesueur and by the best of Philippe de Champaigne—those, I mean, which represent the monastic life. If any of my readers wants to seek these pictures out, I should warn him that they are to be found at the far end of the gallery, in the left part of the building, in the depths of a great square hall where an innumerable multitude of canvases have been confined—so-called religious paintings, for the most part. The general effect of this gallery is so chilly that few people find their way to it, as if it were a corner of a garden unvisited by the sun. It is to this glory-hole of false *ex-votos*, to this immense milky way of chalky ineptitudes that these two modest canvases have been banished.

But the imagination of Delacroix! Never has it flinched before the arduous peaks of religion! The heavens belong to it, no less than hell, war, Olympus and love! In him you have the model of the painter-poet. He is indeed one of the rare elect, and the scope of his mind embraces religion in its domain. His imagination blazes with every flame and every shade of crimson, like the banks of glowing candles before a shrine. All that there is of anguish in the Passion impassions him; all that there is of splendour in the Church casts its glory upon him. On his inspired canvases he pours blood, light and darkness in turn. I believe that he would willingly bestow his own natural magnificence upon the majesties of the Gospel itself, out of superabundance. I remember seeing a little *Annunciation* [1] by Delacroix in which the angel visiting Mary was not alone, but was escorted in ceremony by two other angels, and the effect of this celestial retinue was powerful and touching. One of his youthful pictures, the *Christ in the Garden of Olives* [2] ('O my Father, if it be possible, let this cup pass from me!', in the church of St. Paul, rue St. Antoine) positively melts with feminine sensibility and poetic unction. Anguish and Splendour, which ring forth so sublimely in religion, are never without an echo in his mind.

Very well, my friend, this extraordinary man who has wrestled with Scott, Byron, Goethe, Shakespeare, Ariosto, Tasso, Dante and the

[1] Painted in 1841 (Robaut No. 1707). [2] Exhibited in 1827.

Gospels; this man who has illuminated history with shafts of light from his palette, and has poured out his fantasy in waves upon our dazzled eyes; this man who, though advanced in the number of his years, is yet stamped with the stubbornness of youth, and who since his earliest manhood has consecrated all his time to the exercise of his hand, his memory and his eye for the forging of ever surer weapons for his imagination—this genius, in short, has recently found a master to teach him his art, in a young *journalist*[1] whose ministry had so far confined itself to giving an account of the dress of Madame So-and-so at the latest ball at the Hôtel de Ville. Oh! those *pink* horses, those *lilac-coloured* peasants, and that *red* smoke (red smoke! what a daring touch!)! In what a *bilious-green* manner have they been treated! Delacroix's complete works have been ground to powder and scattered to the four winds of heaven. This kind of article, which you can hear *spoken* in any bourgeois drawing-room, begins invariably with these words: 'I must own that I make no pretensions of being a connoisseur, for the mysteries of painting are a closed book for me, *but nevertheless . . .*' (in that case, why speak of it?), and it generally ends with some acrimonious remark which is equivalent to a glance of envy directed towards those fortunate people who comprehend the incomprehensible.

But what does stupidity matter, you may say, so long as genius triumphs? Nevertheless, my friend, it is by no means time wasted to measure the strength of resistance against which genius is pitted; the whole importance of this young journalist amounts to the fact that he represents the general level of the bourgeois mind—and that is quite enough for our purpose. Please remember that this comedy has been played against Delacroix since 1822, and that ever since that time our painter, always punctual for his engagements, has at every exhibition given us several pictures amongst which there has always been at least one masterpiece, showing untiringly (to use M. Thiers's polite and indulgent expression) 'that spurt of superiority which revives hopes which have already been a trifle dashed by the *too moderate worth of all the others*.' And a little later he added: 'Some strange recollection of the great masters seized hold of me at the sight of this picture (*Dante and Virgil*). Once more I found that power—wild, ardent yet natural—which yields without effort to its own impulse. . . . I do not think that I am mistaken

[1] See the *Exposition Universelle* article (p. 138), where the journalist's name is given; it was Alphonse Karr.

when I say that M. Delacroix *has been given genius*; let him advance with assurance, let him devote himself to *immense* tasks, an *indispensable* condition of talent. . . .'[1] I do not know how many times during his life M. Thiers has been a prophet, but he was so on that day. Delacroix has hurled himself into *immense tasks*—and he has not disarmed opinion. To see this majestic, inexhaustible outpouring of painting, it would be easy to guess the name of the man whom I heard one evening saying: 'Like all men of my age, I have known many passions; but it is only in *work* that I have felt myself perfectly happy.' Pascal said that togas, purple and plumes were very happy inventions to impress the vulgar, to mark with a label what is truly to be respected; and yet the official distinctions of which Delacroix has been the object have done nothing to silence ignorance. But to look carefully at the matter, I think that for those who, like myself, hold that artistic affairs should only be discussed between aristocrats, and believe that it is the scarcity of the elect that makes a paradise, everything is perhaps for the best. He is indeed a privileged man for whom Providence keeps enemies in reserve; fortunate among the fortunate is he whose talent not only triumphs over obstacles, but even creates new obstacles in order to triumph over them. He is as great as the old masters, in a country and a century in which the old masters would not have been able to survive. For when I hear men like Raphael and Veronese being lauded to the skies, with the manifest intention of diminishing the merit of those who came after them, then, although I am quite prepared to bestow my enthusiasm upon these great shades who have no need of it, I ask myself if a merit which is *at least* the equal of theirs (I will even admit for a moment, and out of pure compliance, that it may be inferior) is not infinitely more *meritorious*, since it has triumphantly evolved in an atmosphere and a territory which are hostile to it. The noble artists of the Renaissance would have been positively to blame if they had not been great, prolific and sublime, encouraged and incited as they were by an illustrious company of princes and prelates—but why do I stop here? by the masses themselves, I should say, who were artists to a man in that golden age! But what are we to say of the modern artist who has risen to the heights *in spite of* his century, unless it be things which this age will not accept, and which we must leave to future ages to utter?

[1] Baudelaire had already quoted a long passage from Thiers's *Salon de 1822* (including the sentences quoted here) in his own *Salon de 1846* (see pp. 52–53 above).

But to return to religious painting, tell me if you have ever seen the essential solemnity of the *Entombment*[1] better expressed? Do you honestly believe that Titian could have invented this? He would have conceived it, or rather he did conceive it, differently; but I prefer it this way. The setting is the vault itself, an emblem of the subterranean life which the new religion was to lead for many years. Outside, a spiral of light and air gliding upwards. The Holy Mother is about to faint, she can scarcely support herself. We should note in passing that, instead of turning the most Holy Mother into a little woman from an Easter Album, Eugène Delacroix always bestows upon her a tragic breadth of gesture which is perfectly appropriate to this Queen of Mothers. It is impossible for an amateur who is anything of a poet not to feel his imagination struck, not by an historical impression, but by an impression of poetry, religion and universality, as he gazes at that little group of men who are tenderly carrying the body of their God into the depths of a crypt, into that sepulchre which the world will adore, 'the only sepulchre', as René superbly said, 'which will have nothing to give up at the end of time'.

The *Saint Sebastian*[2] is not only a marvel of painting, but is also an exquisite thrill of sadness. The *Ascent to Calvary*[3] is a complicated, passionate and learned composition. '*It was to have been carried out on a large scale* at St. Sulpice,' we are told by the artist who knows his world, 'in the baptismal chapel, whose purpose has now been altered.' Although he has taken every precaution, and has clearly said to the public, 'I want to show you the small-scale project of a large work with which I had been commissioned,' the critics have not failed, as usual, to rebuke him for only being able to paint sketches!

Look next upon the famous poet who taught the *Art of Love*; there he is, lying on the wild grass, with a soft sadness which is almost that of a woman.[4] Will his noble friends in Rome be able to quell the emperor's spite? Will he one day know again the luxurious pleasures of that prodigious city? No: from this inglorious land the long and melancholy river of the *Tristia* will flow in vain; here he is to live and to die. 'One day, after crossing the Ister near its mouth and becoming

[1] Reproduced Escholier, vol. III, facing p. 240.

[2] Robaut 1353: reproduced *Gazette des Beaux-Arts*, 1859, vol. II, facing p. 138.

[3] Now in the Metz Museum; see pl. 39.

[4] The picture in question is *Ovid in Exile among the Scythians* (now in the National Gallery); see pl. 40.

separated from my band of huntsmen, I found myself within sight of the waves of the Euxine Sea. I came upon a tomb of stone, o'er which a laurel was growing. I tore away the grasses which covered several words of Latin, and soon I succeeded in reading this first line of the elegies of an ill-fated poet:

'You will go to Rome, my book, and you will go to Rome without me.'

'I could not depict to you my feelings on finding the tomb of Ovid in the heart of this desert. You can imagine the sadness of my reflections upon the pains of exile, which were also my own, and upon the uselessness of talents in securing happiness! Rome today delights in the pictures painted by the most ingenious of her poets; but for twenty years Rome could watch the flowing tears of Ovid with dry eyes. But less ungrateful than the peoples of Ausonia, the wild inhabitants of the banks of the Ister still remember the Orpheus who appeared in their forests! They come and dance around his ashes; they have even retained something of his language, so sweet to them is the memory of that Roman who accused himself of being a barbarian because his voice was not heard from the Sarmatic shore!' [1]

It is not without reason that, on the subject of Ovid, I have quoted these reflections of Eudorus. The melancholy tone of the poet of *Les Martyrs* suits this picture, and the languishing sadness of the Christian prisoner is faithfully reflected in it. You will find therein the broadness of touch and feeling which characterized the pen which wrote *Les Natchez*; and in Eugène Delacroix's rough idyll I recognized a 'tale of perfect beauty', because he has put into it 'the desert's flower, the grace of the primitive dwelling and a simplicity in telling a tale of sorrow which I do not flatter myself to have preserved'.[2] I shall certainly not try to translate with my pen all the luxurious melancholy which this verdant exile distils. Perhaps it is better just to quote the catalogue, which speaks in the concise, tidy language of Delacroix's literary works: 'Some of them are examining him with curiosity,' we are told quite simply; 'others are greeting him in their manner, and are offering him wild fruits and mare's milk.' For all his sadness, the poet of fashionable elegance is not insensible to these barbarian graces, to the charm of this rustic hospitality. All the delicacy and fertility of talent that Ovid possessed have passed

[1] The above passage is quoted from Chateaubriand's *Les Martyrs*.
[2] Quoted from the epilogue to Chateaubriand's *Atala*.

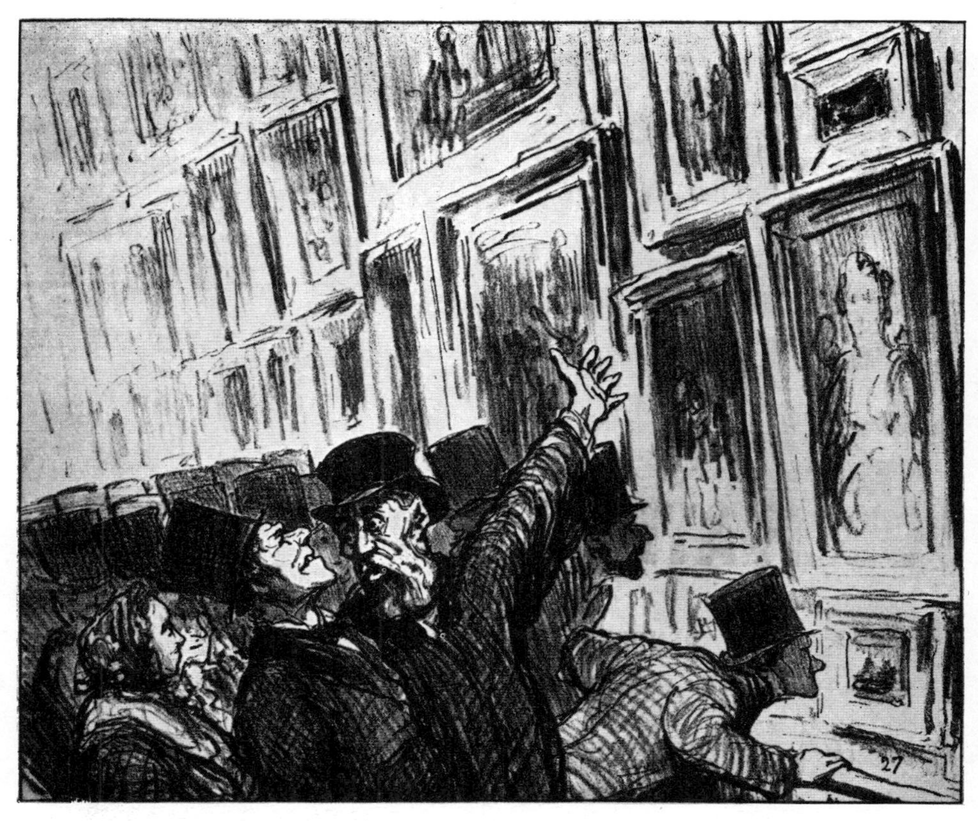

41. DAUMIER: *The Salon of 1859*. Lithograph. London, Victoria and Albert Museum.

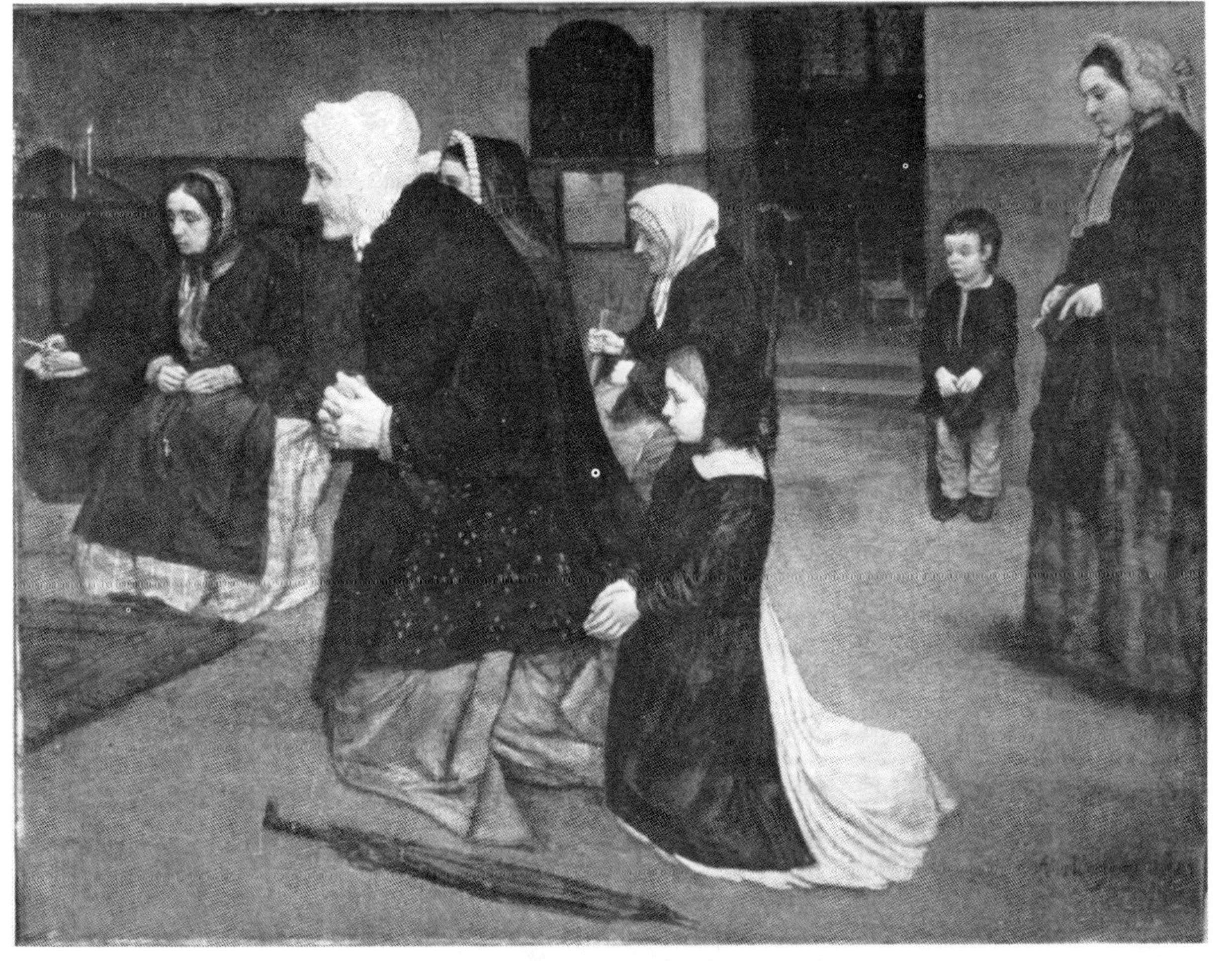

42. LEGROS: *The Angelus*. Salon of 1859. Formerly Cheltenham, Mr. Asa Lingard.

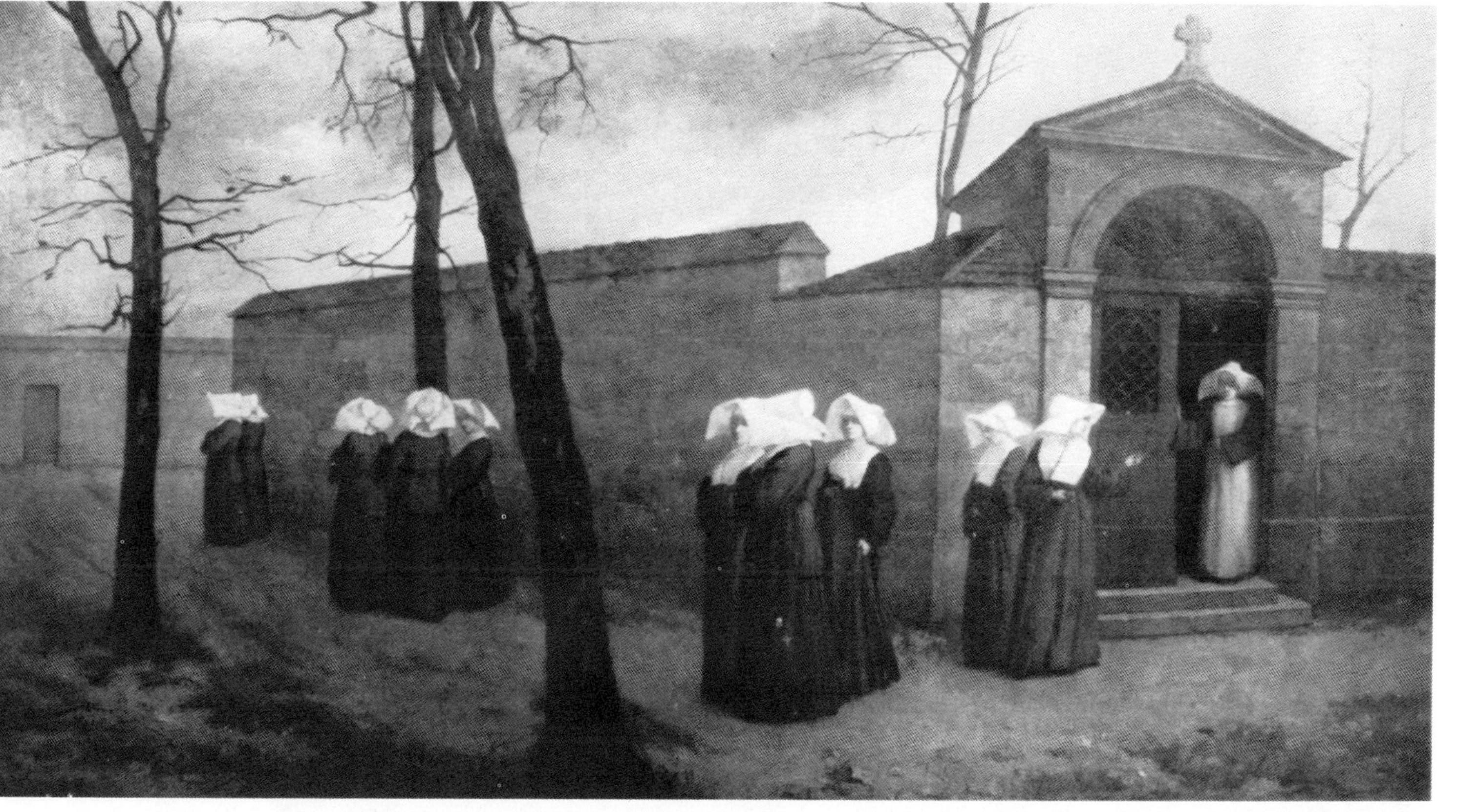

43. AMAND GAUTIER: *Sisters of Mercy*. Salon of 1859. Lille, Musée des Beaux-Arts.

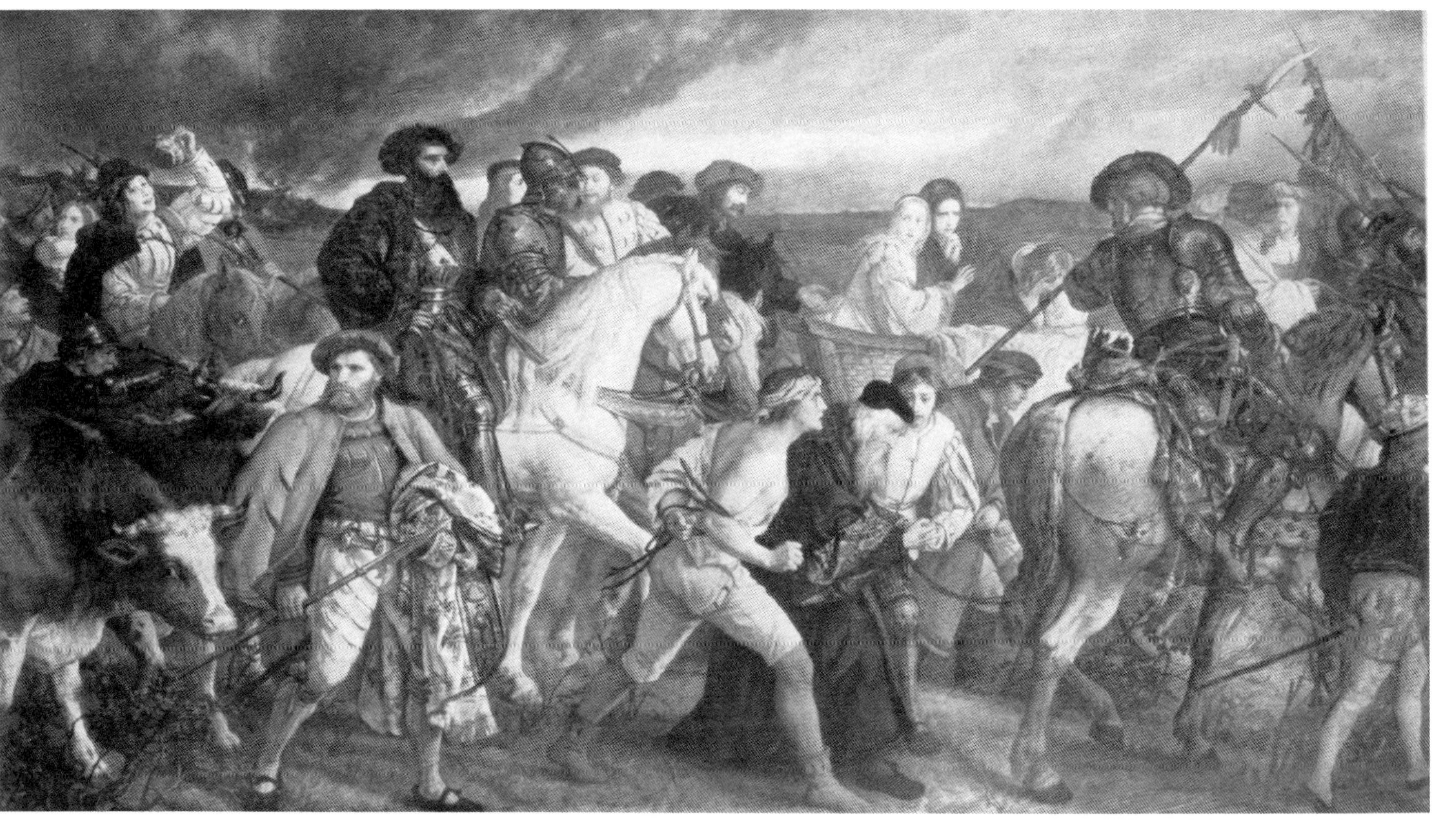

44. Lies: *The Evils of War*. Salon of 1859. Brussels, Musées Royaux.

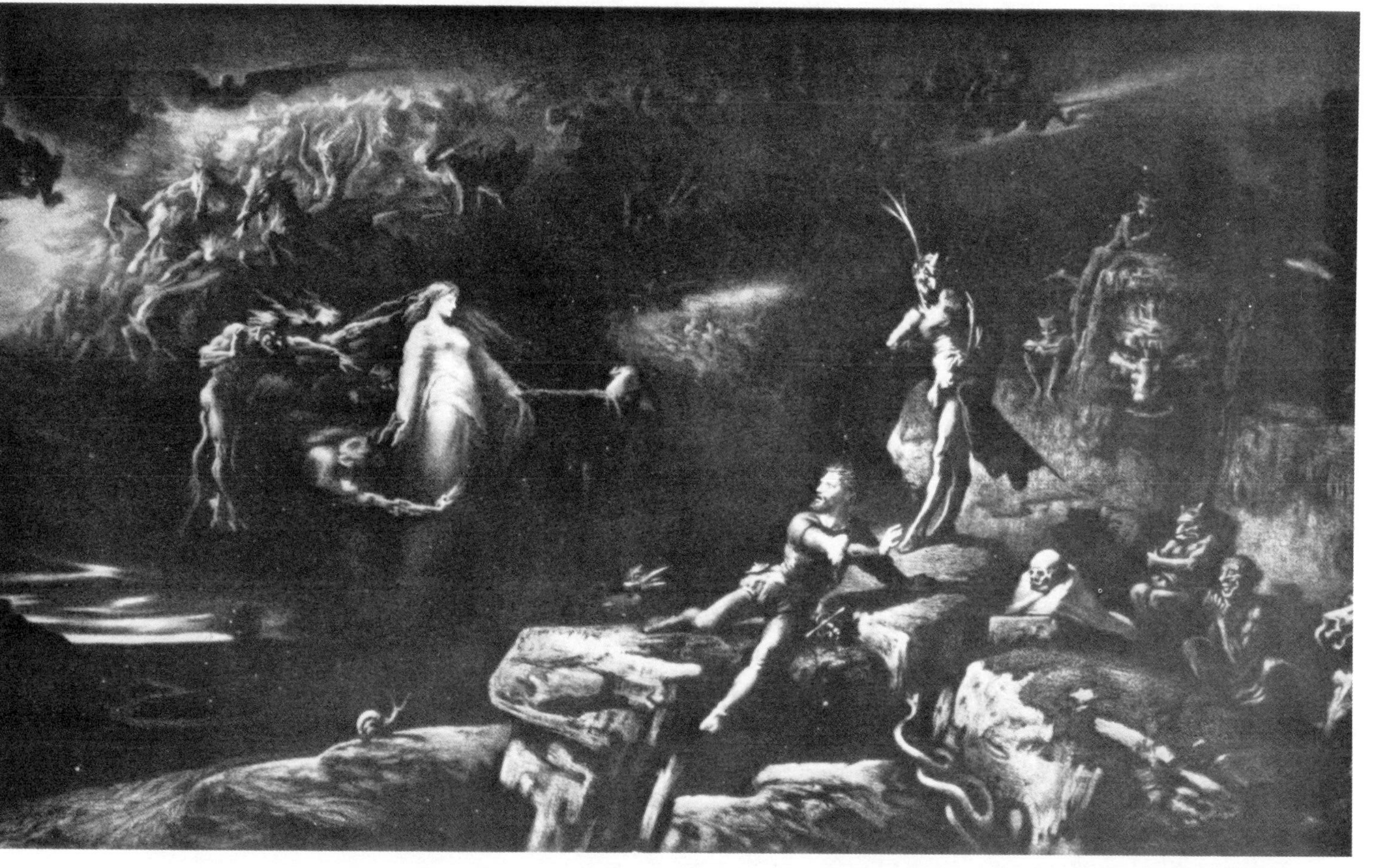

45. CHIFFLART (after): *Faust at the Sabbath* (detail). Salon of 1859. London, Victoria and Albert Museum.

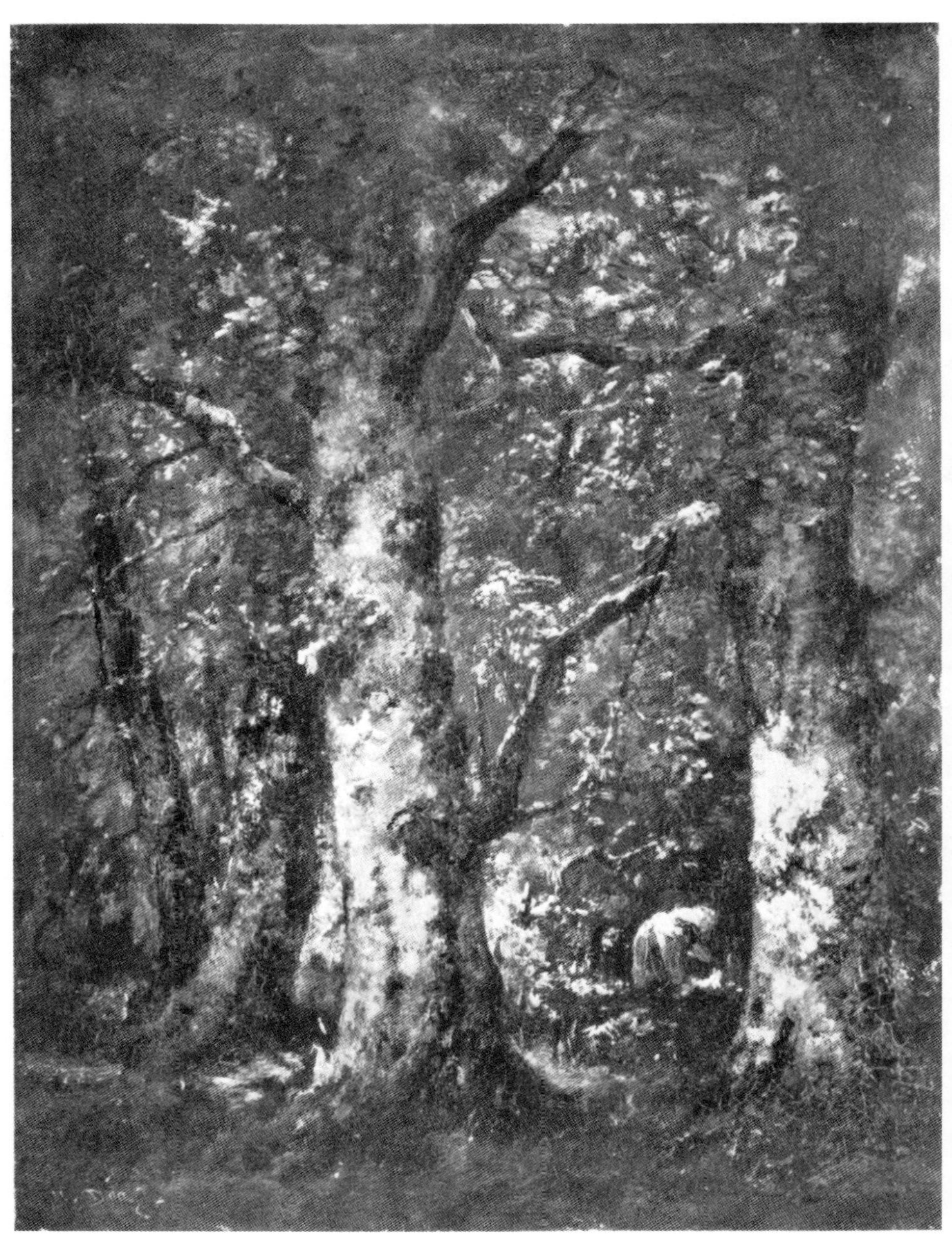

46. Diaz: *Study of Trees*. Formerly New York, Metropolitan Museum of Art.

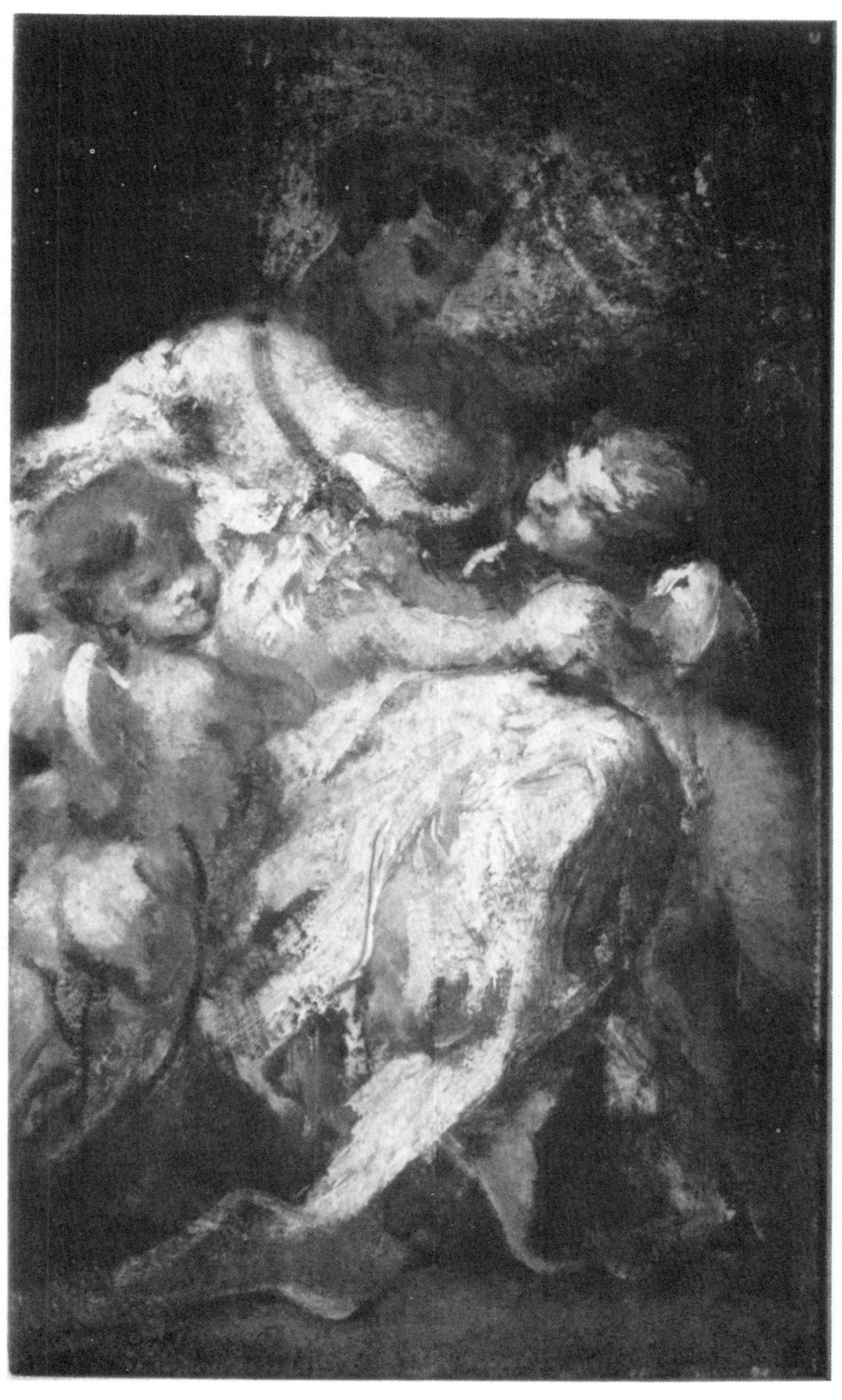

47. Diaz: *Love's Offspring*. Dated 1847. London, National Gallery.

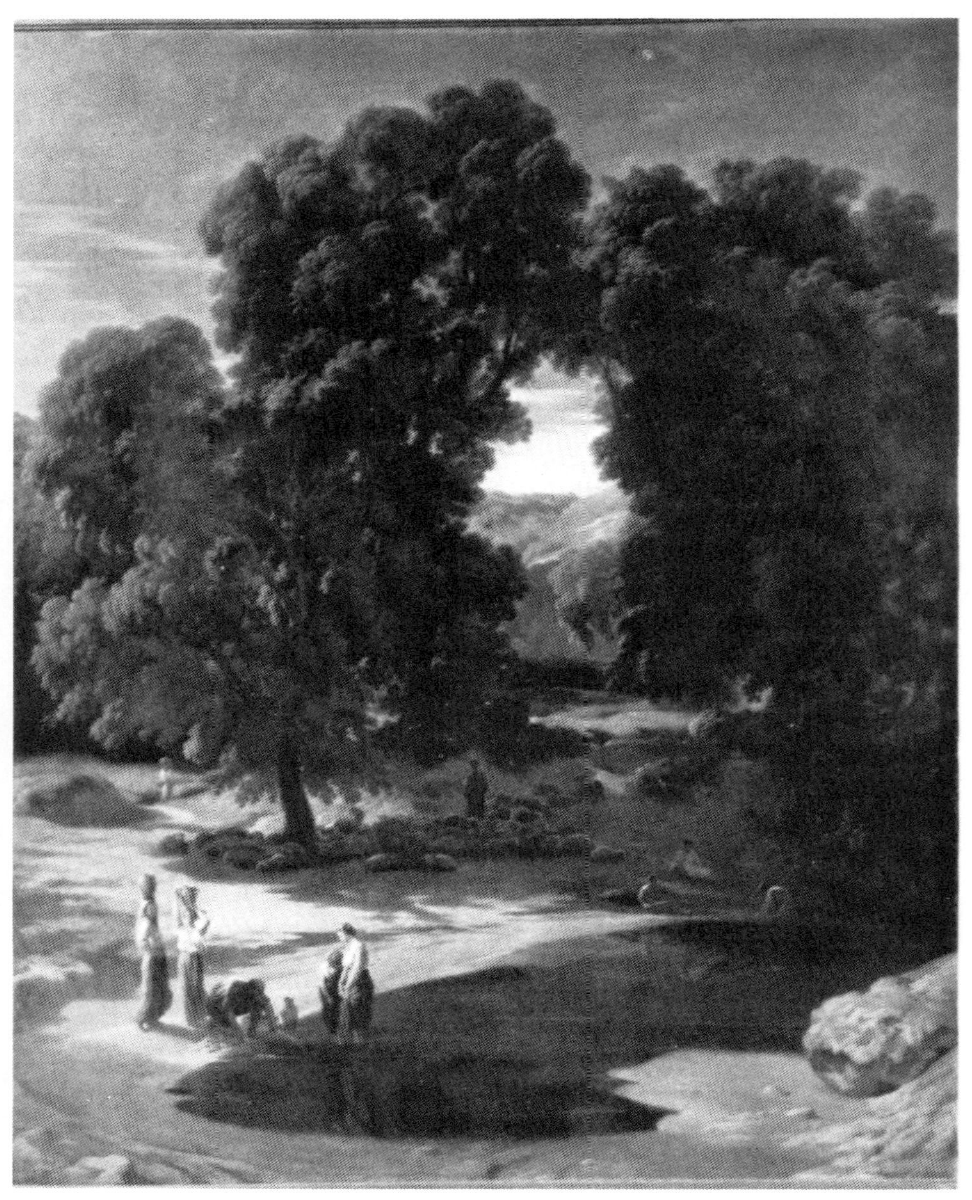

48. Paul Flandrin: *Landscape*. Salon of 1859. Montauban, Musée Ingres.

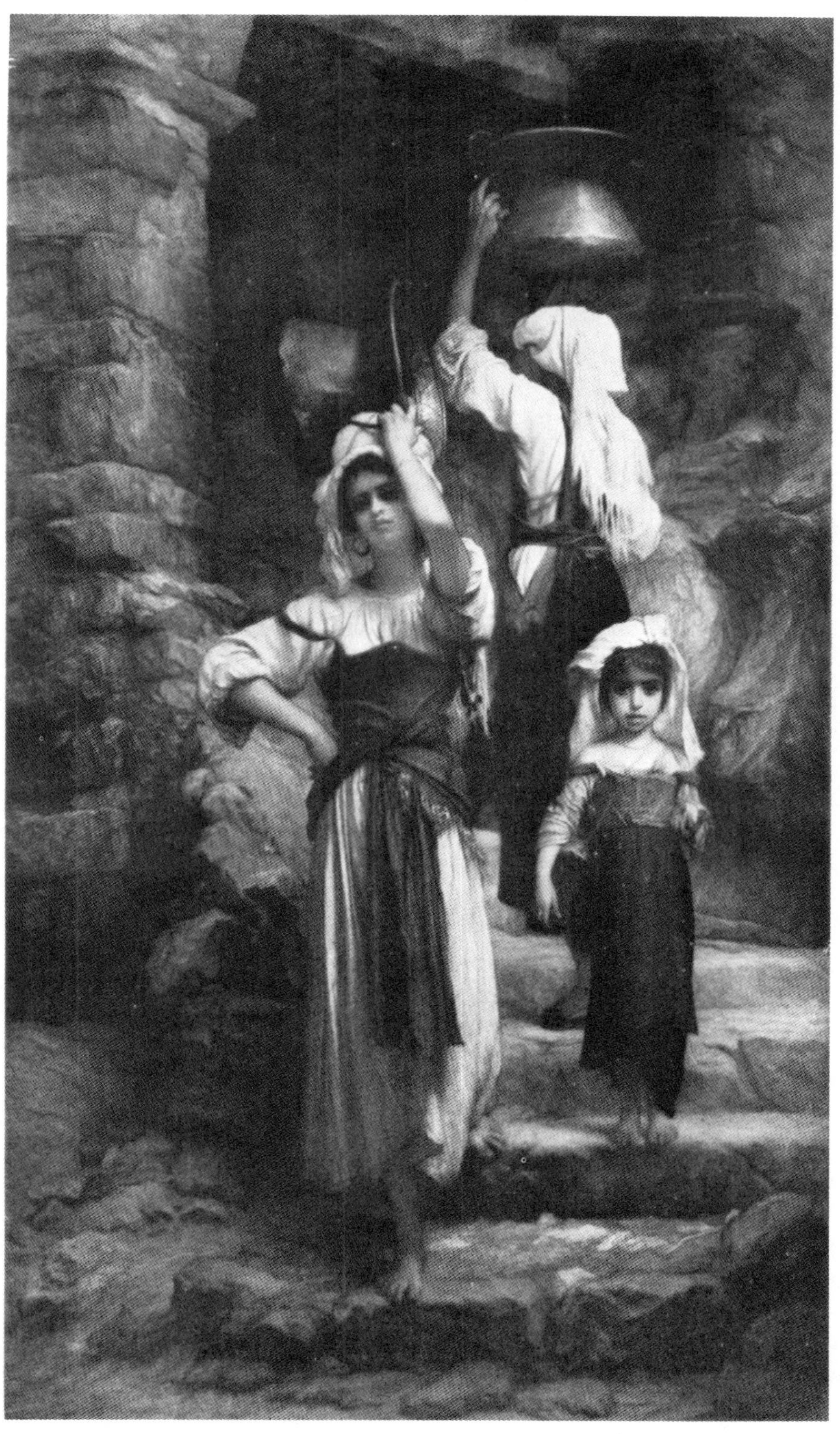

49. HÉBERT: *Peasant Women of Cervaro*. Salon of 1859. Paris, Musée du Louvre.

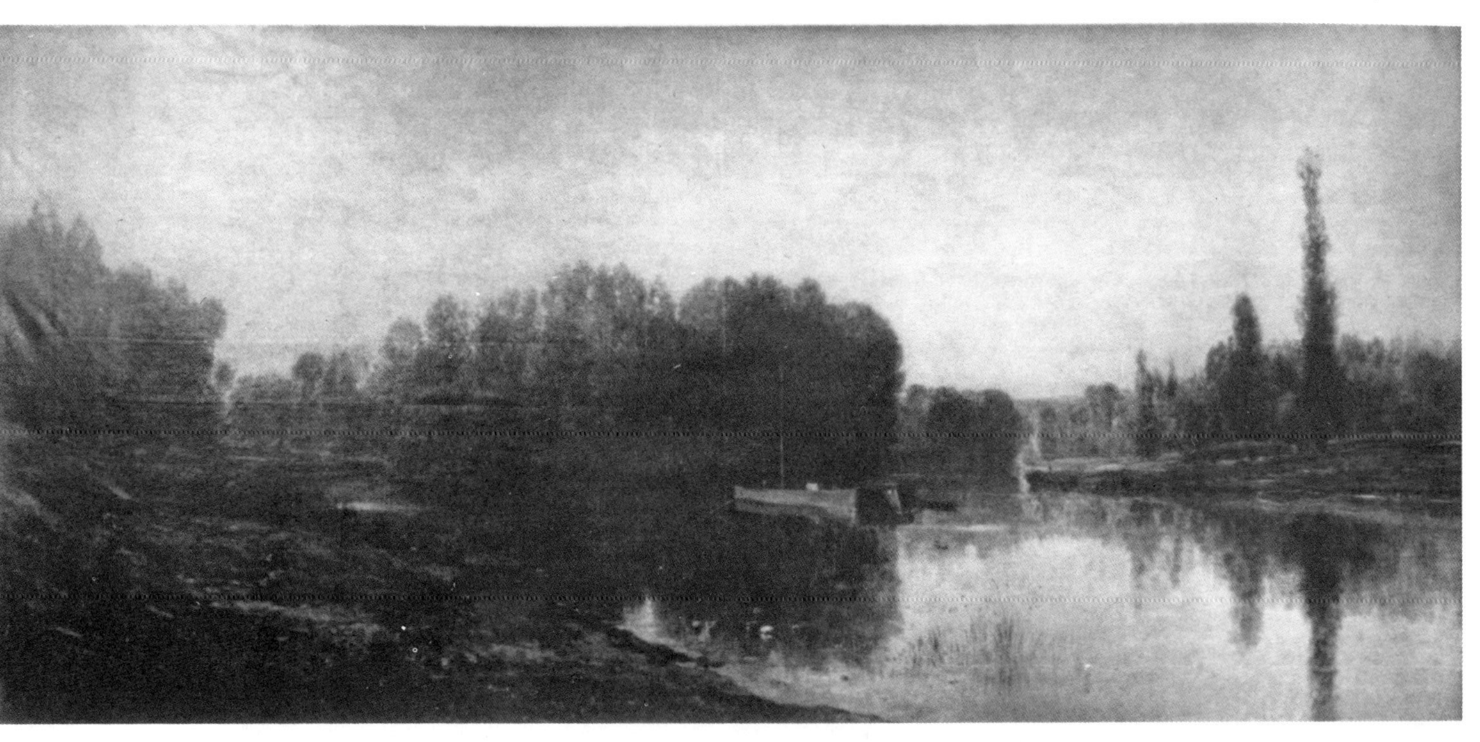

50. DAUBIGNY: *Landscape by the River Oise*. Salon of 1859. Bordeaux, Musée des Beaux-Arts.

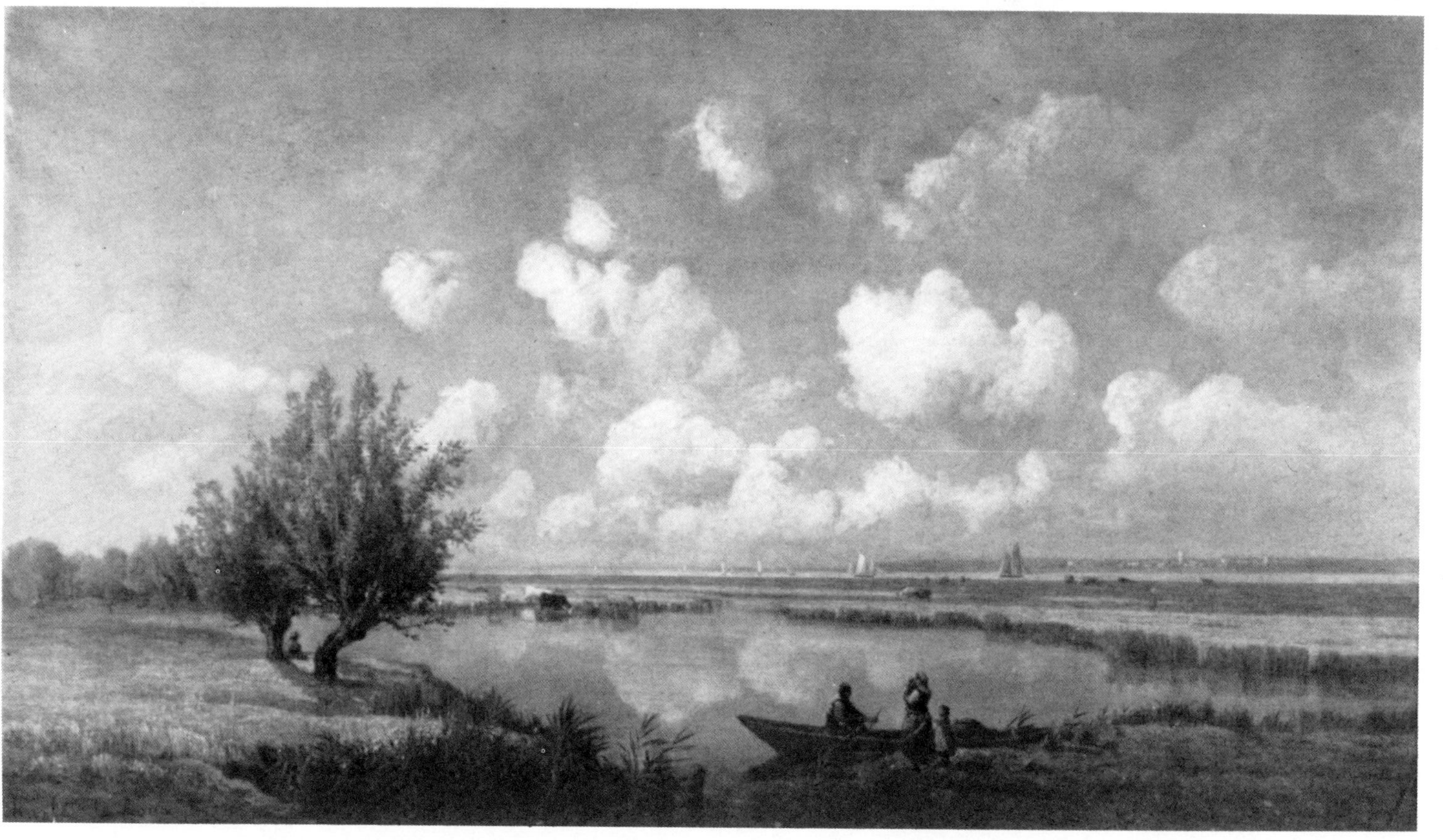

51. Le Roux: *Water-Meadows at Corsept, on the Mouth of the Loire*. Salon of 1859. Paris, Musée du Louvre.

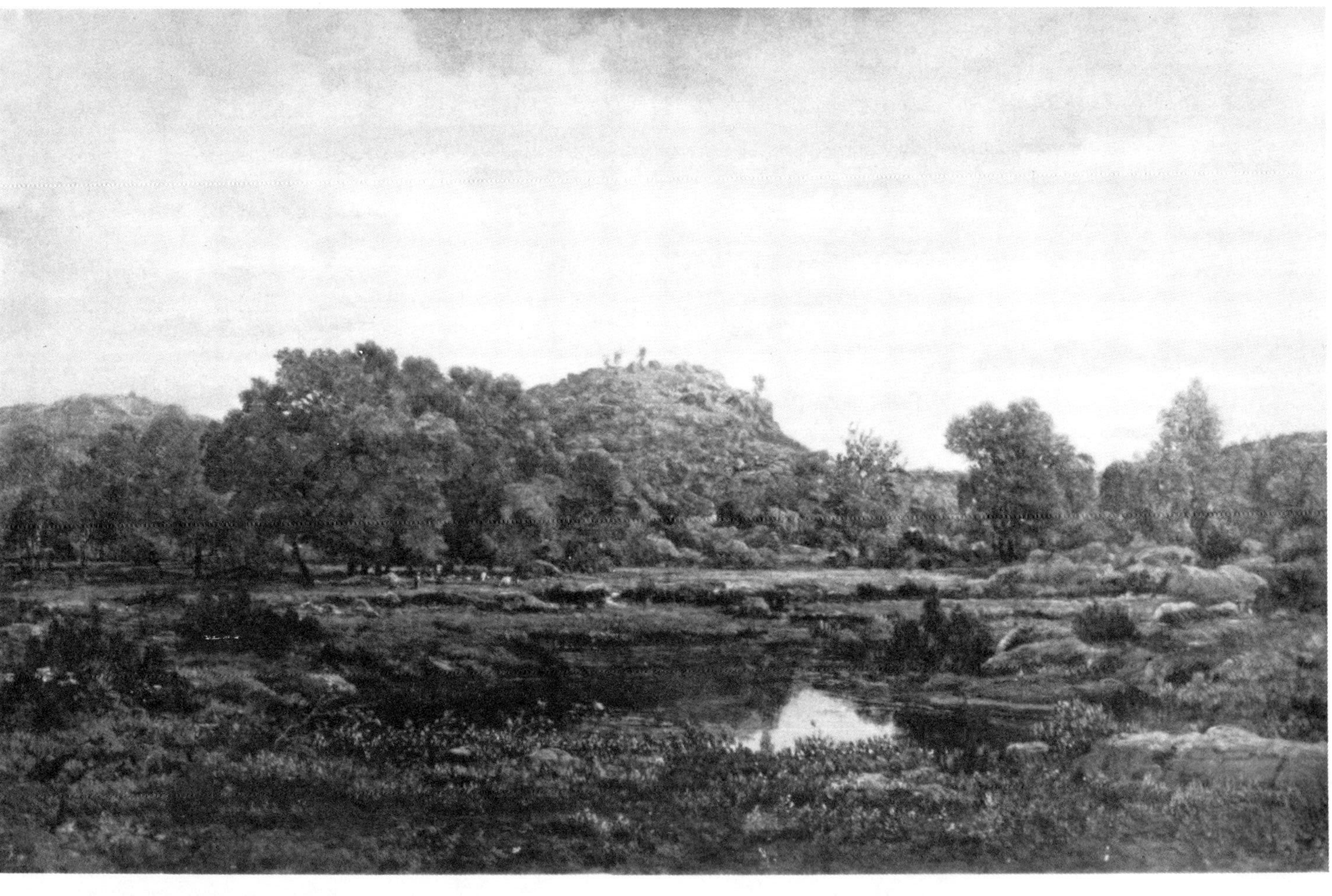

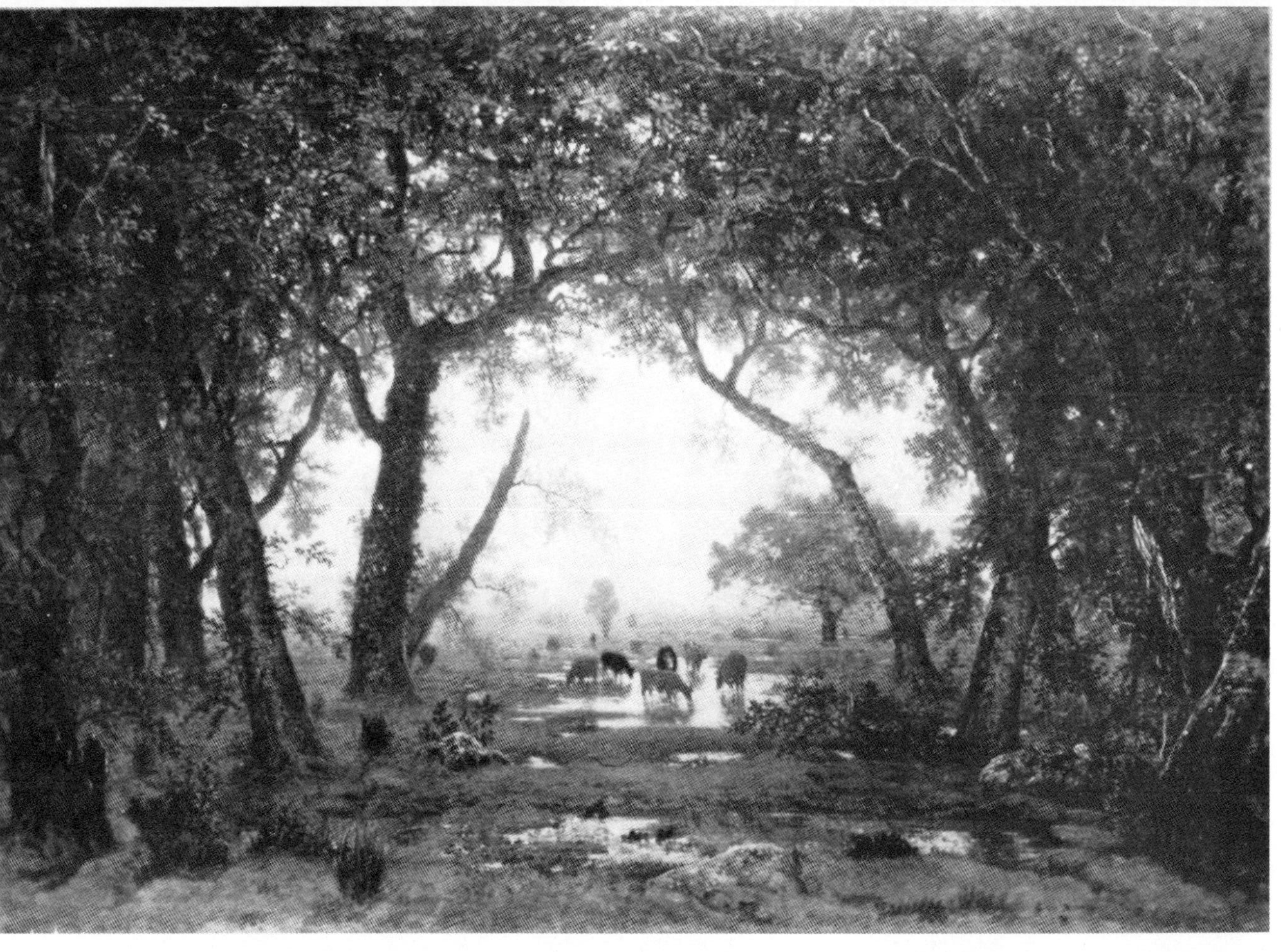

53. Rousseau: *The Forest of Fontainebleau—Morning*. Salon of 1850–1. London, Wallace Collection.

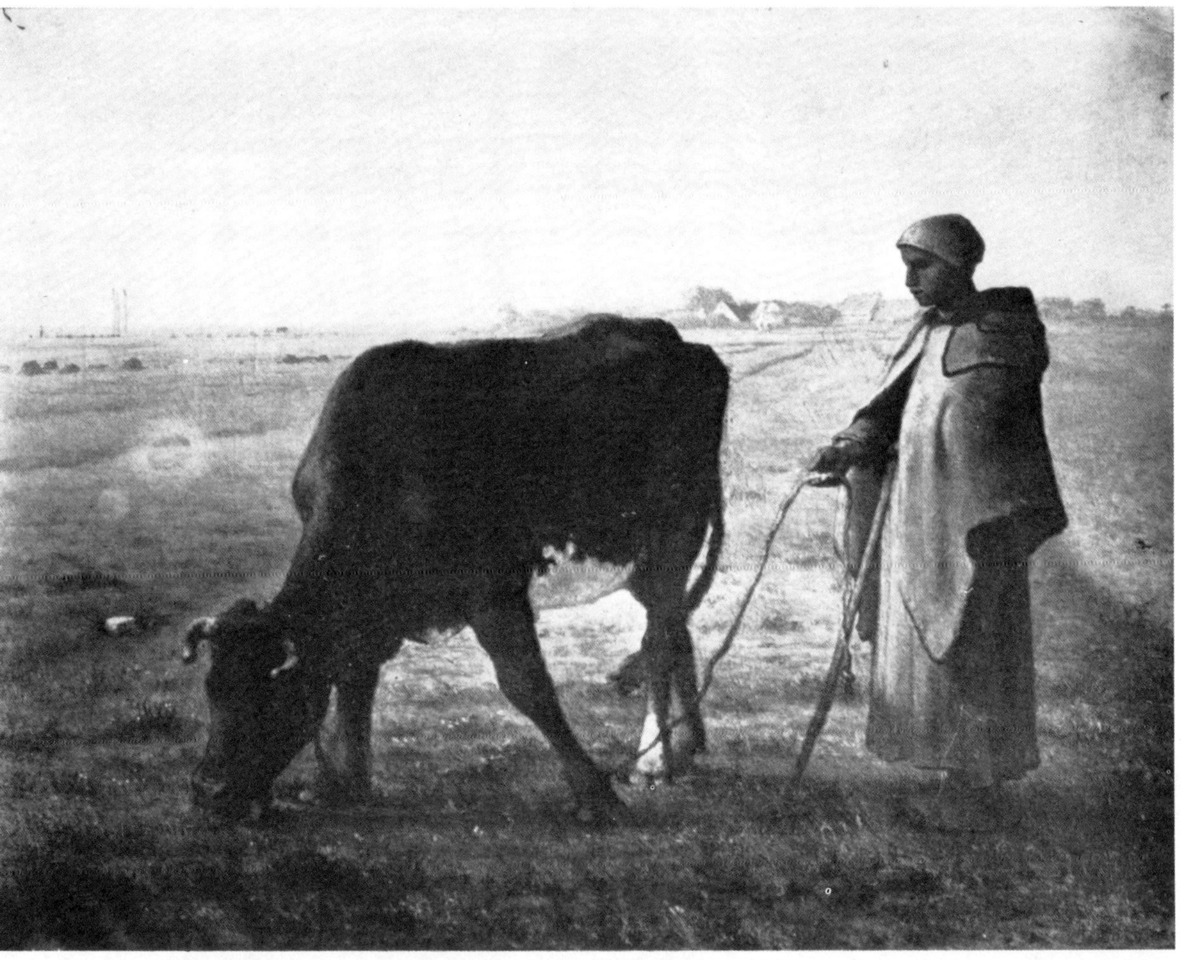

54 MILLET: *The Cowgirl*. Salon of 1859. Bourg-en-Bresse, Musée de l'Ain

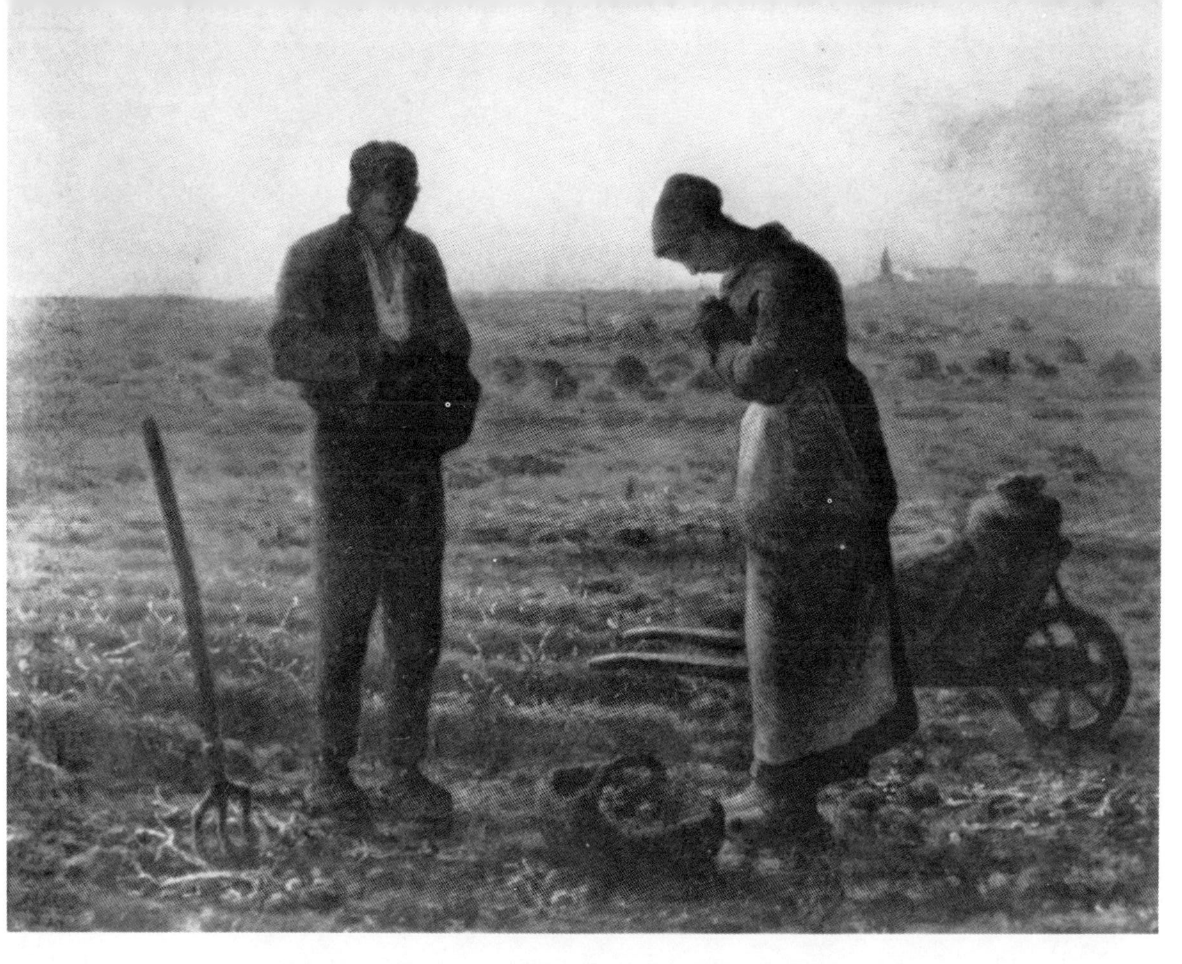

55. MILLET: *The Angelus*. Painted 1858–9. Paris, Musée du Louvre.

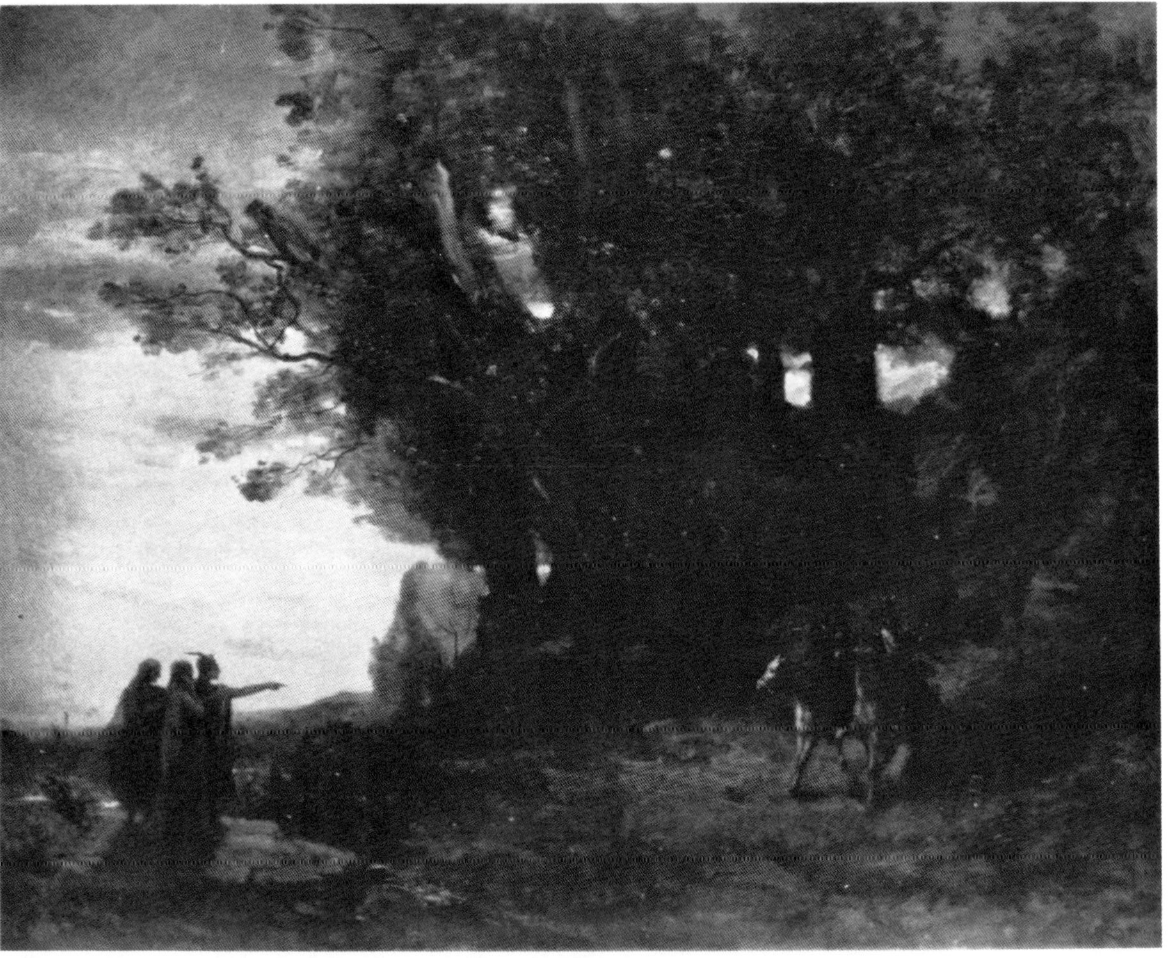

6 Corot, *Macbeth and the Witches*, Salon of 1859. London, Wallace Collection

into Delacroix's picture. And just as exile gave the brilliant poet that quality of sadness which he had hitherto lacked, so melancholy has clothed the painter's superabundant landscape with its own magical glaze. I find it impossible to say that any one of Delacroix's pictures is his best, for the wine comes always from the same cask, heady, exquisite, *sui generis*; but it can be said of *Ovid among the Scythians* that it is one of those wonderful works such as Delacroix alone can conceive and paint. The artist who has painted this can count himself a happy man, and he who is able to feast his eyes upon it every day may also call himself happy. The mind sinks into it with a slow and appreciative rapture, as it would sink into the heavens, or into the sea's horizon—into eyes brimming with thought, or a rich and fertile drift of reverie. I am convinced that this picture has a charm all its own for subtle spirits; I would almost be prepared to swear that, more than others perhaps, it must have pleased highly-strung and poetic temperaments—M. Fromentin, for example, of whom I shall have the pleasure of talking to you presently.

I am cudgelling my brain in order to extract some formula which may properly express Eugène Delacroix's *speciality*.[1] He is an excellent draughtsman, a prodigious colourist, an eager and resourceful composer —all this is obvious, all this has already been said. But how comes it that he produces a sensation of novelty? What does he give us which is more than the past has given us? He is as great as the great, as clever as the clever, but why does he please us more? One might perhaps say that, gifted with a richer imagination, he expresses for us above all the inmost secret of the brain, the *wonderful* aspect of things, so faithfully does his work retain the stamp and temper of its conception. It is the infinite within the finite! It has the quality of a dream! and by this word I do not mean those riotous Bedlams of the night, but rather the vision which comes from intense meditation, or, with minds less naturally fertile, from artificial stimulants. In a word, Eugène Delacroix is above all the painter of the *soul* in its golden hours. Believe me, this man sometimes makes me crave to live as long as Methuselah, or, in spite of all the courage that it would need for a dead man to consent to come alive again ('Send me back to Hell!', as the poor soul cried when the Thessalian witch restored him to life), nevertheless to be revived in time to take

[1] The italicizing of this word by Baudelaire has suggested to Gilman (p. 250, *n*. 27) that he was using it in a Swedenborgian sense, to denote a state of intuitive and immediate vision of all things. See also *Painter of Modern Life*, p. 42.

part in the raptures and the praises which he will provoke in a future age! But what is the good? For even if I should be granted this childish prayer and should see my prophecy fulfilled, what profit would I gain, beyond the shame of having to admit that I was a feeble spirit, possessed by the need of seeing its convictions ratified?

VI. RELIGION, HISTORY, FANTASY
(continued)

COMBINE the epigrammatic wit of France with an element of pedantry, so as to lend a little weight to its natural buoyancy, and you will have the *fons et origo* of a school which Théophile Gautier, in his benevolence, politely calls the 'Neo-Greek', but which I, if you will allow me, propose to dub the 'school of the *pointus*'.[1] In this school the object of erudition is to disguise a lack of imagination. For most of the time it has simply been a matter of transporting common, everyday life into a Greek or Roman setting. Dezobry and Barthélemy [2] will be of great assistance in this, and pastiches of the frescoes of Herculaneum, with their pale tints obtained by means of impalpable washes of colour, will allow the painter to dodge all the difficulties of rich and solid painting. Thus on one side you will find a pile of bric-à-brac (the serious element), and on the other a transposition of the trivialities of life into antique circumstances (the element of surprise and success), and these between them will henceforth take the place of all the conditions required for good painting. So we shall see antique urchins playing at antique ball and with antique hoops, amusing themselves with antique dolls and antique toys; idyllic tots playing at grown-ups (*Ma Sœur n'y est pas*[3]); cupids astride aquatic monsters (*Decoration for a bathroom*[4]); and 'Love-Brokers' in plenty, who offer their merchandise hung up by the wings, like rabbits pinned by the ears—these should be sent back to the Place de la Morgue, where an

[1] According to Crépet, Baudelaire borrowed this phrase from his friend Nadar, who used it to describe pedantic authors.

[2] Both celebrated antiquarian writers, the former of the nineteenth and the latter of the eighteenth century.

[3] By J. L. Hamon (Salon, 1853); it was bought by the Emperor, and perished at the burning of the Tuileries in 1871.

[4] Probably the four *Seasons* by Etex, described in the catalogue as 'panneaux décoratifs d'un salon de bains'.

abundant traffic in more natural birds is carried on. Love, inevitable Love, the immortal Cupid of the confectioners, plays a dominant and universal role in this school. He is the president of this courtly and simpering republic. He is a fish which accommodates itself to every sauce. And yet are we not very weary of seeing paint and marble squandered on behalf of this elderly scamp, winged like an insect or like a duck, whom Thomas Hood has shown us squatting like a cripple and squashing flat his cloud-pillow with his flabby obesity? In his left hand he holds his bow propped against his thigh, like a sabre; with his arrow in his right hand he executes the order 'Shoulder arms!'; his hair is thickly curled like a coachman's wig; his fat wobbling cheeks press against his nostrils and his eyes; it is doubtless the elegiac sighs of the universe which distend his flesh, or perhaps I should rather call it his *meat*, for it is stuffed, tubular and blown out like a bag of lard hanging on a butcher's hook; on his mountainous back is attached a pair of butterfly's wings.

> 'In sober verity,—does such an incubus oppress the female bosom? ... Is this personage the disproportionate partner for whom Pastorella sigheth,—in the smallest of cots?—Does the platonic Amanda (who is all soul), refer, in her discourses on Love, to this palpable being, who is all body? Or does Belinda, indeed, believe that such a substantial Sagittarius lies ambush'd in her perilous blue eye?
>
> 'It is the legend, that a girl of Provence was smitten once, and died, by the marble Apollo; but did impassioned damsel ever dote, and wither, beside the pedestal of this preposterous effigy? or, rather, is not the unseemly emblem accountable for the coyness and proverbial reluctance of maidens to the approaches of Love?
>
> 'I can believe in his dwelling alone in the heart—seeing that he must occupy it to repletion;—in his constancy, because he looks sedentary and not apt to roam. That he is given to melt—from his great pinguitude. That he burneth with a flame, for so all fat burneth—and hath languishings—like other bodies of his tonnage. That he sighs—from his size.
>
> 'I dispute not his kneeling at ladies' feet—since it is the posture of elephants,—nor his promise that the homage shall remain eternal. I doubt not of his dying,—being of a corpulent habit, and a short

> neck.—Of his blindness—with that inflated pig's cheek. But for his lodging in Belinda's eye, my whole faith in heretic—*for she hath never a sty in it*.'[1]

This makes sweet reading, does it not?—and it gives us a little revenge on that great chubby, dimpled dolly which represents the popular idea of Love. For my part, if I were asked to represent Love, I think I should paint him in the form of a maddened horse devouring its master, or perhaps a demon with eyes ringed by debauch and insomnia, dragging noisy chains at its ankles, like a ghost or a galley-slave, shaking a phial of poison in one hand, and in the other a dagger dripping with the blood of its crime.

The school in question, whose principal characteristic (to my eye) is to be perpetually *irritating*, has simultaneous contact with the proverb, the rebus and the neo-archaism. In the rebus, it has not yet reached the standard of *L'Amour fait passer le Temps* and *Le Temps fait passer l'Amour*,[2] which taken together have the merit of an exact, brazen and irreproachable rebus. Next, by their mania for dressing up trivial modern life in antique garments, the adherents of this school are forever perpetrating what I should be inclined to call *counter-caricatures*. If they want to become even more irritating, I fancy that I am doing them a great service by suggesting M. Edouard Fournier's little book[3] as an inexhaustible source of subjects. To clothe all modern history and all the modern professions and industries in the costumes of the past would be, I think, an infallible and infinite means of striking wonder. Even the honorable sage will take some pleasure in it.

It is impossible to fail to recognize some noble qualities in M. Gérôme, chief among which are his quest for the new and his taste for great subjects; and yet his originality (if at least he has such a thing) is often of a laborious nature and scarcely to be detected. Coldly he warms

[1] Translated by Baudelaire from Thomas Hood's sketch, 'On the Popular Cupid', in *Whims and Oddities* (1826). The passage is here given in the original. Against the final pun, Baudelaire added the following footnote: 'Une étable contient *plusieurs* cochons, et, de plus, il y a calembour; on peut deviner quel est le sens du mot *sty* au figuré.' On the whole passage, see Margaret Gilman's 'Baudelaire and Thomas Hood', in *The Romanic Review*, vol. XXVI, No. 3, July-September 1935, pp. 241–4. Hood's essay was accompanied by his own sketch which is described by Baudelaire above, and reproduced here on p. 216.

[2] Cf. *L'Amour et le Temps*, a song by the comte de Ségur.

[3] *Le Vieux-neuf*, 1859.

up his subjects by the addition of little ingredients and by childish devices. The idea of a cock-fight [1] naturally evokes a memory of Manilla or of England. M. Gérôme, however, will seek to beguile our curiosity by transforming this game into a kind of antique pastoral. In spite of great and noble efforts—the *Siècle d'Auguste* [2] for example, which is yet one more proof of his national tendency to look for success elsewhere than in pure painting—M. Gérôme was never yet, nor *will* he be, any more than the first of the *pointus*—at least this is much to be feared. I have no doubt at all that he has exactly portrayed those Roman games,[3] nor that the local colour has been scrupulously observed—I shall not whisper the slightest suspicion on this subject (and yet, seeing that he gives us the *retiarius*, why not also the *mirmillo*?); but if you base your success upon elements of this kind, are you not playing a game which, if not positively dishonest, is at least a dangerous one? and are you not liable to stir up a suspicious resistance among many who will go away shaking their heads and wondering if it is really certain that things happened exactly like this? Even supposing that such a criticism may be unjust (for one can generally recognize in M. Gérôme a mind which is both curious of the past and eager for instruction), it is nevertheless the deserved punishment of an artist who substitutes the amusement of a page of erudition for the joys of pure painting. The *facture* of M. Gérôme's painting, it must be admitted, has never been either strong or original. Indecisive, on the contrary, and but feebly distinguished, it has always oscillated between Ingres and Delaroche. But apart from this I have a sharper criticism to make of the picture in question. Even in order to demonstrate a callousness in crime and debauchery, even to make us suspect the secret abysms of gluttony, it is not necessary to join hands with caricature; and I think that the habit of exercising command—above all when it is a question of commanding the world—confers, in default of virtues, at any rate a certain nobility of attitude which is far too remote from this self-styled Caesar, this butcher, this obese wine-merchant; the most that *he* could aspire to would be the editorship of the *Good Trencherman's Journal*, as his own seductive and trenchermanly pose suggests.

His *King Candaules* is once again a snare and a distraction. Many people go into ecstasies in front of the furnishings and the decoration of its

[1] Gérôme's *Combat de Coqs* was exhibited at the 1847 Salon, and is now in the Louvre. See pl. 58.
[2] Formerly in the Amiens Museum; destroyed by enemy action.
[3] In his *Ave, César!*, which was Lot 165 at Christie's, 30 November 1928.

royal bed. Just look, an Asiatic bedroom! what a triumph! But is it really true that his terrible queen, who was so jealous of her own person that she considered herself no less polluted by a glance than by the touch of a hand, looked like this flat marionette? There is, besides, a great danger in a subject such as this, which is situated at an equal distance between the tragic and the comic. If an Asiatic anecdote is not treated in a way which is itself sinister, bloody and *Asiatic*, it will always raise a laugh; it will invariably call to mind the licentious frivolities of the Baudouins and Biards of the eighteenth century, in which a half-open door allows two wide-open eyes to observe the play of a syringe between the exaggerated adornments of a Marquise.

Julius Caesar! [1] What a sunset splendour this name sheds upon the imagination! If ever a man on earth has seemed like God, it was Caesar. Powerful and charming, courageous, learned and generous, he had every power, every glory and every elegance! He whose greatness always went beyond victory, and who grew in stature even in death! he whose breast, transfixed by the blade, could find utterance only for a cry of a father's love! he to whom the dagger seemed less cruel than the wound of ingratitude! Certainly M. Gérôme's imagination has been carried away this time; it was indeed a happy moment when he conceived his Caesar *alone*, stretched out in front of his overturned throne—when he imagined the corpse of his Roman who was pontiff, warrior, orator, historian and master of the world, filling an immense and deserted hall. This way of showing the subject has been criticized, but to my mind it could not be too highly praised. Its effect is truly great. This terrible summary is enough. We all of us know sufficient Roman history to imagine all that is implied, both the disorder which preceded and the tumult which followed. We can guess at Rome behind this wall, and we can hear the cries of the Roman people, stunned at their deliverance, and thankless at one and the same time towards both victim and assassin: 'Let Brutus be Caesar!' About the picture itself, there remains to explain one thing which is inexplicable. Caesar cannot be made into a Moor; his skin was very fair; besides, it is by no means silly to recall that the dictator took as much care of his person as the most refined dandy. Why then this earthy colour with which his face and arms are veiled? I have heard it suggested that it is the corpse-like hue with which death strikes the face.

[1] See Moreau-Vauthier, *Gérôme*, Paris 1906, pp. 152–3. A version of this subject was in the Corcoran Gallery, Washington.

In that case how long a time are we to suppose it is since the living man became a corpse? Those who put forward such an excuse must regret the absence of putrefaction. Others are content to point out that the arm and the head are enveloped in shadow. But this excuse would imply that M. Gérôme is incapable of representing white flesh in a half light, and that is not to be believed. And so I am forced to abandon the solution of the mystery. Such as it is, and with all its faults, this canvas is the best, and incontestably the most striking, that the artist has shown us for a long time.

French victories in the field are ceaselessly responsible for great quantities of military pictures. I do not know, my dear M—, what you think of military painting considered as a professional speciality. For my part I do not believe that patriotism compels a taste for the false or the insignificant. But if you think about it carefully, this kind of painting positively *exacts* either falseness or nullity. A *real* battle is not a picture; for, in order to be intelligible, and consequently interesting as a *battle*, it can only be represented in the form of black, white or blue lines, which stand for the battalions drawn up. In a composition of this kind, no less than in reality, the *terrain* becomes more important than the men. But in such conditions there is no picture left, or at least there is only a picture of tactics and topography. M. Horace Vernet believed once, or even several times, that he was solving the difficulty by accumulating and juxtaposing a series of episodes. From that moment his picture lost all unity, and began to be like one of those bad plays in which an excess of parasitic incidents prevents one perceiving its central idea, the conception which gave it birth. Thus, apart from pictures made for tacticians and topographers, which we must exclude from pure art, a military picture will only be intelligible and interesting on the condition that it is a *simple episode from military life*. This has been very well understood by M. Pils for example, whose solid and imaginative compositions we have often admired; and in earlier times, by Charlet and Raffet. But even within a simple episode, even within the simple representation of a hand-to-hand fight in a small, enclosed space, how much falseness, exaggeration, and monotony the spectator's eye has often had to endure! I own that what distresses me most of all in this kind of spectacle is not the abundance of wounds, the hideous profusion of slashed limbs, but rather the immobility within the violence, the dreadful cold grimace of a motionless frenzy. How many more criticisms could one not justly make! First of all, those long drab lines of troops, dressed as our modern governments dress them, can hardly sustain a picturesque treatment, and it is rather to the past that our artists turn in their bellicose hours; there they can find a plausible pretext for displaying a fine variety of arms and costumes, as M. Penguilly has done in his *Combat des Trente*. Next, there exists in the heart of man a peculiar love of victory which is not confined by truth, and this often gives to such canvases the false air of an advocate's speech. This is not a little apt to chill an enthusiasm in a rational mind, which is otherwise quite ready to burst into flame. When Alexandre Dumas recently recalled the fable '*Ah! si les lions savaient peindre!*' [1] in this context he drew upon himself a sharp rebuke from one of his colleagues. It is only fair to mention that the moment was not very well chosen,[2] and that he ought to have added that all peoples naïvely display the same fault in their theatres and museums. Just consider, my friend, to what a pitch of madness a patriotic writer can be led by a passion which is exclusive and foreign to the arts. One day I was turning the pages of a famous compilation which depicts the military victories of the French, with the accompaniment of a text. One of these prints represented the conclusion of a Peace Treaty. The French actors in this drama were booted, spurred and haughty in bearing, and their very glances seemed to insult the humble and embarrassed diplomats of the opposing side; and the text praised the artist for having contrived to express the moral vigour of the former by means of their muscular energy, and the cowardice and feebleness of the others by a roundness of form which was quite feminine! But let us set aside these idiocies, whose too lengthy analysis is but an *hors-d'œuvre*, and let us content ourselves with drawing this moral: namely, that it is possible to lack modesty even in the expression of the most noble and the most magnificent of sentiments.

There is one military picture, however, which we must praise, and with all our fervour; it is not a battle-piece; on the contrary, it is almost a pastoral. You will already have guessed that I am referring to M. Tabar's picture. The catalogue says simply: *Guerre de Crimée, Fourrageurs*. What an expanse of grassland, and what beautiful grassland, gently rolling in lines which follow the movement of the hills! Here the soul breathes a complex scent; it is not only the freshness of growing things, the tranquil beauty of a scene which sets us dreaming rather than arguing,

[1] La Fontaine, Book III, No. 10, *Le Lion abattu par l'homme*.

[2] Because of the Austrian war.

but it is at the same time the contemplation of that eager, adventurous life, in which every day commands a different task. It is an idyll shot through by war. The sheaves are stacked, the needful harvest is done and the day's work is doubtless finished, for the bugle's recall is echoing through the air. The soldiers are returning in groups, following the undulations of the landscape up and down with an ease of movement which is at once nonchalant and regular. It would be difficult to turn so simple a subject to better account; all is poetic here—both nature and man; all is true and picturesque, down to the piece of twine or the single strap which here and there supports a pair of red trousers. And the soldiers' uniforms set the gay flame of the poppy to this vast ocean of greenery. Moreover the subject-matter is of an allusive nature; and before I opened the catalogue, as I stood in front of this army of reapers, my thoughts turned first to our African troops, whom the imagination depicts as always so prepared for anything, so active, so truly *Roman*—although, in fact, this scene is set in the Crimea.

Do not be surprised to find an apparent confusion interrupting the methodical gait of my report for several pages. In the triple title of this chapter, it was not without some reason that I chose the word *Fantasy*. *Genre-painting* implies a certain prosaic quality, and *Fancy-painting*,[1] which answered my idea rather better, excludes the idea of the *fantastic*. In this type of painting one's judgement must be more than usually strict; for fantasy is all the more dangerous as it is the more easy and unconstrained; as dangerous as the prose-poem or the novel, it has much in common with the love inspired by a prostitute, which quickly falls into idiocy or degradation; it is as dangerous as all absolute liberty. But fantasy is as vast as the universe, multiplied by the number of all the thinking beings who inhabit it. It is the first thing that comes, interpreted by the first comer, and if he has no soul to throw a magic and supernatural light upon the natural obscurity of things, fantasy is a purposeless horror, it is the first thing that comes, *defiled* by the first comer. Here then you must expect no more analogies, except by chance; on the contrary, you must be prepared for disorder and contrast—a field chequered by an absence of regular cultivation.

First let us throw a passing glance of admiration, and almost of regret, upon the charming productions of some few men who, during that period of noble renaissance of which I spoke at the beginning of this

[1] *Peinture romanesque.*

work, were the artists of the pretty, the precious and the delightful—Eugène Lami, for example, who, between his paradoxical little figures, gives us a glimpse of a world and a taste which have disappeared; and Wattier, that scholar who loved Watteau so much. It was a period of such beauty and fruitfulness, that not one spiritual need was forgotten by its artists. While Eugène Delacroix and Devéria were creating a great and picturesque art, others, witty and noble within a little sphere—painters of the boudoir and of a lighter kind of beauty—were adding incessantly to the present-day album of ideal elegance. This renaissance was great in everything, from the heroic down to the vignette. On the robuster scale of today, M. Chaplin, who is moreover an excellent painter, sometimes continues this cult of the pretty, though he does it with a touch of heaviness; his work smacks less of the world, and a little more of the studio. M. Nanteuil [1] is one of the most nobly productive workers to honour the second phase of this epoch. Admittedly he has poured a finger of water into his wine; but he always paints with energy and imagination. There is a *fatal* quality in the children of that triumphant school: Romanticism is a grace, either from Heaven or Hell, to which we owe eternal stigmata. I can never contemplate that series of dusky and white vignettes with which Nanteuil illustrated the works of his friends, the authors, without feeling a little shiver of the memory, as though caused by a gust of cool air. And in M. Baron have we not also a man of rare gifts? without exaggerating his merit beyond all measure, is it not delightful to see so many faculties employed in such modest and fanciful works? [2] He composes admirably, he groups his figures with ingenuity and colours with ardour, and into all his little dramas he casts an amusing flame; I call them *dramas* because his composition is dramatic, and he possesses something like the genius of opera. I should be really ungrateful if I forgot him; for I owe him a delightful sensation. When a man comes out of a dirty and ill-lit hovel, and finds himself suddenly transported into an apartment which is clean, adorned with well-contrived furniture and clothed with caressing colours, he feels his mind light up and his sensibility prepare itself for the things of happiness. Such is the physical pleasure which the *Hôtellerie de saint Luc* caused me. I had

[1] Nanteuil was a prolific illustrator of such authors as Balzac, Dumas, Eugène Sue and Victor Hugo.

[2] Henri Baron's *Entrée d'un cabaret vénitien où les maîtres peintres allaient fêter leur patron saint Luc* was reproduced *Illustr.*, vol. XXXIII (1859), p. 388.

just been sadly contemplating a whole chaos of horror and vulgarity, constructed as it were of plaster and earth, and when I approached this rich and luminous painting, I felt my heart cry out. At last, we are back again in fine society! How cool they are, these waters which bear those parties of distinguished guests beneath a portico streaming with ivy and roses! How splendid they are, these women, and their escorts, these master-painters who are past-masters in beauty, all plunging into this haunt of joy, to do honour to their patron saint! This composition, which is so rich, so gay, and at the same time so noble and elegant in attitude, is one of the most perfect dreams of happiness which painting has ever attempted to translate.

Because of her noble proportions, M. Clésinger's *Eve* forms a natural antithesis to all these charming, tiny creatures of whom we have just been speaking. Before the Salon opened, I had heard much gossip about this prodigious Eve, and when at last I saw her, I had been so forewarned against her that my first reaction was a feeling that people had mocked far too much. It was quite a natural reaction, and one, furthermore, which was favoured by my incorrigible passion for the *large*. For I must make an admission, my friend, which will perhaps cause you to smile; both in nature and art, supposing an equality of merit, I prefer *large* things above all others—large animals, large landscapes, large ships, large men, large women, large churches; and transforming my tastes into principles, like so many others, I have come to believe that size is no unimportant consideration in the eyes of the Muse. However, to return to M. Clésinger's *Eve*, she possesses other merits too; a happy movement, a tortured elegance in the Florentine taste, and impeccable modelling, particularly in the lower parts of the body, in the knees, the thighs and the stomach—such, in short, as one might expect from a sculptor; it is a very good work which deserved better than it received.

Do you remember the first appearance of M. Hébert, that happy, almost riotous occasion?[1] His second picture claimed particular attention; if I am not mistaken it was the portrait of a woman, sinuous and opalescent—more than that, she was blessed almost with transparence —and writhing (mannered, but exquisite) in an atmosphere of enchantment.[2] Certainly the success was a deserved one, and M. Hébert, like a man of full distinction, announced himself with a flourish, as though he

[1] His first picture, *Le Tasse en prison* (1839), was bought by the state, and is now in the Grenoble Museum.

[2] Probably his *Almée* (Salon, 1849).

would always be a welcome guest. Unfortunately the very thing that caused his just celebrity will one day perhaps cause his decline. For his kind of *distinction* limits itself too readily to the charms of morbidity and to the monotonous languors of the album or the keepsake. It is undeniable that he paints very well indeed, but even so he does it without sufficient authority and energy to hide a weakness of conception. I have tried hard to dig beneath all the engaging qualities which I see in him, and what I have found is a singular degree of wordly ambition, an explicit intention to please by means accepted in advance by the public, and finally a certain fault which it is horribly difficult to define and which, for want of a better term, I shall call the fault of all the *littératisants*. I am eager that an artist should be literate, but it distresses me to see him attempting to woo imagination by means of devices which are situated at the extreme limits of his art, if they be not positively beyond them.[1]

M. Baudry is more of a natural artist, although his painting is not always sufficiently solid. His works betray a serious and loving study of the Italian masters, and his figure of a little girl, who I believe is called *Guillemette*, has had the honour of causing more than one critic to think of the dashing and lively portraits of Velasquez. All in all, however, I cannot help fearing that M. Baudry remains no more than a 'distinguished' artist. His *Madeleine pénitente*[2] is just a little frivolous and facilely painted, and on the whole I prefer his ambitious, complicated and courageous picture of the *Vestal*[3] to his canvases of this year.

M. Diaz is a curious example of an easy fortune achieved by an unique faculty. The time is not yet long past when there was a positive craze for him. The gaiety of his colour, which was scintillating rather than rich, called to mind the happy motley of oriental fabrics. The eye was so honestly entertained that it readily forgot to look for contour and modelling. Like a true prodigal, M. Diaz used up this unique faculty with which nature had prodigally endowed him; and then he felt a more difficult ambition stirring within him. These first impulses expressed themselves in the form of pictures of a greater size than those in which we had generally taken so much pleasure. But it was an ambition which turned out to be his ruin. Everyone noticed the time when his mind was

[1] Of Ernest Hébert's exhibits this year, *Les Cervarolles* is now in the Louvre (see pl. 49) and *Rosa Nera à la fontaine* was reproduced *Illustr.*, vol. XXXIII (1859), p. 276.

[2] Now in the Nantes Museum; see pl. 59.

[3] Exhibited 1857, and now in the Lille Museum.

tormented by jealousy in respect of Correggio and Prud'hon. But it would seem that his eye, which had grown used to noting down the scintillation of a little world, could now no longer see vivid colours on a large scale. His sparkling palette turned to plaster and chalk; or perhaps, seeing that his ambition from now on was to model with care, he therefore deliberately forgot the qualities which had hitherto constituted his glory. It is difficult to define the causes which have so rapidly diminished M. Diaz's lively personality; but perhaps we may be allowed to suppose that these laudable desires have come to him too late. Some reforms are impossible after a certain age, and nothing is more dangerous in the practice of the arts than to be always putting off indispensable studies until the next day. For long years you rely on an instinct which is generally happy, and when at last you want to correct a haphazard education and to acquire principles until then neglected, it is already too late. The brain has adopted incorrigible habits, and the rebellious and unsettled hand can no more express what it once expressed so well than it can give form to the new ideas with which it has now been entrusted. It is truly disagreeable to have to say things like this about a man of such renowned worth as M. Diaz. But I am only an echo; what I am writing today, everyone has already said for himself, either aloud or in a whisper, with malice or with sorrow.

It is quite different with M. Bida; he, on the contrary, seems to have stoically repudiated colour and all its pomps in order to give more value and light to the human characters which his pencil undertakes to express. And he expresses them with a remarkable intensity and depth. Sometimes he agreeably heightens his drawing by the application of a delicate and transparent tint in a luminous passage—but this, however, without breaking its severe unity. One thing that distinguishes M. Bida's works above all is the intimate expression of his faces. It is impossible to attribute them indifferently to one or another race, or to suppose that these individuals profess a religion which is not theirs. Even without the catalogue's explanations (*Prédication maronite dans le Liban*, *Corps de garde d'Arnautes au Caire*), any experienced eye would easily guess the differences.[1]

M. Chifflart won the *grand prix de Rome*, and (what a miracle!) he has his originality. His sojourn in the eternal city has not quenched his mental

[1] Bida's *La Prière* was reproduced *Illustr.*, vol. XXXIV (1859), p. 21, where it is described as a drawing.

powers—which, after all, only goes to prove one thing: namely, that they alone die there who are too weak to live there, and that the 'school' only humiliates those who are dedicated to humility. Everyone justly rebukes M. Chifflart's two drawings (*Faust au combat* and *Faust au sabbat*[1]) for their excess of darkness and gloom, above all in drawings of such complexity. But their *style* is truly fine and imposing. What a dream of chaos! Mephisto and his friend Faust, invincible and invulnerable, are plunging at the gallop through the storm of war, with their swords held high. Marguerite, a long, sinister, unforgettable figure, floats in mid-air and stands out in relief, like a pang of remorse, upon the immense, pale disk of the moon. I count it to M. Chifflart's greatest credit that he has treated these poetic subjects heroically and dramatically, and that he has thrust far from him all the accepted trappings of melancholy. The painter who never tired of doing just one more Christ in the form of his Faust, and one more Faust in the form of his Christ, either of which was indistinguishable from a pianist about to pour forth his private sorrows upon the ivory keys—the good Ary Scheffer,[2] I mean, should really have seen these two vigorous drawings in order to understand that he alone may be allowed to translate the poets who feels in himself an energy equal to theirs. I do not believe that the assured pencil which has drawn this sabbath and this slaughter could ever abandon itself to the silly melancholy of young maidens.

Among the younger reputations, one of the most solidly established is that of M. Fromentin. He is neither precisely a landscape nor a genre painter; these two territories are too restricted to contain his free and supple fancy. If I said of him that he is a teller of travellers' tales, I should not be saying enough, for there are many travellers with neither poetry nor soul, and his soul is one of the rarest and most poetic that I know. His painting, which is properly so called, judicious, powerful, and well-controlled, evidently derives from Eugène Delacroix. With him too we find that expert and innate understanding of colour, which is so rare among us. But light and heat, which cast a kind of tropical madness into certain brains, shaking them with an unappeasable frenzy and driving them to unknown dances, only pour the sweetness and repose of contemplation into his soul. It is ecstasy rather than fanaticism. It is to be presumed that I myself am suffering to some extent from a nostalgia

[1] Both lithographed by Alfred Bahuet. See pl. 45.
[2] He had died the previous year.

which drags me towards the sun; for I find an intoxicating mist arising from these luminous canvases, which soon condenses into desires and regrets. I catch myself envying the lot of those men who are lying outstretched amid their azure shades, and whose eyes, neither waking nor sleeping, express, if anything at all, only love of repose and the feeling of a blissful happiness inspired by an immensity of light. M. Fromentin's mind has something of the feminine about it—just enough to add a grace to his strength. But a faculty which is certainly not feminine, and which he possesses to an eminent degree, is that of snatching up the particles of beauty which lie scattered over the face of the earth, and of tracking out beauty wherever it may have slipped in between the trivialities of a degenerate nature. Therefore it is not difficult to understand the passion with which he loves the grandeurs of the patriarchal life, nor the interest with which he observes those men among whom some trace of an antique heroism still remains. It is not only with gorgeous fabrics or with curiously-wrought arms that his eyes are in love, but above all with that patrician gravity and dandyism which mark the chiefs of powerful tribes. We had the same sensation some fourteen years ago when the painter Catlin[1] brought us his North American Indians, who, even in their state of decadence, made us dream of the art of Pheidias and of Homeric grandeurs. But what is the object of dwelling on this subject? why explain what M. Fromentin has himself so well explained in his two charming books, *Un été dans le Sahara* and *Le Sahel*[2]? Everyone knows that M. Fromentin tells his travellers' tales twice over; that he writes them as well as painting them, in a style which is his alone. The old masters also loved to have a foot in both camps and to use twin tools to express their thought. M. Fromentin has succeeded both as writer and as artist, and both his written and his painted works have such charm that if one were given permission to prune and to cut back some of the shoots of the one in order to give more solidity, more vigour to the other, it would be really very difficult to choose. For in order to achieve a possible gain, we should have to resign ourselves to a great loss.

We remember seeing, at the 1855 Exhibition, some excellent little pictures of a rich and intense colour but of a meticulous finish, whose

[1] In April, 1845. See pp. 70–71 above.

[2] The first of these was published in 1857, the second in 1859. Of Fromentin's exhibits this year, *Une rue à El-Aghouat* was reproduced in the *Gazette des Beaux-Arts*, 1859, vol. II, p. 293.

costumes and figures reflected an intense love of the past; these charming canvases were signed with the name 'Liès'. Not far from them were hanging some other exquisite pictures, no less preciously wrought, and marked with the same qualities and the same retrospective passion; these bore the name 'Leys'. Practically the same painter; practically the same name. This change of a letter is like one of those intelligent sports of Chance, which sometimes shows a subtlety of wit which is almost human. One is the pupil of the other; it is said that a warm friendship unites them. But have they for that reason been raised to the dignity of the Dioscures? In order to enjoy one of them, must we be deprived of the other? M. Liès has taken his bow this year without his Pollux; will M. Leys pay us a visit next year without his Castor? The comparison is all the more legitimate in that M. Leys was, I believe, the teacher of his friend, and it was Pollux too who wanted to cede one half of his immortality to his brother. *Les Maux de la Guerre*![1] what a title! Think of the conquered prisoner with his brutal conqueror lunging after him; think of the disordered bundles of loot, the ravished maidens, that whole world of blood, misery and dejection; the sturdy cavalryman with his shaggy red hair; the camp-follower, who, I believe, is not present, but might easily be—that *painted jade* of the middle ages, who had the authority of the Prince and of the Church to accompany the army, just like the Canadian courtesan who accompanied those other warriors in their beaver-skins—and finally the waggons, harshly and indiscriminately buffeting the young, the weak and the infirm: all this was bound of necessity to produce a thrilling, a truly poetic picture. At first the mind harks back towards Callot; but I do not think that I have seen anything in all the long series of his works which is more dramatically composed. I have nevertheless two criticisms to make of M. Liès. First, his light is too generally spread out—or rather squandered; his colour, monotonously bright, seems to quiver. In the second place, the immediate impression that the eye is fated to receive as it falls upon this picture is the disagreeable, uneasy impression of a piece of trellis-work; M. Liès has put a black line not only around the general contour of his figures, but also around every detail of their accoutrement, and he has done it in such a way that each of these characters has the appearance of a leaded fragment of a stained glass window. Observe too that this annoying effect is only reinforced by the general brightness of the colours.

[1] Now in the Brussels Museum. See pl. 44.

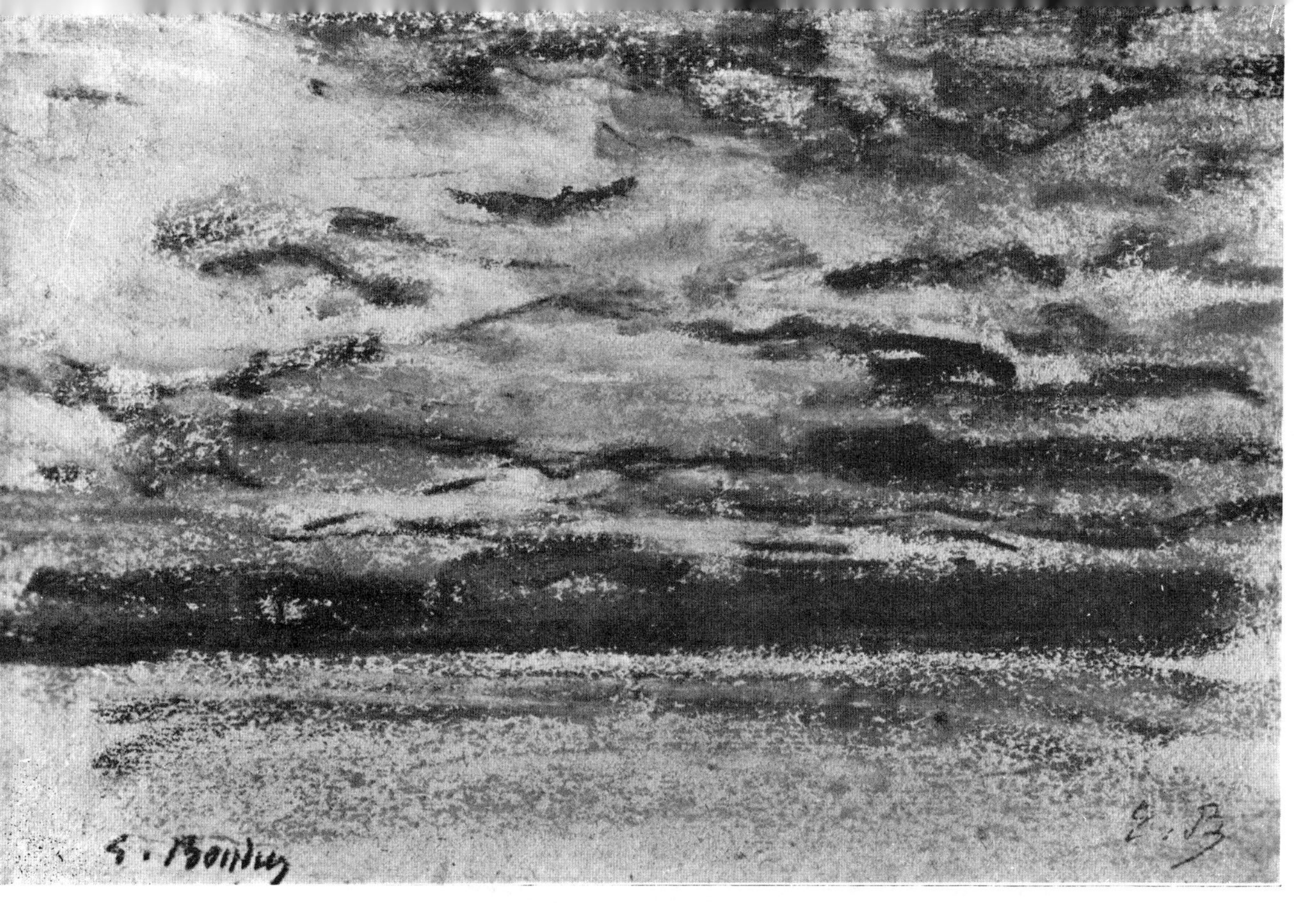

57. BOUDIN: *Sky-Study*. Pastel, c. 1859. London, Mr. Maurice Harris.

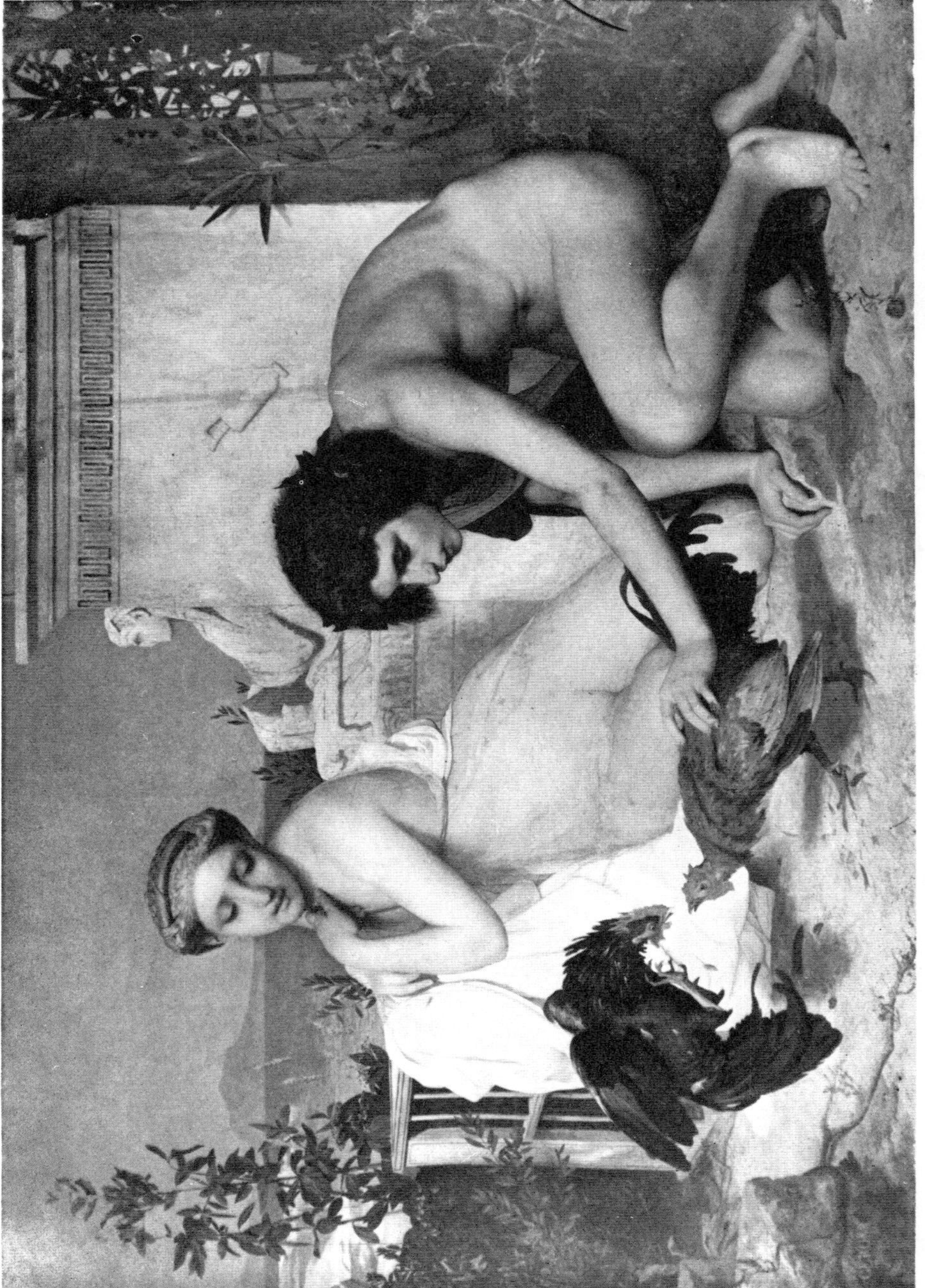

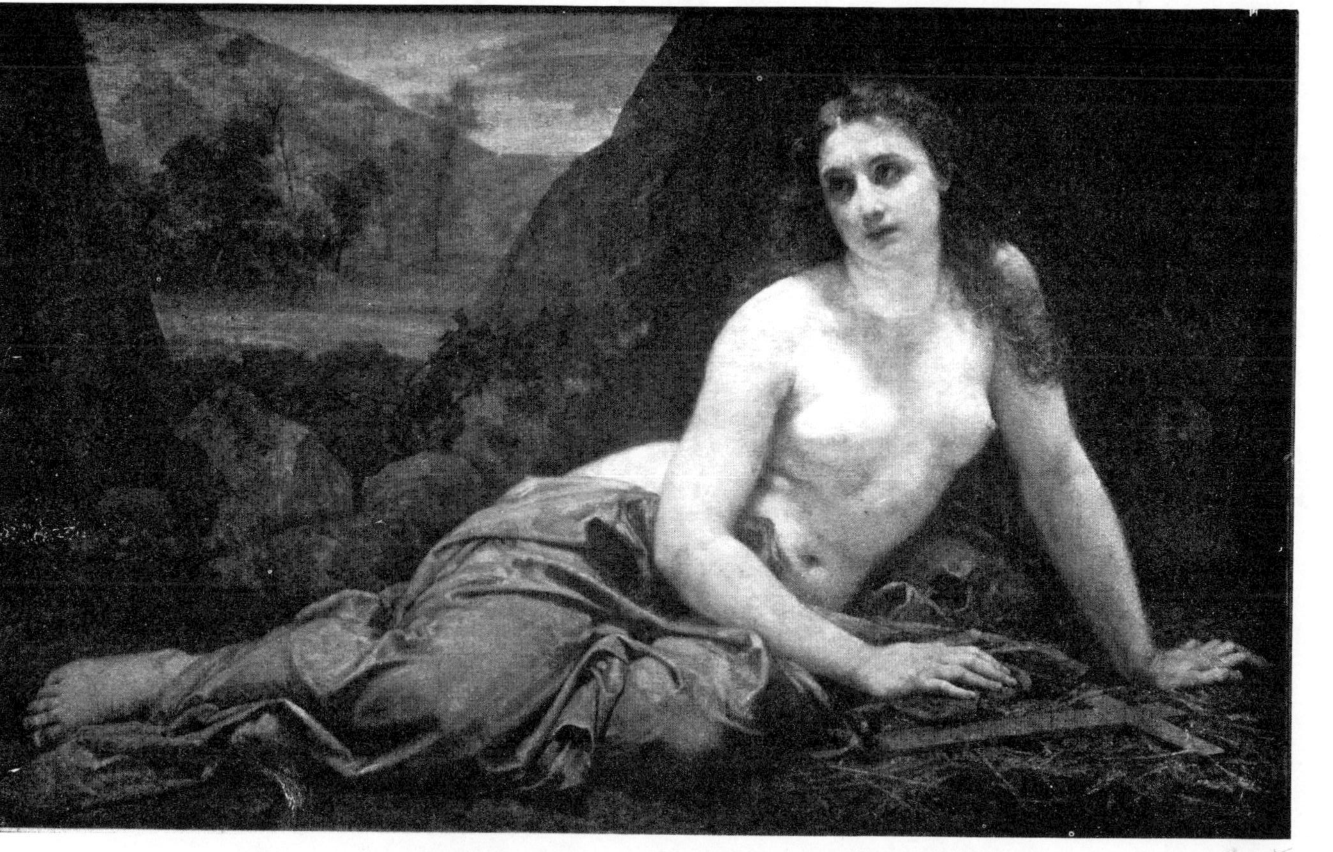

59. BAUDRY: *The Penitent Magdalen*. Salon of 1859. Nantes, Musée des Beaux-Arts.

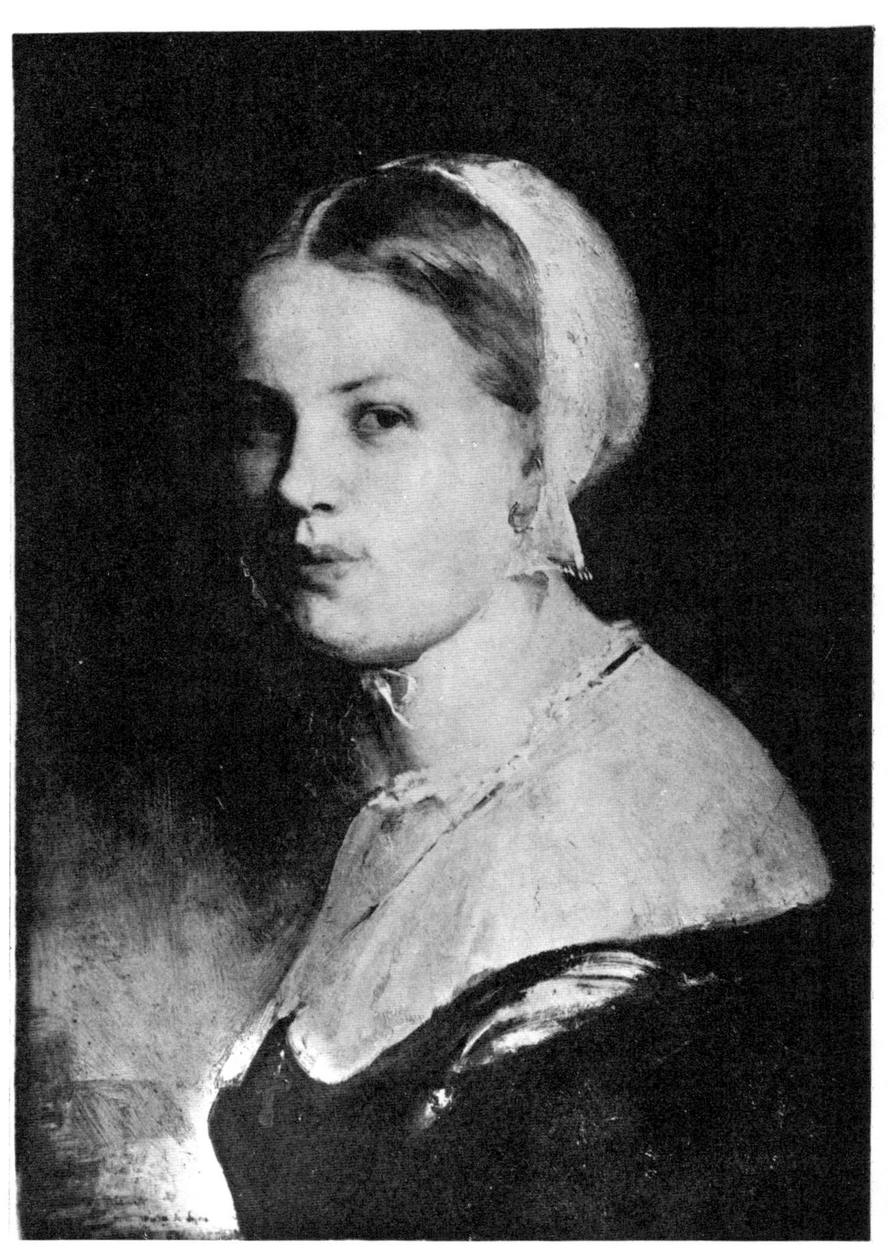

60. Ricard: *Portrait of a Girl*. Lyon, Musée des Beaux-Arts.

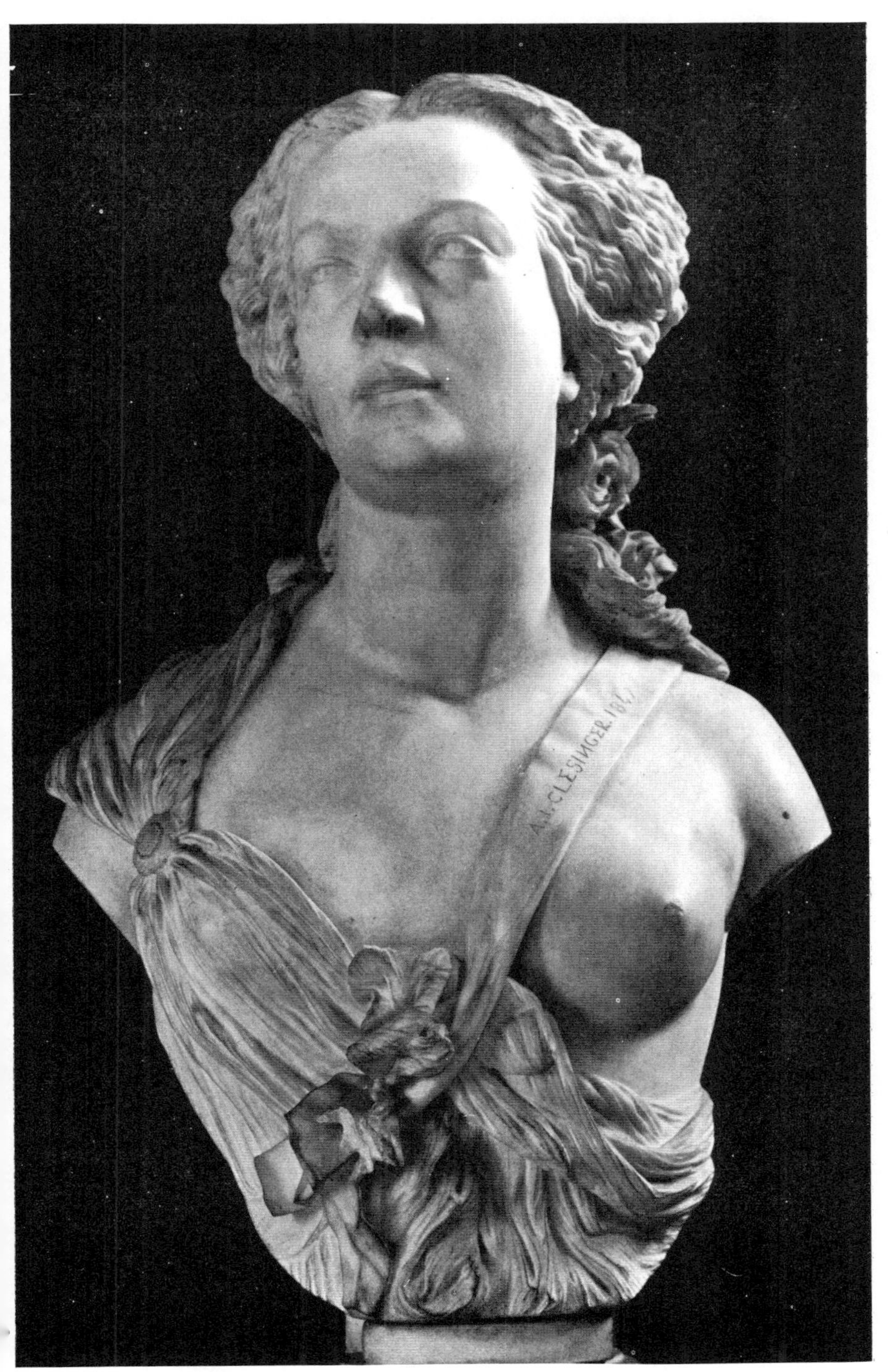

61. Clésinger: *Bust of Mme Sabatier*. Marble, 1847. Paris, Musée du Louvre.

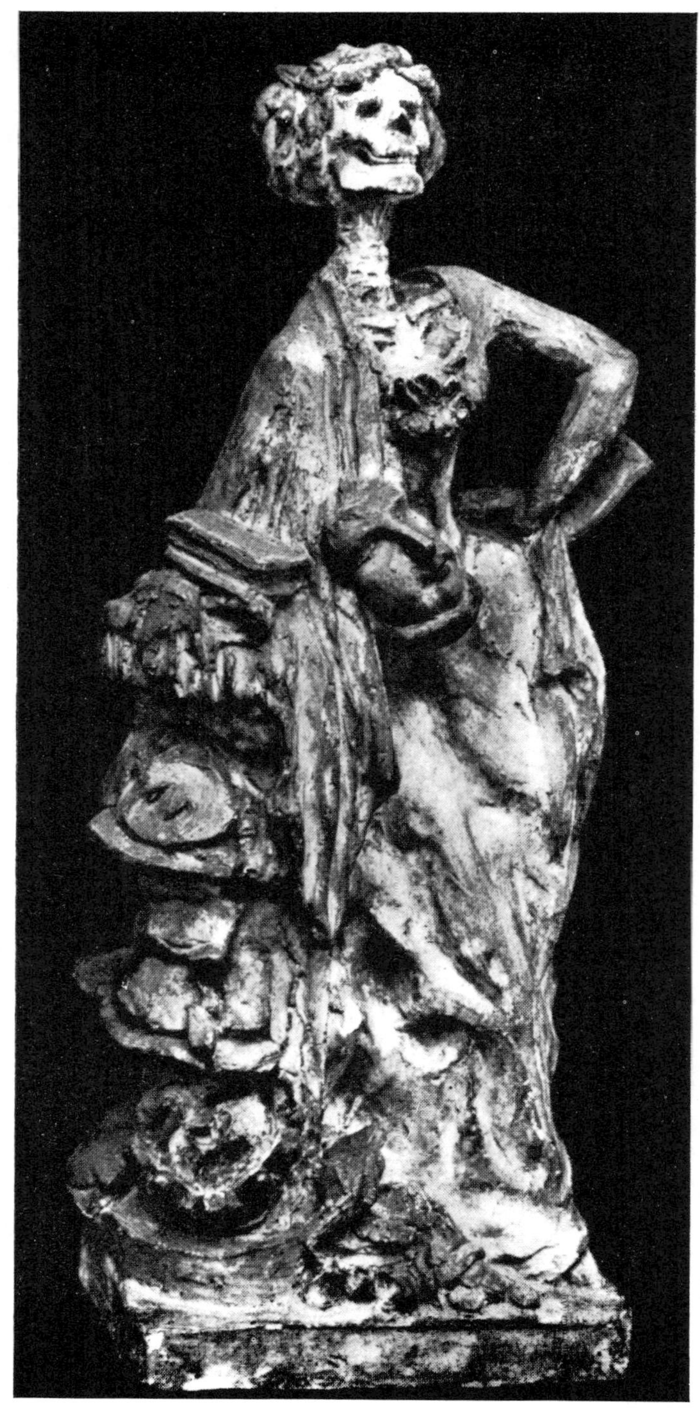

62. CHRISTOPHE: '*Danse macabre*'. Terracotta (?). 1859.
Formerly in the collection of Comte Robert de Montesquiou.

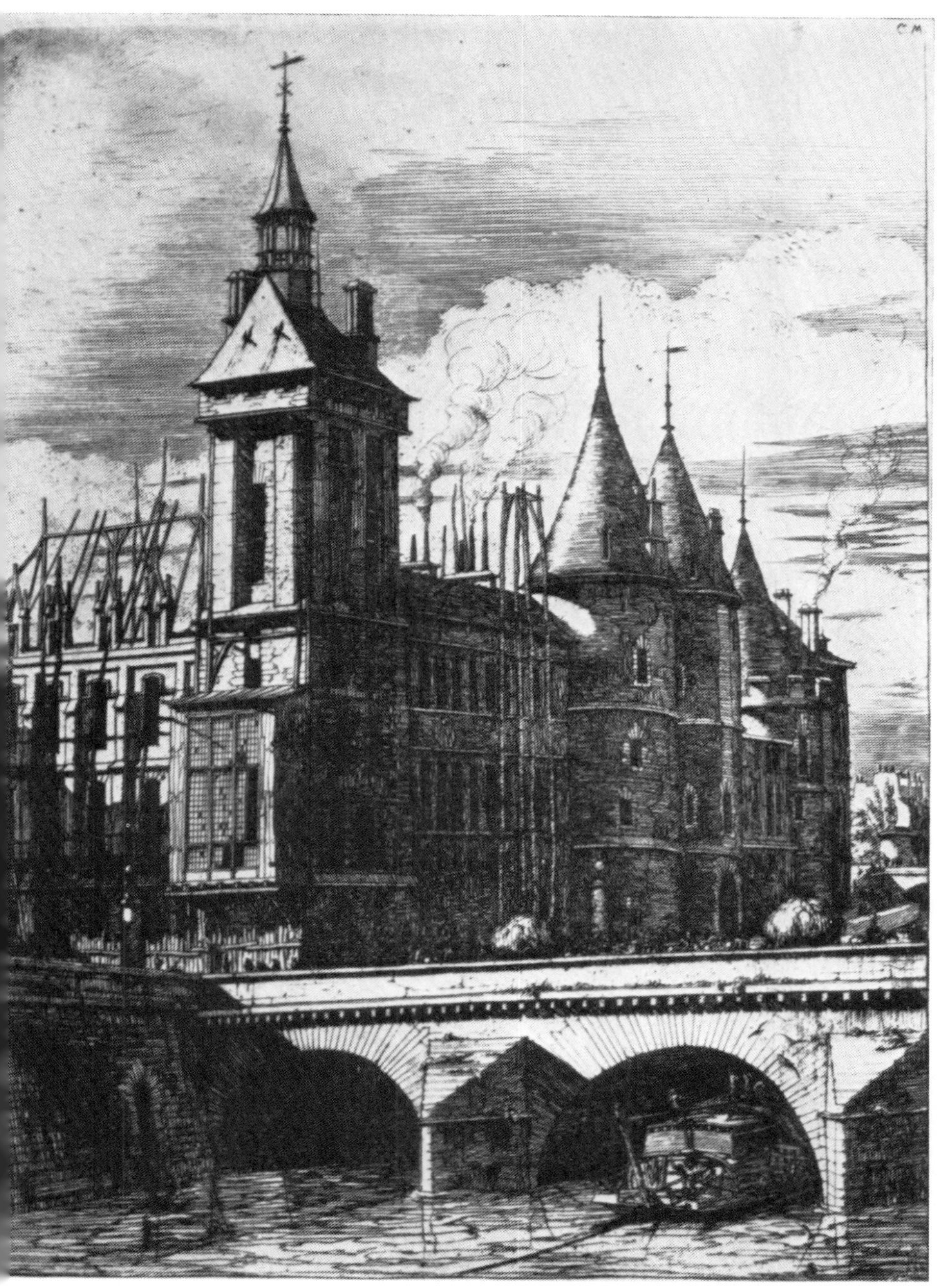

63. MERYON: *The Clock Tower, Paris*. Etching, 1852. London, Victoria and Albert Museum.

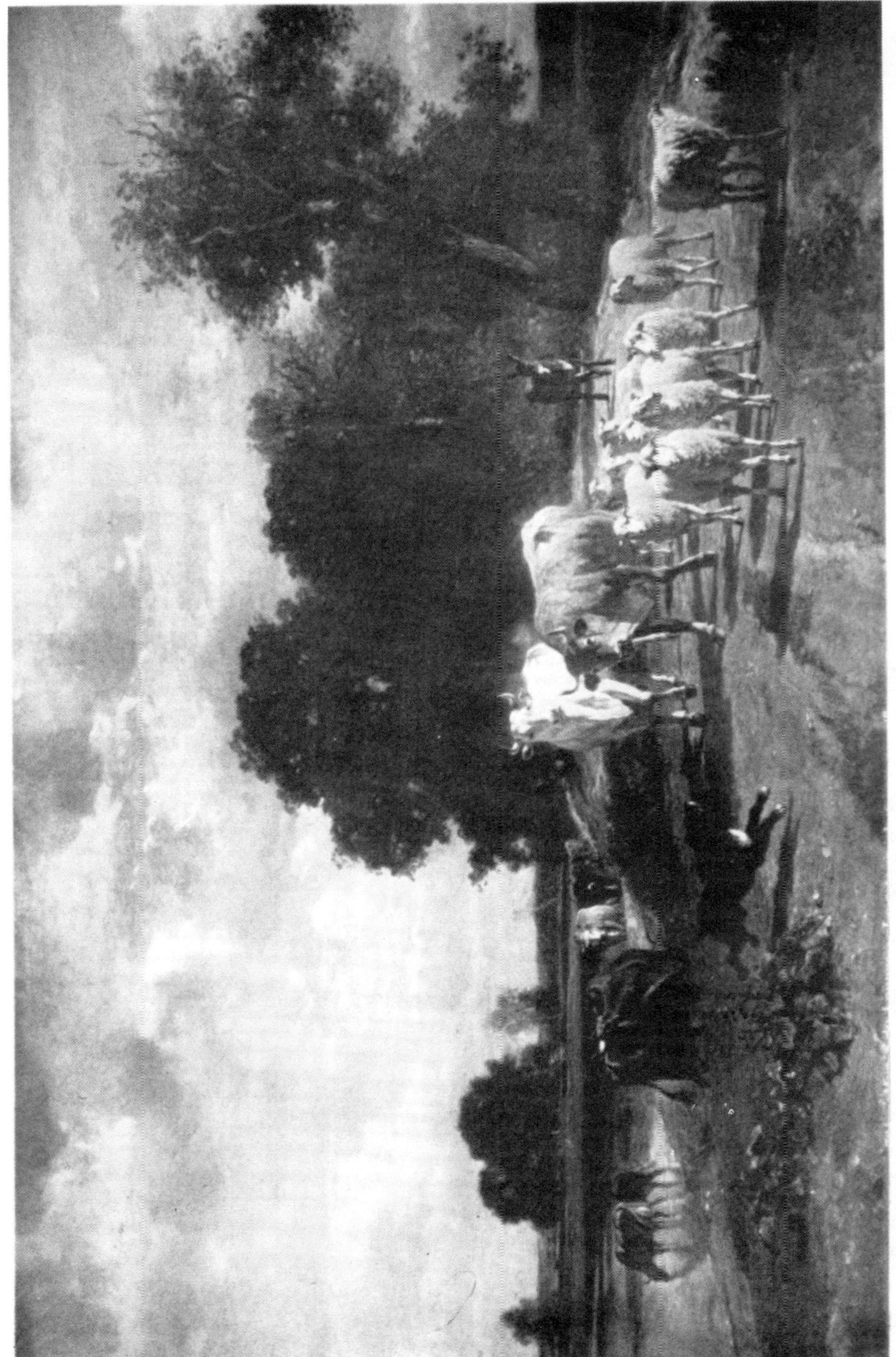

M. Penguilly is also in love with the past. His is an ingenious, enquiring, assiduous mind. Add, if you will, all the most honourable and courteous epithets which can be applied to poetry of the second rank—to poetry which just fails of being nakedly great and simple. He has the minuteness, the burning patience and the neatness of the antiquarian. His works are wrought like the weapons and the furniture of ancient times. His painting has the polish of metal and the cutting-edge of a razor. As for his imagination, I shall not say that it is positively great, but it is singularly active, impressionable and enquiring. I was enchanted by his *Petite Danse Macabre*, which reminded me of a band of belated drunkards, half dragging themselves along, half dancing, in step with their scrawny captain. I beg you to look carefully at each of the little *grisailles* which serve the principal composition both as frame and commentary. There is not one of them which is not an excellent little picture in itself. Modern artists are far too neglectful of those magnificent allegories of the middle ages, in which the grotesque and the horrible entwined themselves in a kind of mad, eternal game, as they do still. Perhaps our nerves have now become too delicate to endure a symbol which is too plainly forbidding. Or perhaps it is charity which exhorts us to avoid anything which may distress our fellows—but this is extremely unlikely! Towards the end of last year a publisher in the rue Royale put on sale a prayer-book of a very choice type; and the advertisements published in the newspapers informed us that all the vignettes which framed the text had been copied from ancient works of the same period, in such a way as to give a rare unity of style to the whole. They went on to say that a unique exception had been made with respect to the macabre figures; according to the note, doubtless drafted by the publisher himself, the greatest care had been taken to avoid reproducing these, *as being no longer to the taste of this age*; 'to such an *enlightened* taste', he should have added, if he had wished to conform entirely to the taste of the said age.

Le mauvais goût du siècle en cela me fait peur.[1]

There is a worthy publication[2] in which every contributor knows all and has a word to say about all, a journal in which every member of the staff is as universal and encyclopedic in his knowledge as the citizens of

[1] Molière, *Misanthrope*, Act I. Molière's text reads 'méchant goût'.
[2] This was *Le Siècle*; the critic referred to below was Louis Jourdan.

ancient Rome, and can instruct us turn and turn about in politics, religion, economics, the fine arts, philosophy and literature. In this vast monument of fatuity, which leans towards the future like the tower of Pisa, and in which nothing less than the happiness of the human kind is being worked out, there is one very honest man who does not want us to admire M. Penguilly. And his reason, my dear M—, his reason? It is because there is a *tedious monotony* in his work. Surely these words do not refer to M. Penguilly's imagination, which is excessively picturesque and varied? This thinker must have meant that he did not like a painter who treated all his subjects in the same style. But Good Heavens! it is his *own* style! Do you want him to change it, then?

I do not want to leave this agreeable artist, all of whose pictures are equally interesting this year, without drawing your attention more particularly to his *Petites Mouettes*; the intense blue of the sky and the water, the two rocky boulders which form a door open upon the infinite (you must know that the infinite seems all the more immense the more it is restricted), a cloud, a multitude, an avalanche, a *plague* of white birds—and solitude! Reflect on that, my dear M—, and then tell me if you think that M. Penguilly's mind is devoid of poetry.

Before concluding this chapter I would also direct your eye to M. Leighton's picture—he was the only English artist, I presume, to be punctual for his appointment: it is called *Count Paris comes to the house of the Capulets to claim his bride Juliet, and finds her apparently lifeless*.[1] This is a rich, meticulous painting, violent in colour and choice in finish; a very dogged work, but dramatic, rhetorical even; for our friends from across the Channel do not paint theatrical subjects as though they were *real* scenes, but as scenes *acted* with the necessary exaggeration; and this fault, if it be one, confers upon their works an element of strange and paradoxical beauty.

In conclusion, if you have time to return to the Salon, do not forget to look at the enamel-paintings of M. Marc Baud. This artist, in a thankless and ill-appreciated genre, displays surprising qualities—those of a true painter. To sum up in a word, he paints *richly* precisely where so many others spread out their poor colours *meanly*; he knows how to make a great gesture in a small space.

[1] Exhibited the previous year at the Royal Academy. Leighton had one other painting at the Salon in 1859.

VII. PORTRAITURE

I DO NOT imagine that the birds of the air would ever make it their business to provide for the expenses of my table, nor that a lion would do me the honour of serving as my grave-digger or undertaker. Nevertheless, in the Thebaid my brain has made for itself, I too, like one of those who knelt alone and wrangled with that incorrigible death's-head, still stuffed with all the false reasoning of the mortal and perishable flesh—I, too, sometimes dispute with grotesque monsters, with phantasms of the daylight, with spectres of the street, the salon and the omnibus. I see in front of me the Soul of the Bourgeoisie; and believe me, if I were not afraid of indelibly staining the hangings of my cell, I would gladly fling my ink-stand in her face, and with a vigour that she does not suspect me of possessing! Just listen to what she said to me today, that wretched Soul, who is no hallucination: 'In truth, our poets are singularly mad to claim that imagination is necessary in all the functions of art. What need is there of imagination in painting a portrait, for example? in painting my soul—my soul which is so visible, so clear, so well-known? I pose, and in reality it is I, the model, who consent to do the bulk of the work. I am the artist's true *supplier*. I myself, all by myself, am the whole thing!' To which I reply: '*Caput mortuum*, be silent! Hyperborean brute of ancient days, eternal Esquimau, be-spectacled, or rather be-scaled, whose eyes not all the visions of Damascus, not all the thunders and lightnings of the heavens, would be able to lighten! The more positive and solid the *thing* appears to be, the more subtle and laborious is the work of the imagination. A portrait! what could be simpler and more complicated, more obvious and more profound? If La Bruyère had had no imagination, would he have been able to compose his *Caractères*, whose raw-material was nevertheless so obvious and presented itself so obligingly to him? And however restricted one may suppose some historical subject or other, what historian can flatter himself that he can paint and *illuminate* it—without imagination?'

The portrait, that type of painting which appears so modest, calls for an immense intelligence. No doubt the artist's submissiveness must be great, but his power of divination must be equally so. Whenever I see a good portrait, I can guess at all the artist's efforts, just as he must not only have seen at once all that lay on the surface, but must also have guessed at what lay hidden. I compared him just now to the historian, and I might also compare him to the actor, whose duty it is to adopt any character and any costume. If you will examine the matter closely, nothing in a portrait is a matter of indifference. Gesture, grimace, clothing, décor even—all must combine to realize a *character*. Great painters, excellent painters—David, for example (both when he was just an eighteenth-century artist, and after he had become a *chef d'école*), or Holbein, in all his portraits—have often aimed at expressing the character which they undertook to paint, with sobriety but with intensity. Others have sought to do more, or to do it differently. Reynolds and Gérard added an element of romance, but always in accord with the natural disposition of the sitter; thus a stormy and troubled sky, light and airy backgrounds, poetic furnishings, a languorous attitude, an intrepid bearing, etc. . . . There you have a dangerous, but not a culpable procedure, which unfortunately demands genius. Finally, whatever may be the means most visibly employed by the artist, whether he be Holbein, David, Velasquez or Lawrence, a good portrait always seems to me to be like a dramatized biography, or rather, like the natural drama inherent in every man. Others have wanted to restrict the means. Was it because of their incapacity to use them all? or was it in the hope of obtaining a greater intensity of expression? I do not know; or rather I should be inclined to believe that in this, as in many other human affairs, both reasons are equally acceptable.

At this point, my friend, I am very much afraid that I am forced to lay hands on one of your idols. I want to speak of the school of Ingres in general, and of his method as applied to the portrait in particular. Not all his pupils have strictly and humbly followed their master's precepts. Whereas M. Amaury-Duval courageously pushes the asceticism of the school to extremes, M. Lehmann makes some attempts to excuse the origin of his pictures by the admixture of alien ingredients. On the whole one might say that his teaching has been despotic, and that it has left a painful scar on French painting. A very stubborn man, gifted with several precious faculties, but determined to deny the utility of those which he does not possess, he has laid claim to an extraordinary and exceptional glory—that of extinguishing the sun. As for the few smoky embers that are still left to wander in space, the master's disciples have undertaken to stamp them out. It is not to be denied that Nature, as expressed by these simplifiers, has turned out to seem more intelligible;

but it is obvious how much less beautiful and exciting she has become in the process. I am bound to admit that I have seen a few portraits by MM. Flandrin and Amaury-Duval which, though falsely disguised as *paintings*, nevertheless offered some admirable specimens of modelling. I will even admit that the visible character of these portraits, save everything relating to colour and light, was vigorously and carefully expressed, and in a penetrating manner. But I ask you if it is playing fair to decrease the difficulties of an art by suppressing some of its parts. I think that M. Chenavard is more courageous and more frank. He has simply repudiated colour as a perilous display, as a reprehensible, emotional element, and has put his trust in the pencil alone to express all the import of his idea. M. Chenavard is incapable of denying all the advantages conferred upon laziness by a procedure which consists in expressing the form of an object without the variously-coloured light which clings to each of its molecules; only he claims that this sacrifice is a glorious and a useful one, and that form and idea are both equally the gainers. But M. Ingres's pupils have very pointlessly retained a semblance of colour. They believe, or they pretend to believe, that they are *painters*.

Here is another charge—a commendation, perhaps, in the eyes of some—which touches them more sharply; it is that their portraits are not true likenesses. Just because I never cease to call for the employment of the imagination and the introduction of poetry into all the functions of art, surely no one will suppose that I desire a conscientious alteration of the model, in the portrait above all? Holbein *knew* Erasmus; he knew him and studied him so well that he created him afresh and evoked him visibly, immortally and superlatively. M. Ingres finds a model that is fine, picturesque and attractive. 'Here we have a curious type to be sure,' he says to himself. 'Beauty or grandeur, I shall express it with care; I shall leave nothing out, but I shall *add to it something which is indispensable*: that is, *style*.' And we know what he means by 'style'. It is not the naturally poetic quality of the subject, which must be extracted so that it may become more visible. It is an alien poetry, usually borrowed from the past. I think that I am justified in concluding that if M. Ingres adds something to his model, it is because he is incapable of making it at once both great and true. But by what right does he add? It is the art of painting that alone should be borrowed from tradition, and not the devices of sophistication. Take that Parisian lady, a ravishing specimen of the butterfly graces of a French *salon*; in spite of herself, he will endow her with a certain heaviness, with a *Roman* complacency. Raphael demands it. Those arms are of the purest curve and the most seductive contour—there is no doubt about it; but they are a trifle slender, and if they are to achieve the preconceived *style*, they require a certain measure of embonpoint—of the sap of matronhood. M. Ingres is the victim of an obsession which relentlessly drives him to displace, to transpose and to alter the beautiful. His pupils do likewise; as each one of them sets to work, he always makes ready, according to his dominant taste, to *distort* his model. Do you find this fault a slight one, or my criticism unmerited?

Among those artists who are content with the natural picturesqueness of the original, the most outstanding are M. Bonvin, who gives a vigorous and surprising vitality to his portraits, and M. Heim, at whom some superficial critics have mocked in the past, and who, this year again, as in 1855, has revealed to us a marvellous understanding of the human *grimace* in a whole cavalcade of sketches. I presume that you will not take this word in a disagreeable sense. I am alluding to the natural and professional grimace which belongs to each one of us.

M. Chaplin and M. Besson both know how to paint portraits. The first has not shown us anything of the kind this year; but enthusiasts who follow the exhibitions attentively, and who know to which of his earlier works I am referring, will have noted their absence with regret, as I did. The second, who is a very good painter, has in addition all the literary qualities and the imagination needed to portray actresses worthily. More than once, while contemplating M. Besson's living and luminous portraits, have I found myself dreaming of all the grace and devotion which the artists of the eighteenth century put into the pictures which they have bequeathed us of their favourite *goddesses*.

At different times, various portrait-painters have caught the fashion, some by reason of their *qualities*, others by their *defects*. The public, which is passionately in love with its own image, knows no half-measures in its love for the artist to whom it most willingly entrusts the task of depicting it. Amongst all those who have managed to snatch this favour, the man who seems to me to have deserved it the most, because he has always remained a frank and genuine artist, is M. Ricard. A lack of solidity in his painting has sometimes been noticed; his taste for Van Dyck, Rembrandt and Titian, and his grace, which is sometimes English, sometimes Italian, have been exaggeratedly rebuked. But such criticisms are just a little unfair. For imitation is the intoxication of supple and brilliant minds, and often even a proof of their superiority. To his painter's instincts, which are altogether remarkable, M. Ricard unites a very wide learning in the history of his art and a critical mind of great finesse; there is not a single work of his in which we do not find evidence of all these qualities. Formerly perhaps he made his models too pretty; and yet I ought to add that in the portraits of which I am speaking, this particular fault may have been *demanded* by his model. Nevertheless the virile and noble part of his mind was quick to prevail. He truly has an understanding which is always ready to grasp and depict the *soul* which poses in front of him. Take the portrait of an old lady, in which there is no cowardly disguising of her age; it immediately reveals a reposeful character, a sweetness and a charity which command confidence. The simplicity of her gaze and of her attitude accords happily with that warm, softly-golden colour which seems to me to have been specially made to convey the sweet thoughts of the evening. But if you want to recognize energy in youth, grace in health, and candour in a countenance which is trembling with life, then consider his portrait of Mlle. L. J. This certainly is a portrait both true and great. If a beautiful model does not *confer* talent, it is certain that at least it adds a charm to existing talent. But how few painters are masters of an execution which could better realize the solidity of this pure and generous nature, and the deep heavens of this eye with its great velvet star! The contour of the face, the curves of this broad, youthful brow with its helmet of heavy tresses, the richness of these lips and the dazzling grain of the skin—all is carefully expressed; and then—the most charming thing of all, and the most difficult to paint—that touch of slyness which is always mingled with innocence, and that strange, nobly ecstatic air which in human beings, no less than in animals, gives such a mysterious appeal to the countenances of the young. The number of portraits painted by M. Ricard is already very considerable; but this one is as good as any, and the activity of this remarkable mind, which is always on the alert and in pursuit, promises us many others.

I think that in a summary but sufficient manner I have explained why the portrait, the true portrait, this genre which is apparently so modest, is in fact so difficult to practise. It is therefore only natural that I have but few specimens to adduce. Many other artists—Mme O'Connell for example—know how to paint a human head; but if I was to deal with them all, I should be obliged to go over the same ground again and again, with reference to this quality or that defect—and we agreed at the beginning that I should content myself as far as possible with explaining what may be regarded as the *ideal*, in respect of each class of painting.

VIII. LANDSCAPE

IF AN assemblage of trees, mountains, water and houses, such as we call a landscape, is beautiful, it is not so of itself, but through me, through my own grace and favour, through the idea or the feeling which *I* attach to it. It amounts to saying, I think, that any landscape-painter who does not know how to convey a *feeling* by means of an assemblage of vegetable or mineral matter, is no artist. I know very well that by a singular effort the human imagination can momentarily conceive of Nature without Man—can conceive of all the suggestive mass of the universe dispersed throughout space without a contemplator to extract from it comparison, metaphor and allegory. It is true enough that all that universal order and harmony would lose none of the inspirational quality with which providence has entrusted it; but in that case, in default of an intelligence to inspire, this quality would be as though it did not exist at all. Those artists who want to express nature *minus* the feelings which she inspires are submitting to an odd sort of operation which consists in killing the reflective and sentient man within them; and believe me, the disaster is that for the majority of them this operation has nothing odd nor painful about it at all! Such is the school which prevails today, and for a long time has prevailed. Like everyone else, I will admit that our modern school of landscape-painters is singularly strong and skilful; but in this triumph and predominance of an inferior genre, in this silly cult of a nature neither purged nor explained by imagination, I see an obvious symptom of general degradation. We shall doubtless seize upon several differences in practical skill between this and that landscape-painter; but these differences are very small. Pupils of various masters, they all of them paint remarkably well, and almost all of them forget that a natural view has no value beyond the immediate feeling that an artist can put into it. Most of them fall into the error to which I drew attention at the beginning of this study. They take the dictionary of art for art itself; they copy a word from the dictionary, believing that they are copying a poem. But a poem can never be copied; it has to be *composed*. Thus, they open a window, and the whole space contained in the rectangle of that window —trees, sky and house—assumes for them the value of a ready-made poem. Some of them go even further. In their eyes a study is a picture. M. Français [1] shows us a tree—an enormous, ancient tree, it is true—and he says to us, 'Behold a landscape'. The technical superiority shown by MM. Anastasi,[2] Leroux,[3] Breton,[4] Belly, Chintreuil, etc., only serves to make the universal lacuna more visible and more distressing. I know that M. Daubigny [5] wishes, and is able, to do more. His landscapes have a grace and a freshness which fascinate the eye at once. They immediately convey to the spectator's soul the original feeling in which they are steeped. But it seems that M. Daubigny has only been able to obtain this quality at the expense of finish and of perfection in detail. Many a picture of his, otherwise ingenious and charming, lacks solidity. It has the grace, but also the flabbiness and impermanence, of an improvisation. Before all else, however, we must record to M. Daubigny's credit the fact that his works are generally poetic, and with all their faults I prefer them to many others which are more perfect, but lack the quality which distinguishes him.

It is style, especially, that M. Millet [6] seeks; he makes no secret, rather he makes a show and glory of it. But part of the ridicule which I directed against M. Ingres's pupils sticks to him. For 'style' has been his disaster. His peasants are pedants who have too high an opinion of themselves. They display a kind of dark and fatal boorishness which makes me want to hate them. Whether they are reaping or sowing, whether they are grazing or shearing their animals, they always seem to be saying: 'We are the poor and disinherited of this earth—but it is we who make it fertile! We are accomplishing a mission, we are exercising a priestly function!' Instead of simply distilling the natural poetry of his subject, M. Millet wants to add something to it at any price. In their monotonous ugliness, all these little pariahs have a pretentiousness which is philosophic, melancholy and Raphaelesque. This disastrous element in M. Millet's painting spoils all the fine qualities by which one's glance is first of all attracted towards him.

[1] His *Soleil couchant* reproduced *Illustr.*, vol. XXXIV (1859), p. 20.
[2] His *Un lac en Tyrol* reproduced *Illustr.*, vol. XXXIII (1859), p. 388.
[3] See pl. 51.
[4] His *Rappel des glaneuses* is now in the Louvre.
[5] Of Daubigny's five exhibits, *Les Graves au bord de la mer, à Villerville* is in the Marseilles Museum and *Les Bords de l'Oise* in the Bordeaux Museum. See pl. 50.
[6] Millet's sole exhibit, his *Femme faisant paître sa vache* is now in the Bourg Museum. See pl. 54.

M. Troyon is the finest example of skill without soul. And so, look at his popularity! With a soul-less public, he deserved it. While still a young man, M. Troyon painted with the same assurance, the same skill and the same insensitivity. Long years ago he had already amazed us by the soundness of his craftsmanship, by the 'directness of his playing', as one says of an actor, and by his unfailing, moderate and continual merit. He *has* a soul—I grant that—but it is a soul too much within the reach of all other souls. The encroachment of these second-class talents cannot take place without injustices being created. When any other beast but the lion takes the lion's share for itself, there cannot fail to be some modest creatures who find their modest portions much too much reduced. I mean that among those second-class talents who are successfully cultivating an inferior branch of art, there are several who are worth every bit of M. Troyon, and who may find it odd that they do not obtain all that is their due, while this man takes much more than is his. I must be careful not to mention names; the victims would perhaps feel themselves no less outraged than the usurper.

The two men who have always been marked out by public opinion as the most important in the field of landscape are MM. Rousseau and Corot. With artists of such eminence one must be full of reserve and respect. M. Rousseau's manner of working is complicated, full of tricks and second thoughts. Few men have had a sincerer love for light, or have rendered it better. But the general silhouette of his form is often difficult to grasp. His luminous haze, which sparkles as it is tossed about, is upsetting to the physical *anatomy* of objects. M. Rousseau has always dazzled, but he has sometimes exhausted me too. And then he falls into that famous modern fault which is born of a blind love of nature and nothing but nature; he takes a simple study for a composition. A glistening marsh, teeming with damp grasses and dappled with luminous patches, a rugged tree-trunk, a cottage with a flowery thatch, in short a little scrap of nature, becomes a sufficient and a perfect picture in his loving eyes. But even all the charm which he can put into this fragment torn from our planet is not always enough to make us forget the absence of construction in his pictures.[1]

If M. Rousseau—who, for all his occasional incompleteness, is perpetually restless and throbbing with life—if M. Rousseau seems like a man who is tormented by several devils and does not know which to

[1] Rousseau exhibited five landscapes this year. See pl. 52.

heed, M. Corot,[1] who is his absolute antithesis, has the devil too seldom within him. However inadequate and even unjust this expression may be, I chose it as approximately giving the reason which prevents this serious artist from dazzling and astonishing us. He does astonish—I freely admit—but slowly; he does enchant—little by little; but you have to know how to penetrate into the science of his art, for with him there is no glaring brilliance, but everywhere an infallible strictness of harmony. More than that, he is one of the rare ones, the only one left, perhaps, who has retained a deep feeling for construction, who observes the proportional value of each detail within the whole, and (if I may be allowed to compare the composition of a landscape to that of the human frame) the only one who always knows where to place the bones and what dimensions to give them. You feel, you guess, that M. Corot draws in a summary and broad manner, which is the only way of making a rapid accumulation of a great quantity of precious raw-materials. If it had been granted to a single man to restrain the modern French school in its impertinent and tedious love of detail, certainly he would have been that man. We have heard this eminent artist criticized because his colour is somewhat too soft and his light is almost crepuscular. It might be said that for him all the light which floods the earth is everywhere dimmed by one or more degrees. His eye, which is keen and judicious, is more concerned with what establishes harmony than with what emphasizes contrast. But even supposing that this criticism is not too unjust, it is well to remark that our exhibitions of painting are not favourable to the effect of good pictures—above all of those which are conceived and executed soundly and with moderation. The sound of a clear voice, but one which is both modest and harmonious, gets lost amid an uproar of deafening or raucous shouts, and even the most luminous Veroneses would often appear pale and grey if they were surrounded by certain modern paintings which are more garish than peasants' scarves.

Among M. Corot's merits one must not forget the excellence of his teaching, which is sound, luminous and methodical. Of the numerous pupils whom he has shaped, sustained or restrained far from the seductions of the times, M. Lavieille is the one who has given me the greatest pleasure. There is quite a simple landscape of his; a cottage on the skirts of a wood, with a road disappearing into it. The snow's whiteness makes

[1] Among Corot's seven exhibits were the *Dante and Virgil* (Boston Museum), the *Macbeth* (Wallace Collection) and the *Idylle* (Lille Museum). See pl. 56.

a pleasant contrast with the conflagration of the evening, which is slowly burning down behind the innumerable mastheads of the leafless forest. For several years now our landscape-painters have been turning more frequently to the picturesque beauties of the sad season. But no one, I think, feels them better than M. Lavieille. Not a few of the effects which he has often realized seem to me, however, to be chosen extracts from the *joys* of winter. In the sadness of this landscape, which wears the sombrely pink and white livery of the fine days of winter as they draw towards their close, there is an irresistible and elegiac thrill of pleasure which is known to all lovers of solitary walks.

Allow me, my friend, to return once more to my obsession—I mean to my feeling of regret when I see the imagination's part in landscape being more and more diminished. Here and there, at long intervals, there appears the trace of a protest, a great and free talent which is no longer in the taste of the age. There is M. Paul Huet, for example; in him we have a *veteran of the old guard*! (I can apply this familiar and grandiloquent expression to the débris of a fighting glory like *Romanticism*, which is already so far behind us). M. Paul Huet remains faithful to the tastes of his youth. His eight paintings of marine or rustic subjects, which are to serve for the decoration of a salon, are veritable poems of lightness, splendour and freshness. It seems superfluous to detail the talents of so exalted an artist, who has produced so much; but what seems to me to be all the more remarkable and praiseworthy in him is that all the time that the taste for minuteness has been everywhere gaining ground step by step, *he* has remained constant in his nature and his method, and has continued to give to all his compositions a character which is lovingly poetic.

Nevertheless this year a little consolation has come my way, from two artists of whom I should not have expected it. M. Jadin, who up to the present has too modestly confined his glory to the hovel and the stable (this is now obvious), has sent a splendid view of Rome, taken from the Arco di Parma. It contains first of all this artist's usual qualities, which are those of energy and solidity, but in addition it reveals the perfect capturing and realization of a poetic impression. It is the glorious and melancholy impression of evening as it falls upon the holy city; a solemn evening, shot with bands of scarlet and blazing with splendour like the Roman religion itself. The second is M. Clésinger, for whom sculpture alone is not enough; he is like those children whose turbulent blood and bounding ardour impel them to scale all heights in order to inscribe their names thereon. His two landscapes, *Isola Farnese* and *Castel Fusana*, are penetrating of aspect, and of a native and austere melancholy. Their waters are heavier and more solemn than elsewhere, their solitude more silent, their very trees more monumental. M. Clésinger's *rhetoric* has often raised a laugh; but he will never lay himself open to mockery on the score of littleness. Vice for vice, I agree with him that excess in everything is better than meanness.

Yes, imagination certainly avoids landscape! I can understand how a mind which is absorbed in taking notes has no time to abandon itself to the prodigious reveries contained in the natural sights which confront it; but why does imagination avoid the landscape-painter's *studio*? Perhaps the artists who cultivate this genre are far too mistrustful of their memory, and adopt a method of immediate copying because it perfectly suits their laziness of mind. If they had been with me recently in the studio of M. Boudin (who, by the way, has exhibited a good and careful picture: *Le Pardon de sainte Anne Palud*[1]), they would have seen several hundred pastel-studies, improvised in front of the sea and sky, and would then have understood what they do not yet seem to understand—the gulf which separates a study from a picture.[2] But M. Boudin, who might pride himself on this devotion to his art, evinces the greatest modesty in showing his curious collection. He knows quite well that all this will have to be turned into a picture, by means of the poetic impression recalled at will; and he lays no claim to be offering his notes as pictures. Later, no doubt, these prodigious enchantments of air and water will be displayed for us in finished paintings. On the margin of each of these studies, so rapidly and so faithfully sketched from the waves and the clouds (which are of all things the most inconstant and difficult to grasp, both in form and in colour), he has inscribed the date, the time and the wind: thus for example, *8th October*, *midday*, *North-West wind*. If you have ever had the time to become acquainted with these meteorological beauties, you will be able to verify by memory the accuracy of M. Boudin's observations. Cover the inscription with your hand, and you

[1] Now in the Museum at Le Havre.

[2] Baudelaire had recently met Boudin at Honfleur. See John Rewald, *History of Impressionism* (New York, Museum of Modern Art, 1946, p. 38). Rewald reproduces one of Boudin's sky-studies. It is hardly necessary to point out the parallel with Constable's activities in the early 1820s. See pl. 57.

could guess the season, the time and the wind. I am not exaggerating. I have seen it. In the end, all these clouds, with their fantastic and luminous forms; these ferments of gloom; these immensities of green and pink, suspended and added one upon another; these gaping furnaces; these firmaments of black or purple satin, crumpled, rolled or torn; these horizons in mourning, or streaming with molten metal—in short, all these depths and all these splendours rose to my brain like a heady drink or like the eloquence of opium. It is rather an odd thing, but never once, while examining these liquid or aerial enchantments, did I think to complain of the absence of man. But I must take care not to allow the abundance of my pleasure to dictate a piece of advice to the world at large, any more than to M. Boudin himself. It would really be too dangerous. Let him remember that man is never loth to see his fellow (as was observed by Robespierre, who was well versed in the *humanities*); and if he wants to win a little popularity, let him take care not to imagine that the public has arrived at an equal enthusiasm for solitude.

There is a lack not only of seascapes—such a poetic genre, moreover; though I do not count as seascapes those military dramas which are played at sea—but also of a genre which I can only call the landscape of great cities, by which I mean that collection of grandeurs and beauties which results from a powerful agglomeration of men and monuments—the profound and complex charm of a capital city which has grown old and aged in the glories and tribulations of life.

Some years ago a strange and stalwart man—a Naval Officer, I am told—began a series of etched studies of the most picturesque views in Paris. By the sharpness, the refinement and the assurance of his drawing, M. Meryon[1] reminded us of the excellent etchers of the past. I have rarely seen the natural solemnity of an immense city more poetically reproduced. Those majestic accumulations of stone; those spires 'whose fingers point to heaven'[2]; those obelisks of industry, spewing forth their conglomerations of smoke against the firmament; those prodigies of

[1] There was at one time a project that Baudelaire should write short texts to accompany a collection of Meryon's etchings of Paris, but unfortunately it came to nothing.

[2] The phrase 'clochers *montrant du doigt le ciel*' (italicized by Baudelaire) deserves a note. Baudelaire probably had it from Gautier, who quoted it (*Fantaisies*, III), with the addition of the adjective 'silencieux', as the only line of Wordsworth that he knew. The line occurs in Wordsworth's *The Excursion* (Book VI, line 19); in the first edition of that poem, Wordsworth has a note to the effect that he had derived the phrase 'point as with silent finger' from Coleridge.

scaffolding round buildings under repair, applying their openwork architecture, so paradoxically beautiful, upon architecture's solid body; that tumultuous sky, charged with anger and spite; those limitless perspectives, only increased by the thought of all the drama they contain —he forgot not one of the complex elements which go to make up the painful and glorious décor of civilization. If Victor Hugo has seen these excellent prints, he must have been pleased; again he will have found worthily depicted, his—

Morne Isis, couverte d'un voile!
Araignée à l'immense toile,
Où se prennent les nations!
Fontaine d'urnes obsédée!
Mamelle sans cesse inondée,
Où, pour se nourrir de l'idée,
Viennent les générations! . . .

Ville qu'un orage enveloppe! [1]

But a cruel demon has touched M. Meryon's brain; a mysterious madness has deranged those faculties which seemed as robust as they were brilliant. His dawning glory and his labours were both suddenly cut short. And from that moment we have never ceased waiting anxiously for some consoling news of this singular naval officer who in one short day turned into a mighty artist, and who bade farewell to the ocean's solemn adventures in order to paint the gloomy majesty of this most disquieting of capitals.

In still regretting the landscape of Romanticism, and even the landscape of Romance (which already existed in the eighteenth century), I am perhaps being unconsciously obedient to the customs of my youth. But surely our landscape-painters are far too herbivorous in their diet? They never willingly take their nourishment from ruins, and apart from a small number of men such as Fromentin, the sky and the desert terrify them. I feel a longing for those great lakes, representing immobility in despair;

[1] 'Gloomy Isis, covered with a veil! Spider with an immense web in which the Nations are caught! Fountain beset with urns! Breast ever-flowing with milk, whither the generations of mankind come to receive the food of ideas! . . . City tempest-wrapped!' *Les Voix intérieures*, IV, 'A l'Arc de Triomphe'. Crépet, in his edition of the *Curiosités esthétiques* (pp. 497–8) quotes an appreciative letter which Baudelaire received from the exiled Hugo.

for immense mountains, staircases from our planet to the skies, from which everything which formerly seemed great now seems small; for castle keeps (yes, I do not even stop at that!); for crenellated abbeys, reflected in gloomy pools; for gigantic bridges, towering Ninevite constructions, haunts of dizziness—for everything, in short, which would have to be invented if it did not already exist!

I must confess in passing that, although he is not endowed with a very decided originality of manner, M. Hildebrandt has given me a keen pleasure with his enormous display of water-colours. As I run through these amusing travel-albums, it always seems to me that I am *seeing again*, that I am *recognizing* what in fact I have never seen. Stimulated by him, my imagination has ranged across thirty-eight [1] romantic countrysides, from the echoing ramparts of Scandinavia to the luminous countries of the ibis and the stork, from the Fiord of Seraphitus to the point of Teneriffe. The moon and the sun have taken it in turns to illumine these scenes, the one pouring forth his explosive light, the other her patient enchantments.

You see, my friend, that I can never regard choice of subject as a matter of indifference, and that, in spite of the necessary love which needs must fertilize the humblest fragment, I hold that *subject-matter* plays a part in the artist's genius, just as it plays a part in my own pleasure—barbarian as I am! On the whole, my examination of the landscape-painters has only yielded a few well-behaved or *little* talents, accompanied by a great idleness of imagination. Not one of them has been able to show me the natural charm, so simply expressed, of Catlin's savannahs and prairies (I'll wager they do not even know the name Catlin!)—let alone the supernatural beauty of Delacroix's landscapes, or the magnificent imagination which streams through the drawings of Victor Hugo, just as mystery streams through the heavens. (I speak of his drawings [2] in Chinese ink, for it is too obvious to mention that in poetry our poet is the king of landscape-painters.)

I would rather return to the diorama, whose brutal and enormous magic has the power to impose a genuine illusion upon me! I would rather go to the theatre and feast my eyes on the scenery, in which I find

[1] Two of these were oil-paintings; the remainder, water-colours. A number of water-colours by this artist are in the Victoria and Albert Museum.

[2] An excellent collection of these is to be seen at the Musée Victor Hugo, in the Place des Vosges, Paris.

my dearest dreams artistically expressed, and tragically concentrated! These things, because they are false, are infinitely closer to the truth; whereas the majority of our landscape-painters are liars, precisely because they have neglected to lie.

IX. SCULPTURE

At the heart of an ancient library, in the propitious gloom which fosters and inspires lengthy thoughts, Harpocrates, standing upright and solemn, a finger placed upon his lips, commands silence and, like a Pythagorean pedagogue, bids you 'Hush!' with an authoritative gesture. Apollo and the Muses, those imperious phantoms whose divine forms shine forth in the half-light, watch over your thoughts, assist at your labours and urge you on to the sublime.

In the fold of a wood, sheltered beneath heavy shades, eternal Melancholy gazes at her august face in the waters of a pool as motionless as she is. And the passing dreamer, both saddened and charmed as he contemplates this great figure whose limbs, though robust, are languid from a secret grief, cries out: 'Behold, my sister!'

As you are hurrying towards the confessional, in the midst of that little chapel which is shaken by the clatter of the omnibus, you are halted by a gaunt and magnificent phantom who is cautiously raising the cover of his enormous tomb in order to implore you, a creature of passage, to think of eternity! And at the corner of that flowery pathway which leads to the burial-place of those who are still dear to you, the prodigious figure of Mourning, prostrate, dishevelled, drowned in the flood of her tears and crushing the powdered remains of some famous man beneath her heavy desolation, teaches you that riches, glory, your country even, are pure frivolities compared to that great Unknown which no one has named, nor defined; which man can only represent by mysterious adverbs such as 'Perhaps', 'Never', 'Always!'—and which contains, as some hope, the infinite beatitude which they so much desire, or else an anguish without respite, whose image is rejected by modern reason with the convulsive gesture of a death-agony.

Your spirit charmed by the music of gushing waters, sweeter still than the tongues of nurses, you tumble into a boudoir of greenery, where Venus and Hebe, those playful goddesses who sometimes presided over your life, are displaying beneath alcoves of leafage the charms of their well-rounded limbs, upon which the furnace has bestowed the rosy sheen of life. But you are hardly likely to find these delightful surprises elsewhere but in the gardens of the past; for of the three excellent substances—bronze, terra-cotta and marble—which are available to the imagination for the fulfilment of its sculptural dream, the last alone enjoys an almost exclusive popularity in our age—and very unjustly so in our opinion.

You are passing through a great city which has grown old in civilization—one of those cities which harbour the most important archives of the universal life—and your eyes are drawn upwards, *sursum, ad sidera*; for in the public squares, at the corners of the crossways, stand motionless figures, larger than those which pass at their feet, repeating to you the solemn legends of Glory, War, Science and Martyrdom, in a dumb language. Some are pointing to the sky, whither they ceaselessly aspired; others indicate the earth from which they sprang. They brandish, or they contemplate, what was the passion of their life and what has become its emblem; a tool, a sword, a book, a torch, *vitai lampada*! Be you the most heedless of men, the most unhappy or the vilest, a beggar or a banker, the stone phantom takes possession of you for a few minutes and commands you, in the name of the past, to think of things which are not of the earth.

Such is the divine role of sculpture.

Who could doubt that a powerful imagination is needed to fulfil such a magnificent programme? It is indeed a strange art, whose roots disappear into the darkness of time and which already, in primitive ages, was producing works which cause the civilized mind to marvel! It is an art in which the very thing which would rightly be counted as *quality* in painting can turn into a defect or a vice, an art in which true perfection is by so much the more necessary as the means at its disposal—which are apparently more complete, but are also more barbarous and childish—will always give a *semblance* of finish and perfection, even to the most mediocre works. Faced with an object taken from nature and represented by sculpture—that is to say, a round, three-dimensional object about which one can move freely, and, like the natural object itself, enveloped in atmosphere—the peasant, the savage or the primitive man feels no indecision; whereas a painting, because of its immense pretensions and its paradoxical and abstractive nature, will disquiet and upset him. We may observe at this point that the *bas-relief* is already a lie, that is to say a step taken in the direction of a more civilized art, departing by that much from the pure idea of sculpture. You will remember that, because he did not understand this, the painter Catlin was all but embroiled in a very dangerous quarrel between two of his native chiefs; after he had painted a profile-portrait of one to them, some of the others started to tease and reprove the sitter for allowing himself to be robbed of half his face! In the same way monkeys have been known to be deceived by some magical painting of nature and to go round behind the picture in order to find the other side. It is a result of the barbarous conditions which restrict sculpture that, as well as a very perfect execution, it demands a very elevated spirituality. Otherwise it will only produce the kind of marvellous object which dumbfounds the ape and the savage. Another result is that even the eye of the true amateur is sometimes so wearied by the monotonous whiteness of all these great dolls, exact in all their proportions of height and thickness, that it abdicates its authority. The mediocre does not always appear contemptible to it, and short of a statue's being aggressively wretched, it is capable of taking it for a good one; but a sublime for a bad one, never! In sculpture, more than in any other medium, beauty imprints itself indelibly on the memory. With what a prodigious power have Egypt, Greece, Michelangelo, Coustou[1] and a few others invested these motionless phantoms! with what a glance these pupil-less eyes! Just as lyric poetry makes everything noble—even passion; so sculpture, true sculpture, makes everything solemn—even movement. Upon everything which is human it bestows something of eternity, which partakes of the hardness of the substance used. Anger becomes calm, tenderness severe, and the flickering and faceted dream of painting is transformed into a solid and stubborn meditation. But if you will stop to think how many different types of perfection must be brought together in order to achieve this austere magic, you will not be surprised at the exhaustion and discouragement which often takes possession of our minds as we hasten through these galleries of modern sculpture, where the divine aim is nearly always misunderstood and a trifling prettiness is indulgently substituted for grandeur.

But our taste is a tolerant one, and our dilettantism can accommodate itself in turn to every sort of grandeur or frivolity. We are capable of

[1] The reference is probably to Guillaume Coustou I (1677–1746), the sculptor of the 'Chevaux de Marly'.

loving the mysterious and sacerdotal art of Egypt and Nineveh; the art of Greece—at once so charming and so rational; the art of Michelangelo—as precise as a science, as prodigious as a dream; and the cleverness of the eighteenth century, which is bravura within Truth: but in all these different manifestations of sculpture we find a power of expression and a richness of feeling which are the inevitable results of a deep imagination only too often lacking amongst us today. And so you will not be surprised to find me brief in my examination of this year's works. Nothing is sweeter than to admire, and nothing more disagreeable than to criticize. But the great and cardinal faculty, like the pictures of the Roman patriots, is only conspicuous by its absence. Now, then, is the moment to thank M. Franceschi for his *Andromède*.[1] While exciting general attention, this figure has given rise to several criticisms which in our opinion were too facile. It has the immense merit of being poetic, exciting and noble. It has been called a plagiarism, and M. Franceschi has been accused of simply taking a recumbent figure by Michelangelo and standing it upright. This is not true. The languor of these forms, which are small in size though great in feeling, and the paradoxical elegance of these limbs are clearly the doing of a modern artist. But even if he should have borrowed his inspiration from the past, I would see in this a ground for praise rather than for rebuke; it is not given to everyone to imitate what is great, and when such imitation is the doing of a young man, who has naturally a great span of life open before him, it gives the critic far more reason for hope than for suspicion.

What a singular man is this M. Clésinger! Perhaps the finest thing that you can say of him is that, to see such an easy production of works so varied, you imagine an intelligence, or rather a temperament, which is always on the alert, a man who has the love of sculpture in his very bowels. You admire a marvellously well-executed fragment; but then some other fragment completely spoils the statue. How thrilling is the slender thrust of this figure! but look at those draperies, which, in the intention of seeming light, are nevertheless tubular and twisted like macaroni! If M. Clésinger sometimes catches movement, he never achieves a complete elegance. The beauty of style and of character, which has been so much praised in his busts of Roman ladies,[2] is neither assured nor perfect. It would seem that in his impetuous passion for his work, he

[1] Reproduced *Gazette des Beaux-Arts*, 1859, vol. II, p. 369.

[2] Mme Sabatier (pl. 61) was represented by Clésinger as a Roman lady.

often forgets muscles and is neglectful of a thing so precious and important as the shifting planes of modelling. I would rather not speak of his unhappy *Sapphos*, for I know that he has frequently done much better; but even in his best-executed statues, the practised eye is distressed by his method of *abbreviation*, whereby the human face and human limbs all have the banal finish and polish of wax cast in a mould. If Canova was sometimes charming, it was certainly not thanks to this defect. His *Taureau Romain* has received well-deserved praise from everybody; it is really a very fine work: but if I was M. Clésinger, I should not like to be praised so magnificently for having created the image of an *animal*, however noble and superb that animal may have been. A sculptor of his calibre ought to have other ambitions and to set his hand to the creation of other images than those of bulls.[1]

The *Saint Sebastian* by a pupil of Rude, M. Just Becquet, is a painstaking and vigorous piece of sculpture. It makes one think at once of the painting of Ribera and of the harsh statuary of Spain. M. Rude's teaching has had a great effect upon the school of our time; but if it has profited some—those, doubtless, who were able to *edit* that teaching with the aid of their own natural intelligence—it has nevertheless plunged others, too docile, into the most amazing aberrations. Look at that Gaulish woman[2] for example! The first shape that a woman of Gaul assumes in your mind is that of a figure of noble bearing, free, powerful, robust and supple of form, a strapping daughter of the forests, a wild and warlike woman, whose voice was heard in the councils of the fatherland. But in the unfortunate object of which I am speaking, there is a complete absence of all that constitutes beauty and strength. The breasts, hips, thighs, legs,—everything in fact, that ought to stand in relief, is hollow. I have seen corpses like this on dissection-tables, ravaged by disease and the continuous poverty of forty years. Can it be that the artist has sought to represent the decay and the exhaustion of a woman who has known no other nourishment but acorns? and has he confused his warrior-woman of ancient Gaul with a decrepit female Papuan? Let us look for a less ambitious explanation and simply assume that, having heard it frequently repeated that one must faithfully copy the model, and not being endowed with the necessary perspicacity to choose a fine one, he has copied the

[1] Three of Clésinger's exhibits, including one of his Sapphos, and the Roman bull, are reproduced in Estignard, *Clésinger* (Paris 1900), facing pp. 56, 72, and 172.

[2] By J. B. Baujault.

ugliest that he could find, with a perfect devotion. This statue has found praise, doubtless because of its far-darting eye, like a 'Keepsake' Velléda. I am not at all surprised.

If you want to study the opposite of sculpture once again, but this time in another form, look at those two little theatrical microcosms invented by M. Butté: they represent, I believe, *The Tower of Babel* and *The Flood*. But subject-matter has little importance, anyway, when by its nature, or by the manner in which it is treated, the very essence of the art is found to have perished. This lilliputian world, these miniature processions, these little crowds which wind in and out among the rocky boulders, put one simultaneously in mind of the relief maps in the Marine Museum, of musical picture-clocks, and of those landscapes with fortress, drawbridge and the changing of the guard which may be seen in pastry-cooks' and toy-sellers' shops. I find it extremely unpleasant to have to write such things, especially when we are concerned with works in which both imagination and ingenuity are otherwise to be found; and if I speak of them, it is only because they are important in this one respect—that they serve to put on record one of the mind's greatest vices, which is a stubborn disobedience to the constituent rules of art. How could one conceive of qualities fine enough to counterbalance such an enormity of error? What healthy brain could imagine without horror a painting in relief, a piece of sculpture mechanically activated, a rhymeless ode, a novel in verse, and so on? When the natural aim of an art is misunderstood, it is natural to call to its aid all the devices which are alien to that art. And in the case of M. Butté, who has wanted to represent, on a small scale, vast scenes demanding an innumerable quantity of figures, we may observe that the ancients always confined such ventures to the bas-relief, and that among the moderns, even very great and clever sculptors have never attempted them without damage and danger to their art. The two essential conditions—unity of impression and totality of effect—are grievously violated thereby, and no matter how great the 'stage director's' talent, the spectator's mind will be troubled and will start wondering if it has not had a somewhat similar impression from Curtius's [1] waxworks. The vast and magnificent groups which adorn the gardens of Versailles are not a complete refutation of my opinion; for, apart from the fact that

[1] The popularizer of waxwork shows in Paris, during the last half of the eighteenth century. He had two museums, one of 'grands hommes et gens de marque' at the Palais-Royal, and another for 'les criminels' on the Boulevard du Temple.

they are not all equally successful, and that some of them, by their chaotic structure, would only serve, on the contrary, to confirm the said opinion (I refer particularly to those in which almost all the figures are vertical), I would like to point out that there you have an entirely special kind of sculpture, whose faults, which are sometimes quite deliberate, vanish altogether beneath a liquid firework display, beneath a luminous rain; in a word, it is an art which is completed by hydraulics, an inferior art on the whole. Yet even the most perfect among these groups are only so because they approach the closer to true sculpture, and because, by means of their leaning attitudes and their interlacings, the figures create that general compositional arabesque which is motionless and fixed in painting, but as mobile and variable in sculpture as it is in a mountainous landscape.

We have already spoken, my dear M—, about the school of the *pointus*, and we recognized that amongst these subtle spirits, who are all more or less tainted with disobedience to the idea of pure art, there were nevertheless one or two of some interest. In sculpture too we find the same misfortunes. Undoubtedly M. Frémiet is a good sculptor; he is clever, daring, and subtle; he searches for the striking effect, and sometimes he finds it; but that is precisely where his misfortune lies, for he often searches for it some little way from the natural road. His *Orang-outang dragging a woman into a wood*[1] (a rejected work, which naturally I have not seen) is very much the idea of a *pointu*. Why not a crocodile, a tiger, or any other animal which is liable to eat a woman? But that is not the point! Be assured that this is no question of eating, but of worse! Now it is the ape alone, the gigantic ape, at once more and less than a man, that has been known to betray a human appetite for woman. So there, he has found his means of astonishing us! '*He* is carrying her off; will *she* be able to resist?' This is the question which will engage the entire female public. A strange and complex feeling, composed partly of terror and partly of priapic curiosity, will sweep it to success. Nevertheless, seeing that M. Frémiet is an excellent workman, both the animal and the woman will be equally well imitated and modelled. But to tell the truth, such subjects are unworthy of so ripe a talent, and the jury has acted well in refusing this wretched melodrama.

[1] Reproduced facing p. 82 in Philippe Fauré-Frémiet, *Frémiet* (Paris 1934); see also pp. 67–70. Frémiet later made several variations on this subject; examples are in the Nantes Museum and at Melbourne.

If M. Frémiet tells me that I have no right to scrutinize the aims, or even to speak, of what I have not seen, I will humbly fall back upon his *Cheval de saltimbanque*.[1] Taken in himself, the little horse is charming; his thick mane, his square muzzle, his intelligent air, his low-hung quarters, his little legs, both solid and spindly at the same time—everything marks him out as one of those humble beasts that have breeding. But I find the owl perched upon his back just a little disturbing (for I suppose I have not read the catalogue), and I start to wonder why Minerva's bird should be placed upon Neptune's creation. Then I notice the puppets which are hooked to his saddle; the idea of wisdom represented by the owl leads me to deduce that the puppets embody the frivolities of the world. It remains to explain the function of the horse, who, in the language of the Apocalypse, may well symbolize Intelligence, Will or Life. In the end I positively and patiently worked it out that M. Frémiet's work represents human intelligence carrying everywhere with it the idea of wisdom and the taste for folly. So here we have the immortal philosophic antithesis, the essentially human contradiction upon which, from the beginning of time, all philosophy and all literature has turned, from the tumultuous reigns of Ormuzd and Ahriman to the Reverend Maturin, from Manes to Shakespeare!... But a bystander whom I pestered with my questions was pleased to inform me that I was 'looking for apples on a pear-tree', and that the statue simply represents a tumbler's horse.... What, then, of that solemn owl, those mysterious marionettes? do they add nothing new to the idea of the horse? In so far as it is simply a horse, in what particular do they increase its merit? Obviously this work should have been entitled *A tumbler's horse in the absence of the tumbler, who has gone off to have a game of cards and a drink in a neighbouring tavern*! That is the real title!

MM. Carrier, Oliva and Prouha are more modest than M. Frémiet or myself; they are content to astonish us by the flexibility and skill of their art. All three of them have an evident sympathy with the living sculpture of the seventeenth and eighteenth centuries, and to this they devote their more or less concentrated faculties. They have loved and studied Caffieri, Puget, Coustou, Houdon, Pigalle and Francin. True enthusiasts have for long admired M. Oliva's vigorously-modelled busts, in which life breathes and even the eyes sparkle. That which represents *General Bizot* is one of the most *military* busts that I have seen, and *M. de*

[1] Reproduced Fauré-Frémiet, op. cit., facing p. 48.

Mercey is a masterpiece of finesse. Everyone will have recently noticed M. Prouha's statue in the courtyard of the Louvre—it recalled the noble and courtly graces of the Renaissance. M. Carrier may congratulate and compliment himself. Like his favourite masters, he possesses energy and spirit, though a slight excess of disorder and disarray in the costume may perhaps be held to contrast unhappily with the vigorous and patient finish of his faces. I am not claiming that it is a fault to crumple a shirt or a cravat, or to give a pleasant twist to the lapel of a coat; I am only referring to a lack of harmony with relation to the total idea. And yet I will readily own that I hesitate to attach too much importance to this observation, for M. Carrier's busts have caused me a pleasure quite keen enough to make me forget this entirely fleeting little criticism.

You will remember, my friend, that we have already spoken of *Jamais et Toujours*; I have not yet been able to discover the explanation of this riddling title. Can it be a last resort, or a motiveless whim, like *Rouge et Noir*? Or perhaps M. Hébert [1] has bowed to the taste of MM. Commerson and Paul de Kock which prompts them to see a thought in the fortuitous clash of any antithesis? However that may be, he has made a charming piece of sculpture (*chamber-sculpture*, shall we call it? although it is doubtful if the ladies and gentlemen of the bourgeoisie would want it to decorate their boudoirs)—a kind of vignette in sculpture, but one which nevertheless might make an excellent funereal decoration in a cemetery or a chapel, if executed on a larger scale. A young girl, generous and supple of form, is being lifted and swung up with a harmonious lightness; and her body, convulsed in ecstasy or in agony, is resignedly submitting to the kiss of an immense skeleton. It is generally held, perhaps because antiquity did not know it, or knew it but little, that the skeleton should be excluded from the realm of sculpture. This is a great error. We see it appear in the middle ages, comporting and displaying itself with all the impudent clumsiness, with all the arrogance of the Idea without Art. But from then until the eighteenth century (the historical climate of love and of roses) we see the skeleton blossom and flourish in every subject in which it is allowed to make an entrance. The sculptor was very quick to understand all the mysterious and abstract beauty inherent in this scraggy carcass which the flesh serves as clothing, and which is itself a kind of map of the human poem. And so this sentimental, sardonic, almost scientific kind of Grace, cleansed and purified of the

[1] I.e. *Emile* Hébert: see p. 151 above.

soil's defilement, took its stand in its turn among the innumerable other Graces which Art had already wrested from ignorant Nature. M. Hébert's skeleton is not, properly speaking, a skeleton at all. Nevertheless I am not suggesting that the artist has tried to *sidestep* the difficulty, as they say. If this redoubtable personage has here assumed the vague character of a phantom, a spectre or a lamia; if in some parts it is still clothed with a parchment-like skin which adheres to its joints like the membranes of a palmiped; and if it is half enfolded and draped in an immense shroud which is raised here and there by its projecting articulations, all this is doubtless because the artist wanted above all to give expression to the vast and floating idea of total negation. He has succeeded, and his phantom is *full of void*.

The pleasant occurrence of this macabre subject has made me regret that M. Christophe has not exhibited two pieces of his composition, the one of an altogether analogous nature, the other more gracefully allegorical. This second [1] represents a naked woman, quite Florentine in the grandeur and vigour of her frame (for M. Christophe is not one of those feeble artists whose imagination has been destroyed by Rude's positive and finicky teaching); seen from the front, she presents the spectator with a smiling and dainty face, an actress's face. A light drapery, cleverly knotted, serves to join this pretty, conventional head to the robust bosom on which it seems to be resting. But if you take a further step to the right or the left, you will discover the secret of the allegory, the moral of the fable—her *real* head, I mean, twisted out of position and in a swoon of agony and tears. What at first had enchanted your eyes was but a mask—the universal mask, your mask, my mask, the pretty fan which a clever hand uses to conceal its pain or remorse from the eyes of the world. This work is all charm and solidity. The robust character of the body is in picturesque contrast to the mystical expression of an entirely worldly idea, and surprise does not play a more important part than is permissible. If ever the artist should agree to let the dealers have this child of his brain, in the form of a small-scale bronze, I can confidently predict it an immense success.

As for the other idea, believe me, for all its charm I would not answer for it; so much the less because, in order to be fully realized, it needs two substances, the one pale and dull (to represent the skeleton), the other

[1] A later version of this statue is now in the Tuileries. It is the subject of Baudelaire's poem, *Le Masque* (*Les Fleurs du Mal*, xx).

dark and shining (to render the clothing), and this would naturally increase the horror of the idea, and its unpopularity.[1] Alas!

Les charmes de l'horreur n'enivrent que les forts! [2]

Imagine a great female skeleton all ready to set out for a revel. With her flattened, negress's face, her lipless and gumless smile, and her gaze, which is no more than a pit of shadows, this horrible thing, which once was a beautiful woman, seems to be vaguely searching in space for the delicious moment of her rendezvous, or for the solemn moment of the sabbath, which is recorded on the invisible clock of the centuries. Her bust, which Time has eaten away, leaps coquettishly from the corsage, like a withered bouquet from its cone, and this whole funereal conception takes its stand upon the pedestal of a sumptuous crinoline. To cut matters short, may I be allowed to quote a fragment of verse in which I have tried, not to *illustrate*, but to explain the subtle pleasure distilled by this figurine—rather in the manner that a careful reader scribbles with his pencil in the margin of his book?

Fière, autant qu'un vivant, de sa noble stature,
Avec son gros bouquet, son mouchoir et ses gants,
Elle a la nonchalance et la désinvolture
D'une coquette maigre aux airs extravagants.

Vit-on jamais au bal une taille plus mince?
Sa robe, exagérée en sa royale ampleur,
S'écroule abondamment sur un pied sec que pince
Un soulier pomponné joli comme une fleur.

La ruche qui se joue au bord des clavicules,
Comme un ruisseau lascif qui se frotte au rocher,
Défend pudiquement des lazzi ridicules
Les funèbres appas qu'elle tient à cacher.

Ses yeux profonds sont faits de vide et de ténèbres,
Et son crâne, de fleurs artistement coiffé,
Oscille mollement sur ses frêles vertèbres.
O charme du néant follement attifé!

[1] See pl. 62.

[2] 'The charms of horror thrill the strong alone!' From *Danse Macabre* (*Les Fleurs du Mal*, XCVII).

Aucuns t'appelleront une caricature,
Qui ne comprennent pas, amants ivres de chair,
L'élégance sans nom de l'humaine armature!
Tu réponds, grand squelette, à mon goût le plus cher!

Viens-tu troubler, avec ta puissante grimace,
La fête de la vie . . . ? [1]

I think, my friend, that we can stop here. I might produce some new specimens, but I could only regard them as superfluous proofs in support of the principal idea which from the beginning has controlled my work—namely, that the most ingenious and the most patient of talents can in no wise do duty for a taste for grandeur and the sacred frenzy of the imagination. For some years past, people have been amusing themselves with more than permissible criticism of one of our dearest friends; very well, I am one of those who can confess, without blushing, that whatever the *skill* that is annually displayed by our sculptors, nevertheless, since the death of David,[2] I look around me in vain for the ethereal pleasures which I have so often had from the tumultuous, even if fragmentary, *dreams* of Auguste Préault.

X. ENVOI

AT LAST the moment has come to utter that irrepressible *ouf!* of relief which is breathed with such joy by every simple mortal who is not devoid of spleen and has been condemned to a forced march, when at

[1] 'As proud of her noble stature as if she were alive, with her huge bouquet, her handkerchief and her gloves, she has the nonchalance and the unconcern of a skinny coquette with extravagant airs. Did you ever see a slimmer figure among the dancers? Her gown, billowing out in its regal abundance, cascades upon a dry foot which is pinched by a tassled shoe, as pretty as a flower. The frill which plays about her shoulder-blades, like a wanton brook foaming against a rock, chastely shields those funereal charms which she is so anxious to hide from stupid jeers. Her deep eyes are wells of darkness and shadow, and her skull, tastefully crowned with flowers, sways slackly on her slender spine.—Oh spell of nothingness, madly bedecked! Some will call you a caricature—those whose drunken love of the flesh does not allow them to understand the nameless elegance of the body's scaffolding. Huge skeleton, you echo my dearest taste! . . . Do you come to disturb the festival of life, with your awesome grimace . . . ?' The earliest published version of the opening stanzas of Baudelaire's *Danse Macabre.*

[2] David d'Angers died in 1856.

last he can throw himself into the longed-for oasis of rest. From the very beginning, I will willingly admit, the blessed characters which spell the word END have been floating before my brain, clothed in their black skins, like tiny Ethiopian dancers ready to execute the most engaging of 'character dances'. My honourable friends the artists—I speak of true artists, of those who agree with me that everything that is not perfection should hide its head, and that everything that is not sublime is useless and blameworthy; of those who know that there is an awesome profundity in the first idea that comes, and that among the innumerable methods of expressing it, there are at the most only two or three excellent ones (in this I am less strict than La Bruyère)—those artists, I mean, who are always restless and unsatisfied, like souls confined, will not take amiss certain mocking thrusts and peevish sallies which they have to suffer as often as the critic does himself. They know as well as I do that nothing is more wearisome than to have to explain what everyone ought to know already. If boredom and contempt can be regarded as emotions, they too will have found contempt and boredom the most difficult of emotions to deny—the most fatal, the most ready to hand. I impose upon myself the same harsh conditions which I should like to see everyone else impose upon himself; I never stop asking myself, 'What is the good?', and whenever I imagine that I have expounded a good argument, I ask myself, 'Whom, and what, can it serve?' Amongst the numerous omissions of which I am guilty, some are deliberate; I have purposely neglected a crowd of obviously gifted artists who are too well-known to be praised, or not unusual enough, either for good or for ill, to serve as a theme for discussion. I set myself the task of seeking Imagination throughout the Salon, and having found it but seldom, I have only had to speak of a small number of men. As for the involuntary omissions or errors which I may have committed, the Muse of Painting will surely forgive me, as being a man who, without having made extended studies, nevertheless has the love of Painting in every fibre of his being. Besides, anyone who may have some reason for complaint will find innumerable allies to avenge and console him, without counting that one of us to whom you will entrust the task of analysing next year's exhibition, and whom you will grant the same liberties as you have been kind enough to accord to me. I hope with all my heart that he may find more subjects for wonder and amazement than I have conscientiously found. The noble and excellent artists whom I was invoking a moment ago will say, as I do:

'To sum up, a great deal of technique and skill, but precious little genius!' That is what everyone says. Alas then, I agree with everyone! You see, my dear M—, it was quite unnecessary to explain what they all of them agree with us in thinking. My only consolation is that, by parading these commonplaces, I may perhaps have been able to please two or three people who will guess that I am thinking of them, and in whose number I beg you to be so kind as to include yourself.

Your very devoted collaborator and friend.

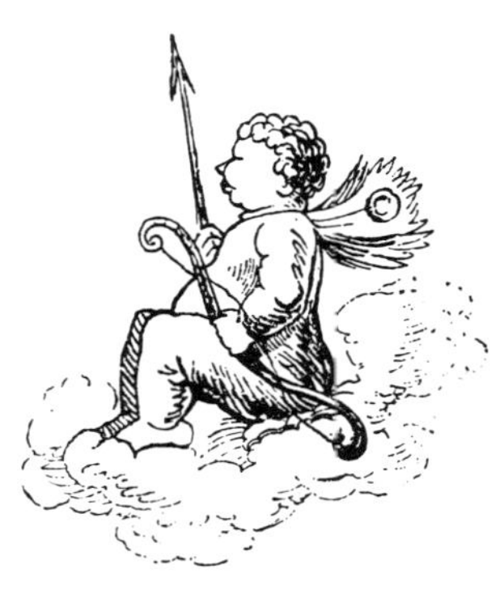

"Tell me, my heart, can this be Love?"

PAINTERS AND ETCHERS

EVER since the grand climacteric when the arts and literature in France exploded in a simultaneous detonation, the sense of the Beautiful, of the Strong, and even of the Picturesque, has continued to dwindle and decay among us. For a number of years the whole glory of the French school seemed to be concentrated in a single man—and I certainly do not mean M. Ingres[1]; but however great his energy and fecundity, they were insufficient by themselves to console us for the paltriness of the others. Only a short time ago, as we can all remember, we witnessed the undisputed sway of the 'neat' in painting—the pretty, the silly, the intricate—and also of those pretentious daubs which, though representing a contrary excess, are no less odious to the eye of a true amateur. This poverty of ideas, this niggling finicality in the expression, and finally all those other notorious absurdities of French painting, are quite enough to explain the immense success of Courbet's pictures from their very first appearance. This reaction, which was carried out with the noisy braggadocio of every other reaction, was positively necessary. We must do Courbet this justice—that he contributed not a little to the re-establishment of a taste for simplicity and honesty, and of a disinterested, absolute love of painting.

More recently still two other artists, both still young, have made their entrances with a quite unusual vigour.

I am alluding to M. Legros[2] and M. Manet.[3] We all remember M. Legros's robust creations—*The Angelus*[4] (1859) which expressed so well the sad, resigned devotion of the congregations of the poor; the *Ex Voto*[5] which was admired at a more recent Salon and at the Galerie

[1] Delacroix, of course.

[2] Baudelaire had already written enthusiastically of Legros in his *Salon of 1859*; cf. pp. 163–5, above.

[3] Baudelaire's not entirely wholehearted admiration for Manet, which was complicated by a close personal friendship for him, has sometimes caused comment; see, for example, P. Rebeyrol's article, 'Baudelaire et Manet', in *Les Temps modernes*, October 1949. It is enough here to remind the reader that the following sentences are the only references to Manet by Baudelaire published during the latter's lifetime. See pls. 65–7.

[4] See pl. 42.

[5] Salon of 1861; now in the Dijon Museum.

Martinet,[1] and was acquired by M. de Balleroy[2]; a picture of monks kneeling before a holy book, as though humbly and piously discussing its interpretation[3]; an assembly of Professors, clad in their official robes, engaged on a scientific debate, which can now be admired in M. Ricord's[4] collection.

M. Manet is the painter of the *Guitarist*[5] which created a lively stir at the last Salon. At the next Salon we are promised several pictures[6] by him spiced with the strongest Spanish flavour, which suggest that the genius of Spain has come to take refuge in France.[7] MM. Manet and Legros combine a vigorous taste for reality, modern reality—already a good symptom—with that lively and abundant imagination, both sensitive and bold, without which, it must be emphasized, even the finest gifts are no more than servants without a master, agents without a government.

It was only natural that in this active movement of renewal, a part should have been allotted to the art of engraving. Into what discredit and indifference that noble art has fallen is, alas!, only too manifest. Formerly, when a plate was advertised reproducing a well-known picture, collectors would flock to subscribe in advance for the first proofs. But it is only by looking through the works of the past that we can understand the splendours of the burin. There was one technique, however, which was even more dead than that of the burin; I refer to etching. To tell the truth, this technique, so subtle and superb, so naif and profound, so gay and severe, a technique which can paradoxically accommodate the most varied qualities and which is so admirably expressive of the personal character of the artist, has never enjoyed a really great popularity among the vulgar. Apart from the prints of Rembrandt, which force themselves

[1] The Galerie Martinet had branches in the Rue Vivienne and the Rue de Rivoli.

[2] A painter and etcher, whose portrait occurs in Manet's *Musique aux Tuileries.*

[3] *The Vocation of St. Francis,* given by the artist to the Alençon Museum in 1862.

[4] A well-known doctor.

[5] Private collection, New York; Jamot, *Manet,* 1932, No. 40, fig. 36; for a related water-colour, see *Edouard Manet,* Phaidon Press, 1958, pl. 4.

[6] For example, the *Mlle. Victorine in the costume of an Espada* (New York, Metropolitan Museum).

[7] Baudelaire was later (1864), in a letter to the critic Thoré, to deny that Manet was guilty of plagiarizing the Spanish painters, and to go so far as to state that at this time Manet had seen practically no Spanish pictures; in his *Manet* (Phaidon Press, 1958, p. 15) Mr. John Richardson discusses this point and suggests that Baudelaire may in fact have been inaccurate.

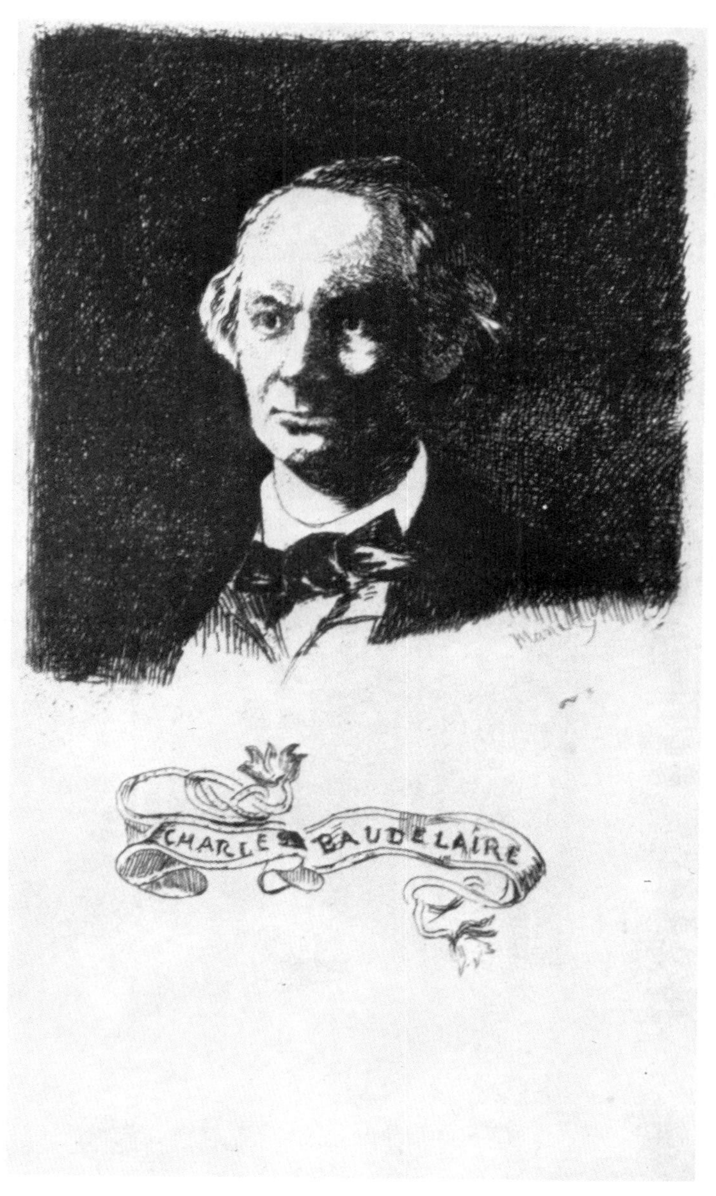

65. MANET: *Portrait of Baudelaire*. Etching, 1865. London, British Museum.

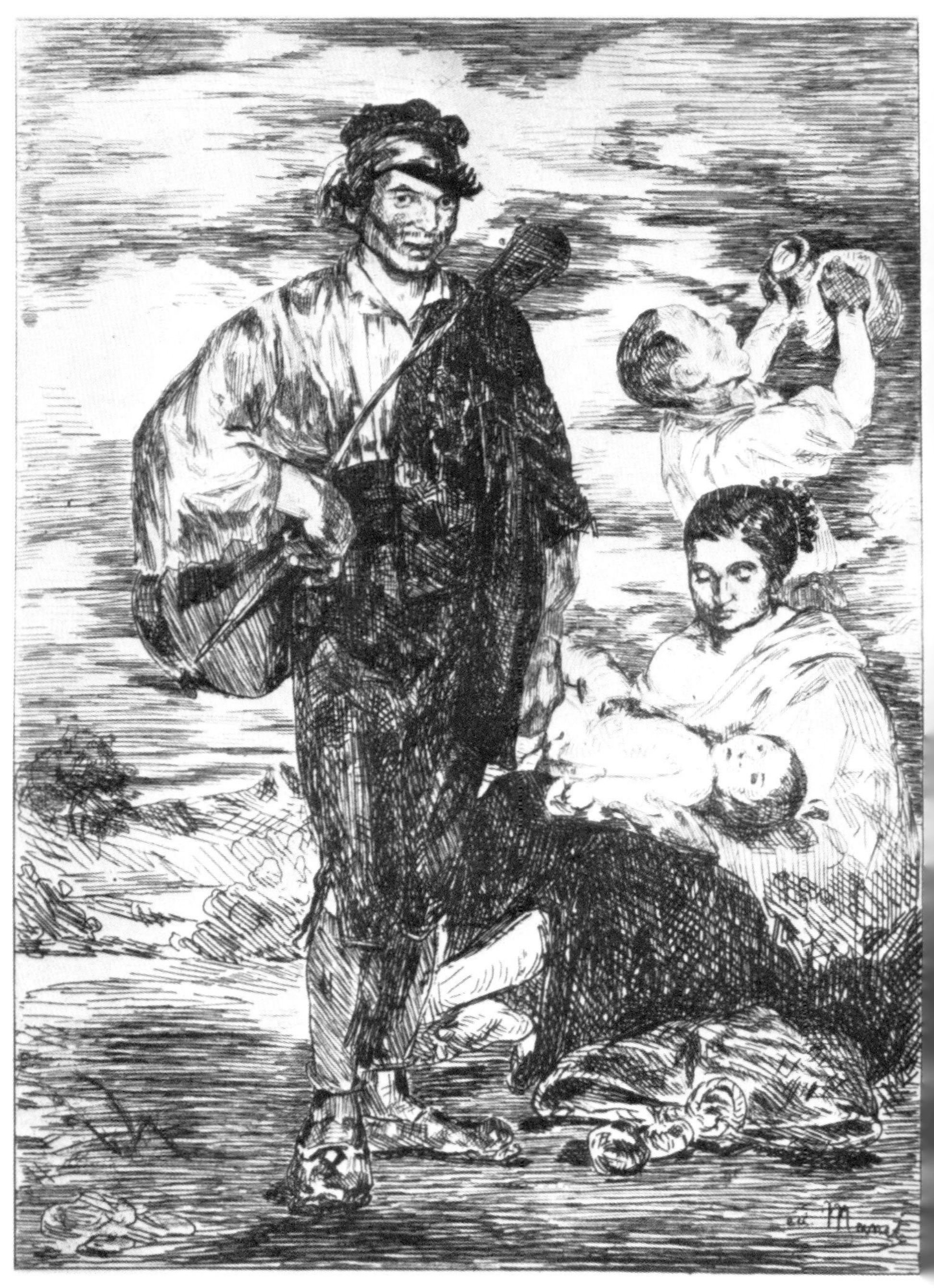

66. MANET: *Les Gitanos*. Etching, 1862. London, Victoria and Albert Museum.

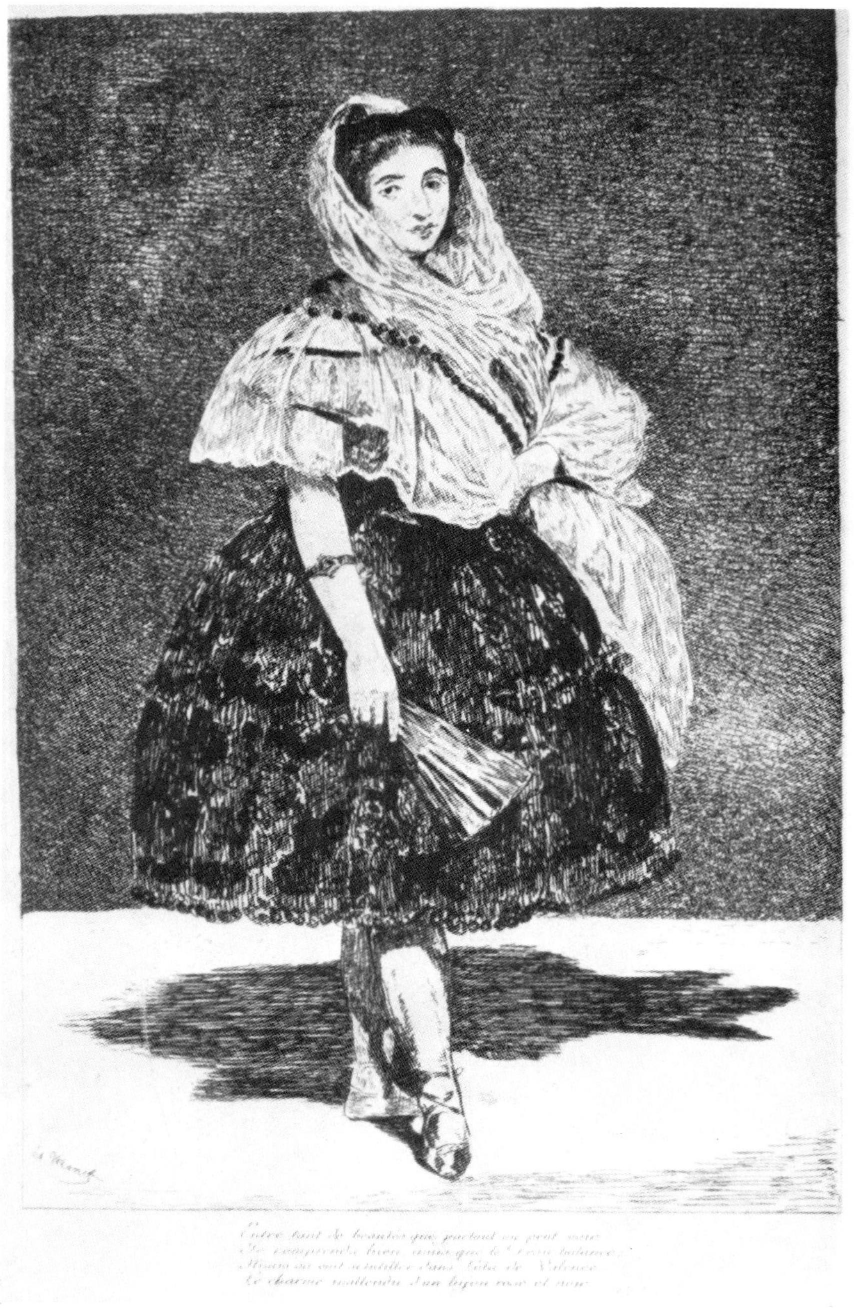

67. MANET: *Lola de Valence*. Etching, 1862. London, British Museum.

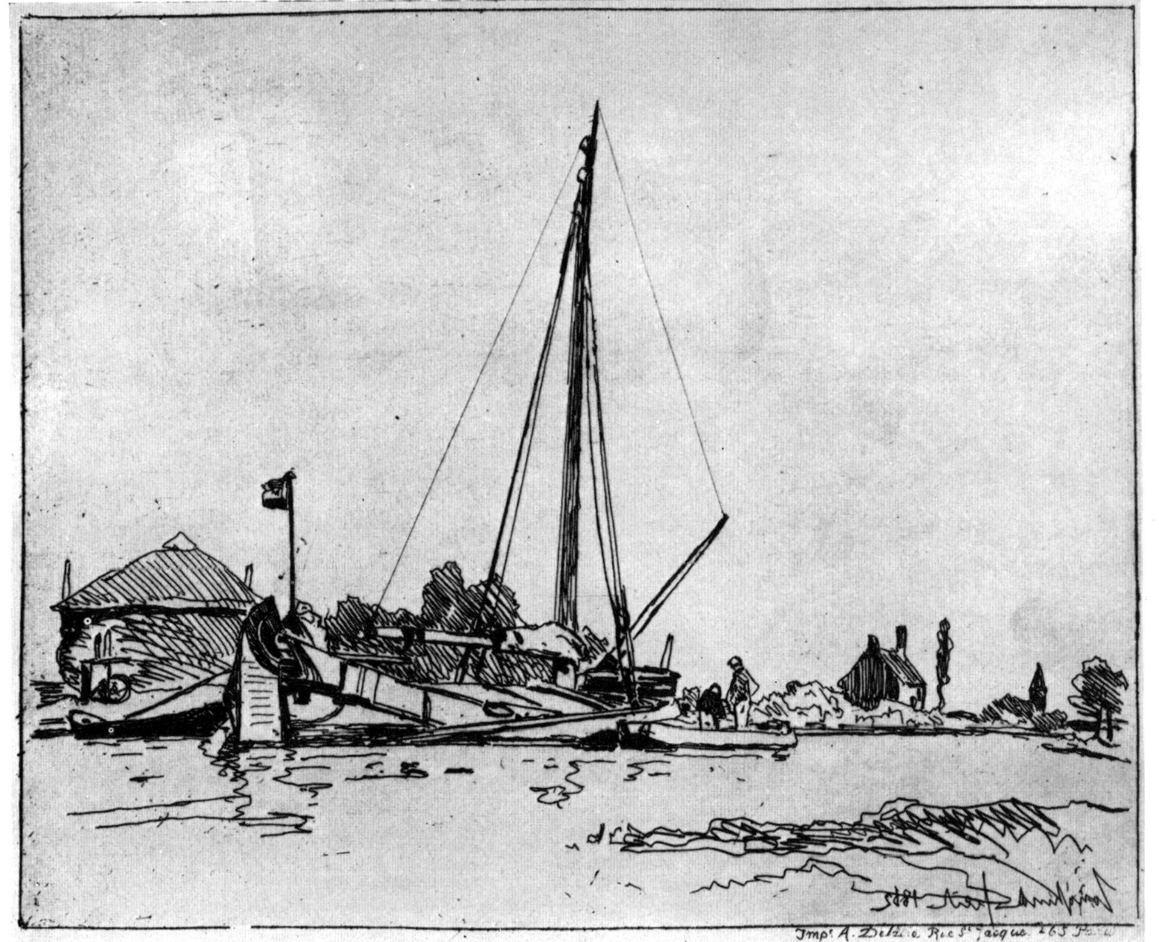

68 JONGKIND: [illegible] Etching, [illegible] London, Victoria and Albert Museum

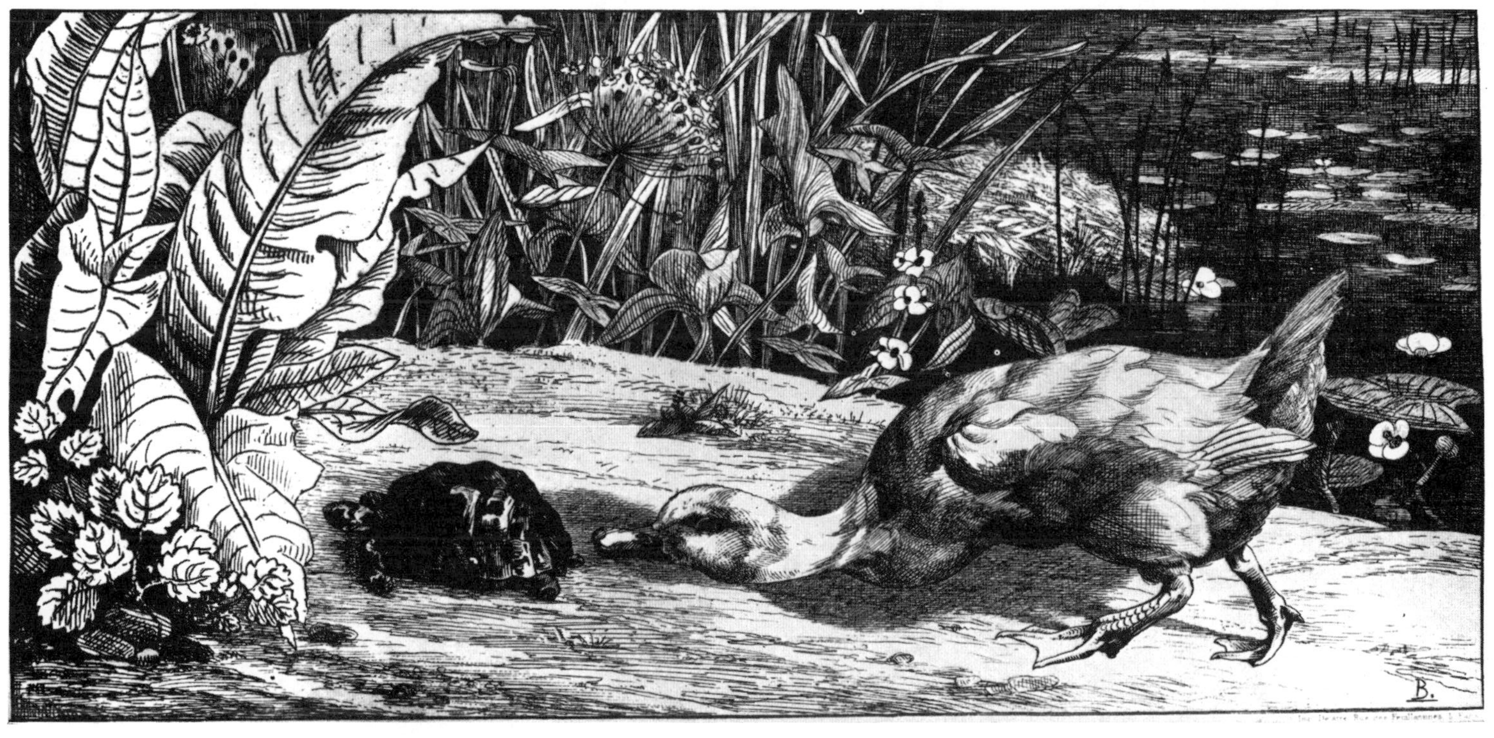

69. BRACQUEMOND: *The Stranger*. Etching, 1862. London, Victoria and Albert Museum.

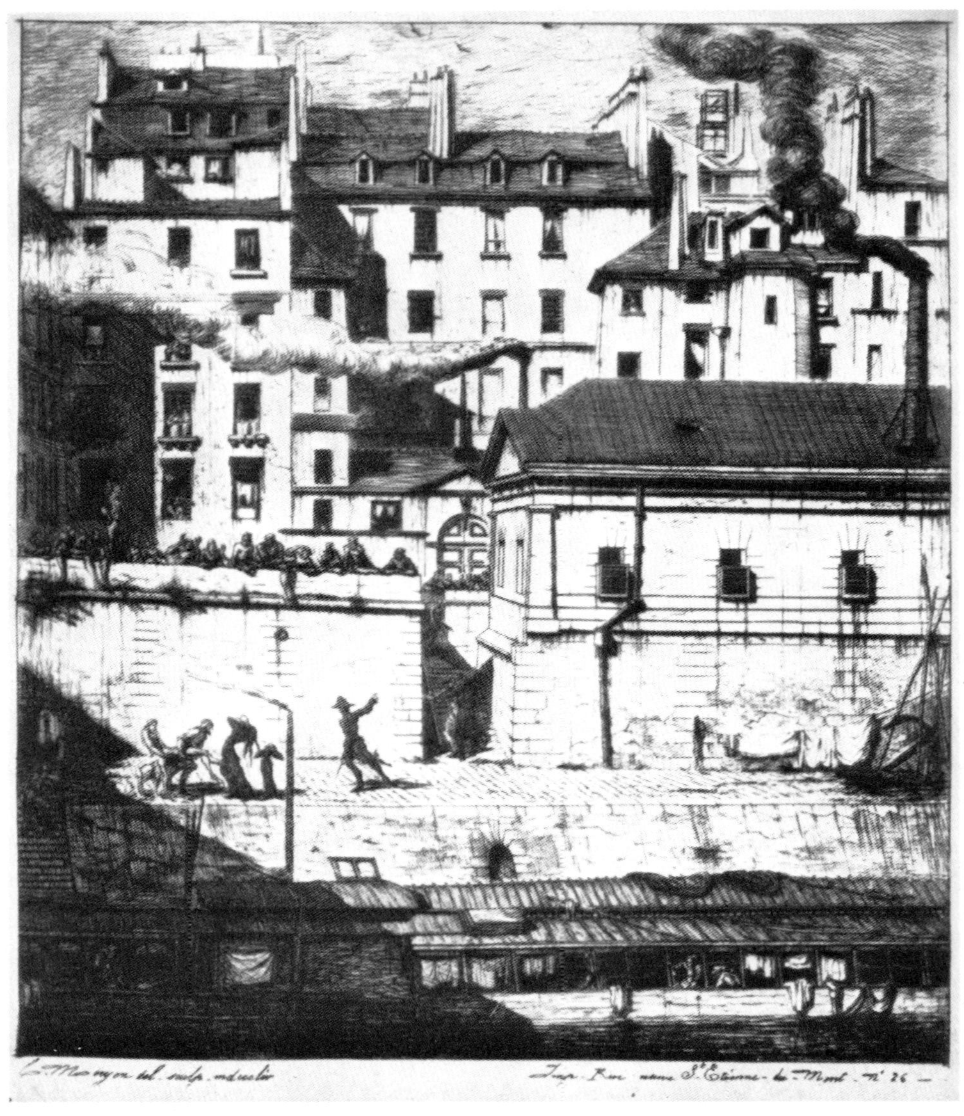

70. MERYON: *The Morgue*. Etching, 1854. London, Victoria and Albert Museum.

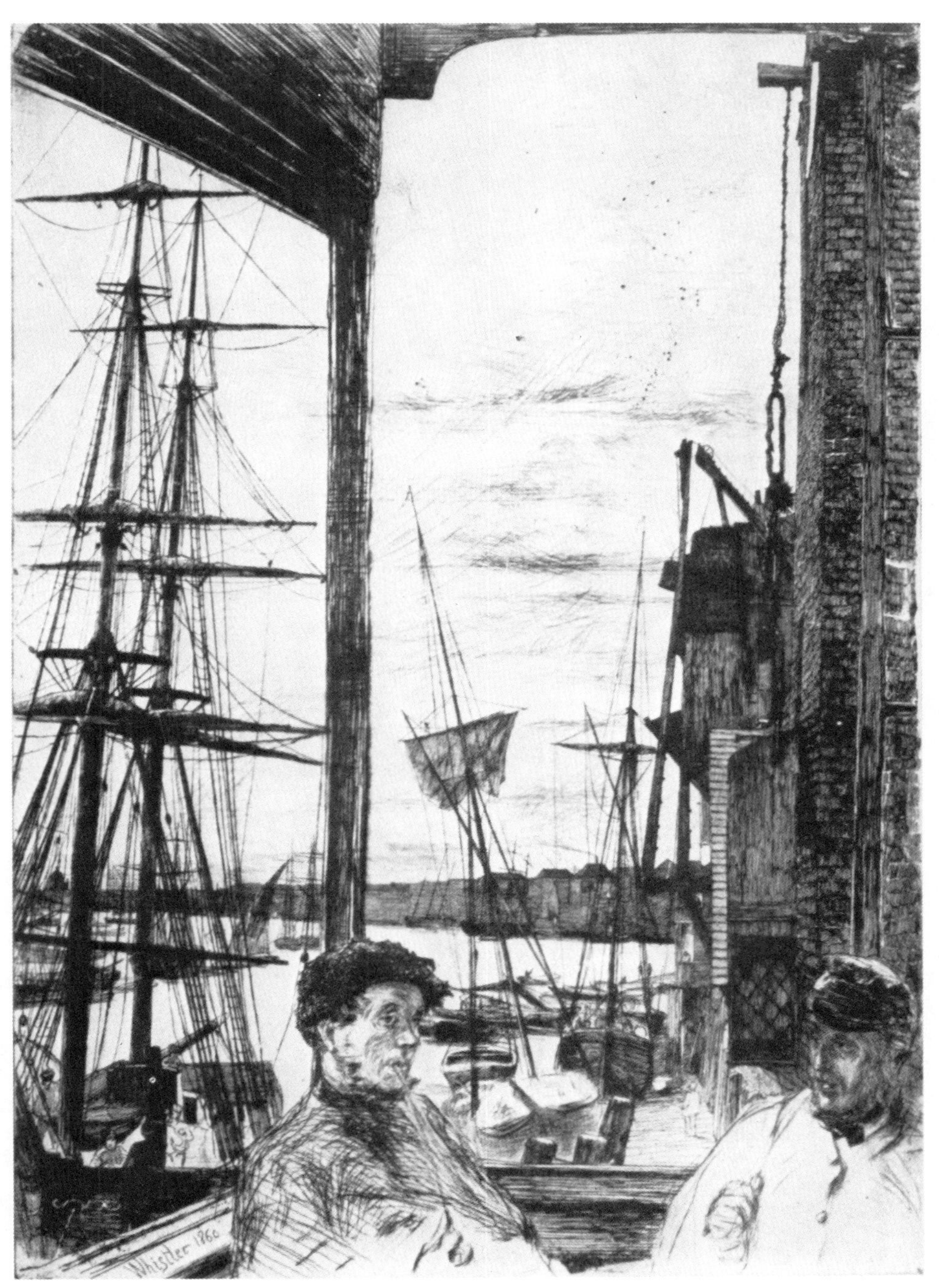

71. WHISTLER: *Rotherhithe*. Etching, 1860. London, British Museum.

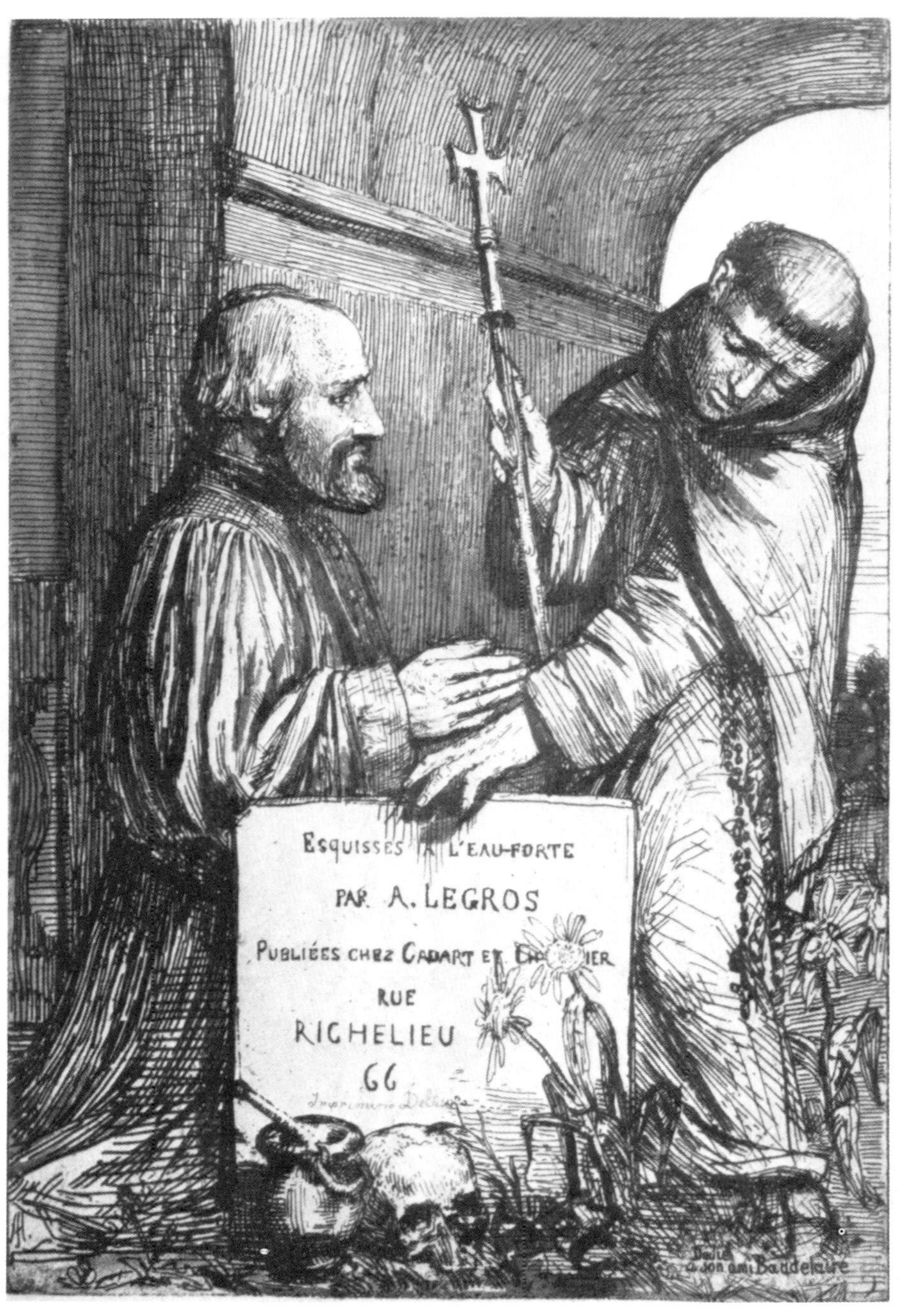

72. LEGROS: *Title-page to a set of etchings*, with dedication to Baudelaire. Etching. London, Victoria and Albert Museum.

with a classic authority even upon the ignorant, and about which there is no room for argument, who really cares about etching? Who, apart from collectors, knows the different forms of perfection in this genre which earlier ages have bequeathed us? The eighteenth century abounds in charming etchings; they are to be had for ten sous apiece in dusty portfolios, and often have to wait a long time for a loving eye to spot them. Are there today, even among the artists, many who know the witty, playful and caustic designs with which Trimolet,[1] of melancholy memory, was enriching the comic Almanacks of Aubert some years ago?

Nevertheless it would seem that we are about to witness a return to etching, or, at all events, attempts may be discerned which permit us to hope so. The young artists of whom I was speaking a moment ago have banded together with several others round an energetic publisher, M. Cadart, and have invited their friends to join with them in founding a regular publication of original etchings—of which, by the way, the first number has already appeared.[2]

It was natural that these artists should turn especially to a genre and a method of expression which together, when fully successful, offer the crispest possible translation of the artist's personality—an expeditious method, moreover, and a cheap one, which is an important point at a time when everyone considers a 'good bargain' as the most important thing, and would be hardly prepared to pay their proper price for the laborious operations of the burin. There is, however, a danger into which more than one of them will fall; the danger, I mean, of slackness, incorrectness, indecision, inadequate execution. It is so easy to run an etching-needle over a blackened sheet of copper which will reproduce only too faithfully all the arabesques of the fancy, all the casual strokes of a momentary caprice! Some of them, I daresay, will even go so far as to pride themselves on their boldness (is this the right word?), like slovenly people who fancy that they are displaying independence. It is all very well for men of a profound and mature talent, like M. Legros, M. Manet or M. Jongkind, for example, to entrust to the public their engraved sketches and studies; indeed they have a perfect right to do so. But they are likely to engender a whole multitude of imitators, and there is a risk that they may inspire the public to a disdain—and in their case a legitimate one—for so charming a genre which will already be guilty, at their

[1] Cf. *Painter of Modern Life*, pp. 183-4.

[2] This was the collection entitled *Eaux-fortes modernes*, first series, 1 September 1862.

hands, of having strayed far outside its range. After all, it must never be forgotten that etching is a deep and dangerous art, full of pitfalls, which exposes the faults of a mind just as clearly as its good qualities. And being very complicated beneath its apparent simplicity, like every great art, it requires a long period of devotion in order to be brought to perfection.

We should like to believe that, thanks to the efforts of artists as intelligent as MM. Seymour Haden,[1] Manet, Legros, Bracquemond,[2] Jongkind, Meryon, Millet, Daubigny, Saint-Marcel, Jacquemart, and others whose names for the moment escape me, etching will regain its old vitality; whatever may be said, however, let us not hope that it win as great a popularity as it did in London, in the heighday of the Etching Club, when even fair 'ladies' prided themselves on their ability to run an inexperienced needle over the varnished plate. A typically British craze, a passing mania, which would bode ill for us.

Just the other day a young American artist, M. Whistler,[3] was showing at the Galerie Martinet a set of etchings, as subtle and lively as improvisation and inspiration, representing the banks of the Thames; wonderful tangles of rigging, yardarms and rope; farragos of fog, furnaces and corkscrews of smoke; the profound and intricate poetry of a vast capital.

We already know the vast, bold etchings of M. Legros, which he has just collected into an album: ecclesiastical ceremonies, as magnificent as dreams, or rather as the reality; processions, nocturnal services, ritual splendours, cloistral austerities; and those few pages in which Edgar Poe finds himself translated with a harsh and simple majesty.[4]

It was at M. Cadart's that M. Bonvin[5] recently put on sale an album of etchings as painstaking, firm and meticulous as his painting.

At the same publisher's M. Jongkind,[6] that charming and unaffected Dutch painter, has placed several plates in which he has enshrined the secret of his memories and reveries—as calm as the banks of the great rivers and the horizons of his noble country; curious abbreviations of

[1] He married Whistler's half-sister, and was associated with him in the revival of etching in England.

[2] See pl. 69.

[3] See pl. 71.

[4] See pl. 72, and *Painter of Modern Life* pls. 34–5.

[5] These were the *Six Eaux-fortes*, a series of figure-subjects.

[6] See pl. 68.

his painting, sketches which will be intelligible to any amateur used to deciphering an artist's soul in his most rapid *scribbles*. 'Scribbles' is the term used a little frivolously by the excellent Diderot[1] in characterizing the etchings of Rembrandt—a frivolity worthy of a moralist who wishes to dissert on something quite other than Morals.

M. Meryon,[2] the true type of the consummate etcher, could not neglect the call. He will shortly be giving us some new works; but M. Cadart still has some of his old ones. These, however, are becoming rare; for in a fit of petulance, which, by the way, was perfectly legitimate, M. Meryon recently destroyed the plates of his Paris album. And straightaway, just round the corner, the Meryon collection was sold twice running at public auctions for four and five times its original value.

In the pungency, the *finesse* and sureness of his drawing, M. Meryon recalls all that was best in the old etchers. We have rarely seen the natural solemnity of a great capital more poetically depicted. Those[3] majestic accumulations of stone; those spires 'whose fingers point to heaven'; those obelisks of industry, spewing forth their conglomerations of smoke against the firmament; those prodigies of scaffolding round buildings under repair, applying their openwork architecture, of such paradoxical and arachnean beauty, upon architecture's solid body; that foggy sky, charged with anger and spite;—he forgot not one of the complex elements which go to make up the painful and glorious décor of civilization.

We also saw at the same publisher's that celebrated perspective of San Francisco,[4] which M. Meryon has a good right to call his veritable masterpiece. The owner of the plate, M. Niel, would be performing a real act of charity if from time to time he had a few impressions printed from it. There would be no difficulty in finding purchasers for them.

In all these facts I discern a happy symptom. But for all that, I would not go so far as to declare that etching is destined shortly for a total popularity. Let us think a moment; a little unpopularity is a sort of consecration. It is really too *personal*, and consequently too *aristocratic*, a genre

[1] This criticism is a little unexpected in a writer who owed so much, and admitted his debt, to Diderot: cf. Gilman, pp. 40 ff.

[2] See pl. 70.

[3] The following sentences, down to the end of the paragraph, are taken, with minor variations, from Baudelaire's *Salon of 1859*; see pp. 200–201, above.

[4] Delteil, *Meryon*, No. 73, of unusual panoramic shape; Meryon used five daguerreotypes in its preparation.

to enchant people other than those who are naturally artists, and thus immediately drawn to any lively personality. Not only does etching serve to glorify the individuality of the artist; it would even be difficult for an artist *not* to describe his most intimate personality on the copper. And so we can safely declare that since the discovery of this kind of engraving, there have been as many manners of cultivating it as there have been etchers. It is not the same thing with the burin, or rather the proportion of the personality in the expression is infinitely less.

After all, however, we should be delighted if we were to turn out to have been bad prophets, and we should be in no wise disgusted to have to share our fruit with a great public. We wish these gentlemen and their publication a good and solid future.

NOTES ON THE ILLUSTRATIONS

NOTES ON THE ILLUSTRATIONS

Unless otherwise stated, the medium is oil on canvas. Dimensions in inches.

Frontispiece. CHARLES BAUDELAIRE (1821–67): Self-Portrait, about 1860. Pen and red chalk, 8 × 5. Chantilly, Spoelberch de Lovenjoul.
One of a series of self-portrait drawings which may have been intended (but were not used) for the second edition of the *Fleurs du mal* (1861). According to Baudelaire's friend and publisher, Poulet-Malassis, this was the best of the group. See *Dessins de Baudelaire* (Paris, 1927), and *Baudelaire: Documents Iconographiques* (ed. Pichois and Ruchon), Geneva, 1960, No. 26.

II. GAVARNI (1804–66): The Artist and his Critic. Lithograph, from *Le Charivari*. See p. 44. London, Victoria and Albert Museum.

III. ETIENNE CARJAT (1828–1906): Photograph of Baudelaire. Carjat took at least two photographs of Baudelaire on the same day, dateable 1861–2. See *Baudelaire: Documents Iconographiques* (ed. Pichois and Ruchon), Geneva 1960, Nos 34 and 35.

1. LOUIS JANMOT (1814–92): Flowers of the Field. Salon of 1845 (Fleurs de champs). Panel, 40½ × 32⅝. See p. 17. Lyon, Musée des Beaux-Arts.

2. WILLIAM HAUSSOULLIER (1818–91): The Fountain of Youth. Salon of 1845 (La Fontaine de jouvence). 51 × 72. See pp. 7–9. London, Mr. Graham Reynolds.
This painting was lot 107 at Christies, 17 December 1937. It is dated 1843. Its intermediate history is unknown.

3. ADRIEN GUIGNET (1816–54): Joseph interpreting the Dreams of Pharaoh. Salon of 1845 (Joseph expliquant les songes du Pharaon). 51⅛ × 78⅜. See p. 23. Rouen, Musée des Beaux-Arts.

4. JEAN-BAPTISTE-CAMILLE COROT (1796–1875): Homer and the Shepherds. Salon of 1845 (Homère et les bergers). 31½ × 50¾. See p. 25. Saint-Lô, Musée.
This painting was inspired by André Chénier's poem, *L'Aveugle*.

5. HORACE VERNET (1789–1863): The Capture of the Smala (detail). Salon of 1845 (La prise de la smalah d'Abd-el-Kader). 16½ × 94⅛ ft. See p. 6. Versailles, Musée.
The capture of the *smalah*—or encampment—of the Emir Abd-el-Kader by the French forces under the duc d'Aumale took place in 1843 and was one of the most picturesque episodes in the North African campaign. This was Horace Vernet's largest composition, the present detail representing only about a quarter of the complete picture.

6. LOUIS DE PLANET (1814–75): The Vision of Saint Teresa. Salon of 1845 (La Vision de sainte Thérèse). Dimensions unknown. See pp. 15–16. France, Private Collection.
See also Louis de Planet, *Souvenirs de travaux de peinture avec M. Eugène Delacroix* (Paris, 1929), pp. 80–4.

7. P.-J. DAVID D'ANGERS (1788–1856): Child with a Bunch of Grapes. Salon of 1845 (L'Enfant à la grappe). Marble, H. 4 ft. $3\frac{1}{8}$ ins. See p. 30. Paris, Musée du Louvre.

8. CHARLES GLEYRE (1806–74): Evening. Salon of 1843 (Le Soir). $53\frac{7}{8} \times 94\frac{1}{2}$. See p. 16. Paris, Musée du Louvre.
This picture achieved a great popular success, and was engraved under the title *Les Illusions perdues*. Clément (*Gleyre*, 1886 edition, p. 98) gives a long quotation from Gleyre's Journal, in which he describes the 'vision' he had in March 1835 beside the Nile, which gave rise to the picture. The seated man in the foreground represents the poetic hero who sadly watches his youthful illusions pass away from him.

9. THÉODORE CHASSÉRIAU (1819–56): The Caliph of Constantine with his Bodyguard. Salon of 1845 (Le Kalifat de Constantine suivi de son escorte). $126 \times 90\frac{3}{4}$. See pp. 13–14. Versailles, Musée.
Ali-ben-Hamet, Caliph of Constantine, had recently paid a lengthy visit to Paris.

10. JACQUES-LOUIS DAVID (1748–1816): The Dead Marat. Inscribed on the wooden box in the right foreground: A MARAT,/DAVID./L'AN DEUX. $63\frac{3}{4} \times 49\frac{1}{4}$. Brussels, Musées Royaux.
Marat was assassinated by Charlotte Corday on the 13th July, 1793. This news was announced to the Jacobins during the presidency of David. On the further announcement to the National Convention, Guiraud, Speaker of the section of the *Contrat Social*, cried: 'Où es-tu, David? Tu as transmis à la postérité l'image de Lepelletier mourant pour la patrie, il te reste un tableau à faire!' 'Aussi le ferai-je,' David replied. On 14 October 1793 he announced to the Convention that his picture was finished, and permission was granted for it, and the portrait of Lepelletier, together with the bath and other objects belonging to Marat, to be exhibited in the courtyard of the Louvre. At least four copies of this painting exist, of which two were supervised by the artist. See pp. 34–35.

11. THE INGRES GALLERY AT THE *Bazar Bonne-Nouvelle*: from a wood-engraving in *l'Illustration*, 14 February 1846, p. 376.
The following works are to be seen, from left to right: M. Bertin the elder, Oedipus and the Sphinx, Comte Molé, the Grande Odalisque, the Dauphin entering Paris, and the Comtesse d'Haussonville.

12. J.-A.-D. INGRES (1780–1867): Stratonice. Signed, and dated 1840. 22½×38¾. Chantilly, Musée Condé.
This painting was commissioned in 1834 by the duc d'Orléans as a companion piece to the *Death of the duc de Guise* by Paul Delaroche. Mme Ingres posed for the doctor, Hippolyte Flandrin for the arm of Antiochus, and Ingres himself for Seleucus. See pp. 37–38.

13. LÉON COGNIET (1794–1880): Tintoretto painting his Dead Daughter. 56¾×62¼. Bordeaux, Musée des Beaux-Arts.
This painting was exhibited at the Salon of 1843. See p. 39.

14. PIERRE-PAUL PRUD'HON (1758–1823): Venus and Adonis. 94½×66. London, Wallace Collection.
This picture, the finished version, was shown at the Salon 1812: the work noticed by Baudelaire (p. 37) at the Bonne-Nouvelle exhibition was a sketch for this, lent by M. Marcille. See the Catalogue of Pictures and Drawings at the Wallace Collection, 1928, p. 226, for a note on this sketch; it differs from the version reproduced here in the features and pose of the head of Adonis, and the disposition of loves and doves

15. PAUL CHENAVARD (1807–95): Dante's Inferno. Salon of 1846 (L'Enfer de Dante). 47¼×44¼. See p. 102. Montpellier, Musée Fabre.
On Baudelaire's opinion of Chenavard, see also Joseph C. Sloane's article 'Baudelaire, Chenavard, and "Philosophic Art" ', in the *Journal of Aesthetics and Art Criticism*, vol. XIII, No. 3, March 1955. Professor Sloane's identification of a portrait-drawing of Baudelaire by Chenavard does not however seem to be entirely convincing. See also *Painter of Modern Life*. pp. 207–9.

16. GUSTAVE LASSALE-BORDES (1814-*c.*1868): The Death of Cleopatra. Salon of 1846 (La Mort de Cléopâtre). 106¼×89. See pp. 67–8. Autun, Musée Municipal.
Like Louis de Planet and Léger Chérelle, Lassale-Bordes was one of Delacroix's assistants in his decorative works.

17. OCTAVE TASSAERT (1800–74): 'Don't play the heartless one!' Lithograph, from the series 'Les Amants et les Epoux'. See pp. 69–70. Paris, Bibliothèque Nationale.

18. COROT: Landscape—The Forest of Fontainebleau. Salon of 1846 (Vue prise dans la forêt de Fontainebleau). 35¾×51. See p. 106. Boston, Museum of Fine Arts.

19. GEORGE CATLIN (1796–1872): Buffalo-Hunt under the Wolf-Skin Mask. 23×27¾. Washington, Smithsonian Institution.
Probably painted in 1832, on the plains of the Upper Missouri. On Catlin, see particularly pp. 70–71.

20. CATLIN: Mah-to-he-ha, the Old Bear. 28 × 23. Washington, Smithsonian Institution.
Painted in 1832, among the Mandan farmers of the Upper Missouri river. The sitter was described by Catlin as 'A very distinguished brave; but here represented in the character of a Medicine Man or Doctor, with his Medicine or mystery pipes in his hands, and foxes' tails tied to his heels, prepared to make his last visit to his patient, to cure him, if possible, by hocus pocus and magic'.

21. JAMES PRADIER (1792–1852): The Frivolous Muse. Salon of 1846 (La Poésie légère). Marble, H. 6 ft. 8¾ in. See p. 113. Nîmes, Musée des Beaux-Arts.

22. THÉODORE CARUELLE D'ALIGNY (1798–1871): The Acropolis, Athens. Salon of 1846. Etching, 13⅛ × 19⅛. See p. 106. London, Victoria and Albert Museum.
No. 5 in Aligny's *Vues des sites les plus célèbres de la Grèce Antique*, Paris 1845.

23. ALEXANDRE-GABRIEL DECAMPS (1803–60): Turkish Landscape. Salon of 1846 (Paysage turc). Panel, 29 × 43. See p. 75. Amsterdam, Fodor Museum.

24. DECAMPS: Souvenir of Turkey in Asia. Salon of 1846 (Souvenir de la Turquie d'Asie). 35⅜ × 28½. See p. 75. Chantilly, Musée Condé.
It is presumably of this picture that Baudelaire observes that the ducks have been given a 'slab of stone to swim on'.

25. ARY SCHEFFER (1795–1858): St. Augustine and St. Monica. Salon of 1846 (Saint Augustin et sainte Monique). 53¼ × 41¼. See pp. 98–99. London, National Gallery.
This is in fact a replica of the Salon picture, which was formerly in the collection of Queen Marie Amélie.

26. HIPPOLYTE FLANDRIN (1809–64): Portrait of Mme Vinet. Dated 1840. 23⅝ × 20½. Paris, Musée du Louvre.
A characteristic example of the Ingres-school portrait, on which see pp. 89–90 and 190–192.

27. FRANÇOIS-MARIUS GRANET (1775–1849): The Interrogation of Savonarola. Salon of 1846 (Interrogatoire de Savonarole). 27¾ × 48. Lyon, Musée des Beaux-Arts.
On Granet's colour, see pp. 92 and 96.

28. THE INGRES GALLERY AT THE EXPOSITION UNIVERSELLE, 1855. Contemporary photograph. See p. 130. London, Victoria and Albert Museum.

The large circular painting in the centre is the *Apotheosis of Napoleon.* To the left can be seen the *Joan of Arc*, the *Grande Odalisque*, the *Venus Anadyomene* and the portrait of Mme Gonse; below, the *Muse de Cherubini* and the portrait of M. Bertin the elder; to the right, the *Bather of Valpinçon, Christ giving the keys to St. Peter, Oedipus and the Sphinx*, and, at the top, three cartoons for stained glass.

29. INGRES: The 'Grande Odalisque'. Dated 1814. $35\frac{3}{4}\times24\frac{3}{8}$. See pp. 38, 69 note, and 84. Paris, Musée du Louvre.

30. INGRES: Cherubini and his Muse. Dated 1842 (La Muse de Cherubini). $41\frac{3}{8}\times37$. See p. 84. Paris. Musée du Louvre.
The composer Cherubini died in Paris in 1842.

31. INGRES: The Comtesse d'Haussonville. Dated 1845. $53\frac{1}{2}\times36\frac{1}{4}$. See p. 84. New York, Frick Collection.

32. INGRES: Apotheosis of Homer. Dated 1827. 152×203. See pp. 61 and 83–4. Paris, Musée du Louvre.

33. EUGÈNE DELACROIX (1798–1863): Dante and Virgil. Salon of 1822 (Dante et Virgile conduits par Phlégias). $74\frac{3}{8}\times96\frac{7}{8}$. See pp. 52–4, 62–3, 136 and 138. Paris, Musée du Louvre.

34. DELACROIX: Women of Algiers. Salon of 1834 (Femmes d'Alger dans leur appartement). $70\frac{7}{8}\times90\frac{1}{8}$. See pp. 55 and 65. Paris, Musée du Louvre.
Among Baudelaire's pictures was a copy of the *Femmes d'Alger* by Emile Deroy.

35. DELACROIX: The Last Words of Marcus Aurelius. Salon of 1845. (Dernières paroles de l'empereur Marc-Aurèle). $100\frac{3}{4}\times129\frac{7}{8}$. See pp. 4–5. Lyon, Musée des Beaux-Arts.

36. DELACROIX: Hamlet and the Gravedigger. Salon of 1839 (Hamlet et Horatio au cimetière). $31\frac{7}{8}\times25\frac{5}{8}$. See pp. 65 and 139. Paris, Musée du Louvre.

37. DELACROIX: Romeo and Juliet. Salon of 1846 (Les Adieux de Roméo et Juliette). $24\frac{3}{8}\times19\frac{5}{8}$. See pp. 64, 139–140. Basle, Dr. Robert von Hirsch.

38. DELACROIX: The Sultan of Morocco with his Bodyguard. Salon of 1845 (Muley Abd-err-Rahman, sultan de Maroc, sortant de son palais de Mequinez). $148\frac{3}{8}\times133\frac{7}{8}$. See p. 6. Toulouse, Musée des Augustins.
A later version is reproduced *Journal*, pl. 56.

39. DELACROIX: The Ascent to Calvary. Salon of 1859 (La Montée au Calvaire). Panel, $22\frac{1}{2}\times18\frac{7}{8}$. See p. 169. Metz, Musée Central.

40. DELACROIX: Ovid in Exile among the Scythians. Salon of 1859 (Ovide en exil chez les Scythes). $34\frac{1}{2}\times51\frac{1}{4}$. See pp. 169–171. London, National Gallery.

41. HONORÉ DAUMIER (1808–79): The Salon of 1859. Lithograph (Delteil 3138) from the series 'L'Exposition de 1859'. London, Victoria and Albert Museum.
The following is a translation of the caption:
—Just look how they have 'skied' my picture!
—Why, my dear fellow—aren't you pleased? But you ought to be enchanted to see that they have hung your little things well above those of Meissonier!

42. ALPHONSE LEGROS (1837–1911): The Angelus. Salon of 1859 (L' Angélus). 25¼ × 31½. See pp. 164–5. Formerly Cheltenham, Mr. Asa Lingard.

43. AMAND-DÉSIRÉ GAUTIER (1825–94): Sisters of Mercy. Salon of 1859 (Les Sœurs de charité). 41¾ × 73⅝. See pp. 165–6. Lille, Musée des Beaux-Arts.

44. JOSEPH LIÈS (1821–65): The Evils of War. Salon of 1859 (Les Maux de la guerre). Panel, 34½ × 59. See p. 186. Brussels, Musées Royaux.

45. NICOLAS-FRANÇOIS CHIFFLART (1825–1901): Faust at the Sabbath (detail). Salon of 1859 (Faust au sabbat). See pp. 183–4. London, Victoria and Albert Museum.
The reproduction is taken from A. Bahuet's lithograph (11⅞ × 32¼) after Chifflart's drawing, whose present whereabouts is not known.

46. NARCISSE DIAZ (1807–76): Study of Trees. Panel, 14 × 10. Formerly New York, Metropolitan Museum of Art.

47. DIAZ: Love's Offspring. Dated 1847. 13¼ × 8¼. London, National Gallery. On Diaz, see particularly pp. 77–8 and 182–3.

48. PAUL FLANDRIN (1811–1902): Landscape. Salon of 1859 (Paysage). 36⅜ × 29⅛. Montauban, Musée Ingres.
Although Baudelaire did not write about Paul Flandrin at the Salon of 1859, he gave him a paragraph in 1845 (p. 26), and in 1846 devoted two pages to an attack on 'Historical Landscape', of which this picture is a good example (pp. 103–6).

49. ERNEST HÉBERT (1817–1908): Peasant Women of Cervaro. Salon of 1859 (Les Cervarolles). 113⅜ × 69¼. See pp. 181–2. Paris, Musée du Louvre.

50. CHARLES DAUBIGNY (1817–78): Landscape by the River Oise. Salon of 1859 (Les Bords de l'Oise). 34¼ × 71¼. See p. 195. Bordeaux, Musée des Beaux-Arts.

51. CHARLES LE ROUX (1814–95): Water-Meadows at Corsept, on the Mouth of the Loire. Salon of 1859 (Prairies et marais de Corsept, à l'embouchure de la Loire, au mois d'août). 44½ × 74⅜. See p. 195. Paris, Musée du Louvre.
The figures are by Corot.

52. THÉODORE ROUSSEAU (1812–67): The Gorges d'Apremont, Fontainebleau. Salon of 1859 (Les Gorges d'Apremont). 26×39½. See p. 196. Princeton, Mrs. F. J. Mather, Jr.

53. ROUSSEAU: The Forest of Fontainebleau—Morning. Salon of 1850–1 (Lisière de forêt—effet de matin). 38×52⅛. London, Wallace Collection. A larger picture representing the same scene at sunset (now in the Louvre), and exhibited at the same Salon, had been commissioned in 1848 by the State. This marked the beginning of Rousseau's official recognition.

54. JEAN-FRANÇOIS MILLET (1814–75): The Cowgirl. Salon of 1859 (Femme faisant paître sa vache). 28¾×36⅝. See p. 195. Bourg-en-Bresse, Musée de l'Ain.

55. MILLET: The Angelus. 21⅞×26. Paris, Musée du Louvre. Although painted in 1858–9, at about the same time as the *Cowgirl*, this picture was not exhibited until the *Exposition Universelle* of 1867.

56. COROT: Macbeth and the Witches. Salon of 1859 (Macbeth; paysage). 43×53. See p. 197. London, Wallace Collection. In the original sketch for this picture, Macbeth was alone and unmounted. The Shakespearian subject shows Corot's orthodox Romantic sympathies.

57. EUGÈNE BOUDIN (1824–98): Sky-Study. Pastel, 5½×9½. See pp. 199–200. London, Mr. Maurice Harris. This pastel, which is not however inscribed, is similar in style to others which have been referred to Baudelaire's description in the *Salon of* 1859.

58. JEAN-LÉON GÉRÔME (1824–1904): The Cock-Fight. Salon of 1847 (Jeunes Grecs faisant battre des coqs). 55⅞×79½. See p. 175. Paris, Musée du Louvre. This was Gérôme's first exhibit at the Salon; it earned him the title of the 'Master of the Neo-Greeks' (see pp. 172 ff.)

59. PAUL BAUDRY (1828–86): The Penitent Magdalen. Salon of 1859 (La Madeleine pénitente). 37×57⅞. See p. 182. Nantes, Musée des Beaux-Arts.

60. GUSTAVE RICARD (1823–73): Portrait of a Girl. Panel, 24¼×19¼. Lyon, Musée des Beaux- Arts. On Ricard, see pp. 192–3.

61. AUGUSTE CLÉSINGER (1814–83): Bust of Madame Sabatier, 1847. Marble, H. 31⅞. Paris, Musée du Louvre. Baudelaire's 'Vénus blanche', and called by Gautier 'la Présidente', Apollonie Sabatier became a celebrated literary and artistic hostess in the 1850s. Whether she was Baudelaire's mistress in the strict sense of the word is still uncertain, but he is known to have addressed anonymous love-letters to her, and a group of poems in the *Fleurs du mal* refers to her. On Clésinger's sculptures, see pp. 206–7.

62. ERNEST CHRISTOPHE (1827–92): 'Danse Macabre'. Terracotta (?), 1859. Dimensions unknown. See pp. 212–214. Present whereabouts unknown.
This *maquette*, which was the source of Baudelaire's poem of the same name, was in 1917 in the collection of Comte Robert de Montesquiou, when it was reproduced as frontispiece to *Le Cinquantenaire de Charles Baudelaire* (Paris, Maison du Livre). In the course of the publication of Baudelaire's articles on the Salon of 1859, Christophe wrote to him hoping that he would not be forgotten when it came to the section on sculpture.

63. CHARLES MERYON (1821–68): The Clock Tower, Paris. Etching, 1852. London, Victoria and Albert Museum.
No. 28 in Delteil and Wright, *Catalogue raisonné of the etchings of Charles Meryon*, 1924. On Meryon, see pp. 200–201.

64. CONSTANT TROYON (1810–65): The Return to the Farm. Salon of 1859 (Le Retour à la ferme). $102\frac{3}{8}\times 153\frac{1}{2}$. See p. 196. Paris, Musée du Louvre.

65. EDOUARD MANET (1832–83): Portrait of Baudelaire. Etching, $6\frac{3}{4}\times 4\frac{1}{8}$. London, British Museum.
The reproduction is of the third state of the third plate of Manet's full-face portrait of Baudelaire, etched in 1865. The fourth state of this plate was published in Charles Asselineau's *Charles Baudelaire, sa vie et son oeuvre*, the first biography of the poet, which appeared in 1869, two years after his death.

66. MANET: Les Gitanos. Etching, $12\frac{1}{2}\times 9\frac{1}{4}$. London, Victoria and Albert Museum.
The reproduction is of the second state of the etching, executed by Manet in 1862 from his oil-painting. It was published by Cadart in the first fascicule of the *Société des Aquafortistes,* 1 September 1862.

67. MANET: Lola de Valence. Etching and aquatint, $10\frac{1}{4}\times 7\frac{1}{8}$. London, British Museum.
The reproduction is of the third state of the etching, executed by Manet from his oil-painting (now in the Louvre) in 1862. Baudelaire's quatrain, engraved at the foot of the etching, was also used on a label under the painting when it was exhibited at the Galerie Martinet in 1863. The quatrain reads as follows:

> Entre tant de beautés que partout on peut voir,
> Je comprends bien, amis, que le Désir balance;
> Mais on voit scintiller dans Lola de Valence
> Le charme inattendu d'un bijou rose et noir.

Lola de Valence was the star of Mariano Camprubi's company of Spanish dancers which had a successful season in Paris, at the Hippodrome, in the

summer and autumn of 1862. Manet also painted a group of dancers, which is now in the Phillips Gallery, Washington.
The etching was published by Cadart in the October 1863 fascicule of the *Société des Aquafortistes*.

68. Johann Barthold Jongkind (1819–91): A Barge. Etching, $7\frac{1}{2}\times 8\frac{1}{4}$. London, Victoria and Albert Museum.
This plate is from the *Cahier d'Eaux-fortes*, published in 1862. See pp. 220–221.

69. Félix Bracquemond (1833–1914): The Stranger (L'Inconnu). Etching and drypoint, $7\frac{1}{4}\times 12\frac{5}{8}$. London, Victoria and Albert Museum.
Published by Cadart as the first plate in the first fascicule of the *Société des Aquafortistes*, 1 September 1862.

70. Charles Meryon: The Morgue. Etching, $9\frac{1}{8}\times 8\frac{1}{4}$. London, Victoria and Albert Museum.
This etching, executed in 1854, is No. 36 in Delteil and Wright, *Catalogue raisonné of the etchings of Charles Meryon.* The reproduction is taken from the fourth state. See pp. 200–201 and 221.

71. James Abbott McNeill Whistler (1834–1903): Rotherhithe. Etching, $10\frac{3}{4}\times 7\frac{3}{4}$. London, British Museum.
This plate, executed in 1860, was published as 'Wapping' in the *Series of Sixteen etchings of scenes on the Thames.* The position of St. Paul's Cathedral, seen through the rigging of the ship to the left, and apparently on the other side of the river, supports the revised title given above. See p. 220.

72. Legros: Title-page to a set of etchings, with dedication to Baudelaire. Etching, $13\frac{3}{8}\times 9\frac{1}{8}$. London, Victoria and Albert Museum.
The dedication is at the bottom righthand corner.

INDEX

INDEX